FOREWORD

This annual report by the Tourism Committee focuses on two topics: employment in the tourism sector and trends in international tourism.

Chapter I summarises the Tourism Committee's recent work on employment, which is further described in the annex. These two papers explain tourism's contribution to job creation in quantitative and qualitative terms. They give details of some of the obstacles to recruiting available labour in the tourist industry: working conditions, productivity, rates of pay and the seasonal aspect of jobs. In conclusion, they identify several areas in which OECD governments could take policy initiatives to improve understanding of the tourism job market and to enhance its operation.

Chapters II and III and the statistical annex deal with supply and demand in OECD Member countries and outline the trends observed in 1992-1993. After a marked resumption of growth in the OECD area in 1992, international tourism stabilised in 1993, although trends varied greatly from country to country.

These studies are based on information supplied by national delegations and by members of the Tourism Committee and its Statistical Working Party.

This report was approved by the Tourism Committee. On the 18 October 1995 the Council decided to make it publicly available.

Tourism Policy
and International Tourism
in OECD Countries

93

re

ployment"

ORGANISATION FOR ECONOMIC CO-OPERATION AND DEVELOPMENT

ORGANISATION FOR ECONOMIC CO-OPERATION AND DEVELOPMENT

Pursuant to Article 1 of the Convention signed in Paris on 14th December 1960, and which came into force on 30th September 1961, the Organisation for Economic Co-operation and Development (OECD) shall promote policies designed:

— to achieve the highest sustainable economic growth and employment and a rising standard of living in Member countries, while maintaining financial stability, and thus to contribute to the development of the world economy;

— to contribute to sound economic expansion in Member as well as non-member countries in the process of economic development; and

— to contribute to the expansion of world trade on a multilateral, non-discriminatory basis in accordance with international obligations.

The original Member countries of the OECD are Austria, Belgium, Canada, Denmark, France, Germany, Greece, Iceland, Ireland, Italy, Luxembourg, the Netherlands, Norway, Portugal, Spain, Sweden, Switzerland, Turkey, the United Kingdom and the United States. The following countries became Members subsequently through accession at the dates indicated hereafter: Japan (28th April 1964), Finland (28th January 1969), Australia (7th June 1971), New Zealand (29th May 1973) and Mexico (18th May 1994). The Commission of the European Communities takes part in the work of the OECD (Article 13 of the OECD Convention).

Publié en français sous le titre :

POLITIQUE DU TOURISME ET TOURISME INTERNATIONAL DANS LES PAYS DE L'OCDE 1992-1993
ÉTUDE SPÉCIALE « TOURISME ET EMPLOI »

Table of Contents

Trends in International Tourism
in the OECD Area

Main Developments

After a significant upswing in international tourism in 1992, 1993 was more a year of consolidation for tourism -- despite economic difficulties and the slowly waning confidence of consumers and businesses. This is shown by the data available for the OECD area:

-- nights spent in various forms of accommodation: up 0.9 per cent (compared with a 4 per cent increase the previous year);

-- arrivals at frontiers: up 0 per cent (compared with a 6 per cent increase);

-- receipts in real terms: up 4 per cent (compared with a 5 per cent increase);

-- receipts in current dollars: down 2 per cent (compared with an 11 per cent increase), to a total of $216 billion in 1993.

The growth rate of tourism, within the various regions, was the following:

-- in North America: nights spent in various forms of accommodation up 3 per cent and arrivals at frontiers down 3 per cent;

-- in the Asia-Pacific region: nights spent in various forms of accommodation up 11 per cent and arrivals at frontiers up 6 per cent;

-- in Europe: nights spent in various forms of accommodation down 0.4 per cent and arrivals at frontiers up 1 per cent.

Trend of international tourism in the OECD area

Per cent change over previous year

	Arrivals at frontiers[1]		Nights spent in means of accommodation[2]		Receipts in national currency		Receipts in real terms[3]	
	% 92/91	% 93/92	% 92/91	% 93/92	% 92/91	% 93/92	% 92/91	% 93/92
Canada	−1.1	2.5	−4.0	3.4	2.3	10.2	0.8	8.4
Mexico	10.3	−9.1	−2.5	3.4	4.8	6.0	−8.2	−3.4
United States	10.8	−3.7			11.3	7.0	8.0	4.2
North America	8.1	−3.3	−3.8	3.4			6.5	4.2
Australia	9.8	15.1	8.3	13.8	11.0	7.0	10.0	4.8
Japan	−0.1	−8.5			−1.7	−13.3	−3.3	−14.1
New Zealand	9.6	9.6	6.3	8.5	4.6	−21.2	3.5	−22.3
Asia and the Pacific	5.9	5.5	7.1	10.5			−1.2	−16.7
Austria			0.1	−2.9	−1.0	−1.1	−4.8	−4.7
Belgium[4]			5.8	0.2	5.0	8.1	2.6	5.2
Denmark			11.1	−9.7	2.8	−18.0	0.7	−18.9
Finland			1.9	15.4	21.6	16.5	18.1	13.1
France	8.5	0.7	7.6	0.9	10.1	−0.1	7.5	−2.3
Germany[6]			2.1	−9.1	−0.2	0.6	−3.9	−3.3
Greece	16.1	0.9	20.9	0.5	52.3	18.8	31.5	4.1
Iceland	−0.6	10.4	−0.3	53.2	−7.9	20.9	−11.4	16.2
Ireland	4.6	6.2	1.5	4.0	1.1	15.0	−2.0	12.5
Italy	−2.4	−0.4	−3.6	2.1	15.7	30.9	9.9	25.3
Luxembourg[4]			−8.8		5.0	8.1	2.6	5.2
Netherlands			5.2	−5.1	14.3	−5.5	10.2	−7.3
Norway			6.2	6.1	14.1	7.0	11.5	4.6
Portugal[7]	2.6	−5.1	−8.6	−9.7	−8.1	31.7	−15.6	23.9
Spain	3.2	4.2	3.4	7.7	13.9	9.1	7.5	4.1
Sweden			3.8	4.5	8.9	15.9	6.5	10.2
Switzerland	1.6	−3.1	−0.1	−0.7	4.7	−2.0	0.6	−5.2
Turkey	28.2	−8.1	73.1	1.7	129.5	74.5	34.9	2.0
United Kingdom	8.0	3.0	0.4	−0.1	6.8	13.5	3.0	9.6
Europe[5]	4.6	0.9	4.4	0.4			4.7	4.2
OECD[5]	5.5	0.0	3.8	0.9			5.1	3.6

1. Arrivals of tourists except in Australia, Ireland, Italy, Spain and Turkey where arrivals concern visitors.
2. Nights spent in all means of accommodation except in Australia, Finland, Iceland and Spain where nights spent concern hotels and similar establishments.
3. After correcting for the effects of inflation. For the regional and OECD totals, the receipts of the individual countries are weighted in proportion to their share in the total expressed in dollars.
4. Receipts apply to both Belgium and Luxembourg.
5. Overall trends for countries with data available from 1991 to 1993.
6. The data relate to the territory of the Federal Republic of Germany prior to 3rd October 1990. Since 1991, data for all means of accommodation include camping sites.
7. Break of series (for payments only) in 1993 due to the liberalisation of capital movements.

In **Europe**, a region where unemployment remained relatively high and the expected economic recovery was weaker than forecast, the growth rate of tourism fell more steeply. Moreover, sharply fluctuating exchange rates in a number of countries, including Sweden, Spain, Finland, Italy, Turkey and the United Kingdom, also had an impact on tourism.

The slight overall increase in the number of overnight stays was the net result of countervailing tendencies. Losses recorded in Germany (down 9 per cent), Denmark and Portugal (down 10 per cent), the Netherlands (down 5 per cent), Austria (down 3 per cent) and Switzerland (down 1 per cent) were partially offset by the very strong performance of international tourism in the other Nordic countries and by favourable figures for Spanish and Irish tourism.

It would appear that strong-currency countries like Germany, the Netherlands, Austria and Switzerland were more adversely affected by the highly fluctuating demand for tourism. For its part, Denmark was hard hit by defections by customers from the other Nordic countries, the Netherlands, Italy and Japan.

Spain was buoyed by the strength of its main markets, although the United States was an exception. The Nordic countries were helped by the depreciation of two of their currencies and by increased demand for nature-oriented tourism, driven primarily by the Germans and the Japanese.

Arrivals of tourists -- the most complete statistical series -- in **North America** (including Mexico) decreased by 3 per cent in 1993. Canada returned to growth after two consecutive years of decline (arrivals up 3 per cent); while its main markets were up significantly, the rise was tempered by a moderate upswing in the US market, which accounted for 80 per cent of total arrivals. The United States (down 4 per cent) was hit harder, due in part to a combination of the dollar's appreciation against all other currencies (with the notable exception of the yen) and the economic weakness of its leading markets. Canadians, Italians and Japanese sharply reduced their visits to the United States in 1993. Lastly, Mexico recorded a substantial decline of 9 per cent.

In the **Asia-Pacific** region, growth continued to be 6 per cent, ensuring the region remained the most dynamic of the major OECD areas. By country, however, the expansion varied. Growth in inward tourism was led by sharp increases in Australia (up 15 per cent) and New Zealand (up 10 per cent), which reaped the full benefits of economic development in Asia (up 18 per cent) and, in Europe, of a buoyant German market (up 23 per cent). In contrast, arrivals of foreign tourists in Japan fell for the second straight year, with the yen's steady appreciation having a significant impact on the price competitiveness of the Japanese tourist industry.

With regard to the main generating countries of international tourism in the OECD area, the contrasts were just as great.

Demand from Germany continued to expand in 1993 (nights spent up 2 per cent), with German tourists heading in particular for the Nordic countries, Canada and Australia. In contrast, the number of nights they spent in Turkey and Portugal declined.

Outbound French tourism in the OECD area increased slightly in 1993, rising by 3 per cent. The rise was especially steep in Turkey (nights spent up 31 per cent) and Australia (visits up 22 per cent).

In 1993, nights spent by Netherlands tourists progressed by 9 per cent and their arrivals by 8 per cent. Growth was sharpest in the Asia-Pacific region, and especially in Australia. Tourists from the Netherlands also increased their travel to France, Norway, Spain and Iceland.

Nights spent by UK tourists in Europe were up a slight 1 per cent, rising to about 15 per cent of the total. In Ireland, where the United Kingdom is the main source of customers, the number of nights spent increased by 5 per cent. Travel to Spain and Finland was also on the rise. In contrast, a number of major destinations (Belgium, France, Iceland, the Netherlands, Norway and Portugal) suffered declines.

The number of nights spent by US tourists was unchanged from the previous year for the OECD area as a whole, although their travel to Europe was down significantly in 1993.

Conversely, the other major generating markets receded. The number of Canadian nationals visiting the United States fell by 7 per cent, causing the overall number of tourists to decrease by 6 per cent. That said, Canadians' trips to other countries rose by 5 per cent in 1993.

In recent years, the Italian market has been one of the most dynamic in Europe, and its potential for growth is still promising. In 1993, however, Italian demand fell sharply: nights spent by Italians declined by 11 per cent in the OECD area. The Italian presence fell in all European destinations except Ireland and Spain.

Japanese demand was down again in 1993, as arrivals fell 3 per cent and expenditure in dollars by 1 per cent. Arrivals of Japanese tourists were down in Europe especially, and this was combined with a shorter average stay. Lastly, there was a 3 per cent drop in Japanese tourism in the United States.

International tourism receipts -- excluding transportation revenue -- represented 5 per cent of OECD-area exports of goods and services. In 1993, those receipts totalled $216 billion in current terms (down 2 per cent from the previous year), or more than 71 per cent of aggregate tourism receipts worldwide.

The countries benefiting most from international tourism were the United States, which accounted for 27 per cent of the OECD total, followed by France (11 per cent) and then Italy (10 per cent). When Spain, Austria and the United Kingdom are added, aggregate receipts for the top six OECD receiving countries represented approximately 69 per cent of the OECD total. Austria again had the highest ratio of tourist receipts to GDP (7.4 per cent in 1993), followed by Greece, Spain and Portugal, for which the proportion ranged between 4 and 5 per cent.

Over the same period, residents of Member countries spent $218 billion on foreign travel. The eight main generating countries mentioned above accounted for about 77 per cent of the aggregate expenditure of the 25 Member countries.

With a more pronounced slowdown of expenditure in 1993 (down 5 per cent), the tourism deficit of the OECD countries was virtually absorbed in 1993, falling to $0.3 billion.

The inflow of foreign currency from tourism is generally expressed in dollars, the unit of account used in the balance of payments. But it is also interesting to note receipts in real terms, *i.e.* eliminating the effects of inflation and currency fluctuations against the dollar. On this basis, North America progressed in 1993 at the same pace as Europe, and slightly faster than the OECD area as a whole (up 4.2 per cent, as opposed to 3.6); the Asia-Pacific region recorded a 17 per cent decrease in 1993.

Trends of international tourism
in North America
(indices 1984 = 100)

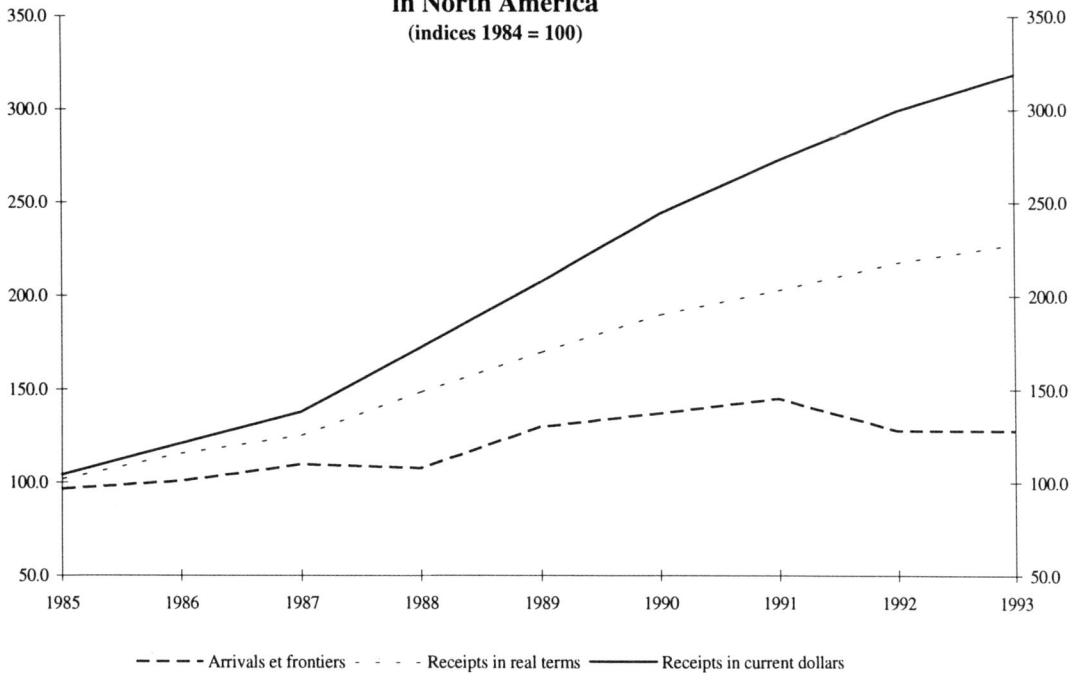

- - - - Arrivals et frontiers - - - - Receipts in real terms ———— Receipts in current dollars

Source : OECD

Trends of international tourism
in Asia and the Pacific
(indices 1984 = 100)

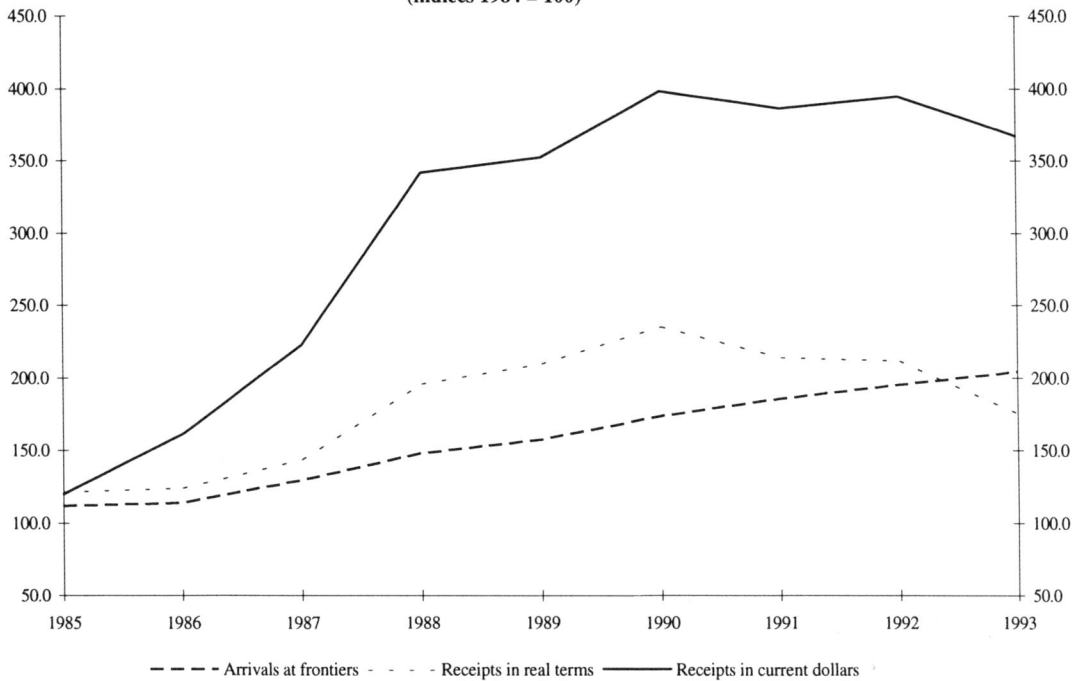

- - - - Arrivals at frontiers - - - - Receipts in real terms ———— Receipts in current dollars

Source : OECD

Trends of international tourism
in Europe
(indices 1984 = 100)

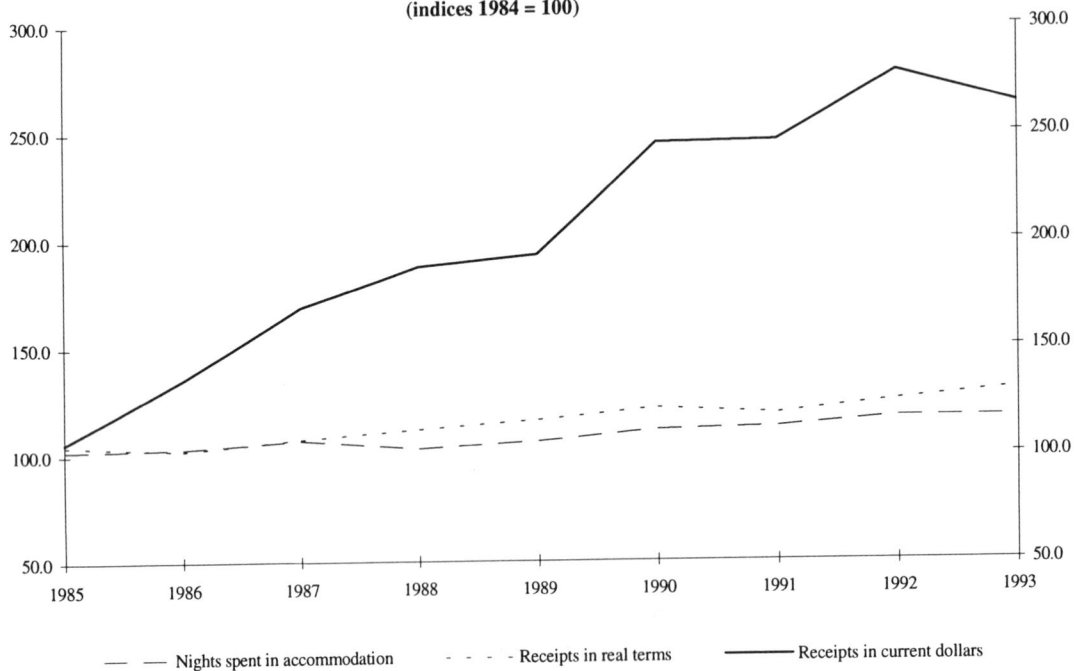

Legend: — — Nights spent in accommodation   - - - - Receipts in real terms   —— Receipts in current dollars

Source : OECD

Apart from the economic trends it observes and analyses each year (through this annual report in particular), the Tourism Committee examines structural change in the sector as well as interactions with other sectoral policies.

Accordingly, since 1988 the Committee has focused on the job market, through an extensive study of the hotel industry in Member countries. More recently, the Committee has embarked upon a wider review of employment in the various segments of the industry.

The OECD has projected that some 35 million people in Member countries were out of work at the end of 1994. Yet for several years the tourism industry has generally been expanding at a faster pace than the economy as a whole, and it is an industry with substantial labour requirements. Because of this, the Tourism Committee decided to undertake a thorough analysis in order to demonstrate the economic importance of tourism in Member countries, to examine the sector's potential for creating employment and to pinpoint obstacles to the recruitment of available labour for jobs in tourism. Lastly, it identified the policy initiatives needed to enhance tourism's contribution to job creation.

This work is based on information available in Member countries, and on discussions at a seminar on "Tourism and Employment" organised by the Tourism Committee in April 1994, with the active co-operation of the Turkish authorities.

Those discussions highlighted the economic impact of the tourist industry, which is one of the largest service sectors of the OECD economies. Tourism is a prime source of employment, as shown in the table.

In addition, tourism-related employment is broken down by sector of activity, and qualitative problems in a number of sectors are described. Drawing on Member country experience, the study examines the role of foreign labour in the tourist industry and shows that tourism creates jobs, in particular for those mainly hit by unemployment -- young people, the unskilled and "visible" minorities.

The report describes obstacles to attracting and retaining workers. *Inter alia*, it discusses the seasonal nature of employment in tourism and the prevalence of part-time work. It is a fact, moreover, that a portion of the jobs in tourism are unskilled and sometimes difficult to fill. However, the report also points out that a large number of positions call for highly skilled individuals. This leads to a discussion of service-sector productivity and wage levels: it is pointed out that in sectors where productivity is low, wages are generally below average (by about 20 per cent), but that there are also highly skilled and extremely well paid jobs. Lastly, while working conditions in the tourism industry (weekends, holidays, nights) are particular, they cannot be described as poor. Except in respect of part-time and seasonal workers, labour laws are generally the same as for other sectors of the economy.

The Committee identified several possible areas in which governments could take policy initiatives and find solutions to the labour problems in tourism. Given its importance for Member countries, employment will continue to be a major focus of the Committee's programme of work.

A summary of this analysis is presented in Chapter I. In addition, the basic report, prepared by Mr. Peter Keller -- head of the tourism department at OFIAMT (Switzerland) and professor at the École des Hautes Études Commerciales of the University of Lausanne -- has been annexed to this report; it is based on Member country responses to a questionnaire from the OECD Secretariat. This

Shares of direct and indirect employment in tourism in the total labour force

	Employment in tourism (in thousand)		Employment in tourism/Total labour force (%)	
	Direct	Indirect	Direct	Indirect
Canada	467.0		4.0	
United-States	6,000.0		5.1	
Australia *	457.7		6.0	
Japan *	990.0		1.6	
Austria	586.0		13.9	
Belgium	54.9	19.1	1.5	0.5
Denmark *	97.0		2.6	
France	895.4	304.6	3.6	1.2
Germany *	1,800.0		6.5	
Greece	220.0	140.0	6.1	3.9
Iceland	3.8		3.0	
Luxembourg *	11.5		6.4	
Netherlands	148.8	51.0	2.1	0.7
Norway	53.7		3.4	
Portugal *	250.0		5.6	
Spain	823.2	576.8	5.4	3.7
Sweden *	153.0		3.4	
Switzerland	204.5	88.7	5.7	2.5
Turkey	129.0		0.7	

* : Indirect employement is included in direct employment.

Shares of direct and indirect employment in tourism in the total labour force

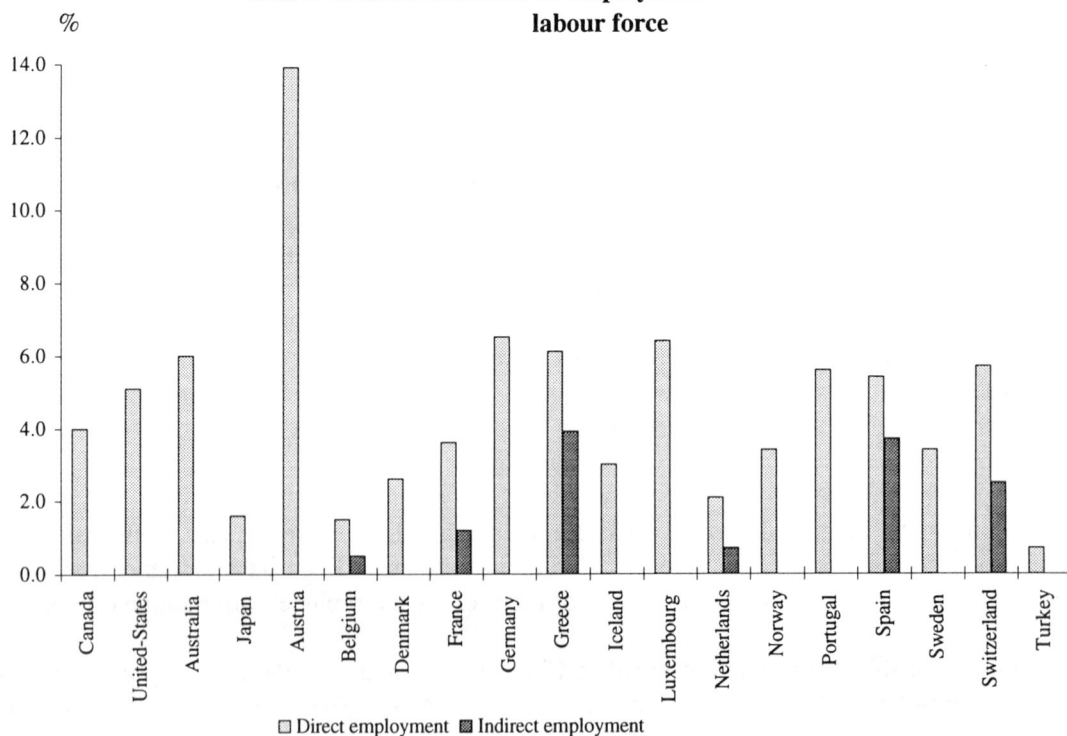

□ Direct employment ▨ Indirect employment

Source : OECD Tourism Committee

work represents an initial outcome of the Tourism Committee's work on this question and has laid the groundwork for further analysis of other, more specific topics, such as regional development and employment in tourism, the impact of structural change in the industry on demand for labour, education and vocational training, immigration issues as they relate to employment in tourism, etc.

Policy shifts and action taken by OECD governments in the realm of tourism will be presented in the Tourism Committee's next annual report. *Inter alia*, the focus is likely to be on changes in the primary objectives of tourism policy, institutional trends and organisation, measures regarding tourism and travel, links with the private sector and international co-operation.

Chapter 1

Tourism and Employment

I. Introduction

The OECD Tourism Committee first attempted to define the contribution of the tourism labour market to Member economies in the 1980s. Although little importance was attached to tourism in labour market policies of the time, there were signs that it had the potential to generate employment on a scale matched by few, if any other sectors.

The results of the Tourism Committee's efforts, which were published in its 1988 annual report, *Tourism Policy and International Tourism in OECD Countries*, were incomplete as they referred only to the hotel sector labour market. It was not possible to analyse and draw conclusions on the complete range of jobs directly or indirectly linked to tourism. This was due to the fact that while tourism is a heterogeneous industry, representing a wide variety of types and sizes of businesses, it is not an industry in the traditional sense of the word. So it does not fit the standard criteria for national accounts.

Nevertheless, the findings clearly demonstrated the favourable impact of tourism on employment and this argument has since been reinforced by evidence from other sources. In the United States, for example, high growth in employment in the private services field in the 1980s - which was an economically robust period - highlighted the importance of the hotel and catering industry for the labour market. And in Western Europe since the beginning of the 1990s - a period over which unemployment overall has risen sharply as a result of the recession - tourist regions have stood up quite well overall to the economic crisis. Regions which are highly diversified and well equipped in terms of tourism have only been slightly affected by unemployment.

Given the projections by OECD of 35 million unemployed by the end of 1994, it is not surprising that unemployment has become a dominant policy issue in the social and economic fabric of OECD countries. It is also one of the most widely feared phenomena of our times, touching all parts of society. It was partly for these reasons that the Tourism Committee decided to organise a seminar on Tourism and Employment to address the issue in depth and try to assess the future implications of tourism for the wider economies of OECD countries.

Organised in co-operation with the Turkish Ministry of Tourism and held in Antalya, Turkey, from 25-26 April 1994, the seminar was planned to coincide with the publication of a first part of the *OECD Jobs' Study*. It was seen as an unique opportunity to bring together policy makers, tourism economists and representatives of the tourism industry for a broad discussion of sector specific policy issues and future prospects.

The Tourism Committee's main objectives were to:

-- highlight the economic importance of tourism to OECD Members;
-- to examine the sector's employment potential; and
-- to identify suitable policy initiatives that could maximise the industry's contribution to reducing unemployment and improving the quality of jobs in the sector.

In order to set the scene for these discussions, a background paper was prepared for the seminar (see Annex I). This was based largely on the results of a questionnaire circulated to the relevant national tourism authorities in OECD Member countries. While the responses did not permit strict comparisons from country to country - and, therefore, no in-depth analysis - they did point to some interesting trends in terms of tourism's contribution to reducing employment. Supplementary reports were also submitted for consideration by seminar participants from different National Tourism Administrations (NTAs), as well as from individual institutions and/or organisations.

The following provides an overview of the substance of these reports, as well as summarising the proceedings of the Antalya seminar.

II. Unemployment: key facts and figures

During the 1950s and 1960s, the total number of unemployed in OECD area averaged less than ten million. This figure tripled during the following decade and, although subsequent economic expansion in the 1980s trimmed back the average unemployment total to 25 million by 1990, it has since risen sharply as a result of the economic recession.

The findings of the OECD Jobs' Study project that there will be about 35 million unemployed in Member countries by the end of 1994, representing some 8.5 per cent of the OECD labour force. Moreover, this official figure does not reflect the full extent of the problem. There is also severe underemployment and a further 14-15 million people have accepted jobs which are well below, or inappropriate to their skills.

The highest levels of unemployment are found in the European Union (EU) and Oceania where - according to the OECD Jobs' Study - rates average between 10-11 per cent, followed by EFTA countries (eight per cent), North America (seven per cent) and Japan (three per cent). The situation in the EU is particularly depressing as around 50 per cent of all those without work have been unemployed for more than 12 months. This compares with 11 per cent long term unemployment in the United States. But the Study shows that in the USA and Canada, while an unemployed person has a much better chance of being rehired quickly, there is a greater risk of becoming unemployed in the first place.

One of the sectors most affected by unemployment are young people, for whom the rate is as high as 30 per cent in some European countries, notably Finland, Ireland, Italy and Spain. More significantly perhaps, the incidence of long term unemployment among unemployed youth rises to between 50-70 per cent in certain parts of Europe. Other sectors of the population which are also more adversely affected by unemployment than the average are unskilled or low-skilled workers, women and visible minority groups.

The problem represents an enormous cost to society and helps to explain why unemployment has become such a central policy issue for all OECD Member governments. There are no ready solutions, either. Although projected economic growth during the 1990s is expected to help reduce unemployment, it is largely a structural problem - one that will not automatically disappear with the end of the recession.

According to the OECD Jobs' Study, structural unemployment is due to an insufficient ability by Member governments and society to adapt to a fast changing world of new technologies, globalisation and intense national and international competition. These forces have undermined many traditional patterns of work and overwhelmed many long established responses to unemployment.

Although tourism is not seen as a panacea that can right all ills, there are signs that its implications for the wider economies of OECD Member countries might be more far-reaching than had previously been realised. By way of example, its economic contribution to national economies and to employment would seem to have been seriously underestimated in the past. According to the research conducted among OECD Members for the Antalya seminar, it already accounts for between five to ten per cent of the total workforce in most OECD countries. Moreover, a significant share of the jobs generated by travel and tourism appear to be in areas not traditionally perceived of as being linked to tourism.

Tourism is now being touted as the world's largest industry and, while there are signs of stagnation in terms of foreign arrivals and international tourism receipts for some of the more mature OECD tourist destinations, the overall growth prospects for tourism are much more bullish than for most other sectors of the economy. Forecasts from the World Tourism Organisation (WTO) project some 660 million international arrivals worldwide by the year 2000 - or an annual growth of 3.8 per cent from 1990 to the end of the century - and US$527 billion in international tourist receipts.

But what further potential does tourism offer as a source of employment creation? What type of jobs are likely to become available? And for whom? Meanwhile, is the industry capable of absorbing jobs lost in other sectors? And is tourism a sector in which governments should be investing their scarce resources to stimulate employment?

III. Tourism in OECD economies

A dearth of statistics

While the importance of tourism for national economies would now seem to be widely recognised, the scattered structure of the industry and its largely unrecorded ramifications in other sectors have resulted in a dearth of solid statistical data demonstrating the extent of its economic contribution. Moreover, there was no attempt until fairly recently at harmonisation of statistical data across countries, with the result that meaningful analyses and comparisons have not been possible in the past.

In 1984, the OECD Tourism Committee decided to improve its statistical base by developing the OECD Manual on Tourism Economic Accounts. The manual contains a new statistical approach to data collection and analysis, which provides for international comparability from one Member country to another, as well as between tourism and other sectors of the economy. It includes practical methods for reviewing the importance of tourism in a national economy and it places much more emphasis on the demand side of tourism - at the same time, linking demand to supply - thereby more clearly defining the range of sectors dependent in one way or another on tourism.

The new system, which is being progressively implemented by OECD Member countries, will not be able to identify the full economic importance of tourism. It has, unfortunately, not been possible to include sectors for which tourism is only part of the bottom line - such as the retail trade, banks and post offices, car rental and garages, and personal services like hairdressers. But OECD has identified those sectors which depend most closely on tourism. And once implementation is achieved throughout the OECD area, the resulting harmonisation of data across countries should greatly facilitate the assessment of tourism's economic importance.

It is expected to take at least five years before the new system of statistical data collection and analysis contained in the Manual is fully operational in Member countries. But existing statistics from OECD Member countries, as well as from other government and industry sources, all tend to reinforce the arguments supporting the favourable economic impact of tourism on national economies. These sources include the annual statistics published by OECD on physical and monetary flows, as well as specific input for the background report to the seminar submitted by OECD Member NTAs - together with written presentations from a number of countries and case studies presented at the seminar itself. The full statistical tables are provided in the Appendices to this chapter and in the following chapters on International Tourist Flows and the Economic Importance of International Tourism in Member Countries.

A prime source of revenues

The shares of international tourism in exports and therefore, its contribution to the balance of payments, differ greatly between Member states, ranging from one to 25 per cent. Some countries rely heavily on tourism to boost their balance of payments. The positive balance from Spain's international tourism account, for example, entirely wipes out what would otherwise have been a negative trade balance. And in many other less developed countries, in which outbound travel is still in its infancy, tourism's favourable impact on the balance of payments is usually even greater.

However, tourism can be just as important, economically speaking, for countries at high levels of industrial development - as a case study of Germany presented at the Antalya seminar showed. Although Germany's international tourism balance is consistently in negative figures, the deficit masks a high volume of earnings from domestic tourism - both overnight and same day travel. At the same time, while Germany's massive outbound travel volumes impact unfavourably on the country's balance of tourism account, this sector of the industry does generate significant employment.

The shares of tourism in GDP, as reported by Members, cannot be strictly compared since methodologies used to calculate them differ from one country to another. Nevertheless, all Members rate tourism among the major sectors of their national economies, alongside construction and the retail trade.

IV. The job creation potential of tourism

Already a major generator of jobs

Tourism is already a powerhouse in terms of employment, ranking among the major sources of jobs in most OECD and non-OECD Member countries. As an indication of its global significance, it is interesting to cite the results of research conducted on behalf of the World Travel and Tourism Council (WTTC). It should, nevertheless, be pointed out that individual OECD Member states do not necessarily agree with the respective individual country figures from WTTC.

However, the global research from WTTC suggests that travel and tourism generates direct and indirect employment for around 200 million people worldwide - some 10.6 per cent of the global labour force, or one in nine jobs. More significantly, WTTC forecasts that the industry will provide an additional 144 million new jobs by the year 2005.

According to data provided by individual OECD Members, tourism's share in employment exceeds five per cent in ten Member countries, including the USA (5.1 per cent), Germany (6.5 per cent) and Canada (9.6 per cent[1]). In some of the more mature tourist destinations of the OECD area, the relative share is over eight per cent - 13.8 per cent in Austria, for example, ten per cent in Greece and 8.1 per cent in Switzerland. It should once again be stressed that although these figures do provide a useful indication of trends, they are not strictly comparable, since they involve varying definitions and methodologies, notably for estimations of employment indirectly linked to tourism. So they should be interpreted with caution.

Absolute figures relating to tourism employment are also impressive. Even in OECD countries with small labour forces, the numbers of people working in tourism are surprisingly high - from 250 000 in Portugal and 293 000 in Switzerland to 360 000 in Greece and 586 000 in Austria. In the larger countries of the OECD area, total employment ranges from around one million in Japan to 1.2 million[1] in Canada, 1.4 million in France and Spain, 1.6 million in Germany and six million in the USA.

What type of jobs?

A statistical breakdown of tourism related employment between the different sectors of the industry shows that the main employer is hotel and catering, probably accounting for around one third of total jobs - depending on the exact definitions used for tourism related employment. Second in the overall ranking is the transport sector - that is, air, rail and road transport combined - and data provided by some Member countries puts this share at around 15 per cent.

In terms of direct employment, the travel trade is an interesting case, since all retail and wholesale travel services are tourism related. But the overall workforce is relatively small, accounting for an estimated three-five per cent only of total tourism jobs in the OECD area. As far as other sectors are concerned, reliable statistics are not readily available. But numbers and shares tend to be governed by the structure of the industry overall in the different countries.

Tourism has been one of the fastest growing industries over the last 30 to 40 years, so it is hardly surprising that it has generated above average growth in employment. Except during occasional cyclical slowdowns, its highly diversified structure has also stood up well to recession so that in most OECD countries, the growth in tourism jobs has continued more or less uninterrupted through to the

1990s. This growth has not only been evident in sectors directly related to tourism, either. Reflecting the large share of tourist expenditure that goes directly to areas of the economy not normally recognised as part of the tourism industry, a significant share of the jobs generated by travel and tourism appear to be in areas not directly linked to tourism.

While trends in different OECD Member countries suggest that the hotel and catering sector has contributed most to employment in the OECD area in absolute terms, this is also the sector that has proved the most sensitive to cyclical slowdowns. So it registered the highest share of job losses during the recession of the 1990s. In terms of percentage growth, the travel agency sector has grown the fastest and growth rates have also been high in sectors partly dependent on tourism, such as transport, cultural and sporting activities.

Despite the growth, most of the jobs created have been either in regions with a low level of development, or in tourist centres and towns which are cultural and administrative centres. Tourism's ability has so far not stretched to providing substitute jobs for those lost in industry, although evidence from some OECD Member countries suggests that good progress has been made with solutions combining the possibilities of tourism with agriculture.

Employing the unemployed

The results of a major study commissioned by Tourism Canada specifically for the OECD seminar, Tourism-Related Employment in Canada, suggest that tourism is capable of taking up unemployed labour in Canada at a rate around 1.5 times faster than that of the economy as a whole. While all the jobs it provides may not be of high quality, these findings are of great interest to other OECD Member countries, given the extent of the unemployment problem in the OECD area overall. For the young in particular, the study findings are of particular significance as tourism would seem to offer a way back into the labour force, as well as being a popular first time entry point.

The Canadian study - which used a longitudinal survey, enabling the labour market behaviour of participants to be tracked over 36 months - covered six of the more traditional sectors of the industry: food and beverage, accommodation, transportation, adventure tourism and outdoor recreation. The main objectives of the study was to identify:

-- the people who gained tourism jobs after unemployment, their characteristics, the characteristics of their unemployment, and the tourism jobs they obtained;
-- tourism's share of the people who obtained work after unemployment;
-- the tourism sectors and occupations projected to have the greatest employment growth over the next decade; and
-- whether the tourism jobs obtained after unemployment were in the same tourism sectors and occupations projected to have the greatest future employment growth.

The detailed findings of the study indicated that the people being employed in tourism related jobs after unemployment are mainly from among the young (60 per cent are under 25 years old), women, the unskilled and visible minority groups. This highlights the fact that tourism has the ability to generate jobs for those at the very core of OECD's unemployment.

Those entering tourism after unemployment come from a range of industries, the study shows. Less than one third (30 per cent) were previously in a tourism job, with 70 per cent coming in almost equal shares from other service industries and public administrations; trade and finance; primary, construction and manufacturing; school; or from outside the labour force altogether. The study findings also indicated that when people who obtain a job in tourism looked for a job, they found one very quickly - 50 per cent were re-employed in less than four weeks.

The tourism sectors and occupations which are projected to have the greatest growth in the next decade are the same sectors and occupations in which the unemployed have gained work, according to the Canadian study. Food and beverage seems to take up the largest share of the unemployed, attracting young, female employees in particular, and the growth in job creation in this sector is expected to be the fastest over the next decade.

V. Obstacles to attracting and retaining labour

While tourism clearly has the ability to generate jobs for the unemployed, the industry has traditionally been faced with a number of obstacles to attracting and retaining labour at all levels. These must clearly be addressed if job creation potential is to be maximised.

The industry's poor image

Tourism has a much higher proportion of part-time and seasonal workers than other industries, and most of the vacancies for employment are for unskilled or low-skilled jobs. This is highlighted by the results of the Canadian study.

Some 41 per cent of the participants in the study who gained jobs after unemployment were offered part-time jobs, with fewer hours of work than they really wanted. And the jobs were also characterised by low wages and benefits. The majority were also not unionised and provided no pension plan - thus contributing to the inherent instability of this sector of employment and to its poor image.

Another contributing factor is high turnover. The industry is a major entry point to working life for many first time employees, who are often attracted by the glamorous image of travel and tourism. But a significant share of these same young people leave the industry after a few years, disenchanted with its working conditions and limited training and career prospects.

Seasonality of demand

The strong seasonal fluctuations in tourism demand have a marked impact on many enterprises in tourism and tourism related fields, since they in turn demand flexibility in the supply of services, with obvious consequences on employment. As an example, for every full-time job in tourism, there are several seasonal, or casual jobs.

Research suggests that in some of the major OECD tourism destinations, at least 90 per cent of all contracts in the restaurant sector are for fixed terms. Peak seasons, which are marked by a shortage of labour, are followed by seasonal troughs when there is little work available. The shorter the season, the greater the risk of unemployment.

It should, nevertheless, be pointed out that not all potential employees are deterred from working by the seasonal nature of available jobs. As an example, many young people actively look for part-time and seasonal jobs during their undergraduate or post-graduate studies.

Low skills, low wages and poor conditions

The low skills applicable to some tourism jobs pose a problem in highly developed economies. While the development level of an economy can influence the availability of unskilled and low-skilled labour, the level of unemployment can be just as, if not more important. Indeed, technology and economic restructuring in some developed economies is reducing the number of unskilled jobs available, creating a need for positions for less-skilled people. The shortfall is usually made up by recruiting foreign labour, but this is also not without problems as the experiences of countries like Switzerland have shown. During periods of heavy immigration, certain jobs may be set aside for immigrants with the result that in time, nationals consider these jobs beneath them.

This contributes to a perception that many of the jobs available in tourism and tourism related fields are at the lower end of the social scale, since few people want them. In many countries, working conditions in this sector have lagged behind other sectors and the gap has even widened over the years. Fluctuating demand patterns also pose constraints on the organisation of working hours, with frequent recourse to split shifts and night work. So it is not surprising that another common perception of the tourism industry is of one with long, unsociable working hours.

In addition, the remuneration system in some countries still includes uncertainty of income. In the restaurant sector especially, employees often have to rely on gratuities rather than fixed wages. And although high salaries in the tourism sector obviously do exist, average wages do not compare well with those in other sectors of industry or business. One of the problems is that the high proportion of unqualified and low-skilled workers in the industry and the rising import of cheap foreign labour have kept wages low. Social benefits like pensions and insurance cover are not generally good, either. And in many countries, large categories of workers in tourism are not covered by legal provisions or collective agreements.

Education and training ill-adapted to industry needs

The changing nature of tourism demand has also contributed to inadequacies in the tourism employment sector, largely because formal education and vocational training programmes have failed to adapt to the changing needs of the industry.

On the one hand - as in all sectors of the economy - there is a need for higher academic skills and increasing technological know-how, to respond to the demands of this increasingly technology driven world. Yet there is also a need for more broad based training, which helps develop a variety of skills. These are essential since tourists have become more sophisticated in their travel expectations and thus more demanding of quality and value for money. This puts an added burden on the staff themselves.

There appears to be a growing shortage of skilled labour in all sectors of the tourism and related industries. Yet the inadequacies of training - particularly on the job training, or job enrichment - and the perceived lack of career prospects, make it difficult to attract and retain qualified personnel. Some countries have added problems as well, as case studies presented during the Antalya seminar showed.

In Ireland, for example, the population of young people is in decline and employment opportunities in tourism and related sectors tends to be very decentralised, since so many tourism businesses are located in remote parts of the country. This does not appeal to many young people looking for jobs.

Overcoming the obstacles

What clearly emerged from the Antalya seminar is that many of the obstacles to attracting and retaining labour in the tourism industry can be overcome, as Member states' efforts have already proved.

Ireland, in common with a number of other OECD Member countries, has gone a long way to identifying some of the key problems of supply and demand in the tourism employment sector, through training needs' analyses and other market research, and is developing successful strategies to address them. Similarly, a survey was conducted in Portugal in 1992 to try to assess both the quantitative and qualitative needs of the tourism industry, to forecast labour demand over the coming years, and articulate it with the existing training supply. Changing demands clearly imply changing needs in terms of employment and, therefore, education and training.

Not surprisingly, the different approaches used from one country to another to address the issues have resulted in different strategies. These include distance learning and day release, or off-season courses, enabling students to learn at their own pace within the restrictions of their daily environment. The overall goal is to adapt training and educational schemes to meet the diverse and ever changing nature of the industry. Traditional course models and schools are clearly no longer valid.

Most OECD Members seem to agree that flexibility is essential, as is an emphasis on quality training. This helps to ensure that educational and training programmes meet the needs of all interested parties: the industry, the customers or tourists, the trainees themselves and the government, which is often the prime source of funds.

In Canada, in order to ensure involvement of both governments and the operating sector of the industry in human resource issues, a system of sector councils has been adopted - not just for tourism, but for all other industries and sectors. The Canadian Tourism Human Resources Council (CTHRC) provides the private sector with a forum to co-ordinate its human resources' activities, as well as to communicate with the federal government. Governments, meanwhile, obtain advice and a greater understanding of the policy implications on tourism.

Key to the whole concept is the partnering, or combining of resources which helps to avoid conflicts and duplication. Both parties have a responsibility and vested interest in ensuring effective and efficient policies and programmes.

VI. Conclusions and recommendations

An economic and social challenge

As has already been demonstrated, tourism is by some measures the largest single sector of OECD economies. It is also a major growth industry and as such, one that generates a large number of jobs. Moreover, given the projected growth forecasts for the industry well into the 21st century, its potential for future employment creation would seem to be even greater.

At a time when unemployment is of prime concern to governments and has been firmly placed at the top of their agendas, it clearly makes sense for OECD Members to look more closely at tourism's job creation potential with a view to helping maximise the industry's contribution to reducing unemployment.

This would provide not only for the development needs of the industry, but also for the career aspirations of young people, who are at the core of OECD's unemployment problem. Unemployment represents an enormous burden to society and Member economies in terms of under-utilised resources, not to mention the redistribution costs of welfare payments and taxation.

Admittedly, the opportunities for direct government intervention in the tourism labour market are limited. It is up to the tourism industry itself to develop its competitive edge in national and international labour markets by offering quality jobs and thus reversing the negative image of tourism as an employer. This implies an improvement of current working conditions - such as low pay and unsociable hours - increased promotional flexibility and career prospects.

But there are a number of ways in which governments can help ease some of the problems and encourage the industry's development.

Specific policy recommendations for governments

The main role for governments is to develop policies and measures that demonstrate their recognition of the importance of tourism as a generator of employment and help create favourable conditions for its growth.

These policies, none of which are unique to tourism, should cover such diverse areas as education and training, infrastructure developments - such as airports and satellite air traffic control systems - transport planning, and active regional and labour market programmes.

Government involvement and co-operation with the industry and with educators are also critical. As an example, the quality of jobs in tourism and related fields needs constant monitoring, especially since certain sectors are characterised by a high share of part-time, seasonal and casual jobs. While these are all forms of employment with inherent instability these jobs can, at the same time, provide a much needed work experience for new entrants to the labour force for young people, students, women and foreign immigrants.

Given its significance to Member economies, the issue of tourism and employment will continue to be a major focus of the OECD Tourism Committee's work programme and activities in the short and medium term future. These activities, the Committee members believe, should increasingly be developed in partnership with the private sector of the industry and could address issues such as education and training, the development of a statistical data base and the co-ordination of marketing strategies.

However, in order to ensure its overall objectives are achieved, certain specific issues need to be addressed in addition by governments. These include:

i)   Improved statistical data measures

Given the fragmented nature of the tourism industry and the fact that it does not fit the standard criteria for national accounts measurements, existing data do not permit an assessment of the size of the industry, nor its real economic impact. This is a major reason why its impact is often underestimated by governments, why they do not know how to tailor their policies to ensure they have the right effects on the sector, nor judge the effect of policy changes.

Improved data collection and analysis, in line with the approach proposed in the OECD Manual on Tourism Accounts and harmonised across OECD Member countries, would help provide a calculable indication of tourism's impact across the many different sectors of Member economies. This would facilitate governments' understanding of the linkages between tourism and employment - as well as identifying the quantitative and qualitative needs of the sector - and assist them in their policy decision-making.

Research into identifying manpower needs would also help ensure stabilisation of the workforce and a reduction of labour turnover.

ii)   The reduction of barriers and rigidities in labour markets

The economic growth projected for the second half of the 1990s should encourage structural change in the tourism sector. Governments should not prevent this change from taking place through protectionist measures, nor by regulating the labour market. Rather, they should continue their policies of liberalisation and the further reduction of barriers within OECD economies to reduce rigidities within labour markets.

Governments should also look at improving welfare cover for employees, especially for seasonal and part-time workers. Non-wage costs, such as employers' contributions to social benefits, should be reduced, as should other disincentives to hiring, and wage systems could be greatly simplified.

iii)   Adapting education and training to industry needs

The close involvement of OECD Member governments in human resource development through the organisation of formal education and training programmes is essential to the efficient operation of the tourism sector. Programmes should improve general as well as vocational skills and quality of service. Manpower and education policies could also go a long way to correcting some of the mismatches between labour supply and demand.

Programmes should, as far as possible, be developed in partnership between employers and employees to ensure they respond to industry needs and so attract the right kind of people to the industry. Joint collaboration should also aim to improve the working conditions in tourism and help define occupational standards.

Training programmes should go hand in hand with clearly identified career paths, offering increased job security, career prospects and further on-the-job training. This is vital for middle and upper level management as well as entry level employees. The motivation of workers, at whatever level, is improved if they are able to demonstrate the skills they have acquired and share in the advantages accruing from their level of performance.

Key findings of the *OECD Jobs' Study* that are of particular interest to the tourism industry suggest that unskilled workers receive less training than workers in general and also tend to seek training less. Less training is also given by small companies and enterprises and by those with high turnover such as those found within the tourism industry.

National education and training policies should take into account labour and social issues, and should be geared to stabilising the workforce and reducing labour turnover. Rather than considering personnel a cost to be reduced whenever possible, they should increasingly be seen as a resource which can help provide a competitive edge.

Background Report for the Seminar on Tourism and Employment

Prepared by Mr. Peter Keller
Head of the Tourism Department, OFIAMT
and Professor at the University of Lausanne, Switzerland

Introduction

Unemployment in western industrialised countries has grown as a result of the recession which began in the early 1990s. The OECD projects that by the end of 1994 there will be approximately 35 million unemployed in Member countries[2]. There are no ready answers to the unemployment problem, which is a complex one, although it can be partially explained by the difficulties of adjusting the economy to external shocks, technological change and globalisation. One other contributing factor commonly mentioned is the decrease in labour productivity, which is probably related to a lower savings ratio and rising interest rates.

In the post-war period strong, steady growth rates resulted in high stability and comparatively low unemployment. Since the first oil shock in 1973/74, macro-economic growth has slowed considerably. Over the same period, international tourism has expanded much faster than the general economy. And according to medium and long-term forecasts, this trend should continue. It may, therefore, be assumed that tourism has made and will continue to make a significant contribution to employment in the OECD area.

The OECD Tourism Committee tried to define the contribution of the tourism labour market to national economies in the 1980s[3]. At the time, little importance was attached to tourism in labour market policy. In the United States, high growth in employment in the private services field during the 1980s -- which was an economically robust period -- demonstrated the importance of the hotel and catering sector for the labour market because of its large workforce. In Western Europe, those concerned with the labour market have realised, for the first time since the start of the recession of the 1990s, that tourist regions are standing up quite well to the crisis. Regions which are highly diversified and well-equipped in terms of tourism are only slightly affected by unemployment.

The Tourism Committee studies published in the 1988 annual report refer only to the labour market for the hotel sector. No conclusions could be drawn at the time on the complete range of jobs in tourism. Since then, following proposals from the Committee, it has been possible to include tourist activities in national accounts, thereby allowing for a more detailed statistical survey of the tourism labour market. On this basis, the OECD developed its "Manual on Tourism Economic Accounts"[4] -- hereafter called the manual -- which permits, in particular, the use of the "production" account (shown in standard table 2) to obtain data on all jobs in tourism. However, the methods and instruments are not yet standardised and comparisons can only be made in certain cases.

It is now acknowledged that the impact of tourism on employment has been underestimated in OECD countries. Although there is a relatively high share of sectors dependent on tourism in the total labour force, they do not provide any indication about the quality of jobs in tourism. One of the economic policy goals in all OECD countries is to provide the most attractive kinds of jobs possible and high salaries for their citizens. The question, therefore, is whether jobs in tourism can meet these requirements.

Answering this question is something of a challenge because labour markets in the various OECD countries do not conform to the same pattern, and tourism's contribution to employment depends on the specific way in which labour markets work. This contribution is at its lowest in countries where institutionally rigid markets exist and where activities with a high value added are encouraged. Macro-economic models for the labour market mean that problems have to be stated in a particular way. The analysis is complicated by the fact that, at present, no model gives a very good grasp of cyclical and structural change.

The present background paper is based on replies to a questionnaire circulated to the relevant tourism authorities in Member countries. The responses, some of which were rather general, do not allow for in-depth and comparable quantitative analyses. They do, however, point to some interesting trends which are instructive as regards tourism's actual contribution to reducing unemployment.

I.   Role of tourism in the economies of OECD countries

i)   *Economic particularities of tourism*

Tourism is often identified simply with the hotel and catering sector. There can be no doubt that the hotel sector in particular is a pilot branch of tourism. Anyone spending a night in a hotel is a tourist. The image of tourism, as perceived in the economy, by society and in policy, is marked by the characteristics of this sector which has a large workforce and accounts for a relatively low value added compared with other sectors. This definition, however, is too narrow.

According to the definition of the World Tourism Organisation (WTO), tourism covers "the activities of persons travelling to and staying in places outside their usual environment for not more than one consecutive year for leisure, business and other purposes". Tourism is therefore defined on the demand side.

In developed countries, many sectors benefit from tourism demand. The tourist or group of travellers decides before a trip and/or at the destination point on the 'package' of services to be included in his, her or their travel budget. This means that in practice, a uniform tourist 'product' and a homogeneous tourism 'industry' do not exist.

The OECD manual covers economic sectors which depend largely on tourism. Only a few sectors produce exclusively for tourism. The main one is the travel agency sector. All other sectors which -- according to the OECD definition -- form the tourism industry, actually depend on tourism, but this dependence is not total. For example, only 30 to 80 per cent of hotel, catering, railway and road transport activities are concerned with tourism. Hotels can be used to accommodate military personnel and refugees. Restaurants meet the needs of the local population. In Switzerland, for example, where the share of tourism exceeds average values, tourism accounts for only 35 per cent of catering turnover.

Before they decide on their trip, tourists opt firstly for a destination and only afterwards for the services available on the market. They regard the destination as a whole or as a system of tourist services. Anyone studying the tourism job market must therefore know what the demand is for a given destination. The "demand" and "destination" criteria make it possible to aggregate the sectors dependent on tourism.

ii)　New statistical methods in tourism

So far, these economic particularities of tourism have not been adequately taken into account. This explains why this sector does not form one specific area for statistical study. Tourism as an entity is not an industry in the usual sense of the word, so it is hardly surprising that tourism is not classified internationally as an independent sector of the economy. Data are compiled on certain sectors which can be clearly defined on the supply side and are dependent on tourism, such as the hotel and catering sector and air transport. But there are no statistical surveys on tourism as a whole, which covers a large number of economic sectors. This explains why until very recently, tourism's contribution to the gross domestic product (GDP) and to employment could not be calculated directly and simply on the basis of supply.

In 1984, the OECD Tourism Committee decided to improve its statistical basis by developing the manual as a tool which would permit international comparability, based on the principles of national accounts. This method allows for the collection of data from the tourism industry; it creates a link between demand and supply. The tourism data compiled so far are based on the number of visitors recorded at frontiers and/or in establishments providing accommodation (arrivals/nights). On the basis of these physical flows, currency receipts are calculated or estimated by banks and statistical institutes. Since tourism supply can be assessed only through expenditure by visitors, the traditional statistical methodology is still being used. However, the OECD has produced a manual on a new statistical approach which integrates tourism in national accounts[5]. Comparisons with other sectors of the national economy are thus possible. This approach includes practical methods for assessing the importance of tourism in a national economy. It relates demand to supply and thereby defines the sectors which -- at least through some of their activities -- are dependent on tourism.

The OECD approach cannot, however, fully identify the importance of tourism for GDP and for certain sectors. Only representative goods and services can be covered. The direct relationship between services in demand (consumed) and specific sectors of the economy has not been established. Various Member countries have therefore tried to make up for these shortcomings, independently of the OECD concept. In particular, they have estimated tourism's share in the production of the main sectors concerned with tourism.

For studies on share of tourism in GDP, value added in the tourism sector has first to be calculated. This can be done by filling in table 2 of the manual - "derivation of value added in tourism industries at market prices". This table includes gross output, intermediate consumption and value added which is composed of compensation of employees, operating surplus, consumption of capital and indirect taxes. Direct tourist demand for goods and services should be expressed as a proportion of gross output. Tourist demand not only includes spending by foreigners but also spending by residents in their own country, consumption by the authorities and intermediate consumption.

In addition to this directly induced gross value added, tourism also contributes indirectly to GDP. Firstly, it requires 'intermediate consumption' (the difference between gross output and gross value added) which, at a subsidiary level, again indirectly induce demand within other sectors of the economy. For example, the purchase of a restaurant results in demand for the wholesale trade with the food or farming industries. Secondly, tourism also creates a demand for investment which should be taken into account.

OECD has identified the sectors which depend the most closely on tourism and has identified them as the 'tourist industry'. But it has not taken into account sectors for which tourism is only a part of the bottom line. These are, for example, the retail trade, banks, car rental or personal services, such as those provided by a hairdresser. It is not the intention of this report to provide detailed calculations either of value added (whether generated directly or indirectly from tourism) or of the number of people employed. These are relatively complex operations since they include estimates of the share of intermediate consumption, labour productivity and imports.

The inclusion of tourism in national accounts also gives rise to definition problems, such as the inclusion of the costs of private car transport or expenditure on owner-occupied second homes. In addition, this approach does not cover the underground economy, which is widespread in tourism, nor external social costs and benefits.

iii) Importance of tourism for the national economy

The annual data published by the OECD on physical and monetary flows focus on international tourism. They help Member countries to follow trends in the world's main tourist markets. Each OECD country can thus see how it is placed on the international market. From the point of view of the national economy, available data can be used to assess the contribution of tourism to the balance of payments. In the post-war period which was marked by the liberalisation of currency operations, this was of prime importance. Tourism has played a significant role, particularly in the reconstruction of Europe, since it is the prototype of an 'invisible export'. Today, currency contributions from tourism still play an important role in the economies of Member countries.

The shares of international tourism in exports -- and, therefore, the contribution to the balance of payments -- differ greatly among Member countries, ranging from 1 to 25 per cent. The respective share expresses the degree of a country's specialisation in tourism, which generally results in a balance of tourism surplus. But it says nothing about the country's actual market position in international tourism. The OECD countries where the share of receipts in exports of goods and services is low are also among the top 20 tourism destinations (Japan: share of tourism in exports 0.6 per cent, ranking 19th; Germany: 2.0 per cent, ranking seventh). The explanation for this is that these are major exporting countries, so that the share of tourism which is high in absolute figures is low in percentage terms.

It is interesting to note that, in OECD countries with a relatively low degree of specialisation in international tourism, the share of tourism in value added at macro-economic level is high (Sweden 6 per cent, Germany 5.6 per cent). Tourism shares in GDP, as reported by Member countries, are in fact not comparable since different kinds of methods are obviously used to calculate them. Surprisingly, however, these countries still place tourism among the major sectors of the economy, like construction and the retail trade. Tourism therefore has a great impact on the domestic economy.

Comparison of the weight of tourism in employment and in GDP

	Direct and indirect employment in tourism (in thousand)	Share of employment in tourism in the total labour force (%)	Share of tourism in GDP (%)
Canada	467.0	4.0	4.0
United-States	6,000.0	5.1	6.0
	0.0		
Australia	457.7	6.0	5.5
Japan	990.0	1.6	1.8
	0.0		
Austria	586.0	13.9	14.0
Belgium	74.0	2.0	4.0
Denmark	97.0	2.6	2.5
France	1,200.0	4.8	2.6
Germany	1,800.0	6.5	5.6
Greece	360.0	10.0	8.0
Iceland	3.8	3.0	5.0
Luxembourg	11.5	6.4	5.0
Netherlands	199.8	2.8	2.1
Norway	53.7	3.4	2.9
Portugal	250.0	5.6	8.0
Spain	1,400.0	9.1	8.0
Sweden	153.0	3.4	6.0
Switzerland	293.2	8.2	5.6
Turkey	129.0	0.7	3.4

Relative shares of tourism and construction in GDP

	Tourism/GDP (%)	Construction/GDP (%)	Reference year (construction)
Canada	4.0	6.3	1991
United-States	6.0	4.4	1992
Australia	5.5	6.9	1989
Japan	1.8	9.4	1991
Austria	14.0	7.0	1990
Belgium	4.0	5.8	1990
Denmark	2.5	5.2	1990
France	2.6	5.2	1990
Germany	5.6	4.9	1990
Greece	8.0	4.7	1990
Iceland	5.0		
Luxembourg	5.0	7.0	1990
Netherlands	2.1	6.9	1990
Norway	2.9	5.4	1989
Portugal	8.0	6.3	1989
Spain	8.0	8.6	1990
Sweden	6.0	9.9	1990
Switzerland	5.6	8.4	1990
Turkey	3.4	6.7	1990

Comparison of the weight of tourim in employment and in GDP

%

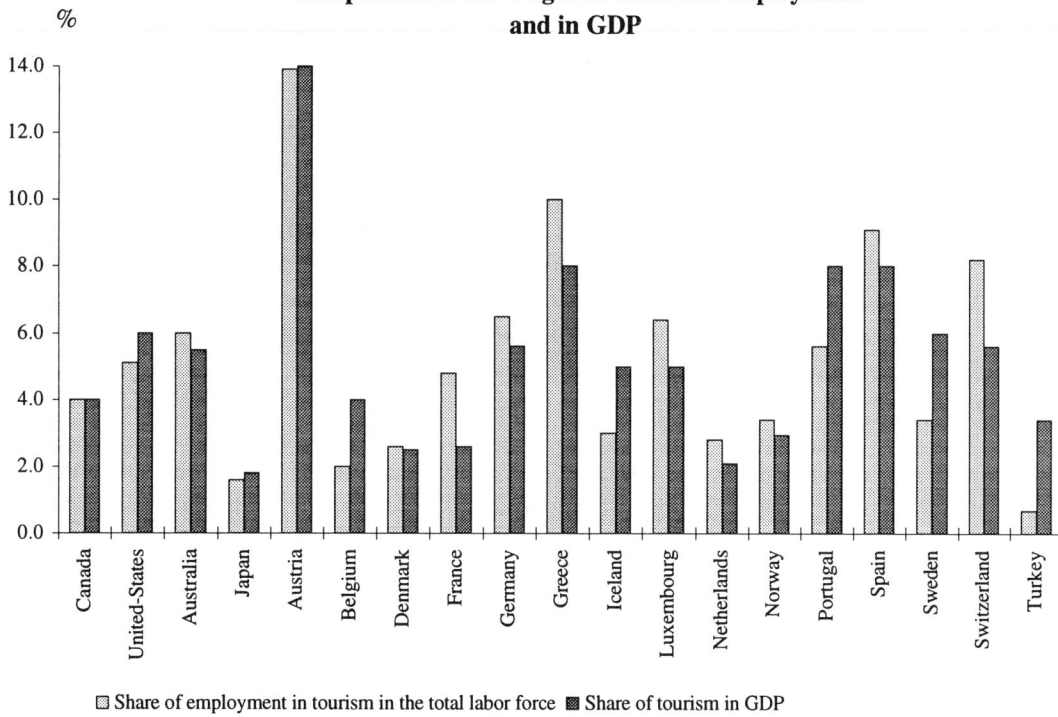

☐ Share of employment in tourism in the total labor force ■ Share of tourism in GDP

Source : OECD

Relative shares of tourism and construction in GDP

%

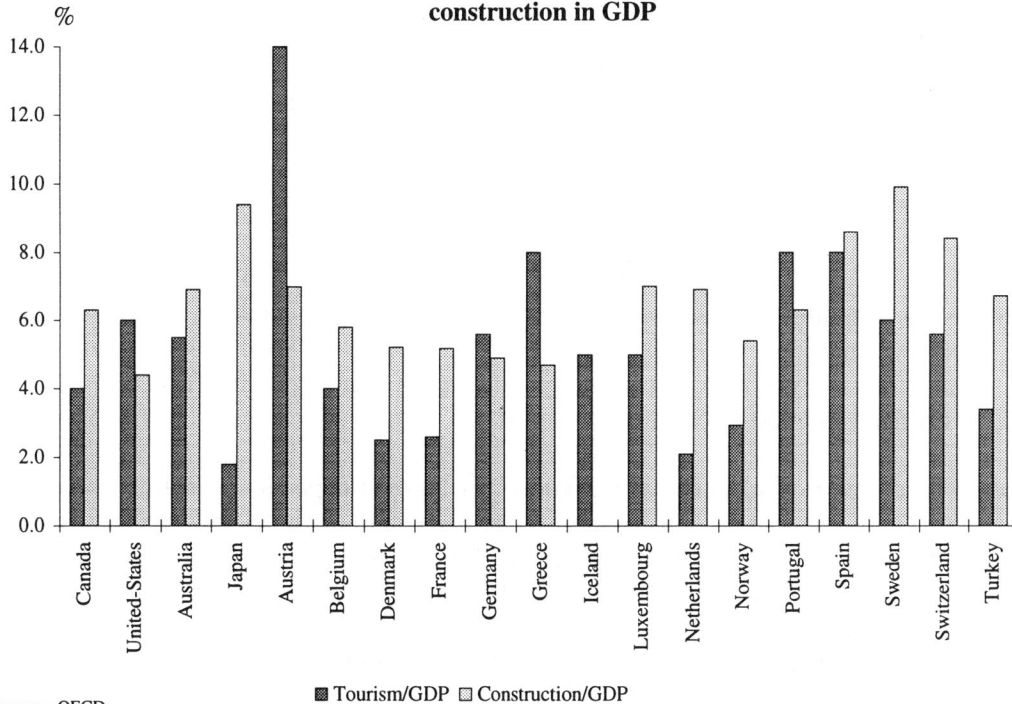

■ Tourism/GDP ☐ Construction/GDP

Source : OECD

Thus, it would be interesting to see how the value added from tourism is broken down between the various sectors. On the basis of a major study by the Swiss tourist authorities, it has been possible to obtain details of such a breakdown. The tourist industry, as defined by the OECD, accounts for about 50 per cent of the value added from tourism. The hotel and catering sector has the highest value added. According to the study, however, it accounts for only 20 per cent of tourism's total value added, but for half the tourist industry's value added. The attempt to grasp the macro-economic importance of tourism has given the following result: sectors which at first sight are not considered dependent on tourism do benefit from this activity (the retail trade, post offices, road transport activities, etc.). In addition, the construction and rental of holiday accommodation, intermediate consumption and investment are fields with a comparatively high value added. These fields which do not belong to the tourist industry as defined by the OECD, account for about half the value added from tourism.

The importance of tourism for a national economy can therefore be determined using new statistical methods in tourism. In this context, the regional aspect of the economy must be taken into account since, within national economies, some localities and regions are 50 to 80 per cent dependent on tourism.

iv) *Contribution of tourism to employment*

Tourist expenditure generates employment directly and indirectly in many sectors. Direct employment is that which depends on services used directly by tourists without intermediate transactions. Indirect employment relates to intermediate consumption and investment.

Tourism is a powerhouse in terms of employment. In most OECD countries, it is among the major sources of employment. On the basis of the data provided by Member countries, tourism's share in employment exceeds 5 per cent in ten OECD countries, including major countries such as the United States (5.1 per cent), Germany (6.5 per cent) and Canada (9.6 per cent[1]). In certain traditional tourist countries in the OECD area, the share exceeds 8 per cent (Austria 13.8 per cent, Greece 10 per cent, Switzerland 8.1 per cent). These figures must, however, be interpreted with caution since they are not entirely comparable. In most cases, they also include direct and indirect employment dependent on tourism. The World Travel and Tourism Council (WTTC) [5], which represents the tourist industry's interests internationally, estimates the shares of tourism in direct and indirect employment in the OECD region at 5.1 and 5.5 per cent respectively for 1994[6].

The absolute figures relating to employment dependent on tourism are also impressive. The United States has 6 million jobs in tourism, Germany 1.6 million, Spain and France 1.4 million each, Canada 1.2 million[1] and Japan 990 000. Similarly, in the case of Member countries where the labour force is smaller, the shares of employment in tourism are surprisingly high: Austria 586 000, Greece 360 000, Switzerland 293 000 and Portugal 250 000.

As one would expect, a statistical breakdown of tourism dependent employment between the different sectors confirms that the major employer in tourism is the hotel and catering sector. In the OECD area, this sector accounts for an average of one third of total tourist jobs and almost half of those in the tourist industry as defined by the OECD. The share of jobs in the accommodation sector is higher than in catering. The second-ranking employer in tourism is obviously the transport sector, *i.e.* air, rail and road transport combined. According to the data provided by some Member countries, its share is around 15 per cent.

In terms of direct employment, the travel agency field is an interesting case study since all its services are tourist related. This highly organised sector, which is geared to organising services, does not have a large workforce. The share of travel agencies in tourist jobs is between 3 to 5 per cent in most OECD countries.

The numbers employed in other sectors dependent on tourism are governed by the tourism structure of the respective Member countries. The number of jobs dependent on tourism in the retail trade is greater in cases where the share of para-hotel accommodation is high.

II.   Tourism's contribution to reducing unemployment

i)   Development of tourism and job creation

Tourism is a growth activity. In the post-war years it generated a wide range of jobs in many sectors and this growth in employment has been sustained to the present day. In most OECD countries, the sectors dependent on tourism have recorded above average growth in employment -- without any interruption in the 1980s and at the start of the 1990s -- both in absolute terms and compared with the economy as a whole. In OECD Member countries, a substantial part of the growth in the services sector is generated by jobs dependent on tourism.

Of the different activities dependent on tourism, the hotel and catering sector has contributed most to employment in a number of OECD countries. In absolute terms, this sector has to a large extent exceeded growth in all the other sectors dependent on tourism. In percentage terms, the travel agency sector has seen the highest growth in several OECD countries. Growth rates have also been high in sectors partly dependent on tourism such as transport and cultural, training and sporting activities.

The recession which has marked the OECD area since the start of the 1990s has had no great impact on employment in tourism as a whole. Most job losses have been reported in the hotel and catering sector which saw high growth in the boom period. The accommodation sector is the most sensitive to cyclical slowdowns. There are few alternative possibilities of employment for its workforce. Geographical mobility is very limited, since a high proportion of jobs in hotels and catering are filled by women and foreigners. The first are generally limited by family ties, the latter by specific work permit restrictions. Broadly speaking, however, the increased diversification of local and regional supply ensures steady demand and, therefore, stability of employment in tourist regions.

On the whole, it can be shown that tourism has contributed to employment. But it is also obvious that it cannot replace jobs lost in industry. Only a few industrial regions can be developed for tourism. Most jobs have been created in tourist centres and in towns which are cultural and administrative centres. In many OECD countries, rural areas are still lying fallow as far as tourism is concerned.

Some of the growth in jobs dependent on tourism concerns relatively low-skilled, often part-time jobs. Tourism has therefore contributed to marked growth in employment in the services sector, but this growth has given only a limited productivity gain.

ii) *Future impact of tourism on employment*

According to all medium and long-term forecasts, OECD countries can expect above average growth in tourism. The WTO projects that nominal growth rates in tourist expenditure for the period 1994-2005 will be between 4.6 and 12.7 per cent a year depending on the country concerned. During the 1990s, the actual international tourist flows (arrivals, nights) generating these growth rates should increase by 3.5 per cent.

The expected growth in tourism is justified in the short term by the economic recovery in OECD countries, and in the longer term by the spin-off from the emerging market globalisation which could mark the 1990s. Tourism will develop not only in the countries moving towards a market economy. Owing to the higher level of development in the newly industrialising countries (NIC), the traditional tourist regions in the OECD countries should attract more tourists. This trend will be strengthened by the increasing integration of regional economic groups (Europe, North America, Australia/Japan). It will result in greater competition in tourism and meet the as yet unsatisfied demand for tourist travel among wide sections of the population.

In the course of the next cyclical upswing, which is already imminent in the OECD area, higher productivity can be expected. And this will provide scope for wage increases in real terms and reductions in working time. In Switzerland, it has been calculated that a 5 per cent reduction (neutral, in terms of costs) in working time in the form of a fortnight's holiday would make it possible to create some 80 000 jobs. Promoting part-time work has the same effect. If working time was to be shortened, firms would have to recruit more employees in the recovery phase and there would be a greater likelihood of an increase in tourist expenditure.

Rising tourist expenditure creates jobs. In this field, the impact on employment occurs sooner than in other sectors of the economy. Research and development are, on the whole, not major factors in the tourism industry. Compared with industry, the utilisation of tourist facilities is low. In OECD countries, average occupancy in hotels is between 40 and 60 per cent a year (in industry: capacity utilisation is 80 per cent or higher). Initially, higher tourist expenditure creates jobs through the better use of available facilities. The next phase is one of additional investment, which also has an effect on employment.

WTTC forecasts high investment in tourist facilities in 1994. According to OECD's estimates, these figures seem overly optimistic. However, they do give an accurate picture of tourism's future contribution to employment in the OECD area, if the forecast expenditure are examined in detail. Experience, as shown by the number of additional jobs per hotel bed, for example, confirms the positive effects of tourism on employment.

iii) *The qualitative aspects of the tourism labour market*

The unemployment rate is comparatively high in OECD countries where productivity growth is strong. The jobless are often unskilled and are affected by long term unemployment. In these countries, some of the growth in tourism jobs is not very consistent with labour market policy. It is feared that unskilled jobs in tourism will result in low wages, considerable fluctuations in the workforce, a rise in the current unemployment level and greater segmentation of the labour market.

This argument is only partially sound. Tourism does generate unskilled jobs, particularly in the hotel and catering sector, where the workforce fluctuates greatly. But the fact remains that it generates a large number of full-time and part-time jobs that are particularly appreciated by young people, workers seeking re-employment, and housewives. These jobs reduce unemployment in regions where labour markets are flexible and deregulated. They also provide work for those who are not highly skilled.

It is worth pointing out that the share of the hotel and catering sector in countries with flexible and open labour markets is considerably higher than in countries with more rigid and segmented markets. In Switzerland, receipts from international tourism total over US$ 1,000 per capita. But the share of hotels and catering in employment is only 5.9 per cent. In the United States, the share is 6.7 per cent (1992 figures).

Jobs in the hotel and catering sector are the most visible part of tourism employment and very much influence the image of the sector. But they only provide a limited picture of the overall employment situation. Many of the other jobs dependent on tourism are well paid and interesting. If a wider approach is taken to tourism, it is found that, for every unskilled job in the hotel and catering sector, there is one skilled job in fields directly dependent on tourism. Moreover, all jobs in the hotel and catering sector are not unskilled. According to Swiss employment statistics, 74.2 per cent of jobs in the hotel and catering sector are unskilled, as compared with 60.6 in the economy as a whole.

The qualitative problems of the tourism labour market mainly concern the inbound tourism sector. In the tourism field, the economic structure is based on small enterprises and is dominated by the hotel and catering sector which needs a large number of personnel and is difficult to rationalise. Although some inbound services concern the export side of tourism, the structure is dominated by small enterprises and is geared to the domestic market. This does not make for an attractive work environment.

In contrast, jobs in the outbound or tourist generating sector are usually greatly appreciated. Demand for jobs in travel agencies and airlines is extremely high in OECD countries where leisure activities have a prominent place. Such jobs are considered ideal, particularly for young people. Technology is changing the face of outbound tourism, which is dominated by large firms that combine technical progress with significant economies of scale. Firms engaged in outbound tourism have an industrial-type structure and an international outlook, which makes the jobs in this field particularly attractive.

iv) Jobs in tourism and level of development

Tourism helps to speed up development in poor countries. It is easier to attract tourists than to sell high-tech products on the world market. In all OECD countries, tourism has contributed to the establishment and strengthening of economic structures and to the integration of the national economy in international markets. In some OECD countries, tourism was already contributing to development a hundred years ago or during the post-war years while in others, it has only been important since the 1970s or 1980s.

During such development phases, tourism rapidly creates jobs when the assets of the location are highlighted through substantial investment and efficient marketing. Under these circumstances, tourism has a competitive advantage since it has -- in comparison with other sectors -- many attractive jobs to offer. Judging by per capita income, some OECD countries are still benefiting from this advantage. However, the advantage tends to decline as the development level rises. Wages and prices increase as the country's national economy integrates with the world economy. It then becomes difficult to fill unskilled jobs in tourism.

The very highly developed economies of the OECD area have had to recruit foreigners for low-skilled jobs. The higher a country's development level and the higher the wages, the greater the proportion of foreigners employed in the hotel and catering sector. Although data supporting this phenomenon are not complete, the proportion tends to be consistent with a country's position in the per capita income ranking. The proportion of foreigners in the hotel and catering workforce is, on the basis of a weighted estimate, 14 per cent in France, 27 per cent in Germany, 33 per cent in Austria and 45 per cent in Switzerland. During the last boom period in Switzerland, many Swiss nationals left the hotel and catering sector. By recruiting foreigners, rich countries have managed to guarantee quality services in the tourism sector while, at the same time, enabling their nationals to take on well paid, interesting jobs.

III. Obstacles to the recruitment of available labour for jobs in tourism

i) Seasonal aspect of demand and hidden unemployment

The seasonal fluctuations in tourism demand result in partial unemployment for structural reasons. For every year round job in tourism, there are one or more seasonal jobs. The peak periods, where there is a shortage of labour, are followed by seasonal troughs where there is little work. The shorter the season, the greater the risk of unemployment. Where they have the choice, workers generally prefer year-round work to a seasonal job.

However, the fact that jobs in tourism are seasonal clearly does not matter to some employees, particularly young people who have a career in mind and who take seasonal jobs for training purposes. Foreign workers are also interested in taking seasonal jobs without having to emigrate from their country of residence, so that they can send home savings from their wages. This is a common practice throughout Europe. The seasonal nature of tourism also gives young people an opportunity to travel and work in a holiday atmosphere in seasonal or part-time jobs. This type of seasonal work is greatly appreciated, as shown by the excess demand for jobs as animators or sports instructors in holiday clubs.

As a rule, part-time workers and trainees are taken on during peak periods. Together with those recruited for the whole season, they contribute to the considerable fluctuations in employee numbers which characterise all activities dependent on seasonal jobs in tourism. In a large town, the fluctuation rate in the hotel and catering sector may be as high as 50 per cent. In such cases, there can be a complete turnover of the workforce in only two years. High geographic and professional mobility has an effect on productivity and wages. Seasonal jobs in tourism are not an alternative for workers seeking a permanent job. They are, however, appreciated given the present development of part-time work in OECD countries.

ii) Low skills and a segmented job market

The low skills applicable to some tourist jobs are a problem in highly developed economies. The higher the development level, the more difficult it is to find employees for unskilled work. The shortfall is made up by recruiting foreign labour from other OECD countries and, increasingly, from

Comparison between employees in the tourism sector and employees in other sectors

	Tourism sector		Other sectors	
	Women %	Foreigners %	Women %	Foreigners %
Canada	61.0			
United-States				
Australia	58.0			
Japan		20.0		
Austria	59.9	33.0	50.2	6.5
Belgium				
Denmark	70.0	20.0		
France	49.0	14.0		
Germany		27.0		
Greece	36.7			
Iceland				
Luxembourg		90.0		
Netherlands	52.0		39.0	
Norway	65.0	10.7		
Portugal	53.0			
Spain	46.0			
Sweden	75.0	20.0		
Switzerland	50.4	45.0		
Turkey	63.3		12.0	

non-OECD countries that are not highly developed. The recruitment problem becomes more serious in the up-swing phases of the business cycle.

The use of low-skilled foreign workers is problematic when they enjoy freedom of movement on the labour market. In Switzerland, the switch by unskilled labour from the hotel and catering sector to industry has resulted in productivity losses in the economy as a whole. Some unskilled workers in this sector who, during the boom period, moved from tourism activities and regions to industrial areas are now out of work.

The decrease in the number of nationals in unskilled jobs and the recruitment of foreign or part-time labour may result in segmentation of the labour market. In the dualistic theory of the labour market, a distinction is made between primary and secondary markets. The primary market consists of jobs with high salaries and a foreseeable career structure, good working conditions and guaranteed stability. The secondary market, in contrast, provides less well paid jobs offering little opportunity for promotion and little or no stability of employment. The barriers between these two labour markets are very high, since these various types of jobs are also identified with people of different 'cultures', representing different systems of values or lifestyles. This theory applies most markedly to the labour market in the hotel and catering sector.

In the event of lengthy periods of heavy immigration, some jobs may be set aside especially for immigrants in some parts of the tourism sector. This results in an interaction between immigration and the structure of the labour market. In time, nationals end up avoiding certain jobs. In such cases, these jobs will be taken only by new immigrants since nationals now consider that these jobs are beneath them. This is an important fact with regard to finding work for the unemployed. OECD countries cannot force people to work in the hotel and catering sector, especially when the available jobs are in remote areas.

iii) *Low productivity and wage levels*

It is difficult to increase productivity in jobs providing personal services. From the macro-economic point of view, productivity in this sector is relatively low. As a rule, the net value added per employee in a high-class urban hotel is three to four times less than in the case of a bank employee. In Switzerland, it is no higher in the hotel and catering sector than in agriculture. In that country, however, it has been shown that the net value added per employee for all activities dependent on tourism is only slightly less than in the economy as a whole.

Tourism also includes fields in which the value added per employee is high. These are fields which have benefited from technical progress and can be rationalised to some extent. In the transport field, for example, technical and telematic innovations (high-performance transport modes, reservation systems and yield management) have made it possible to achieve higher output at lower cost. In the hotel and catering field, para-hotel accommodation and standardised catering are increasingly common in some parts of the market. These types of accommodation and catering which are consistent with market realities, provide minimum service and fewer staff, so that the net value added per employee is higher.

However, the potential for productivity gains has been almost entirely exhausted in the traditional hotel and catering establishments which are still attached to quality of service. These establishments are suffering from 'cost disease' as they have to reflect their rising costs in higher prices, which are due to the difference between productivity gains in the general economy and the productivity trend in the sector. It is thus difficult to offer attractive wages and working conditions.

The fact that tourism expenditure has risen more than income enables a number of small and medium sized enterprises to survive in this sector, particularly if they have developed specific quality strategies. Visitors are prepared to pay relatively high prices for quality. Establishments focusing on quality have, however, less and less room for manoeuvre. In many cases, it is a buyer's market. In addition, the market is increasingly in the hold of intermediaries. A hotel which is located in an urban area and belongs to a chain usually pays commissions of 20 to 30 per cent to various intermediaries, including credit card and reservation companies.

It is therefore not surprising that wage levels are far below average in tourist sectors where productivity is low, as is shown by the results of the survey conducted in Member countries. The difference is 20 per cent on average. Average wages in the hotel and catering sector are comparable with those in the retail trade. It should not be concluded, however, that high wages are non-existent in this sector. Highly skilled employees -- whether cooks, receptionists or wine waiters -- sometimes command very high salaries. But it is notable that a significant share of jobs in this field are not competitive in national labour markets.

iv) Special working conditions

The fact that attractive and well paid jobs in many Member countries sometimes suffer from a shortage of staff raises the issue of working conditions in tourism. It would not be fair to say these conditions are generally poor. In most OECD countries, regulations on working time, holidays and welfare benefits are much the same in tourism as in other sectors of the economy. But the exceptions are seasonal workers and part-time employees who generally have no unemployment insurance in Member countries.

Nothing or almost nothing can be done about the particularities of working conditions in tourism. Some kinds of service involve undesirable working times (weekends, holidays, nights). The workload varies with demand. The personal nature of services requires considerable personal commitment. Peak hours result in stress. The work is quite often repetitive. This is why many individuals are not qualified for employment in tourism and others are not willing to accept the sector's employment disadvantages.

Working conditions are particularly difficult in catering. While hard physical work is on its way out in industry and the working environment is becoming healthier, working conditions are still quite often physically demanding and the environment unhealthy for kitchen staff and, to some extent, for service personnel (heat, steam, draughts, poor lighting, noise). It is not surprising that catering jobs are not generally held in high esteem.

IV. Policy initiatives for the solution of labour market problems in tourism

i) Creation of favourable conditions for tourism

The possibilities of government intervention on the labour market are limited in the tourism field. It is up to the tourist sector to develop its competitiveness in international and national labour markets by offering attractive, well paid jobs. Governments can contribute to the process by creating favourable conditions for tourism.

The economic growth expected in the second half of the 1990s will assist structural change in the tourism sector. Governments must not prevent this change from taking place through protectionist measures, or by regulating the labour market. Their task is rather to provide welfare cover for employees in the sector, including seasonal and part-time workers.

Governments can help to protect and create jobs in tourism by investing in infrastructure, telecommunications, land-use planning and protection of the countryside. To achieve more direct sectoral effects, they can also promote tourism demand by supporting the marketing operations of national tourist bodies.

Governments can also improve quality in tourism by ensuring that vocational training is consistent with market conditions. The quality approach plays a decisive role in international competition among OECD countries.

ii) *Freedom of movement for workers and deregulation of the labour market*

The survey conducted in Member countries clearly shows that freedom of movement for workers in the tourist sector does not exist in the OECD area. It exists only in the EU countries. Some countries issue temporary permits for the recruitment of foreign workers for the unskilled and seasonal jobs which are rejected by nationals. These permits generally include rules setting minimum wages in order to prevent social dumping.

Such restrictions create difficulties on national labour markets as far as tourism is concerned. These difficulties, which are especially marked in a boom period, have a positive side, in that they prevent wages from plummeting in sectors that employ foreigners. This raises the question as to whether it would be reasonable to reduce these restrictions in the OECD area.

The OECD countries have concluded agreements on the exchange of trainees and workers. These agreements generally cover a period of 18 months to two years and can be extended on a bilateral or even multilateral basis.

The recession which is persisting in some OECD countries has led to a change in thinking about what is 'acceptable work' for the jobless. A number of Member countries have taken specific action to encourage young, unemployed people to work in tourism. In certain circumstances, for example, a job in catering is increasingly seen as 'acceptable' work. Japan does not allow foreigners to be recruited for seasonal jobs, which are reserved for elderly people whose unemployment benefits are coming to an end.

iii) *Vocational training geared to market needs*

All OECD countries now have a well developed training system for the tourism sector, which includes apprenticeships, higher vocational education and continuing training at all levels. Attempts have been made in recent years to adapt the system more closely to market needs. Over-specialised basic training has been eliminated, and comprehensive courses have been set up. Training increasingly includes marketing and management courses.

Some OECD countries have an excessive number of graduates in tourism studies (Belgium, Netherlands). It is also frequently claimed that the needs of employers and the salaries they offer are not up to prospective employees' expectations. The question of government support for vocational training has to be reconsidered. Excellence of training will not solve all the problems on the labour market. In the case of unskilled personnel and part-time employees, in-house, or on-the-job training seems to be the most appropriate. Broadly speaking, OECD countries will have to develop vocational training strategies which could help to revitalise a tourism sector that has now reached maturity.

The hotel, catering and transport sectors require early specialisation -- *i.e.* from the basic training stage -- but all the other activities directly connected with tourism have openings for personnel from other sectors. The concentration and horizontal co-operation processes, however, are leading to professional standards requiring tourism specialisation in the management and marketing fields.

iv) *Encouraging innovation in tourism*

In OECD countries, the encouragement of tourism by governments is not so much to boost employment as to help maintain tourism infrastructure and activities. The more mature an economy is, the greater the risk of a deteriorating infrastructure. The quality of jobs available is then often not up to expectations.

The new approach to tourism statistics, which facilitates the calculation of value added per worker, can be used as a starting point for a better targeted labour market policy. The aim should primarily be to support fields that will create value added and give priority to qualitative growth. Lastly, individual productivity must be improved.

The accent must be less on promoting buildings and facilities than on innovation with regard to organisation, products and marketing, which contribute to greater rationalisation and to more attractive jobs. This kind of innovation should be encouraged, particularly in the hotel and catering sector.

New facilities should not be advocated except in areas which have sufficient labour reserves. For example, in rural areas from which agricultural activity will progressively disappear.

Notes

1   These figures refer to available estimates of "all persons employed" in "all tourism-related industries in Canada". Canada has developed more precise estimates as a part of the recently released Tourism Satellite Account for 1988. These estimates measure tourism employment share somewhat differently and therefore give different estimates of tourism-related employment. The TSA results suggest that in 1988 tourism activities represented 4 percent of total employment in Canada when measured in terms of full time equivalent person years which were estimated at a total of 467 000 FTE in "tourism activities".

2   OECD Jobs' Study, SG/EUS (94 No. 1), Paris 1994.

3   OECD, International Tourism and Tourism Policy in OECD Member Countries, Paris 1988.

4   OECD, Tourism Committee, Manual on Tourism Economic Accounts, OECD/GD(91)82, Paris 1991.

5   World Travel and Tourism Council (WTTC), Brussels 1993.

6   World Tourism Organisation (WTO), Global Tourism Forecasts to the Year 2000 and Beyond, Madrid 1993.

Chapter II

International Tourist Flows in Member Countries

This Chapter brings together, in the form of summary tables, data on international tourist flows to OECD Member countries. The tables give regional totals for each of the three geographical areas of the OECD -- North America, Asia-Pacific and Europe -- plus the OECD total.

Henceforth, Mexico, having become the Organisation's 25th Member country, is incorporated into all of the summary tables, under North America. As a result, figures for the region are not comparable with past data, which included only the United States and Canada. In addition, for the sake of consistency with other OECD publications, the order in which regions are presented has been changed, and the name of the "Australasia-Japan" region has become "Asia-Pacific".

Annual data by country of origin of foreign tourists or visitors, for 1992 and 1993, are set out in the Statistical Annex.

Section A outlines the general trends noted in 1993 over the whole OECD area.

Section B records changes in international tourist flows in each Member country in 1993. The data cover:

a) Arrivals at frontiers either of tourists (persons spending more than one night in the country being visited) or, where such figures are not available, all visitors (tourists plus same-day visitors). For further details of how travellers are classified, please refer to Chart A in the Statistical Annex.

b) The number of nights spent by foreign tourists in hotels and similar establishments (generally speaking, hotels, motels, inns and boarding houses).

c) The number of nights spent in all forms of accommodation (*i.e.* in all forms combined).

For further details on the types of accommodation covered by data for each receiving country, please refer to Table C in the Statistical Annex.

Lastly, Section C describes international flows from the OECD's main generating countries: Canada, France, Germany, Italy, Japan, the Netherlands, the United Kingdom and the United States.

I. International tourism in the OECD area

After a significant upswing in international tourism in 1992, 1993 was more a year of consolidation for tourism -- despite economic difficulties and the slowly waning confidence of consumers and businesses:

-- nights spent in all forms of accommodation in the OECD area: up 0.2 per cent (compared with a 4 per cent increase the previous year);

-- nights spent in hotels in the OECD area: up 0 per cent (compared with a 5 per cent increase);

-- arrivals at frontiers in the OECD area: up 0 per cent (compared with a 6 per cent increase).

According to the World Tourism Organisation (WTO), in 1993 international tourism, expressed in terms of arrivals, rose worldwide by 2 per cent to about 513 million arrivals. The fastest growth was observed in the Far East/Pacific region (up 11 per cent), followed by Africa (up 3 per cent), Europe (up 1 per cent) and the Americas (up 0.2 per cent). Lastly, slight decreases were recorded in South Asia (down 1 per cent) and the Middle East (down 1 per cent).

From 1989 to 1993, worldwide arrivals were up by 20 cent. Growth was decidedly brisker in the Far East/Pacific region (up 50 per cent) and in Africa (up 33 per cent), whereas Europe (up 14 per cent), South Asia (up 13 per cent) and the Middle East (up 10 per cent) each lost market share.

Nevertheless, Europe remained the largest tourist market in the world, with 60 per cent of arrivals. Tourism activity within the EU remained buoyant in spite of weak European economies and high unemployment.

The 1993 figures for the OECD area are as follows:

-- arrivals at frontiers in North America: down 3 per cent (compared with an 8 per cent increase the previous year);

-- arrivals at frontiers in the Asia-Pacific region: up 6 per cent (as in 1992);

-- nights spent in all forms of accommodation in Europe: down 0.2 per cent (compared with a 5 per cent increase);

-- nights spent in hotels in Europe: down 1 per cent (compared with a 5 per cent increase);

-- arrivals at frontiers in Europe: up 1 per cent (compared with a 5 per cent increase);

Arrivals at frontiers (Table 1)

Of the 19 European Member countries, only 12 collect data or provide estimates on foreign tourist or visitor flows at frontiers. Two of these 12 countries -- Austria and Germany -- record all traveller arrivals at frontiers, which is a much broader yardstick than is used for analysing tourist flows, since it includes travellers in transit. These figures have not, therefore, been included in Table 1 but are shown for information in Table 6 of the Statistical Annex.

Sixteen countries, including ten in Europe, collect figures on arrivals at frontiers. Regional trends show significant divergencies.

In **Europe**, a region where unemployment remained relatively high and the expected economic recovery was weaker than projected, the growth rate of tourism fell significantly. Moreover, sharply fluctuating exchange rates in a number of countries, including Sweden, Spain, Finland, Italy, Turkey and the United Kingdom, also had an impact on tourism.

After a brisk upswing in 1992, when they enjoyed a return of their long-haul customers, the OECD's Mediterranean countries had a more mixed year in 1993. Spain improved its position (arrivals up 4 per cent, compared with a 3 per cent increase in 1992), as did Italy, which was slowly returning to equilibrium by cutting its decline from 15 per cent in 1991 to 0.4 per cent in 1993. All of the other countries suffered an deterioration of their relative positions in terms of arrivals at frontiers. France and Greece both had fewer Japanese and US visitors, while the numbers of Italians visiting France and of Netherlands tourists visiting Greece also declined. Portugal recorded a drop in customers from the main OECD generating countries, with the notable exception of Japan. Lastly, Turkey was mostly hit by the weak German and Italian markets.

Growth was sustained in the United Kingdom (arrivals up 3 per cent).

Lastly, Iceland and Ireland had the highest growth rates (at respectively 10 and 6 per cent).

Arrivals in **North America** (including Mexico) decreased by 3 per cent in 1993 (compared with an 8 per cent increase). Canada returned to growth after two consecutive years of decline (arrivals up 3 per cent); while its main markets were up significantly, the rise was tempered by a moderate upswing in the US market (up 1.7 per cent), which accounted for 80 per cent of total arrivals. The United States (down 4 per cent) was hit harder, due in part to a combination of the dollar's appreciation against all other currencies (with the notable exception of the yen) and the economic weakness of its leading markets. Canadians, Italians and Japanese sharply reduced their visits to the United States in 1993. Lastly, Mexico recorded a substantial decline of 9 per cent.

The **Asia-Pacific** region remained the most dynamic of the major OECD areas, with arrivals increasing at the same pace as the previous year (up 6 per cent). By country, however, the expansion varied. Growth in inward tourism was led by steep increases in Australia (up 15 per cent), which reaped the full benefits of economic development in Asia; inbound from Europe, the German (up 18 per cent), French (up 22 per cent) and Netherlands (up 17 per cent) markets rose sharply.

For the second consecutive year, robust growth was also recorded in New Zealand. Asian markets were the most dynamic (arrivals up 49 per cent), while Germany (up 23 per cent) also made a substantial contribution to these strong results.

The yen's steady appreciation had a significant impact on the price competitiveness of the Japanese tourist industry, and arrivals of tourists in Japan dropped by 9 per cent.

Nights spent in hotels and similar establishments (Table 2)

Eighteen European countries plus Australia and Mexico compile data on nights spent in hotels and similar establishments; generally speaking, these data concern nights recorded in hotels, motels, boarding houses and inns (see Table C in the Statistical Annex).

After a 5 per cent rise from 1991 to 1992, Europe recorded a 1 per cent drop in visits in 1993. This figure masks very different trends, however, from one country to another.

The sharpest declines were recorded in Portugal (nights spent down 10 per cent), Germany (down 8 per cent), France (down 7 per cent) and the Netherlands (down 6 per cent).

Finland, Sweden, Norway, Turkey and Spain experienced growth. Lastly, Iceland enjoyed a 53 per cent gain, driven largely by a substantial contingent of German and US customers.

Outside Europe, Australia performed well, with strong growth (up 14 per cent, hotels only), as did Mexico (up 3 per cent).

Nights spent in all forms of accommodation (Table 3)

Nineteen countries (16 in Europe plus Australia, Canada and New Zealand) compile aggregate data on nights spent in all forms of accommodation. This category includes hotel and non-hotel accommodation -- youth hostels, camp sites, holiday villages etc. -- (for further details see Table C in the Statistical Annex).

Data on all forms of accommodation combined showed that the number of nights spent remained flat between 1992 and 1993. In Europe, the performance of international tourism in the Nordic countries, except for Denmark (nights spent down 10 per cent), was strong, with the upswing led primarily by the Germans and the Japanese. For its part, Denmark was hard hit by defections by customers from other Nordic countries, the Netherlands, Italy and Japan.

In Germany, nights spent declined by 9 per cent, reflecting a fall-off of all its main markets, and especially Sweden (down 31 per cent), Italy (down 18 per cent), Spain (down 16 per cent) and the United States (down 11 per cent).

In the Mediterranean area -- apart from Portugal, which recorded a downturn (of 10 per cent) for the second consecutive year -- Greece (up 1 per cent), France (up 1 per cent), Italy (up 2 per cent) and Turkey (up 2 per cent) experienced moderate growth.

Canada had a 3 per cent increase in nights spent, representing a gain of more than 2.6 million nights. This strong performance stemmed chiefly from a greater number of nights spent by tourists from the United States (up 3 per cent) and the United Kingdom (up 6 per cent).

Australia and New Zealand were also on the rise (up by 9 per cent).

Table 1. **Annual growth rates of number of arrivals of foreign tourists at frontiers**[1]

	T/V	% 91/90	% 92/91	% 93/92	1993 Millions of arrivals
Canada	T	−2.0	−1.1	2.5	15.1
Mexico	T	−9.2	10.3	−9.1	9.8
United States	T	8.5	10.8	−3.7	45.8
North America		3.1	8.1	−3.3	
Australia	V	7.0	9.8	15.1	3.0
Japan	T	12.0	−0.1	−8.5	1.9
New Zealand	T	−1.3	9.6	9.6	1.2
Asia and the Pacific[1]		7.3	5.9	5.5	
Austria					
Belgium					
Denmark					
Finland					
France[4]	T	3.5	8.5	0.7	60.1
Germany					
Greece	T	−9.4	16.1	0.9	9.4
Iceland	T	1.2	−0.6	10.4	0.2
Ireland	V	−2.3	4.6	6.2	3.3
Italy	V	−14.9	−2.4	−0.4	49.9
Luxembourg					
Netherlands					
Norway					
Portugal	T	7.9	2.6	−5.1	8.4
Spain	V	3.5	3.2	4.2	57.9
Sweden					
Switzerland[2]	T	−4.5	1.6	−3.1	12.4
Turkey[3]	V	2.4	28.2	−8.1	6.5
United Kingdom	T	−6.1	8.0	3.0	17.9
Europe[1]		−3.2	4.6	0.9	
OECD[1]		−1.6	5.5	0.0	

V Visitors.
T Tourists.
Note: Canada, Italy and Portugal dispose of both series (V and T); see annex.
1. Overall trend for all countries with data available from 1990 to 1993.
2. Estimates.
3. Travellers.
4. Changes of series in 1991: new frontiers' survey.

Table 2. **Annual growth rates of nights spent by foreign tourists in hotels and similar establishments**[1]

	% 91/90	% 92/91	% 93/92	1993 Millions of beds-nights
Canada				
Mexico	1.3	−2.5	3.4	19.9
United States				
North America[1]				
Australia	−8.3	8.3	13.8	14.2
Japan				
New Zealand				
Asia and the Pacific[1]				
Austria	3.5	0.2	−3.4	62.0
Belgium	−4.4	17.0	−2.7	7.5
Denmark	9.8	3.6	−4.3	5.9
Finland	−10.8	1.9	15.4	2.6
France	−2.8	10.8	−7.1	54.6
Germany[2]	−6.7	2.2	−8.1	26.1
Greece	−14.7	21.4	0.6	36.5
Iceland	3.5	−0.3	53.2	0.7
Ireland	13.8	−1.0	2.4	9.6
Italy	−0.3	−3.7	1.8	64.6
Luxembourg	−0.4	−6.1		
Netherlands	−1.3	6.3	−6.2	8.0
Norway	10.7	9.2	6.6	4.6
Portugal	14.2	−6.3	−9.5	16.2
Spain	3.8	3.4	7.7	82.9
Sweden	−11.5	−0.8	6.4	3.0
Switzerland	−3.2	−0.6	−2.3	19.8
Turkey	−21.1	66.8	5.9	14.4
United Kingdom				
Europe[1]	−0.8	4.8	−0.6	
OECD[1]	−1.0	4.5	0.0	

1. Overall trend for all countries with data available from 1990 to 1993.
2. The data relate to the territory of the Federal Republic of Germany prior to 3rd October 1990.

Table 3. **Annual growth rates of nights spent by foreign tourists in all means of accommodation[1]**

	% 91/90	% 92/91	% 93/92	1993 Millions of beds-nights
Canada	0.7	−4.0	3.4	82.1
Mexico				
United States				
North America[1]				
Australia			9.1	35.4
Japan				
New Zealand	−6.6	6.3	8.5	22.2
Asia and the Pacific[1]	−6.6	6.3	8.5	
Austria	5.1	0.1	−2.9	96.8
Belgium	−5.6	5.8	0.2	12.9
Denmark	11.7	11.1	−9.7	10.5
Finland				
France[3]	2.3	7.6	0.9	430.3
Germany[2]	7.4	2.1	−9.1	34.7
Greece	−15.9	20.9	0.5	37.1
Iceland				
Ireland	−1.2	1.5	4.0	35.1
Italy	0.0	−3.6	2.1	85.4
Luxembourg	5.9	−8.8		
Netherlands	4.5	5.2	−5.1	17.2
Norway	4.5	6.2	6.1	6.9
Portugal	13.5	−8.6	−9.7	18.1
Spain				
Sweden	−14.8	3.8	4.5	6.1
Switzerland	0.4	−0.1	−0.7	36.7
Turkey	−26.9	73.1	1.7	17.1
United Kingdom	−5.0	0.4	−0.1	187.0
Europe[1]	0.0	4.5	−0.2	
OECD[1]	−0.1	3.9	0.2	

1. Overall trend for all countries with data available from 1990 to 1993.
2. The data relate to the territory of the Federal Republic of Germany prior to 3rd October 1990. Since 1991 includes camping sites.
3. Changes of series in 1991: new frontiers' survey.

52

II. International tourism in each member country in 1993

Australia. The number of nights spent by foreign tourists in registered tourist accommodation rose by 9 per cent, after declining for two years; the number of nights spent in hotels advanced more sharply (up 14 per cent). Total nights spent by tourists from Europe (excluding those from the United Kingdom and Ireland) in all forms of accommodation progressed by 13 per cent, while nights spent by tourists from North America rose by 10 per cent. Significant decreases were recorded for tourists from the United Kingdom and Ireland (down 7 per cent) as well as for those from Japan (down 10 per cent).

Using arrivals at frontiers (the most comprehensive statistical series), a more detailed analysis of recent trends in tourism by foreign visitors in Australia shows that growth rates were sustained, especially for tourists from emerging markets in Asia. The number of visitors to Australia reached nearly 3 million for the first time in 1993, rising 15 per cent from the previous year.

In terms of arrivals, Japan remained the largest market for Australia with 671 000 visitors in 1993. This accounted for 22 per cent of aggregate arrivals and represented a 7 per cent increase over 1992.

Arrivals from the rest of Asia rose by 40 per cent. This reflects both the economic buoyancy of the region, which is inducing more and more people to travel, but also the attractiveness of Australia as a destination. A weaker Australian dollar relative to many Asian currencies also improved the competitiveness of Australian tourism for Asian visitors. The inbound Asian markets that grew most strongly were Korea (up 85 per cent) and Taiwan (up 71 per cent). Indonesia and Thailand also expanded (up 56 and 38 per cent respectively).

Arrivals from the United Kingdom/Ireland and from the rest of Europe grew by 8 and 13 per cent, respectively, in 1993. The only major market segment to have declined in 1993 was the Nordic countries (visitors down 1 per cent).

Austria. All indicators show that Austrian tourism fell off significantly in 1993. The number of nights spent in registered tourist accommodation, and those spent in hotels and similar establishments, decreased by about 3 per cent.

The number of nights spent in registered tourist accommodation in Austria -- the series considered to be the most representative for analytical purposes -- fell by 2.8 per cent for tourists from Europe in spite of the 0.4 per cent increase from the leading market, Germany (67 per cent of nights spent). The other major markets -- the Netherlands and the United Kingdom -- were down by 6 and 9 per cent respectively. Other substantial decreases were recorded for tourists from the Nordic countries, Italy (down 23 per cent), Spain (down 14 per cent) and France (down 7 per cent). Finally, European non-Member countries performed well.

From outside Europe, after a sharp upswing in 1992, North American tourists curtailed their visits to Austria (down 10 per cent), as did those from Australia and Japan (down 14 and 3 per cent respectively).

Belgium. In 1992, there had been growth in the number of foreign tourists staying in terms of registered tourist accommodation (up 5 per cent).

Since 1991, official statistics no longer include one sector that is growing rapidly -- that of rentals. The reasons for this are technical: the methods of calculation are too different from those used for other forms of accommodation.

In 1993, foreign markets remained stable for registered tourist accommodation (up 0.2 per cent), whereas nights spent in hotels declined by 3 per cent. These mediocre results were due in part to heightened competition, from "sun" destinations in particular. Furthermore, the year was affected by a fall-off of business tourism; this element was a major factor in the temporary downturn in hotel stays by travellers from the United Kingdom (down 11 per cent), Italy (down 13 per cent), the United States (down 16 per cent) and Japan (down 17 per cent).

Neighbouring markets continued to grow, albeit more slowly than in 1992: Germany (up 8 per cent for registered tourist accommodation), the Netherlands (up 4 per cent) and France (up 8 per cent).

Canada. In 1993, inbound international tourism picked up moderately: nights spent in tourist accommodation rose by 3 per cent, and the number of tourists grew at the same rate, to a total of about 15 million arrivals.

The devaluation of the Canadian dollar relative to most other currencies (including the US dollar), along with marketing efforts undertaken in co-operation with the industry and the development of new products (casinos, museums, natural attractions), had a relatively positive impact on travel to Canada.

The improved figures were due to strong demand from Canada's biggest customers -- those from the United States (58 per cent of nights spent; up 3 per cent over 1992) and the United Kingdom, its number two market (8 per cent of nights spent; up 6 per cent).

Overall, nights spent by tourists from OECD-Europe increased by 9 per cent, but this masked big differences in trend: Austria, Finland, Germany and France were up by between 12 and 22 per cent; Iceland, Norway and Portugal were down by between 16 and 18 per cent.

The increase in the number of nights spent by Japanese tourists (up 15 per cent) should also be noted, as should the appreciable rise in Latin American markets (up 5 per cent).

Denmark. After expanding for several years in succession, the number of nights that foreign tourists spent in registered tourist accommodation (excluding furnished accommodation and holiday homes) fell by 10 per cent in 1993. The decline was attributable to fewer tourists from other Nordic countries (down 19 per cent) and from the Netherlands (down 32 per cent), Italy (down 21 per cent) and Japan (down 10 per cent).

In particular, Denmark was hurt by the lowering of VAT rates on accommodations in the other Nordic countries and by the devaluation of the Swedish krona, which caused Norwegians and Swedes to curtail their visits and prompted tourists from some countries, such as Germany, to go to Sweden rather than Denmark.

It needs to be pointed out that the form of accommodation most commonly used by tourists in Denmark is summer homes and private accommodation and that this category is not included in OECD statistics. In 1993, given that accommodation of this sort recorded growth of 13 per cent, tourist stays in all forms of accommodation combined were actually up by 2 per cent.

Finland. After the reversal in trend that took place in 1992, 1993 was another record year as the number of nights spent in hotels rose by 15 per cent. One of the main reasons for this was improved competitiveness due to the weakness of a floating Finnish markka, together with a strengthened marketing policy -- a policy that was carried out in partnership with the private sector and that relied in particular on the "green" tourism segment, in which demand remained especially buoyant.

All of the main markets were on the rise. Inbound tourism continued to grow from Germany (up 34 per cent), Norway (up 19 per cent) and the United States (up 9 per cent). After falling in 1992, growth resumed in the Swedish (up 6 per cent), United Kingdom (up 11 per cent), Canadian (up 16 per cent) and Japanese (up 25 per cent) markets.

On the other hand, visits by Danes (down 6 per cent), Austrians (down 7 per cent) and Icelanders (down 18 per cent) fell off appreciably.

France. Despite a gloomy economic situation in Europe and devaluations in several large neighbouring countries, the level of international tourism held steady in 1993. The number of nights spent in tourist accommodation rose by 1 per cent, to 430 million nights; arrivals of tourists grew at the same rate. Only nights spent in hotels experienced a significant drop, falling by 7 per cent.

In terms of nights spent in tourist accommodation, the lower number of tourists from Italy (down 12 per cent), Spain (down 12 per cent), Switzerland (down 17 per cent) and the United Kingdom (down 2 per cent), as well as from the United States (down 2 per cent) and Japan (down 31 per cent), was more than offset by the sharp increase in arrivals from Belgium (up 6 per cent), the Netherlands (up 15 per cent) and Canada (up 15 per cent), and by continued growth in the number of German visitors (up 2 per cent).

Unlike the previous year, 1993 did not feature any special events of interest to tourists (such as the Winter Olympics and the opening of Eurodisney). Nevertheless, because the Eurodisney complex opened in mid-1992, the full-year effect of the additional inflow of tourists had a positive impact on 1993.

Germany. Since 1992, statistics on registered tourist accommodation have included camp sites and therefore cannot be compared with statistics from earlier years.

The downward trend in overnight stays that had been observed in 1991 and 1992 continued in 1993: the total number of nights spent was 35 million, down 9 per cent on 1992.

This tendency was due chiefly to the lower number of nights spent by tourists from the main generating countries, such as the Netherlands (down 10 per cent), Japan (down 8 per cent), the United States (down 11 per cent), Sweden (down 31 per cent), Italy (down 18 per cent) and France (down 6 per cent).

One positive development was the marked increase in the number of nights spent by tourists from former republics of the USSR (up 16 per cent), Portugal (up 8 per cent) and Turkey (up 7 per cent).

Greece. Tourism in Greece was consolidated in 1993 after an excellent year in 1992. Over 9 million tourists went to Greece (1 per cent more than in 1992), including a greater number of German (up 6 per cent), Italian (up 1 per cent) and UK tourists (up 2 per cent). Also of note was the very sharp growth of one of the neighbouring markets -- Turkey (up 179 per cent from 1991 to 1993). Nevertheless, this strong showing was offset by a fall-off in tourists from the Netherlands (down 7 per cent), Austria (down 16 per cent) and Finland (down 32 per cent). Tourists from all OECD countries outside Europe were down significantly.

The number of tourists from the Central and Eastern European countries continued to grow.

Figures for nights spent in hotels were also up, by 2 per cent

The resumption of growth stemmed from the end of the Gulf War, but also because additional access routes had been developed to offset the impact of war in the former Yugoslavia.

Iceland. The number of arrivals of tourists rose very significantly in 1993 (up 10 per cent). All of the country's five main markets except Sweden recorded good performances. Together, Germany (up 28 per cent), the United States (up 16 per cent), the United Kingdom (up 12 per cent) and Denmark (up 6 per cent) accounted for 56 per cent of total nights spent. The upswing was just as great for visitors from smaller markets, such as the Netherlands (up 40 per cent), Spain (up 33 per cent) and Ireland (up 26 per cent).

The good results were offset, however, by the lesser performance of Iceland's fourth-largest market -- Sweden (down 3 per cent) -- as well as Switzerland (down 11 per cent), Italy (down 13 per cent) and France (down 5 per cent), in decline for the second year running.

Ireland. Arrivals of foreign visitors increased by 6 per cent in 1993, and the number of overnight stays rose by 4 per cent, with nights spent in hotels recording a 2 per cent gain.

Growth was driven by tourists from continental Europe, in terms of both arrivals of visitors (up 8 per cent) and nights spent (up 7 per cent), with Germany and Italy especially strong (overnight stays up by 14 and 34 per cent, respectively). The other good performances were from the Nordic countries, Belgium and Luxembourg.

The United Kingdom market, which accounted for nearly 43 per cent of all overnight stays, rebounded by 5 per cent after two consecutive years of decline.

That said, the number of nights spent by French tourists in tourist accommodation fell by 2 per cent in 1993, the same trend being apparent for visitors from Switzerland (down 10 per cent), the Netherlands (down 4 per cent), the United States (down 2 per cent) and Japan (down 7 per cent).

Italy. International tourist flows rose moderately in 1993. Nights spent in all means of accommodation and in hotels were up by 2 per cent, while arrivals of visitors at frontiers were down by just 0.4 per cent.

In terms of nights spent in all means of accommodation, the three main markets -- Germany, United Kingdom and France -- were up 2 per cent. The trend was the same for other OECD regions -- North America and Asia Pacific -- which expanded by 9 and 12 per cent respectively.

Non-OECD European markets were also sharply up on 1992 (4 per cent).

Trends in international tourist flows were affected by several factors. On the one hand, the persisting economic weakness of the major generating countries and the normalisation of international tourist movements in Italy, in the wake of changes in tourist demand, international crises and competition from other countries played a rather negative role. On the other hand, the devaluation of the Italian lira in 1992 continued to positively influence international tourist flows.

Japan. Arrivals of foreign tourists (down 9 per cent) fell more sharply than arrivals of visitors (down 5 per cent). The downturn was especially pronounced for arrivals from Asia/Oceania (down 9.4 per cent; 65 per cent of nights spent). Among OECD regions, the decline was generally less steep, ranging between 6 and 7 per cent.

The United Kingdom market, which accounted for about 50 per cent of the nights spent by Europeans, dropped by 10 per cent after a significant rise (up 17 per cent) a year earlier. Fewer Germans came to Japan (down 3 per cent), but the French market swung back to growth (up 7 per cent).

The Canadian market confirmed that its revival (up 5 per cent), as did tourism from Australia, which was up 7 per cent in 1993.

Lastly, the number of tourists from the United States decreased by 9 per cent, with about 25 000 fewer tourists over the course of the year than in 1992.

Luxembourg. Data were unavailable to the Secretariat at the time this chapter was drafted.

Mexico. This is the first edition of the annual report to incorporate Mexico as a new Member of the OECD. However, Mexico is not yet completely integrated into all of the tables; it is fully included in the Introduction and in Chapters II and III and appears in a number of special tables in the Statistical Annex. Mexico will be totally incorporated into the various tables and aggregates presented herein for the Tourism Committee's next annual report.

In terms of tourist flows, nights spent in hotels rose by 3 per cent, whereas arrivals of visitors declined by 9 per cent in 1993.

At the time this chapter was drafted, the Secretariat had no information available on nights spent in hotels and similar establishments, nor on arrivals of visitors at frontiers, broken down by country of origin.

Netherlands. In 1993, the number of arrivals of tourists dropped by 11 per cent. Nights spent, both in registered tourist accommodation and in hotels alone, fell less sharply (down respectively 5 and 6 per cent), indicating that the length of stay per arrival increased significantly.

For registered tourist accommodation, the leading market -- Germany, which represented just over half of aggregate nights spent -- was up by 1 per cent, and the number-three market -- Belgium -- by 3 per cent. There was a fall-off in all other customers from the OECD area: the sharpest drops were for the Nordic countries (down 20 per cent), as well as for Australia, Italy and Japan (also down by about 20 per cent each).

More generally, economic weakness in the major markets, combined with a strong guilder, was chiefly to blame for the decline in inbound tourism. Moreover, the lack of any special event such as the 1992 Floriade flower exhibition, which had drawn 3.2 million visitors, 37 per cent of whom from abroad, also had a negative effect on inbound international tourism.

New Zealand. The number of arrivals of tourists increased in 1993 by 10 per cent over the previous year, while that of nights spent in registered tourist accommodation increased by 9 per cent.

The four main markets accounted for 56 per cent of total nights spent. Australia was down 3 per cent, and the United Kingdom remained at the same level as the previous year; the other two large markets -- the United States and Japan -- expanded by 9 and 17 per cent respectively.

Among the other major customers, it should be noted that there were a larger number of Germans (up 14 per cent, on the heels of a 21 per cent increase in 1992).

On the other hand, Canada (down 2 per cent) and Sweden (down 4 per cent) declined for the second consecutive year.

Asia continued to be a dynamic market, with arrivals increasing by 50 per cent on 1992; the region now accounts for 15 per cent of total arrivals. Strong growth was recorded for arrivals from South Korea (up 114 per cent), Taiwan (up 79 per cent) and Thailand (up 66 per cent).

Norway. Inbound tourism in Norway, as measured by the number of nights spent in hotels, expanded by 30 per cent from 1990 to 1993 and by 7 per cent between 1992 and 1993. All of Norway's main European markets -- except Sweden (down 3 per cent) and the United Kingdom (down 4 per cent) -- were up: Germany (up 22 per cent), Denmark (up 5 per cent), France (up 10 per cent) and the Netherlands (up 8 per cent). From outside Europe, Japanese visitors were up 21 per cent, whereas the number of US tourists fell by 11 per cent.

According to the national marketing organisation, the primary reasons for this growth were the competitiveness (especially in terms of prices) of the tourism and travel industry and the development of nature-based activities packaged with a "green" profile.

Portugal. Throughout 1993, the recession that had already affected tourism in 1992 continued to make an impact. Statistical indicators of tourist flows declined, in part because of the international recession, from which Portugal did not begin to recover until 1994, but also because Portugal, as a tourist destination, is somewhat out of the way for the main European generating markets.

Nights spent in registered tourist accommodation -- which is deemed the most significant statistic -- declined by 10 per cent, as did nights spent in hotels. At the same time, arrivals of tourists at frontiers fell off less sharply (down 5 per cent), whereas the number of visitors was virtually unchanged. This interesting trend stemmed primarily from changes in the Spanish market (which accounted for 50 per cent of tourists and 77 per cent of visitors): in two years, the number of Spanish same-day visitors rose five times faster than the volume of Spanish tourists (up by 11 per cent, as opposed to 2 per cent, between 1991 and 1993).

In terms of nights spent in registered tourist accommodation, the three leading markets -- the United Kingdom (down 6 per cent), Germany (down 7 per cent) and Spain (down 6 per cent) -- were in decline, as were most other OECD countries. It is worth noting, however, that nights spent by Japanese were up by 38 per cent.

There were some strong figures for tourists from Central and Eastern Europe, Asia/Oceania (up 27 per cent) and Africa (up 13 per cent).

The average stay of tourists visiting Portugal in 1993 was down slightly from the previous year (from 7.2 to 7 days).

Spain. In 1992, the organisation of two major events had spurred the development of international tourism. In 1993, the various indicators were still on the rise: the number of nights spent in hotels grew by 8 per cent (up by 6 million nights), and Spain received 58 million visitors.

In terms of nights spent in hotels (the most significant data), German tourists (34 per cent of the market) increased their visits to Spain (up 6 per cent), as did those from the United Kingdom (Spain's second-largest market, accounting for 27 per cent of nights spent), whose volume increased by 15 per cent, representing 3 million additional nights. The other large markets expanded as well: France (up 7 per cent), Italy (up 8 per cent) and Belgium (up 22 per cent).

Long-haul markets were less robust: North America was down 4 per cent and Japan 17 per cent. Of note, lastly, was the vitality of the Greek market (up 123 per cent between 1991 and 1993).

Sweden. In 1993, the number of nights spent in registered tourist accommodation increased by 4 per cent, to a total of 6 million nights, while that of nights spent in hotels rose by 6 per cent.

Nights spent by tourists from other Nordic countries were down by 1 per cent due to a 19 per cent decline in the Finnish market. The number of nights spent by tourists from Denmark rose by 12 per cent, and those by Norwegian tourists changed little (down 0.4 per cent). Demand from other European countries rose by about 6 per cent. Since 1991, Germany has been Sweden's leading market with, in 1993, about 1.8 million nights spent in registered tourist accommodation (up 16 per cent). A 6 per cent increase was recorded for North America. Lastly, the Japanese market grew by 17 per cent.

The depreciation of the Swedish krona at the end of 1992, together with the fact that value added tax for hotel services and camping was reduced to 12 per cent in July 1993, made Sweden's prices more competitive.

Switzerland. Foreign visitors spent some 36.7 million nights in registered tourist accommodation, or about 271 000 fewer than in 1992 (down 0.1 per cent). Hotels lost 459 000 overnight stays (down 2 per cent), whereas similar establishments gained 188 000 (up 1 per cent).

Demand declined on the part of almost all European countries and especially Italy, for which 340 000 fewer overnight stays were recorded (down 17 per cent). Ninety per cent of this was due to a drop in the number of nights spent in hotels. One positive development was that demand from Germany rose by 4 per cent; despite a gloomy economic situation (relatively high unemployment along with tax increases and rent rises), a greater number of Germans still travelled to Switzerland.

The only overseas markets for which an increase was recorded were India and Israel (up 8 and 1 per cent respectively). Fewer tourists went to Switzerland from all other countries, particularly the United States and Japan (down 3 per cent).

The breakdown of nights spent by form of accommodation shows that 55 per cent of foreign tourists stayed in hotels. A closer look at the breakdown shows that the alternatives to hotels were popular with tourists from the Netherlands (up 73 per cent), Germany (up 56 per cent) and Belgium (up 53 per cent).

Turkey. After international tourism revived in 1992 (up 73 per cent) following the Gulf War, 1993 more or less consolidated those results. Nights spent in registered tourist accommodation rose by 2 per cent and those in hotels by 6 per cent, whereas arrivals at frontiers declined by 8 per cent (after climbing by 28 per cent); these data confirm an increase in the average stay, which lengthened to 9.9 nights.

This growth was driven primarily by non-Members of the OECD, and in particular by Central and Eastern European countries and by Asia/Oceania (both up 23 per cent). Among OECD markets, the most spectacular increases involved the United Kingdom (up 70 per cent, after a 108 per cent increase the previous year), France (up 31 per cent, after a 129 per cent increase), Spain (up 34 per cent, after a 95 per cent increase) and -- from outside Europe -- the United States (up 29 per cent) and Australia (up 27 per cent). This was due to the fact that calm had been restored in the region, as well as to efforts to promote tourist activities.

Nevertheless, demand from Germany -- the leading market, with 39 per cent of nights spent -- was down by 12 per cent, with a loss of 900 000 nights spent for the full year.

United Kingdom. In 1993, the number of nights spent in all means of tourist accommodation held steady (down 0.1 per cent) after two years of decrease, whereas arrivals of visitors at frontiers were up 5 per cent. The average length of stay in the country visited recorded a slight decrease (down to 9.5 nights).

In terms of nights spent, two of its main markets were up -- Ireland (up 10 per cent) and the United States (up 2 per cent). The other three main markets -- Australia, France and Germany -- decreased by 17, 1 and 4 per cent respectively.

The number of nights from the OECD Asia-Pacific region fell by 13 per cent. However, this decrease was balanced by the increase from non-OECD tourists from the region (up 13 per cent). Overall, the total number of nights for non-OECD tourists increased by 3 per cent.

United States. Despite an overall decline in 1993 (to 45.7 million arrivals, down 4 per cent, compared to an 11 per cent increase in 1992), the number of European tourists continued to rise (up 4 per cent in 1993 and 13 per cent in 1992). Visitors from the three main European markets -- the United Kingdom (up 6 per cent), Germany (up 8 per cent) and France (up 6 per cent) -- increased their travel to the United States.

In contrast, tourism from OECD countries in the Asia-Pacific region decreased by 4 per cent. The main market, Canada, which accounted for 38 per cent of arrivals, also fell, by 7 per cent.

The number of tourists from Latin America, which represented 30 per cent of arrivals, fell by 6 per cent after a sharp, 35 per cent surge in 1992.

III. Main generating countries

This section describes recent trends in the main countries generating international tourism to the OECD area (see Tables 4, 5, 6 and 7), namely Canada, France, Germany, Italy, Japan, the Netherlands, the United Kingdom and the United States. For a more detailed picture of historical trends in these main generating countries as a whole, summary tables for the period 1982-1993 are available in annex.

Table 4. Annual growth rates of number of arrivals at frontiers from main generating countries

	T/V	Total Variation % 93/92	From France		From Germany		From United Kingdom		From United States	
			Relative share % 92	Variation % 93/92	Relative share % 92	Variation % 93/92	Relative share % 92	Variation % 93/92	Relative share % 92	Variation % 93/92
Canada (R)	T	2.5	2.1	16.4	2.0	16.7	3.6	4.7	80.2	1.7
Mexico (R)										
United States (R)	T	−3.7	1.7	6.2	3.6	8.0	5.9	6.2		
North America		−2.3	1.8	9.0	3.2	9.3	5.4	6.0	19.0	1.7
Australia (R)	V	15.1	1.0	22.0	3.5	17.5	11.1	7.0	10.1	7.0
Japan (N)	T	−8.5	1.0	6.7	1.3	−2.5	6.8	−10.1	14.2	−8.6
New Zealand (R)	T	9.6	0.5	9.5	4.3	22.9	9.1	7.1	12.4	9.3
Asia and the Pacific		5.5	0.9	14.6	2.8	15.6	9.2	2.4	12.0	0.7
Austria										
Belgium										
Denmark										
Finland										
France (R)	T	0.7			21.2	3.0	13.9	−1.7	3.4	−2.2
Germany										
Greece (N)	T	0.9	5.8	2.3	20.8	6.4	23.1	1.7	3.0	−8.0
Iceland (N)	T	10.4	5.6	−5.1	17.2	28.2	9.8	11.5	15.2	15.5
Ireland (R)	V	6.2	6.9	9.7	7.0	14.5	56.0	7.2	11.7	−2.5
Italy (N)	V	−0.4	17.6	−6.2	17.5	−12.4	3.2	7.7	2.6	−6.5
Luxembourg										
Netherlands										
Norway										
Portugal (N)	T	−5.1	7.3	−15.7	9.1	−10.9	14.4	−4.2	1.8	−6.7
Spain (N)	V	4.2	21.2	2.4	14.0	12.3	11.7	14.9	1.5	−5.1
Sweden										
Switzerland										
Turkey (N)	V	−8.1	3.5	21.6	16.5	−4.0	4.4	40.4	2.6	39.8
United Kingdom (R)	T	3.0	11.5	−0.2	12.2	3.4			15.7	−1.1
Europe		1.1	11.5	−1.2	16.8	1.0	10.4	5.4	3.7	−2.1
OECD		0.4	9.1	−0.7	13.5	1.5	9.2	5.4	7.3	0.2

V Visitors.
T Tourists.
(R) Tourist count by country of residence.
(N) Tourist count by country of nationality.

This section does not aim to present a detailed account of the stays and travellers from the main generating countries in OECD, but to outline the main patterns followed by the residents of these countries when travelling abroad. Destinations are analysed in terms of nights spent or arrivals at frontiers, depending on the data available in the receiving countries. This section is chiefly concerned with flows within the OECD area.

The eight countries were selected on the basis of their contribution to international tourism growth as expressed in terms of dollar expenditures, the standard unit of account for the "travel" item in the balance of payments. Taken together, they accounted for about 77 per cent of total expenditure by the 25 OECD Member countries in 1993 (for further information, see Table 2 in Chapter III).

For **Canadian** outbound travel, the weakness of the Canadian dollar was reflected in a decrease in the number of Canadians visiting the United States (down 5 per cent). On the whole, there was a 6 per cent fall in the number of tourists and a 5 per cent fall in dollar expenditures. Canadian travel to countries other than the United States rose by 7 per cent in 1993, thus rebounding from the depressed levels recorded in 1991 as a result of the Gulf war. In Europe, there was an increase in Canadian travel to France (nights spent up 15 per cent), Turkey (nights spent up 48 per cent) and Iceland (nights spent up 28 per cent).

French outbound travel in the OECD area increased slightly in 1993 -- by 3 per cent -- accounting for about 3 per cent of total nights spent in Europe. Expenditure in dollars, however, fell by 8 per cent on 1992. The number of French visitors continued to rise in Turkey (up 31 per cent) and also in Canada, Finland, New Zealand and Norway. Conversely, demand slumped for some of the popular destinations such as the Netherlands (down 15 per cent), Sweden (down 8 per cent), Austria (down 6 per cent) and Germany (down 6 per cent). All the other, non-European OECD countries received more French tourists, and particularly Australia (up 22 per cent on visits).

In Europe, the **German** market is in the lead with 26 per cent of the total number of nights spent. In 1993, German demand rose by only 2 per cent in terms of nights spent compared with 1992, and expenditure on international tourism expressed in dollars rose by 3 per cent. In 1993, Germany continued to absorb the financial cost of unification, which has turned out to be higher than expected. The number of German tourists rose markedly for the Nordic countries (Finland, Norway, Sweden and Iceland), Canada (up 19 per cent) and Australia (up 17 per cent). There were also big declines, however, in Turkey (down 12 per cent, or 900 000 fewer nights) and Portugal (down 9 per cent) for the second consecutive year.

The **Italian** market has continued in recent years to be one of the most flourishing in Europe and retains a promising growth potential. In 1993, however, Italian demand fell sharply, the number of nights spent by Italian tourists diminishing by 11 per cent in the OECD area, and arrivals by 9 per cent. During the same period, expenditure in dollars fell by 15 per cent. Italians travelled less to all European countries (down by between 9 and 23 per cent), with the exception of Ireland (up 34 per cent) and Spain (up 8 per cent). Arrivals of Italian tourists increased by 10 per cent in the Asia-Pacific region, despite the fall recorded in Japan (down 1 per cent), and dropped by 5 per cent in North America.

After picking up in 1992, **Japanese** demand fell again in 1993 with negative growth of 3 per cent in terms of arrivals and 1 per cent for expenditure in dollars. Arrivals of Japanese tourists fell in Europe above all (down 10 per cent) and the decline in the average length of their stay in Europe was confirmed, with a sharper drop in the number of nights spent (down 15 per cent). That said, nights

Table 5. **Annual growth rates of number of arrivals at frontiers from main generating countries**

	T/V	Total Variation % 93/92	From Japan		From Netherlands		From Canada		From Italy	
			Relative share % 92	Variation % 93/92	Relative share % 92	Variation % 93/92	Relative share % 92	Variation % 93/92	Relative share % 92	Variation % 93/92
Canada (R)	T	2.5	2.7	4.1	0.6	−1.2			0.6	1.9
Mexico (R)										
United States (R)	T	−3.7	7.7	−3.0	0.7	10.8	39.1	−7.0	1.2	−5.8
North America		−2.3	6.5	−2.3	0.7	8.4	29.9	−7.0	1.1	−4.7
Australia (R)	V	15.1	24.2	6.5	0.9	17.0	1.9	3.5	1.1	15.3
Japan (N)	T	−8.5			0.3	8.3	2.1	5.0	0.5	−1.4
New Zealand (R)	T	9.6	12.2	5.4	0.9	10.4	2.4	7.4	0.4	8.7
Asia and the Pacific		5.5	13.2	6.3	0.7	14.0	2.1	4.9	0.7	10.4
Austria										
Belgium										
Denmark										
Finland										
France (R)	T	0.7	0.8	−27.6	10.5	13.4	1.0	17.9	12.1	−10.5
Germany										
Greece (N)	T	0.9	1.2	−18.0	5.9	−6.5	0.6	−13.9	6.7	0.5
Iceland (N)	T	10.4	1.0	27.8	2.7	39.5	0.8	27.8	2.9	−13.0
Ireland (R)	V	6.2	0.4	38.5			1.2	2.6		
Italy (N)	V	−0.4	1.5	−1.4	2.4	−11.8	0.7	−7.9		
Luxembourg										
Netherlands										
Norway										
Portugal (N)	T	−5.1	0.3	27.1	3.8	−2.8	0.7	−7.1	2.9	−8.9
Spain (N)										
Sweden										
Switzerland										
Turkey (N)	V	−8.1	0.5	30.0	2.9	5.6	0.4	33.3	2.2	−14.9
United Kingdom (R)	V	5.1	3.0	−11.4	5.4	21.8	3.4	−6.7	4.2	1.1
Europe		0.2	1.2	−10.4	6.2	9.2	1.1	1.8	5.9	−8.7
OECD		−0.4	3.0	−3.6	4.5	9.2	9.2	−6.2	4.4	−8.4

V Visitors.
T Tourists.
(R) Tourist count by country of residence.
(N) Tourist count by country of nationality.

spent increased in Portugal (up 38 per cent), Norway (up 21 per cent) and Turkey (up 2 per cent). There continued to be large numbers of Japanese visitors to the Asia-Pacific region (up 6 per cent) and Canada (up 4 per cent on arrivals). Lastly, fewer Japanese tourists went to the United States (down 3 per cent).

In 1993 the nights spent by **Dutch** tourists rose by 9 per cent and arrivals by 8 per cent. Growth was faster in the Asia-Pacific region (up 14 per cent) and especially Australia (up 17 per cent). Most Netherlands tourists went to France (up 15 per cent), Norway (up 8 per cent), Spain (up 21 per cent) and Iceland (up 40 per cent on arrivals), but fewer went to Germany (down 10 per cent), where they accounted for 21 per cent of nights spent. Two other destinations also suffered losses: Portugal (down 22 per cent) and Denmark (down 32 per cent). Expenditure by Dutch tourists fell in dollar terms by 6 per cent.

In the **United Kingdom**, residents reduced their dollar expenditures by 12 per cent in 1993. The number of nights spent by British tourists rose slightly in Europe -- by 1 per cent -- now accounting for about 15 per cent of total nights spent. In Ireland, where British tourists are the main clients -- 43 per cent of the total -- the number of nights spent rose by 5 per cent. Spanish and Finnish destinations also showed an upward trend (up 15 and 11 per cent, respectively). Similarly, as in all the other big generating countries, the number of visitors to Turkey picked up again (up 70 per cent). However, in a number of countries where British tourists account for more than 10 per cent of total nights spent, the trend was downward, this being the case of Belgium, France, Iceland, Norway, the Netherlands and Portugal.

Where North America is concerned, the number of nights spent in Canada rose by 6 per cent and the number of visits to the United States by 6 per cent also. Arrivals in the Asia-Pacific region increased less rapidly (up 2 per cent), largely because of a 10 per cent fall in Japan.

The number of nights spent by **United States** residents remained at the same level as the previous year throughout the OECD area. Europe, however, recorded a distinct fall in the number of American visitors in 1993 (down 3 per cent in terms of nights spent and down 2 per cent in terms of arrivals), the countries most affected being Belgium, Germany, Norway and Portugal. Americans have, however, been returning in greater numbers to Iceland (up 15 per cent) and Turkey (up 29 per cent). Fewer of them, on the other hand, visited Japan in 1993 (down 9 per cent on arrivals), this being the only OECD country whose currency appreciated against the dollar. American arrivals in Australia and New Zealand rose by 7 and 9 per cent respectively. In monetary terms, American spending abroad increased slightly on 1992 -- by 2 per cent.

Table 6. **Annual growth rates of nights spent in the various means of accommodation from main generating countries**

	H/A	Total Variation % 93/92	From France		From Germany		From the United Kingdom		From the United-States	
			Relative share % 92	Variation % 93/92	Relative share % 92	Variation % 93/92	Relative share % 92	Variation % 93/92	Relative share % 92	Variation % 93/92
Canada (R)	A	3.4	4.8	11.9	4.5	19.3	7.7	5.7	58.3	2.6
Mexico (R)										
United States (R)										
North America		3.4	4.8	11.9	4.5	19.3	7.7	5.7	58.3	2.6
Australia (R)	A	9.1			10.0	14.7	40.3	−7.1	19.1	9.8
Japan (N)										
New Zealand (R)	A	8.5	0.5	28.4	6.7	14.3	15.5	−0.3	9.6	9.1
Asia and the Pacific		8.5	0.5	28.4	6.7	14.3	15.5	−0.3	9.6	9.1
Austria	A	−2.9	2.9	−7.3	64.9	0.4	4.1	−9.5	1.5	−10.2
Belgium	A	0.2	10.2	1.7	17.6	8.4	11.7	−9.6	4.8	−15.7
Denmark	A	−9.7	1.3	−5.2	39.5	−0.9	3.3	−1.7	2.8	−5.5
Finland	H	15.4	3.7	13.3	16.8	33.8	5.7	10.9	6.7	8.5
France (R)	A	0.9			20.2	1.8	14.4	−2.4	4.1	−1.5
Germany	A	−9.1	4.7	−6.1			8.7	−4.7	9.5	−10.6
Greece (N)										
Iceland (N)	H	53.2	6.2	−2.6	22.8	16.1	10.6	−9.0	7.1	15.1
Ireland (R)	A	4.0	9.8	−2.2	10.1	14.2	42.6	4.8	12.6	−1.8
Italy (N)	A	2.1	6.7	2.4	39.7	2.0	6.5	1.7	5.9	9.3
Luxembourg	A		5.2		8.9		4.3		2.5	
Netherlands	A	−5.1	4.4	−14.8	50.1	1.2	11.4	−16.8	5.2	−7.2
Norway	H	6.6	5.7	10.3	19.9	21.9	10.0	−3.9	8.2	−11.4
Portugal (N)	A	−9.7	6.0	−5.5	19.1	−9.3	29.0	−5.5	2.7	−13.5
Spain (N)	H	7.7	7.9	6.7	34.3	6.3	25.3	14.7	2.0	−5.1
Sweden	A	4.5	2.9	−7.7	26.0	16.0	5.0	−2.4	4.8	5.7
Switzerland	A	−0.7	6.3	−1.6	43.3	3.7	7.0	−6.0	5.8	−3.3
Turkey (N)	A	1.7	8.6	31.4	45.1	−12.0	5.2	70.4	2.3	28.6
United Kingdom (R)	A	−0.1	8.0	−0.5	10.3	−3.5			14.4	2.4
Europe		0.3	3.9	0.8	26.0	1.5	11.4	1.0	6.2	−0.1
OECD		0.7	3.9	1.8	24.2	1.8	11.2	1.2	9.7	1.2

H Hotels and similar establishments.
A All means of accommodation.
(R) Tourist count by country of residence.
(N) Tourist count by country of nationality.

Table 7. Annual growth rates of nights spent in the various means of accommodation from main generating countries

	H/A	Total Variation % 93/92	From Japan		From Netherlands		From Canada		From Italy	
			Relative share % 92	Variation % 93/92	Relative share % 92	Variation % 93/92	Relative share % 92	Variation % 93/92	Relative share % 92	Variation % 93/92
Canada (R)	A	3.4	3.1	15.4	1.3	9.4			1.1	9.3
Mexico (R)										
United States (R)										
North America		3.4	3.1	15.4	1.3	9.4			1.1	9.3
Australia (R)	A	9.1	13.1	1.4			3.1	21.2		
Japan (N)										
New Zealand (R)	A	8.5	7.1	16.7	1.8	1.3	3.0	−2.3	0.3	25.4
Asia and the Pacific		8.5	7.1	16.7	1.8	1.3	3.0	−2.3	0.3	25.4
Austria	A	−2.9	0.5	−2.6	9.0	−6.2	0.2	−1.2	3.6	−22.9
Belgium	A	0.2	1.8	−16.6	32.8	4.4	0.7	−16.4	3.3	−12.8
Denmark	A	−9.7	1.0	−9.8	8.7	−31.6			2.0	−21.3
Finland										
France (R)	A	0.9	0.5	−30.5	14.1	15.3	1.3	15.0	10.0	−11.6
Germany	A	−9.1	3.3	−7.6	21.2	−9.6	0.9	−10.6	5.0	−18.3
Greece (N)										
Iceland (N)										
Ireland (R)	A	4.0			2.4	−4.2	1.7	−2.5	4.0	34.3
Italy (N)	A	2.1	2.3	13.0	3.4	1.2	0.8	6.9		
Luxembourg										
Netherlands	A	−5.1	1.3	−19.5			0.9	−13.0	3.6	−21.0
Norway	H	6.6	2.3	21.1	4.1	7.9			3.7	−17.9
Portugal (N)	A	−9.7	0.4	38.3	9.2	−22.3	1.1	−12.1	3.2	−14.1
Spain (N)	H	7.7	0.9	−17.4	3.2	20.6	0.2	4.3	6.8	8.2
Sweden	A	4.5	1.5	17.1	5.8	0.6	0.3	6.9	2.2	−9.1
Switzerland	A	−0.7	2.3	−2.5	9.2	−0.7	0.6	−5.6	5.4	−16.9
Turkey (N)	A	1.7	1.3	2.0			0.2	42.4	3.8	−21.7
United Kingdom (R)	A	−0.1	2.2	−3.2	3.1	5.0	4.1	1.0	4.7	−0.6
Europe		0.2	1.2	−6.6	9.8	8.6	1.5	5.5	6.6	−9.7
OECD		0.6	1.4	−1.1	9.0	8.6	1.4	5.2	6.1	−9.4

H Hotels and similar establishments.
A All means of accommodation.
(R) Tourist count by country of residence.
(N) Tourist count by country of nationality.

Trends of international tourism
in Europe, from :
(Overnights in accommodation, indices 1984 = 100)

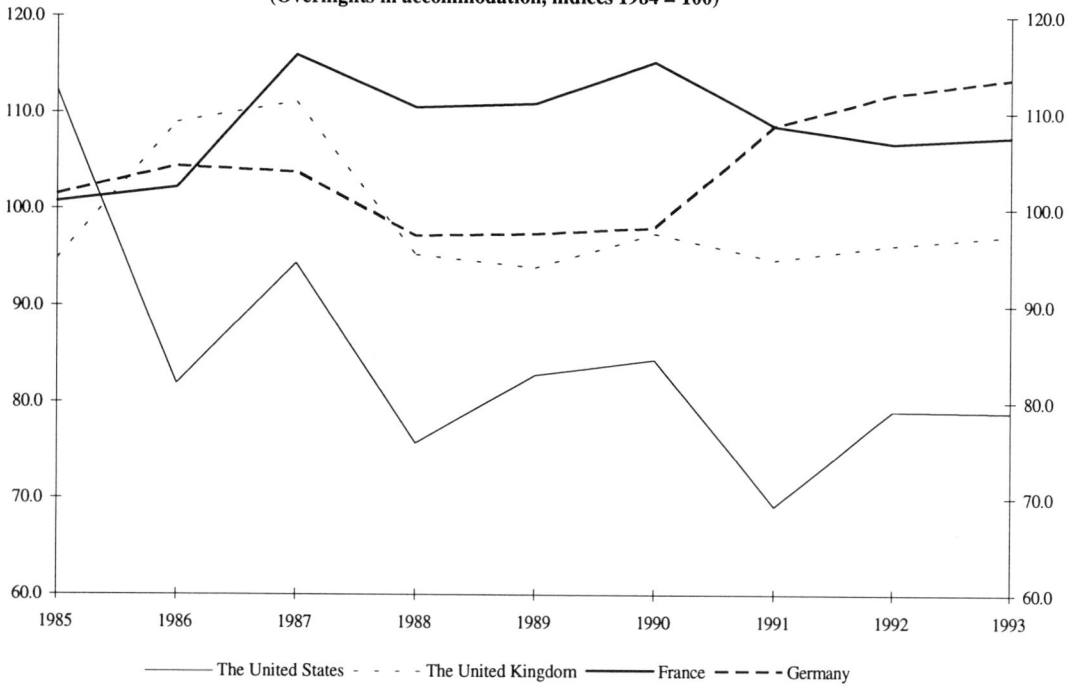

———— The United States - - - - The United Kingdom ━━━━ France ━ ━ ━ Germany

Source : OECD

Trends of international tourism
in Europe, from :
(Overnights in accommodation, indices 1984 = 100)

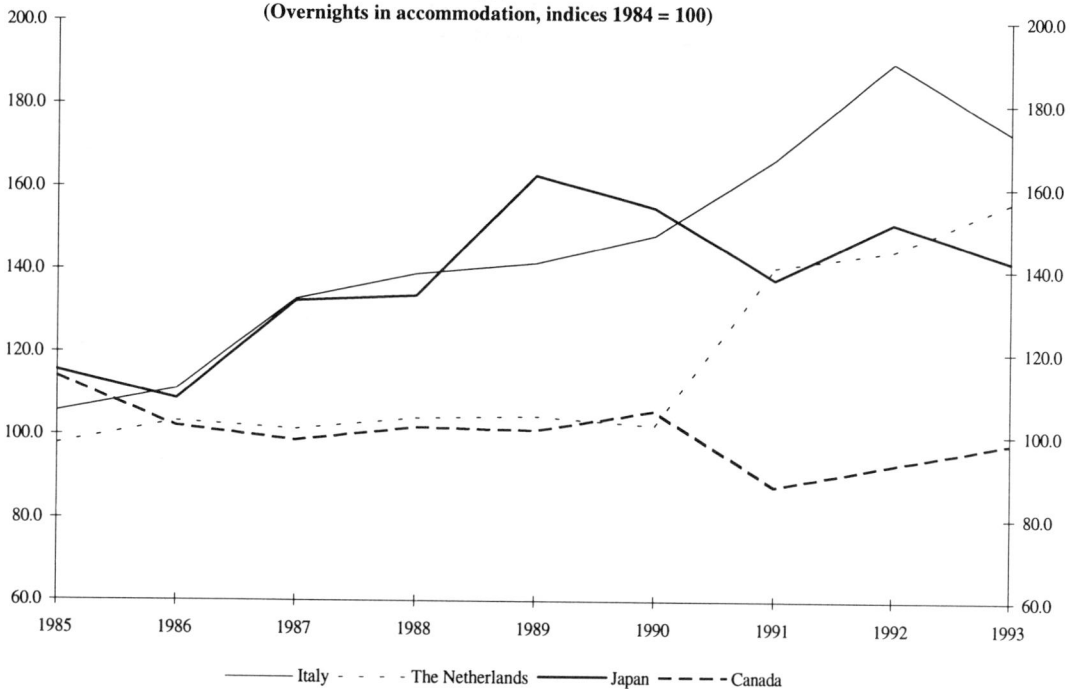

———— Italy - - - - The Netherlands ━━━━ Japan ━ ━ ━ Canada

Source : OECD

Trends of international tourism
in North America, from :
(Arrivals at frontiers, indices 1984 = 100)

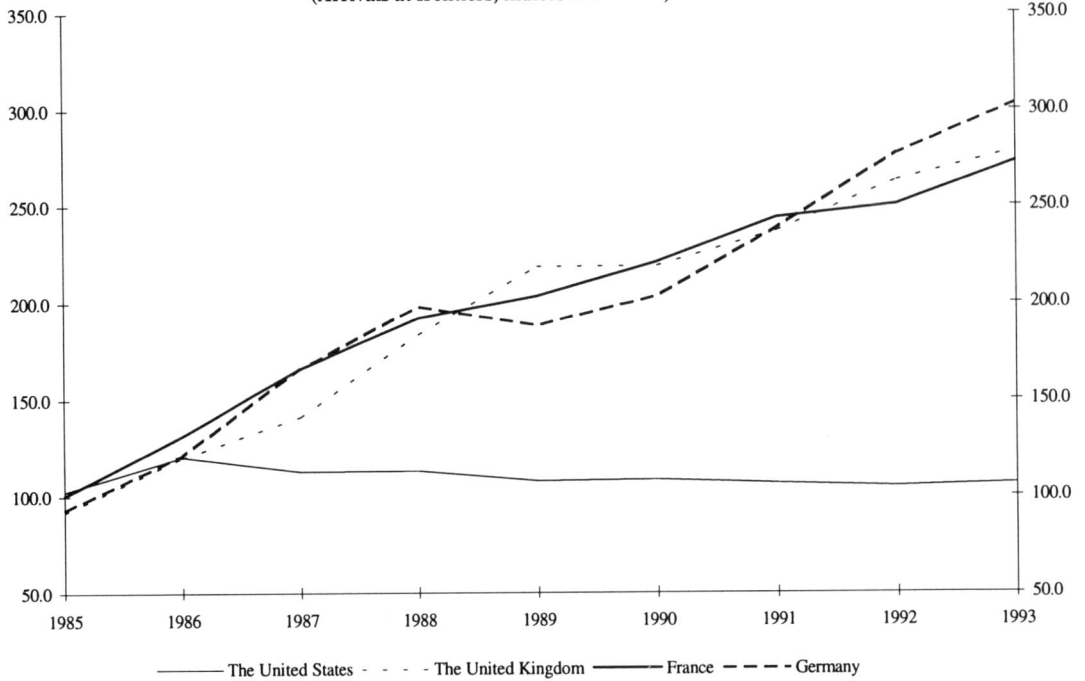

The United States - - - - The United Kingdom ——— France — — — Germany

Source : OECD

Trends of international tourism
in North America, from :
(Arrivals at frontiers, indices 1984 = 100)

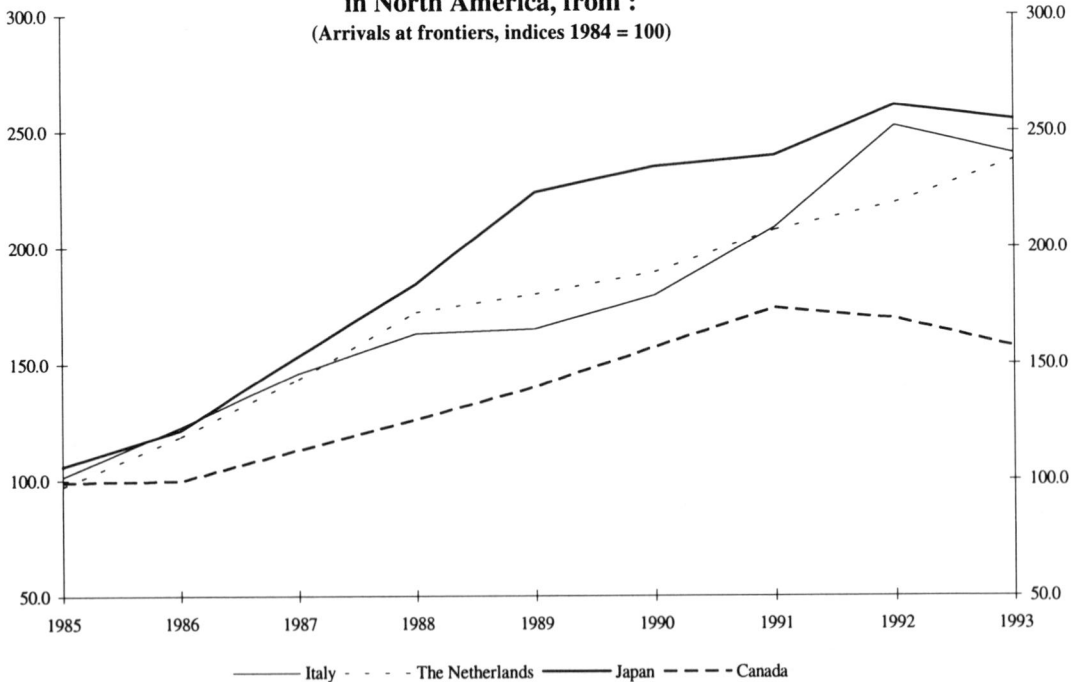

——— Italy - - - - The Netherlands ——— Japan — — — Canada

Source : OECD

**Trends of international tourism
in Asia and the Pacific, from :**
(Arrivals at frontiers, indices 1984 = 100)

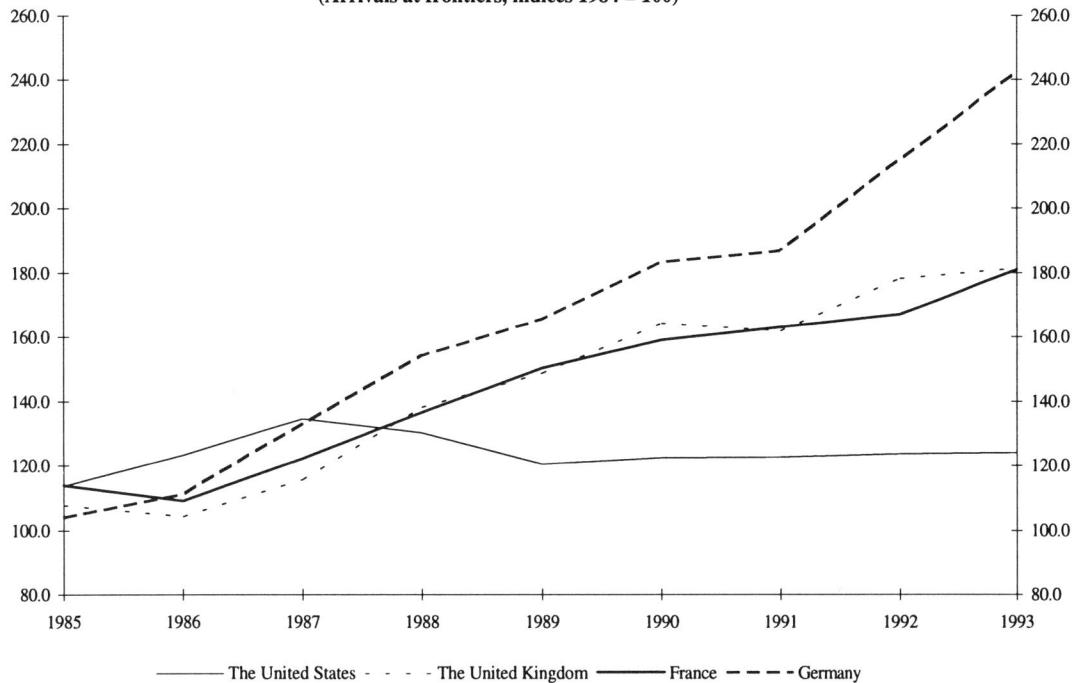

——— The United States - - - - The United Kingdom ——— France — — — Germany

Source : OECD

**Trends of international tourism
in Asia and the Pacific, from :**
(Arrivals at frontiers, indices 1984 = 100)

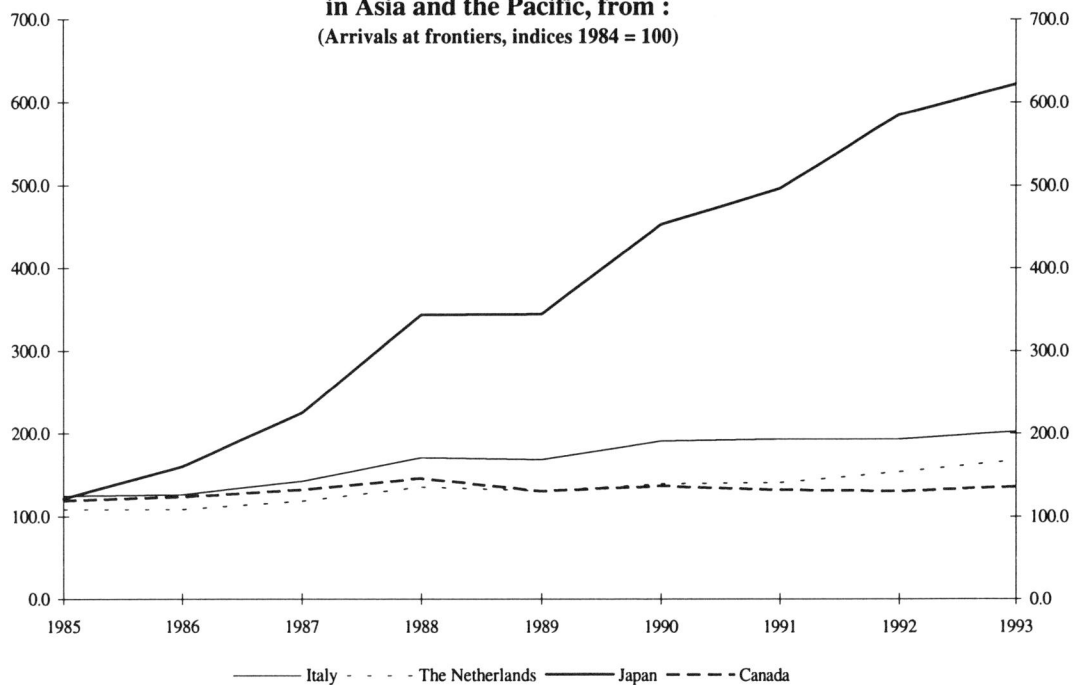

——— Italy - - - - The Netherlands ——— Japan — — — Canada

Source : OECD

Chapter III

The Economic Importance of International Tourism
in Member Countries

This chapter brings together the data available on international tourism receipts and expenditure in 1993 for the 25 OECD Member countries. The figures do not include international fare payments, except where explicitly stated (see Table 18 in the Statistical Annex).

The first part of the chapter (Section I) considers:

a) receipts expressed in both national currencies and US dollars, first in current terms and then in real terms, *i.e.* adjusted for the effects of inflation and for parity changes between the dollar and national currencies;

b) expenditure, again in both national currencies and US dollars, in current terms;

c) the tourism balance sheet for the OECD area and its three constituent regions.

The dollar was used as the common unit of account to evaluate trends for a range of countries. However, when considering the tables that give figures in "current dollars", the reader must take into account the marked fluctuations that have taken place in recent years in most OECD currencies against the dollar.

In 1993, the dollar rose against all the OECD currencies, with the exception of the yen and the New Zealand dollar (see Table 17 of the Annex). The biggest rises were against the Turkish lira (up 60 per cent), the Swedish kroner (up 34 per cent), the Italian lira and the Finnish markka (up 28 per cent) and the Spanish peseta (up 24 per cent). Outside Europe, the pattern was generally the same but much more moderate, in the region of + 1 per cent to + 8 per cent.

These figures are of limited analytical usefulness, so any conclusions drawn from data expressed in dollars must be viewed with some caution.

Section II compares the data on receipts and expenditure with a number of major macroeconomic indicators -- gross domestic product, private final consumption, and exports and imports of goods and services for the period 1991-1993.

The comparability of the figures provided by Member countries on receipts and expenditure for international tourism is still insufficient, and its improvement is a continuing priority for the Statistical Working Party of the OECD Tourism Committee.

The main source of divergence lies in the different survey methods used. Most countries use the "bank reporting method", which is based on sales and purchases of foreign currency before or after travel abroad. The main drawback of this method is that it gives data on the currency concerned but not on the country visited. The "estimation method" is based on sample surveys carried out among residents at entry or departure points. Such surveys can provide extensive information but, because of their cost, they are conducted by only a few countries. Lastly, some countries use a "mixed method" involving limited surveys to give adjustment factors to apply to bank-derived data. Progress towards data comparability is being made, however. (For further information, the notes in the Statistical Annex should be consulted.)

I. International tourism receipts and expenditure

Dollar receipts and expenditure for the OECD area as a whole were down by 2 and 5 per cent respectively (compared, respectively, with rises of 11 and 14 per cent in 1992) -- a trend that was amplified by the strengthening of the dollar against most other currencies (there being two exceptions).

In Europe, dollar receipts fell by 5 per cent and expenditure by 8 per cent. In the Asia-Pacific region, expenditure declined by 1 per cent and receipts by 4 per cent. In North America, finally, receipts rose by 7 per cent while expenditure remained stable. In real terms, receipts in the OECD area increased by 4 per cent, *i.e.* at virtually the same pace as in 1992 (up 5 per cent).

Where Portugal is concerned, payments data are not meaningful because of a change in series in 1993, following the introduction of a new system of data collection and production.

International tourism receipts

The consolidation of international tourism flows in 1993 (see Chapter II) is confirmed by the rise in receipts expressed in national currencies (see Table 1), these being up in 17 of the OECD's 25 Member countries. Eight countries saw a decline in their receipts in national currency terms, but in only three of them was the fall substantial (Japan, New Zealand and Denmark, with - 13, - 21 and - 18 per cent respectively).

The increase in receipts in current dollars was negative in 1993 (see Table 2), with Denmark (down 24 per cent), New Zealand (down 21 per cent), Sweden (down 13 per cent) and Spain (down 12 per cent) experiencing the biggest shortfalls. In Europe, Turkey, Iceland, Italy, Portugal and Belgium/Luxembourg saw increases in their dollar receipts. In volume terms, receipts rose by $4 billion in the United States.

For the OECD area as a whole, receipts totalled $216 billion in 1993, whereas worldwide, according to the World Tourism Organisation, the total came to $305.7 billion (compared with 304 billion in 1992), *i.e.* an increase of 0.6 per cent. This slightly reduced -- to 71 per cent -- the OECD countries' share of the overall total.

Table 1. International tourist receipts and expenditure in national currencies
In millions

	Currency	Receipts			Expenditure		
		1992	1993	%93/92	1992	1993	%93/92
Canada	Dollar	6 846	7 546	10.2	13 563	13 708	1.1
Mexico	Mexican Peso	11 968	12 687	6.0	6 439	6 546	1.7
United States	Dollar	53 861	57 622	7.0	39 872	40 564	1.7
Australia	Dollar	5 932	6 349	7.0	5 135	5 482	6.8
Japan	Yen	454 653	394 072	–13.3	3 396 060	2 944 432	–13.3
New Zealand	Dollar	2 734	2 155	–21.2	1 914	1 855	–3.1
Austria	Schilling	159 540	157 714	–1.1	92 160	95 059	3.1
Belgium-Luxembourg	Franc	130 124	140 632	8.1	212 063	219 595	3.6
Denmark	Krone	22 839	18 726	–18.0	22 811	19 430	–14.8
Finland	Markka	5 893	6 863	16.5	10 716	9 061	–15.4
France	Franc	132 621	132 536	–0.1	73 659	72 502	–1.6
Germany	Deutsche Mark	17 265	17 375	0.6	57 199	62 022	8.4
Greece	Drachma	611 759	726 628	18.8	220 322	228 048	3.5
Iceland	Krona	7 396	8 943	20.9	16 563	17 917	8.2
Ireland	Pound	949	1 091	15.0	804	835	3.9
Italy	Lira	26 441 462	34 625 046	30.9	20 368 274	22 072 946	8.4
Netherlands	Guilder	9 131	8 630	–5.5	16 750	16 528	–1.3
Norway	Krone	12 264	13 118	7.0	24 033	25 056	4.3
Portugal [1]	Escudo	496 137	653 458	31.7	155 723	304 572	95.6
Spain	Peseta	2 268 100	2 474 500	9.1	565 900	599 400	5.9
Sweden	Krona	17 792	20 622	15.9	41 565	36 040	–13.3
Switzerland	Franc	10 590	10 375	–2.0	8 610	8 595	–0.2
Turkey	Lira	25 390 934	44 305 829	74.5	5 346 827	10 357 281	93.7
United Kingdom	Pound	7 891	8 954	13.5	11 243	11 604	3.2

Notice: for statistical coverage, see notes in table 18 in annex.
1. Break of series in 1993 due to a new collection and statistical production system.

Table 2. International tourist receipts and expenditure in current dollars
In millions

	Receipts			Expenditure		
	1992	1993	%93/92	1992	1993	%93/92
Canada	5 663.7	5 849.1	3.3	11 219.7	10 625.5	–5.3
Mexico	3 866.8	4 072.8	5.3	2 080.5	2 101.3	1.0
United States	53 861.0	57 622.0	7.0	39 872.0	40 564.0	1.7
North America	63 391.5	67 543.9	6.6	53 172.2	53 290.8	0.2
Australia	4 354.6	4 310.3	–1.0	3 769.5	3 721.7	–1.3
Japan	3 589.2	3 544.6	–1.2	26 809.7	26 484.5	–1.2
New Zealand	1 469.9	1 164.5	–20.8	1 029.0	1 002.4	–2.6
Asia and the Pacific	9 413.7	9 019.3	–4.2	31 608.3	31 208.6	–1.3
Austria	14 515.8	13 559.8	–6.6	8 385.2	8 172.9	–2.5
Belgium-Luxembourg	4 047.9	4 069.6	0.5	6 596.8	6 354.7	–3.7
Denmark	3 782.4	2 888.9	–23.6	3 777.7	2 997.5	–20.7
Finland	1 313.7	1 199.7	–8.7	2 388.9	1 583.9	–33.7
France	25 052.8	23 406.8	–6.6	13 914.6	12 804.4	–8.0
Germany	11 053.7	10 509.4	–4.9	36 620.8	37 514.6	2.4
Greece	3 211.9	3 171.1	–1.3	1 156.7	995.2	–14.0
Iceland	128.4	132.2	3.0	287.5	264.9	–7.9
Ireland	1 615.3	1 596.8	–1.1	1 368.5	1 222.1	–10.7
Italy	21 461.8	22 030.9	2.7	16 532.3	14 044.4	–15.0
Netherlands	5 193.8	4 646.9	–10.5	9 527.5	8 899.7	–6.6
Norway	1 973.5	1 849.6	–6.3	3 867.3	3 532.8	–8.7
Portugal	3 680.1	4 067.5	10.5	1 155.1	1 895.8	64.1
Spain	22 149.6	19 447.1	–12.2	5 526.4	4 710.7	–14.8
Sweden	3 054.7	2 648.8	–13.3	7 136.4	4 629.2	–35.1
Switzerland	7 533.5	7 022.9	–6.8	6 125.0	5 818.0	–5.0
Turkey	3 701.0	4 040.4	9.2	779.0	944.5	21.2
United Kingdom	13 851.8	13 444.8	–2.9	19 735.8	17 423.9	–11.7
Europe	147 321.4	139 733.2	–5.2	144 881.9	133 809.1	–7.6
OECD	220 126.6	216 296.4	–1.7	229 662.3	218 308.4	–4.9

The countries benefiting most from international tourism -- in dollar terms -- were the United States, which accounted for 27 per cent of the OECD total, followed by France (in second place with 11 per cent) and Italy (with 10 per cent). The combined receipts of the OECD's top six receiving countries (*i.e.* including Spain, Austria and the United Kingdom) accounted for approximately 69 per cent of the OECD total.

In real terms (see Table 3), *i.e.* after adjustment for the effects of inflation and exchange rate fluctuations against the dollar, North America experienced much the same growth as the OECD area as a whole (up 4.2 per cent, compared with 3.6 per cent), and the Asia-Pacific region recorded a fall of 17 per cent in 1993. The highest growth rates were achieved by Italy, Iceland, Finland, Ireland and Sweden, while a number of countries recorded falls for the second consecutive year: Japan (down 14 per cent), Germany (down 3 per cent), Austria (down 5 per cent) and Mexico (down 3 per cent).

International tourism expenditure

Expenditure in national currencies rose in 16 of the 25 OECD Member countries, the main exceptions being Japan (down 13 per cent), Denmark and Finland (down 15 per cent) and Sweden (down 13 per cent) (see Table 1). The steepest increases were in Turkey (up 94 per cent), Germany and Italy (up 8 per cent).

Taking the OECD countries as a whole, dollar expenditure amounted to $218.3 billion in 1993, which was 5 per cent down on the previous year (see Table 2). The biggest falls were recorded by Sweden (down 35 per cent), Finland (down 34 per cent) and Denmark (down 21 per cent).

Only in North American did expenditure increase slightly (up 0.2 per cent). Europe, on the other hand, recorded the biggest fall (down 8 per cent), despite increases in Turkey (up 21 per cent) and Germany (up 2 per cent).

The tourism balance sheet

With expenditure slowing more markedly in 1993, the OECD countries' deficit on tourism account (see Table 4) was virtually wiped out in 1993, standing at $0.3 billion. This was attributable mainly to the rapid increase in receipts in North America (up 16 per cent between 1991 and 1993) where the surplus now stands at $14 billion. In the Asia-Pacific region, the deficit stabilised in 1993 at around $23 billion. In Europe, with expenditure falling faster than receipts, the surplus grew and was back almost to the 1991 level.

II.   The economic importance of the "travel" account in the balance of payments

For some years, the Tourism Committee's Statistical Working Party has been working to apply the System of National Accounts (SNA) to pinpoint the economic importance of tourism, principally in monetary terms. The SNA is the only available framework for coherent analysis of the economic contribution of tourism, because it brings together commodities, supply and use and sets them against activities and final users. It also allows links with other parts of the system, such as income and outlays.

The Manual on Tourism Economic Accounts was adopted in April 1991. Available free of charge under the reference OECD/GD(91)82, it provides a basis for the compilation of data on production, consumption, value added, gross fixed capital formation and employment in the tourist industries. Testing of the Manual began in 1992 and is still going on. During the period in question, countries are to compare experience, conduct new surveys to provide the best possible responses to the Manual's requests for data and resolve methodological problems. At the same time, the OECD Secretariat is examining data quality for purposes of comparative international analysis. Ultimately, this system will be used as a basic tool to assess the importance of tourism to Member country economies. The Secretariat is considering preparing a publication on this subject for 1996.

Inasmuch as data on the economic accounts of tourism are not yet ready for publication, the Secretariat is still using other indicators which, albeit less satisfactory, are the only ones that give an idea of the macroeconomic importance of tourism.

The final section of this chapter considers the importance of tourism in individual Member countries as measured by four indicators. The tables cover the period 1991 to 1993. It would, admittedly, have been useful to include international passenger transport payments but, as only a few Member countries break down their "transport" account in this way (see Table 16 in the Statistical Annex), the data would not be comparable.

Share of "travel account" receipts in Gross Domestic Product

"Travel account" receipts (see Table 5) in 1993 amounted to 1.2 per cent of GDP for the OECD area as a whole. The increase in receipts as a proportion of GDP between 1991 and 1993 was especially significant in Italy (from 1.6 to 2.2 per cent), Greece (from 3.6 to 4.6 per cent), Sweden (from 1.1 to 1.4 per cent), Australia (from 1.5 to 1.7 per cent) and Turkey (from 1.8 to 2.3 per cent). By contrast, the ratio declined in Germany (from 0.6 to 0.5 per cent), Denmark (from 2.7 to 2.3 per cent) and Austria (from 8.4 to 7.4 per cent). Austria remained the country where the share of tourism receipts in GDP was highest (7.4 per cent in 1993), and it was followed by Greece, Spain and Portugal, where the share was between 4 and 5 per cent.

Share of "travel account" expenditure in private final consumption

From 1991 to 1993, "travel account" expenditure as a proportion of private final consumption in all Member countries combined remained stable at 1.9 per cent (see Table 6). The sharpest increases took place in Portugal (from 2 to 3.4 per cent) and Italy (from 1.6 to 2.3 per cent), whereas the steepest declines were in Finland (from 3.9 to 3.3 per cent), Japan (from 1.3 to 1.1 per cent) and Sweden (from 4.9 to 4.4 per cent).

Share of "travel account" receipts in exports of goods and services

The share of international tourism receipts in OECD-area exports of goods and services is gradually increasing and in 1993 stood at 5.3 per cent (see Table 7). The most pronounced increases were in Greece (from 17.6 to 23.4 per cent) and Turkey (from 11.5 to 14.4 per cent), while two substantial falls were recorded: in Denmark (from 5.8 to 4.2 per cent) and Canada (from 4.5 to 4 per cent).

Share of "travel account" expenditure in imports of goods and services

Between 1991 and 1993, the share of "travel account" expenditure in imports of goods and services rose from 5.2 to 5.5 per cent (see Table 8). The only region to decrease was North America, from 5.6 to 5.4 per cent, as a result of the fall in Canada and in Mexico. In Europe, falls in the majority of Nordic countries, with the exception of Iceland and Norway, were very largely offset by big increases in Portugal (from 3.4 to 5.8 per cent), Italy (from 4.5 to 5.8 per cent) and Germany (from 5.8 to 7.1 per cent). In the Asia-Pacific region, expenditure in Japan accounted in 1993 for 6.4 per cent of imports of goods and services (compared with 5.9 per cent in 1991).

Table 3. Trends in international tourist receipts in real prices[1]

	1988 = 100					Relative share in percentage of total	
	1989	1990	1991	1992	1993	1992	1993
Canada	99.8	104.3	101.7	102.5	111.1	2.8	3.0
Mexico	102.5	104.8	101.6	93.3	90.2	1.4	1.3
United States	116.6	131.2	141.6	153.0	159.4	27.4	27.6
North America[1]	113.5	126.0	133.9	142.6	148.5	31.7	31.9
Australia	87.4		105.9	116.5	122.1	2.3	2.4
Japan	114.8	132.6	114.4	110.6	95.1	1.9	1.6
New Zealand	94.9	101.1	101.0	104.6	81.3	0.9	0.7
Asia and the Pacific[1]	108.1	121.9	109.9	108.6	90.4	2.9	2.3
Austria	110.9	115.5	118.2	112.4	107.2	6.9	6.3
Belgium-Luxembourg	93.3		89.1	91.4	96.2	1.9	1.9
Denmark	99.0	117.1	123.3	124.1	100.7	1.8	1.4
Finland	99.3	95.9	99.9	118.0	133.5	0.7	0.8
France	122.0	125.1	133.0	143.0	139.7	11.9	11.2
Germany[3]	105.3	107.4	106.4	102.3	98.9	5.2	4.9
Greece	82.6	86.0	71.3	93.8	97.6	1.4	1.4
Iceland	108.7	124.2	115.2	102.0	118.5	0.1	0.1
Ireland	110.8	124.4	129.2	126.6	142.5	0.8	0.8
Italy[2]	95.6	129.6	117.6	129.3	161.9	9.7	11.7
Netherlands	112.7	111.8	130.8	144.2	133.6	2.5	2.2
Norway	92.3	92.9	99.9	111.4	116.5	1.0	1.0
Portugal[4]	108.0	112.8	108.8	91.8	113.7	1.3	1.6
Spain	92.7	84.8	84.8	91.2	94.9	9.2	9.2
Sweden	107.1	101.7	88.3	94.1	103.7	1.3	1.4
Switzerland	105.7	103.7	104.7	105.3	99.9	3.7	3.3
Turkey	94.8	93.5	71.4	96.4	98.3	1.4	1.4
United Kingdom	103.2	105.2	94.8	97.6	107.0	6.5	6.9
Europe[1]	103.8	108.6	106.8	111.9	116.6	65.4	65.8
OECD[1]	106.5	113.7	114.1	119.9	124.3	100.0	100.0

1. After correcting for the effects of inflation in each country. For the regional and OECD totals, the receipts of the individual countries are weighted in proportion to their share in the total expressed in dollars.
2. Break of series in 1990 due to the liberalisation of capital movements.
3. The data relate to the territory of the Federal Republic of Germany prior to 3rd October 1990. Since July 1990, data include all transactions of the former German Democratic Republic with foreign countries.
4. Break of series in 1993 due to a new collection and statistical production system.

Table 4. Tourism balance sheet
In billions of current dollars

	1991	1992	1993
North America			
Receipts	58.0	63.4	67.5
Expenditure	48.5	53.2	53.3
Balance[1]	9.5	10.2	14.3
Asia and the Pacific			
Receipts	4.9	5.1	4.7
Expenditure	25.0	27.8	27.5
Balance[1]	−20.0	−22.8	−22.8
Europe			
Receipts	126.8	143.3	135.7
Expenditure	117.8	138.3	127.5
Balance[1]	9.1	5.0	8.2
OECD			
Receipts	189.8	211.7	207.9
Expenditure	191.2	219.3	208.2
Balance[1]	−1.5	−7.6	−0.3

1. Minus signs indicate deficits. Due to rounding of figures, balances are not always equal to difference between receipts and expenditure.

Table 5. Ratio of the "Travel" account receipts to the gross domestic product (%)

	1991	1992	1993
Canada	1.2	1.2	1.2
Mexico	2.1	1.8	1.7
United States	0.9	0.9	0.9
North America	0.9	1.0	1.0
Australia	1.5	1.5	1.7
Japan	0.1	0.1	0.1
New Zealand	2.4	2.5	2.7
Asia and the pacific	0.2	0.2	0.2
Austria	8.4	7.8	7.4
Belgium-Luxembourg	1.8	1.8	1.9
Denmark	2.7	2.7	2.3
Finland	1.0	1.2	1.4
France	1.8	1.9	1.9
Germany	0.6	0.6	0.5
Greece	3.6	4.2	4.6
Iceland	2.0	1.9	2.2
Ireland	3.3	3.2	3.3
Italy	1.6	1.9	2.2
Netherlands	1.5	1.6	1.5
Norway	1.6	1.8	1.8
Portugal	4.8	3.9	4.8
Spain	3.6	3.8	4.1
Sweden	1.1	1.2	1.4
Switzerland	3.1	3.1	3.0
Turkey	1.8	2.3	2.3
United Kingdom	1.3	1.3	1.5
Europe	1.8	1.8	1.9
OECD	1.1	1.2	1.2

Source: OECD, Balance of Payments Division and *National Accounts of OECD Member Countries*.

Table 6. Ratio of the "Travel" account expenditure to the private final consumption (%)

	1991	1992	1993
Canada	3.8	3.9	3.9
Mexico	2.8	2.6	2.2
United States	0.9	1.0	1.0
North America	1.3	1.3	1.2
Australia	2.1	2.2	2.1
Japan	1.3	1.3	1.1
New Zealand	3.8	3.9	3.8
Asia and the Pacific	1.4	1.4	1.2
Austria	8.1	8.2	8.2
Belgium-Luxembourg	4.5	4.8	4.9
Denmark	5.0	5.2	4.6
Finland	3.9	3.9	3.3
France	1.7	1.8	1.7
Germany	3.2	3.3	3.4
Greece	2.0	2.1	1.9
Iceland	6.9	6.7	7.2
Ireland	4.2	4.5	4.6
Italy	1.6	2.4	2.3
Netherlands	4.8	4.9	4.7
Norway	6.4	6.9	6.9
Portugal	2.0	1.9	3.4
Spain	1.4	1.5	1.6
Sweden	4.9	5.2	4.4
Switzerland	4.3	4.3	4.3
Turkey	0.6	0.7	0.8
United Kingdom	2.7	3.0	3.1
Europe	2.8	3.0	3.0
OECD	1.9	2.0	1.9

Source: OECD, Balance of Payments Division and *National Accounts of OECD Member Countries*.

Table 7. Share of "Travel" account receipts in exports of goods and services

	1991	1992	1993
Canada	4.5	4.2	4.0
Mexico	13.8	13.7	13.0
United States	6.7	7.4	7.6
North America	6.7	7.2	7.2
Australia	7.8	7.7	8.2
Japan	0.7	0.7	0.6
New Zealand	8.4	8.3	8.7
Asia and the Pacific	1.6	1.5	1.5
Austria	18.4	17.8	17.6
Belgium-Luxembourg	1.7	1.7	1.8
Denmark	5.8	5.3	4.2
Finland	4.1	4.4	4.1
France	6.0	6.2	6.1
Germany	1.9	1.9	2.0
Greece	17.6	21.3	23.4
Iceland	6.1	5.9	6.3
Ireland	5.1	4.6	4.7
Italy	7.7	8.5	8.6
Netherlands	2.4	2.7	2.5
Norway	3.3	3.8	3.9
Portugal	16.1	14.3	15.5
Spain	19.8	20.2	19.9
Sweden	3.4	3.8	3.8
Switzerland	6.4	6.6	6.4
Turkey	11.5	14.4	14.4
United Kingdom	3.4	3.8	3.9
Europe	5.2	5.5	5.5
OCDE	5.0	5.3	5.3

Source: OECD, Balance of Payments Division.

Table 8. Share of "Travel" account expenditure in imports of goods and services

	1991	1992	1993
Canada	7.6	7.5	6.7
Mexico	9.5	8.5	7.6
United States	4.8	5.1	5.3
North America	5.6	5.7	5.7
Australia	5.8	5.7	5.4
Japan	5.9	6.7	6.4
New Zealand	7.3	7.1	6.7
Asia and the Pacific	5.9	6.5	6.3
Austria	9.8	10.4	10.8
Belgium-Luxembourg	2.7	2.8	3.0
Denmark	5.9	5.8	4.8
Finland	7.7	7.0	5.3
France	3.4	3.5	3.5
Germany	5.8	6.3	7.1
Greece	4.5	5.0	4.7
Iceland	11.6	12.0	12.7
Ireland	3.6	3.9	3.6
Italy	4.5	6.2	5.8
Netherlands	4.8	5.2	5.2
Norway	7.8	8.6	8.8
Portugal	3.4	3.4	5.8
Spain	3.8	4.1	4.4
Sweden	7.7	8.1	6.3
Switzerland	5.9	6.3	6.5
Turkey	2.1	2.6	2.5
United Kingdom	4.5	5.2	5.3
Europe	4.9	5.4	5.5
OECD	5.2	5.6	5.6

Source: OECD, Balance of Payments Division.

International tourist receipts
in real terms
(Shares of the various regions within the OECD)

Relatives shares   1984 = 100

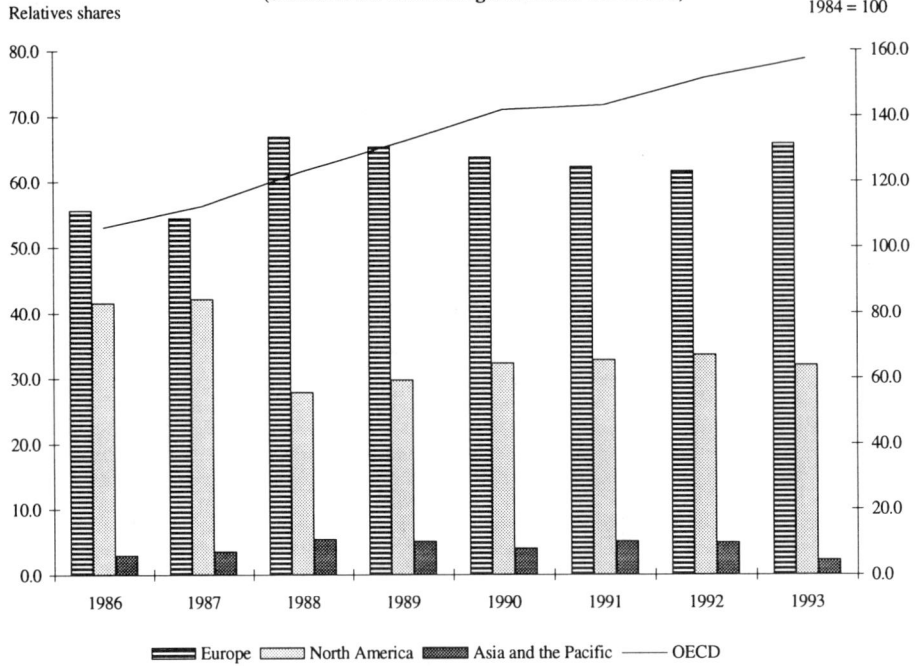

■ Europe   ☐ North America   ■ Asia and the Pacific   —— OECD

Source : OECD

International tourist receipts
Importance of the OECD area in the world total
(1993 in dollars)

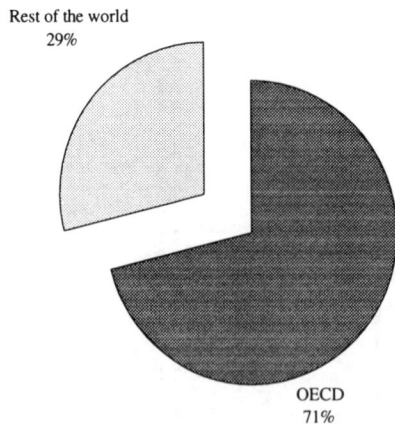

Rest of the world
29%

OECD
71%

Source : OECD

International tourist receipts
Share of the various regions within the OECD
(1993 in real terms)

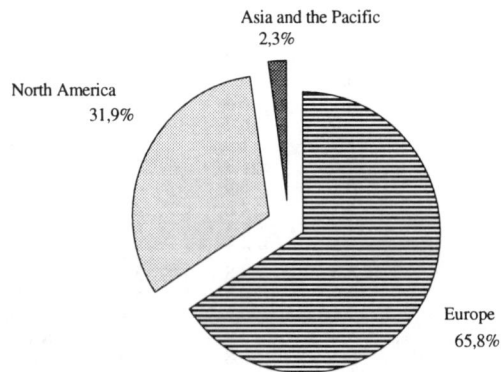

Asia and the Pacific
2,3%

North America
31,9%

Europe
65,8%

Source : OECD

Statistical Annex

Transport

Employment

Prices

International tourist flows from main generating

International tourist flows by receiving country

Notes

This Annex reproduces the main international tourism statistical series available in Member countries. It illustrates recent tourism developments in the OECD (over a two or three-year period).

Some of the data contained in the text itself may not always correspond exactly to that included in the Annex: the discrepancies can be explained by a different statistical coverage (e.g. the use of GNP instead of GDP) or by the use of material of a more analytical nature (data derived from gross figures).

Finally, certain tables are prepared from data available for other OECD work (e.g. Balance of Payments and National Accounts). In some cases, these statistics, which have been standardised to follow existing international guidelines, may differ from the ones supplied by countries in response to the annual questionnaire of the Tourism Committee.

Three tables of general interest for the use of the statistical series are presented at the beginning of the Annex:

A. Classification of travellers;

B. Series available by countries;

C. Types of establishments covered by the statistics.

Main elements of the terminology used

This section indicates the main methods used for collecting statistics and deals with international tourism.

Table A gives an overview of the international classification of travellers.

International inbound tourism (*i.e.* tourism performed in a given country by non-residents) is usually measured by the receiving country as monthly, quarterly or annual number of arrivals and/or nights spent, using one of three methods:

-- *Border controls*: these can provide only a limited amount of information about volumes, means of transport, etc. (as used in Japan, New Zealand and Spain);

-- *Sample surveys*: these provide a large amount of quantitative and qualitative information (as used in Canada, Portugal and the United Kingdom);

-- *Registration in means of accommodation*: this method, which is used in Finland, Italy and Switzerland among others, provides more accurate information, but with a more limited scope. However, by definition, it excludes excursionists and certain types of accommodation that are not registered for tax or other reasons, such as that provided by relatives or friends.

In estimating tourism supply, it is necessary to take account of all the goods and services required by tourism *i.e.* the resources, infrastructure and industries producing such goods and services, whether in the tourism field itself or indirectly related to the tourist industries.

The various means of accommodation are an essential part of this supply. They can be divided into two broad categories: hotels and similar establishments, and supplementary means of accommodation.

The first category (hotels and similar establishments) normally covers four types of establishments: hotels, motels, boarding houses and inns. However, in order to reflect the actual situation in a country more accurately, similar establishments are also often included (in which case the statistical coverage is indicated in Table C or in the methodological notes for each country).

The second category (supplementary means of accommodation) can include seven types of establishment: youth hostels, camping sites, holiday villages, mountain huts and shelters, rented rooms, houses and flats, sanatoria and health establishments and children's holiday camps. The list can also be extended in some cases.

The data on international tourism receipts and expenditure are those found under the "travel" heading in the Balance of Payments. They are available in varying degrees of disaggregation by country/region of origin or country/region of destination.

Data concerning international tourism payments follow, in practice, the recommendations of the World Tourism Organisation.

International tourism receipts: they are defined as the receipts of a country resulting from consumption expenditures, *i.e.*, payments for goods and services, made by visitors out of foreign currency. They should, however, exclude all forms of remuneration resulting from employment, as well as international fare receipts.

International tourism expenditure: they are defined as consumption expenditures, *i.e.*, payments for goods and services, made by residents of a country visiting abroad. They should, however, exclude all forms of remuneration resulting from employment, as well as international fare payments.

Three different methods are currently used by the Member countries.

In most countries, data are collected by the central bank using a method called the *bank reporting method*. When a traveller purchases or sells currency before or after a trip abroad, the bank or authorised agency records the transaction. Under this method, data are broken down according to the currency used and not according to the traveller's country of origin or destination.

The *estimation method* is based on sample surveys that are usually carried out at the points of entry or departure for non-residents, or at the re-entry points for returning residents. Data are broken down according to tourists' country of origin or destination. These surveys provide the most reliable and most detailed statistics.

The *mixed method*, which is used by only a few countries, was developed to remedy the shortcomings of the bank reporting method. It uses parallel sources (surveys of visitors, comparison with data provided by receiving countries, etc.), allowing the statistics obtained by the bank reporting method to be adjusted.

However, these data have their limitations. First, the volumes obtained by the bank reporting method in most countries are not an accurate measure of international tourist trade, since they represent net balances and not gross volumes; tourist transactions therefore tend to be understated. Second, it was noted that items unrelated to international tourism were included under the "travel" heading. Third, large discrepancies are found when any attempt is made to compile bilateral balances by comparing a given country's receipts, broken down by country of origin, with the expenditure reported by generating countries, broken down by country of destination.

Geographic coverage

Belgium-Luxembourg: Balance of payments statistics refer to the Belgium-Luxembourg Economic Union.

Other OECD-Europe: include OECD European countries for which no breakdown is available.

Other European countries: include non-OECD European countries for which no breakdown is available.

Origin country unspecified: includes non-OECD countries which cannot be broken down into any specific large geographic (other European countries, Latin America, Asia-Oceania, Africa).

North America includes Canada, Mexico and United States.

Sources

The principal national bodies for each OECD Member country dealing with tourism statistics are as follows:

Australia

    Bureau of Tourism Research
    Australian Bureau of Statistics

Austria

    Osterreichisches Statistisches Zentralamt
    Osterreichische Nationalbank

Belgium

    Institut National de Statistiques
    Banque nationale de Belgique
    Institut Belgo-Luxembourgeois du Change

Canada

    Statistics Canada, International Travel Section
    Industry, Science and Technology Canada, Tourism

Denmark

    Statistik Denmark
    Danmarks National Bank

Finland

    Central Statistical Office
    Bank of Finland

France

    Ministère du Tourisme, Direction des Industries touristiques
    Banque de France

Germany

Statistisches Bundesamt
Deutsche Bundesbank

Greece

National Statistical Service of the National Tourist Organisation of Greece
Bank of Greece

Iceland

Icelandic Immigration Authorities
Iceland Tourist Board
Central Bank of Iceland

Ireland

Central Statistics Office
Irish Tourist Board (Bord Failte)

Italy

Ministero del Turismo e dello Spetacolo
Istituto Centrale di Statistica
Banca d'Italia

Japan

Ministry of Transport, Department of Tourism
Japan National Tourist Organisation
Bank of Japan

Luxembourg

Service Central de la Statistique et des Etudes Economiques (STATEC)
Institut Belgo-Luxembourgeois du Change

Mexico

Secretaria de Turismo
Instituto Nacional de Estadistica, Geografia e Informatica (INEGI)
Banco de Mexico

Netherlands

Ministry of the Economy
Central Bureau of Statistics
Dutch Central Bank

New Zealand

New Zealand Tourism Department

Norway

Central Bureau of Statistics
Bank of Norway

Portugal

Direcçao-Geral de Turisme
Instituto Nacional de Estatistica
Banco de Portugal

Spain

Instituto Nacional de Estadisticas
Banco de Espana

Sweden

Statistics Sweden
Central Bank of Sweden

Switzerland

Office Fédéral de la Statistique, Section du Tourisme

Turkey

Ministry of Tourism
Central Bank

United Kingdom

Department of National Heritage
Central Statistical Office
British Tourist Authority

United States

Department of Commerce, United States Travel and Tourism Administration (USTTA)
Department of Commerce, Bureau of Economic Analysis

Graph A. **Classification of international visitors**

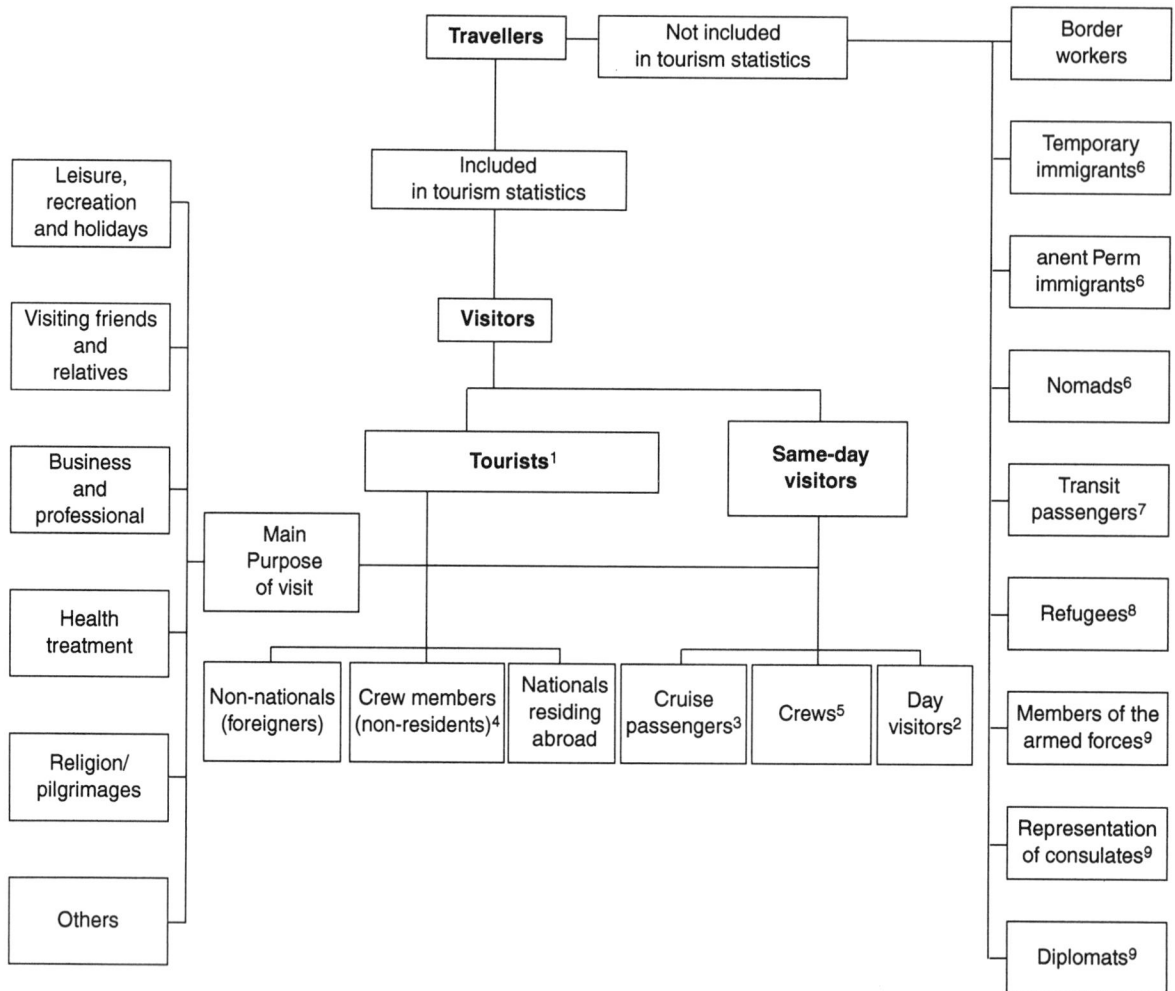

Travellers

Not included in tourism statistics
- Border workers
- Temporary immigrants[6]
- anent Perm immigrants[6]
- Nomads[6]
- Transit passengers[7]
- Refugees[8]
- Members of the armed forces[9]
- Representation of consulates[9]
- Diplomats[9]

Included in tourism statistics

Visitors

- **Tourists**[1]
- **Same-day visitors**

Main Purpose of visit
- Leisure, recreation and holidays
- Visiting friends and relatives
- Business and professional
- Health treatment
- Religion/ pilgrimages
- Others

Tourists[1]:
- Non-nationals (foreigners)
- Crew members (non-residents)[4]
- Nationals residing abroad

Same-day visitors:
- Cruise passengers[3]
- Crews[5]
- Day visitors[2]

1. Visitors who spend at least one night in the country visited, but less than one year.
2. Visitors who arrive and leave the same day for leisure, recreation and holidays; visiting friends and relatives; business and professional; health treatment; religion/pilgrimages and other tourism purposes, including transit day visitors en route to or from their destination countries.
3. Persons who arrive in a country aboard cruise ships [as defined by the international Maritime Organization (IMO), 1965] and who spend the night aboard ship even when disembarking for one or more day visits.
4. Foreign air or ship crews docked or in lay over and who use the accommodation establishments of the country visited.
5. Crews who are not residents of the country visited and who stay in the country for the day.
6. As defined by the United Nations in the Recommendations on Statistics of International.
7. Who do not leave the transit area of the airport or the port, including transfer between airports or ports.
8. As defined by the United Nations High Commissioner for Refugees, 1967.
9. When they travel from their country of origin to the duty station and vice-versa (including household servants and dependants accompanying or joining them).
Source: World Tourism Organisation (WTO).

B. Series available by country

Arrivals of foreign tourists at frontiers

Canada	Iceland	Portugal
France	New Zealand	United States
Greece	Japan	

Arrivals of foreign visitors at frontiers

Australia	Italy	Spain
Canada	Japan	Turkey (travellers)
Ireland	Portugal	United Kingdom

Arrivals of foreign tourists at hotels and similar establishments

Austria	Ireland	Spain
Finland	Italy	Switzerland
France	Netherlands	Turkey
Germany	Portugal	

Arrivals of foreign tourists at all means of accommodation

Austria	Italy	Switzerland
Germany	Netherlands	Turkey
Ireland	Portugal	

Nights spent by foreign tourists in hotels and similar establishments

Australia	Germany	Portugal
Austria	Ireland	Spain
Belgium	Italy	Sweden
Denmark	Netherlands	Switzerland
Finland	Norway	Turkey
France		

Nights spent by foreign tourists in all means of accommodation

Australia	Germany	Portugal
Austria	Ireland	Sweden
Belgium	Italy	Switzerland
Canada	Netherlands	Turkey
Denmark	New Zealand	United Kingdom
France		

C. Types of accommodation covered by the statistics

Countries	Hotels and similar establishments[11]					Supplementary means of accommodation[12]							
	Hotels[1]	Motels[2]	Boarding houses[3]	Inns[4]	Others[5]	Youth hostels	Camping/caravan sites[7]	Holiday villages	Mountain huts and shelters	Rented rooms, flats and houses	Sanatoria, health establishments	Recreation homes for children[8]	Others[9]
Australia	X	X	X		X	X	X			X			X
Austria[10]	X					X	X	X	X	X	X	X	X
Belgium	X	X			X		X			X	X	X	X
Canada	X						X						X
Denmark[10]	X					X	X						X
Finland	X		X		X		X						
France	X		X	X	X		X	X		X			
Germany	X	X	X	X	X	X	X	X			X		X
Greece	X	X	X	X	X		X						
Ireland	X		X										
Italy	X		X		X	X	X			X			X
Netherlands	X				X	X	X						
Norway[10]	X					X	X						
Portugal	X	X	X	X	X		X					X	
Spain	X	X					X						
Sweden	X	X	X	X		X	X	X		X			
Switzerland	X	X		X		X	X			X	X		X
Turkey	X	X	X	X	X		X	X					X

Countries not listed in this table do not dispose of data by type of accommodation.

1. Includes: Germany: hotels serving breakfast only; Belgium: motels, boarding houses and inns; Finland: motels; France: motels; Ireland: motels; boarding houses ("Fondas" and Casas de Huespedes"); Sweden: motels; Switzerland: boarding houses; Turkey: thermal hotels.
2. Includes: Greece: bungalows.
3. Includes: Finland: inns; Ireland: inns; Sweden: resort hotels.
4. Includes: Portugal: private and state-owned inns.
5. Includes: Australia: hotels and motels without facilities in most rooms and not necessarily providing meals and alcoholic drinks; Belgium: non-licensed establishments; Finland: lodging houses and part of youth hostels; Greece: bungalow-hotels, studio-hotels and recreation homes for children; Netherlands: youth hostels in Amsterdam; Portugal: holiday flats and villages; Spain: fondas; Sweden: boarding houses, inns, and resort hotels; Turkey: special licensed hotels, studio-hotels and thermal hotels.
6. Includes: Germany: mountain huts and shelters.
7. Includes: Australia: cabins and flats; Finland: holiday village cottages.
8. Includes: Portugal: youth hostels.
9. Includes: Australia: rented farms, house-boats, rented camper-vans, boats, cabin cruisers, camping outside commercial grounds; Austria: mountain huts and shelters; Belgium: youth hostels, holiday villages and social tourism establishments; Canada: homes of friends or relatives, private cottages, commercial cottages and others (universities, hostels); Germany: recreation and holiday homes, institutions providing educational services; Greece: holiday centres; Italy: recreation homes for children, mountain huts and shelters, holiday homes and religious establishments; Spain: secondary residences, private appartments, chalets and bungalows; Switzerland: dormitories in recreation homes for children, tourist camps, mountain huts and shelters, holiday villages.
10. Total available without breakdown for "hotels and similar establishments".
11. Includes: Denmark: hotels with more than 40 beds.
12. Includes: Denmark: January and February (hotels only), March (hotels and campings January to march), October (hotels and campings October to December), November and December (hotels only).

1. Tourism from European Member countries[1]

	Arrivals at frontiers[2]			Arrivals at all means of accommodation[3]			Nights spent in all means of accommodation[4]		
	Volume 1993 (thousand)	% 93/92	% 92/91	Volume 1993 (thousand)	% 93/92	% 92/91	Volume 1993 (thousand)	% 93/92	% 92/91
Canada	1 739.8	8.3	2.9				20 774.0	8.8	0.5
Mexico									
United States	8 413.1	4.3	12.8						
Australia	621.0	10.4	9.2				24 178.0	2.0	– 10.3
Japan	239.0	– 6.4	9.9						
New Zealand	219.3	11.5	14.2	120.9			6 462.2	5.6	5.4
Austria				16 119.9	– 3.9	– 1.2	91 155.8	– 2.8	– 0.3
Belgium							11 275.5	2.4	4.8
Denmark							9 593.0	– 10.6	11.9
Finland				1 279.5			2 111.4		
France	52 988.0	0.9	8.2	52 988.0	0.9	8.2	361 338.0	1.4	7.4
Germany				9 536.9	– 10.9	– 1.7	23 099.5	– 10.2	– 1.8
Greece	7 771.1	1.1	23.0						
Iceland	123.2	8.4	– 0.6						
Ireland	2 808.0	7.5	2.4	2 489.5	7.5	– 7.3	28 740.0	17.6	– 0.8
Italy	36 210.8	– 8.7	– 4.1	14 233.3	1.0	– 5.2	66 033.5	1.2	– 7.4
Luxembourg									
Netherlands				4 801.8	– 5.0	2.7	15 140.8	– 4.8	4.5
Norway							3 807.8	6.6	7.6
Portugal	7 899.7	– 4.7	2.6	3 449.8	– 9.7	– 10.1	16 567.0	– 10.5	– 9.0
Spain	31 144.9			10 976.1	5.5	5.3	78 960.4	8.7	7.2
Sweden							4 811.7	4.2	3.8
Switzerland				7 290.1	– 3.6	– 1.9	30 762.2	– 0.5	– 1.0
Turkey	3 164.9	5.2	63.7	2 855.3	7.2	75.4	13 952.4	– 2.4	85.9
United Kingdom	12 351.0	6.6	5.7				91 207.0	0.5	– 1.2

1. Derived from tables by receiving country (see corresponding notes.)
2. *Tourist* or *visitor* arrivals. When both available : *tourist arrivals.*
3. Arrivals *in all means of accommodation* or *in hotels and similar establishments*. When both available : arrivals *in all means of accommodation.*
4. Nights spent *in all means of accommodation* or *in hotels and similar establishments*. When both available : nights spent *in all means of accommodation.*

2. Tourism from Canada Mexico and the United States[1]

	Arrivals at frontiers[2]			Arrivals at all means of accommodation[3]			Nights spent in all means of accommodation[4]		
	Volume 1993 (thousand)	% 93/92	% 92/91	Volume 1993 (thousand)	% 93/92	% 92/91	Volume 1993 (thousand)	% 93/92	% 92/91
Canada	12 097.7	1.8	– 1.5				48 141.3	2.7	– 6.1
Mexico									
United States	27 117.0	– 8.9	10.9						
Australia	334.0	6.5	– 4.0				8 729.0	10.2	– 11.3
Japan	325.0	– 6.8	4.5						
New Zealand	172.8	9.2	– 3.3	172.8			2 775.8	7.0	0.9
Austria				616.7	– 13.2	30.0	1 576.6	– 9.1	25.0
Belgium							619.8	– 14.8	16.6
Denmark							306.4	– 5.5	4.2
Finland				100.7			191.2		
France	2 665.0	2.3	21.9	2 665.0	2.3	21.9	23 587.0	2.4	21.8
Germany				1 723.7	– 12.6	7.4	3 640.6	– 10.7	6.2
Greece	313.5	– 9.2	49.4						
Iceland	26.7	16.0	– 2.3						
Ireland	397.0	– 2.0	18.1	422.0	1.2	17.1	4 736.0	– 1.8	11.9
Italy	1 651.5	– 7.2	14.0	2 372.5	4.6	27.2	6 344.0	8.8	22.6
Luxembourg									
Netherlands				492.1	– 7.2	8.5	1 016.4	– 8.1	9.5
Norway							311.5	– 11.4	25.4
Portugal	207.7	– 6.8	8.0	244.4	– 9.7	3.3	682.5	– 13.5	– 1.0
Spain	854.3			794.6	– 4.8	20.3	1 764.0	– 7.8	21.9
Sweden							317.3	5.8	10.8
Switzerland				997.1	– 8.0	20.7	2 307.3	– 3.7	15.8
Turkey	297.2	38.8	116.1	230.9	32.2	73.3	549.2	29.6	37.7
United Kingdom	3 402.0	0.7	17.8				35 277.0	2.1	6.1

1. Derived from tables by receiving country (see corresponding notes.)
2. *Tourist* or *visitor* arrivals. When both available : *tourist arrivals.*
3. Arrivals *in all means of accommodation* or *in hotels and similar establishments*. When both available : arrivals *in all means of accommodation.*
4. Nights spent *in all means of accommodation* or *in hotels and similar establishments*. When both available : nights spent *in all means of accommodation.*

3. Tourism from Australia, Japan and New Zealand [1]

	Arrivals at frontiers [2]			Arrivals at all means of accommodation [3]			Nights spent in all means of accommodation [4]		
	Volume 1993 (thousand)	% 93/92	% 92/91	Volume 1993 (thousand)	% 93/92	% 92/91	Volume 1993 (thousand)	% 93/92	% 92/91
Canada	533.0	1.7	0.6				4 141.6	4.1	− 0.7
Mexico									
United States	4 124.8	− 3.6	8.7						
Australia	1 170.1	8.6	6.8				12 439.0	0.1	− 6.0
Japan	40.9	3.9	15.8						
New Zealand	501.3	0.5	8.4	501.3			7 154.4	2.1	3.7
Austria				280.8	− 6.1	8.1	607.9	− 6.1	5.0
Belgium							194.7	− 16.6	47.7
Denmark							100.0	− 9.8	18.7
Finland				49.9			86.9		
France	325.0	− 27.6	6.4	325.0	− 27.6	6.4	1 405.0	− 30.5	2.3
Germany				830.3	− 9.1	10.6	1 438.5	− 8.1	6.8
Greece	152.9	− 18.4	40.9						
Iceland	2.5	22.1	9.8						
Ireland	73.0	10.6	32.0	74.0	4.2	31.5	528.0	− 6.7	− 35.2
Italy	932.6	− 2.6	26.1	1 344.3	11.9	29.9	2 861.2	11.5	27.8
Luxembourg									
Netherlands				155.4	− 21.2	22.1	323.1	− 20.3	21.3
Norway							120.9	21.1	17.5
Portugal	32.5	− 28.5	− 0.9	68.5	24.0	2.1	149.3	20.6	− 4.9
Spain	227.8			325.5	− 12.2	8.5	586.8	− 17.4	15.1
Sweden							100.6	17.1	− 4.4
Switzerland				604.8	− 4.6	15.1	1 043.9	− 4.1	6.9
Turkey	85.5	14.6	61.8	156.6	14.8	126.6	258.0	5.1	119.0
United Kingdom	1 076.0	− 8.3	13.4				15 919.0	− 13.4	− 7.5

1. Derived from tables by receiving country (see corresponding notes.)
2. *Tourist* or *visitor arrivals.* When both available : *tourist arrivals.*
3. Arrivals *in all means of accommodation* or *in hotels and similar establishments.* When both available : arrivals *in all means of accommodation.*
4. Nights spent *in all means of accommodation* or *in hotels and similar establishments.* When both available : nights spent *in all means of accommodation.*

4. Tourism from all OECD countries [1]

	Arrivals at frontiers [2]			Arrivals at all means of accommodation [3]			Nights spent in all means of accommodation [4]		
	Volume 1993 (thousand)	% 93/92	% 92/91	Volume 1993 (thousand)	% 93/92	% 92/91	Volume 1993 (thousand)	% 93/92	% 92/91
Canada	14 370.5	2.5	− 1.0				73 056.9	4.5	− 4.1
Mexico									
United States	39 654.9	− 5.8	11.1						
Australia	2 125.1	8.8	5.5				45 346.0	2.9	− 9.3
Japan	604.9	− 6.0	7.3						
New Zealand	893.4	4.6	7.3	795.1			16 392.4	4.3	3.9
Austria				17 017.4	− 4.3	− 0.1	93 340.4	− 2.9	0.1
Belgium							12 090.0	1.0	6.1
Denmark							9 999.4	− 10.4	11.7
Finland				1 430.1			2 389.5		
France	55 978.0	0.8	8.8	55 978.0	0.8	8.8	386 330.0	1.3	8.1
Germany				12 090.9	− 11.0	0.3	28 178.7	− 10.2	− 0.4
Greece	8 237.5	0.2	24.3						
Iceland	152.4	9.8	− 0.7						
Ireland	3 278.0	6.3	4.7	3 158.0	4.9	3.5	34 004.0	14.0	0.1
Italy	38 794.8	− 8.5	− 3.0	17 950.2	2.2	− 0.1	75 238.8	2.2	− 4.6
Luxembourg									
Netherlands				5 449.3	− 5.7	3.7	16 480.3	− 5.4	5.1
Norway							4 240.2	5.4	9.2
Portugal	8 139.9	− 4.9	2.7	3 762.6	− 9.3	− 9.2	17 398.8	− 10.5	− 8.7
Spain	32 227.0			12 096.3	4.2	6.4	81 311.2	8.0	7.6
Sweden							5 229.6	4.5	4.1
Switzerland				8 892.0	− 4.1	1.3	34 113.4	− 0.9	0.3
Turkey	3 547.7	7.6	66.3	3 242.9	9.0	77.1	14 759.6	− 1.4	84.5
United Kingdom	16 829.0	4.3	8.6				142 403.0	− 0.9	− 0.4

1. Derived from tables by receiving country (see corresponding notes.)
2. *Tourist* or *visitor arrivals.* When both available : *tourist arrivals.*
3. Arrivals *in all means of accommodation* or *in hotels and similar establishments.* When both available : arrivals *in all means of accommodation.*
4. Nights spent *in all means of accommodation* or *in hotels and similar establishments.* When both available : nights spent *in all means of accommodation.*

5. Tourism from non-Member countries [1]

	Arrivals at frontiers [2]			Arrivals at all means of accommodation [3]			Nights spent in all means of accommodation [4]		
	Volume 1993 (thousand)	% 93/92	% 92/91	Volume 1993 (thousand)	% 93/92	% 92/91	Volume 1993 (thousand)	% 93/92	% 92/91
Canada	738.8	1.7	– 11.0				9 035.2	– 4.9	– 6.8
Mexico									
United States	6 123.9	12.4	– 57.1						
Australia	871.9	34.3	25.9				19 370.0	11.4	8.2
Japan	1 320.6	– 9.5	– 3.3						
New Zealand	263.5	30.7	20.2				5 856.0	22.3	15.5
Austria				1 239.3	– 5.4	22.8	3 483.4	– 3.0	23.6
Belgium							809.5	– 11.0	– 0.1
Denmark							460.6	9.0	– 3.6
Finland				58.7			114.2		
France	4 122.0	– 0.7	4.9	4 122.0	– 0.7	4.9	43 970.0	– 1.8	3.6
Germany				2 256.8	– 2.8	20.9	6 532.8	– 4.4	25.2
Greece	1 175.4	5.6	22.2				36 475.0	0.6	21.4
Iceland	5.0	29.0	9.7						
Ireland	52.0	– 1.9	1.9	50.0	– 84.0	194.3	1 126.0	– 71.4	13.6
Italy	11 114.9	44.4	130.2	3 075.2	7.4	13.9	10 192.0	1.9	12.7
Luxembourg									
Netherlands				257.4	– 14.8	12.2	697.5	3.0	7.0
Norway							316.6	25.2	8.6
Portugal	294.0	– 9.1	– 0.4	199.1	0.5	– 3.7	725.3	15.0	– 6.7
Spain	3 753.8	2.0	6.7	853.3	– 25.8	– 4.4	1 561.0	– 6.8	– 64.0
Sweden							845.0	4.2	2.4
Switzerland				1 009.3	2.1	8.7	2 615.5	1.0	1.4
Turkey	2 953.0	– 21.9	11.9	854.5	14.6	9.8	2 304.5	27.0	19.3
United Kingdom	2 659.0	11.0	8.0				44 560.0	2.6	5.0

1. Derived from tables by receiving country (see corresponding notes.)
2. *Tourist* or *visitor* arrivals. When both available : *tourist arrivals.*
3. Arrivals *in all means of accommodation* or *in hotels and similar establishments.* When both available : arrivals *in all means of accommodation.*
4. Nights spent *in all means of accommodation* or *in hotels and similar establishments.* When both available : nights spent *in all means of accommodation.*

6. Tourism from all countries [1]

	Arrivals at frontiers [2]			Arrivals at all means of accommodation [3]			Nights spent in all means of accommodation [4]		
	Volume 1993 (thousand)	% 93/92	% 92/91	Volume 1993 (thousand)	% 93/92	% 92/91	Volume 1993 (thousand)	% 93/92	% 92/91
Canada	15 109.3	2.5	– 1.5				82 092.1	3.4	– 4.4
Mexico									
United States	45 778.8	– 3.7	– 6.1						
Australia	2 997.0	15.1	10.0				35 392.0	9.1	– 49.8
Japan	1 925.5	– 8.5	– 0.3						
New Zealand	1 157.0	9.6	9.5	795.1			22 248.4	8.5	6.4
Austria[5]				18 256.8	– 4.4	1.2	96 823.8	– 2.9	0.8
Belgium							12 899.5	0.2	5.6
Denmark							10 460.0	– 9.7	11.1
Finland				1 488.8			2 503.7		
France	60 100.0	0.7	8.5	60 100.0	0.7	8.5	430 300.0	0.9	7.6
Germany				14 347.7	– 9.8	2.8	34 711.4	– 9.1	3.4
Greece	9 412.9	0.9	24.1				36 475.0	0.6	21.4
Iceland	157.3	10.4	– 0.5						
Ireland	3 330.0	6.2	4.6	3 274.0	5.1	3.3	35 130.0	4.0	1.5
Italy	49 909.7	– 0.4	6.5	21 025.4	2.9	1.7	85 430.8	2.1	– 2.8
Luxembourg									
Netherlands				5 706.7	– 6.2	4.1	17 177.8	– 5.1	5.2
Norway							4 556.8	6.6	9.2
Portugal	8 433.9	– 5.1	2.6	3 961.7	– 8.8	– 8.9	18 124.1	– 9.7	– 8.6
Spain	32 227.0			12 949.5	1.5	5.3	82 872.3	7.7	3.1
Sweden							6 074.6	4.5	3.8
Suisse[6]				9 901.3	– 3.5	2.0	36 728.9	– 0.7	0.4
Turkey[5]	6 500.6	– 8.1	32.0	4 097.4	10.1	57.7	17 064.1	1.7	74.2
United Kingdom	19 488.0	5.1	8.5				186 963.0	– 0.1	0.8

1. Derived from tables by receiving country. See corresponding notes, except for the countries mentioned in notes 5 and 6 below.
2. *Tourist* or *visitor* arrivals. When both available : *tourist arrivals.*
3. Arrivals *in all means of accommodation* or *in hotels and similar establishments.* When both available : arrivals *in all means of accommodation.*
4. Nights spent *in all means of accommodation* or *in hotels and similar establishments.* When both available : nights spent *in all means of accommodation.*
5. *Traveller* arrivals at frontiers.
6. *Tourist* arrivals at frontiers : estimates.

Table 7. **Tourism from the United States**
Expenditure of US Residents Travelling Abroad
In millions of dollars

	1989	1990	1991	1992	1993
Expenditure abroad[1]	33 418	37 349	35 322	39 006	40 563
Canada[2]	3 396	3 541	3 705	3 554	3 691
Mexico	4 276	4 879	5 111	5 159	5 158
Total overseas	25 746	28 929	26 506	30 293	31 714
Western Europe	11 668	13 615	11 073	13 155	14 190
United Kingdom	3 319	3 657	3 168	3 220	4 040
Germany	2 664	2 671	2 191	2 306	2 612
France	1 553	1 788	1 533	2 056	2 225
Italy	1 425	1 631	1 459	1 591	1 486
Eastern Europe	299	381	451	796	247
Caribbean, South and Central America	5 123	5 395	3 072	6 351	6 987
Japan	1 872	2 210	2 760	2 473	2 924
Australia, New Zealand and South Africa	1 049	1 249	1 124	1 770	1 058
Australia	726	867	783	837	719
Other	5 735	6 079	4 966	6 341	6 308
Fare payments					
Foreign-flag carriers	8 248	10 530	10 012	10 608	11 410

1. Excluding travel by military personnel and other Government employees stationed abroad, their dependents and United States citizens residing abroad; includes shore expenditure of United States cruise travellers.
2. Excluding fare payments and crew spending.

Source: US Department of Commerce, US Travel and Tourism Administration and Bureau of Economic Analysis.

Table 8. **Tourism from the United States**
Number and Expenditure of US Residents Travelling Overseas

	Number of travellers in thousands			Total expenditure Millions of dollars[1]			Average expenditure per traveller		
	1991	1992	1993	1991	1992	1993	1991	1992	1993
Total overseas	14 521	15 945	17 102	26 506	30 293	31 714	1 925	1 950	2 212
Europe	6 316	7 136	7 491	11 524	13 951	14 417	1 825	1 918	2 419
Caribbean, South and Central America	5 155	5 285	5 729	3 072	6 351	6 987	596	672	993
Japan	897	1 017	1 043	2 760	2 473	2 924	3 078	3 107	3 709
Australia, New Zealand and South Africa	684	639	719	1 124	1 770	1 058	1 643	1 856	1 952
Other	1 469	1 888	2 838	4 966	6 341	6 308	3 381	2 996	3 721

1. Excludes travel by military personnel and other Government employees stationed abroad, their dependents and United States citizens residing abroad and cruise travellers.

Source: US Department of Commerce, US Travel and Tourism Administration and Bureau of Economic Analysis, based on data of the US Department of Justice, Immigration and Naturalisation Service.

9.   Average length of stay of foreign tourists

	Tourists from all foreign countries			Tourists from Europe (OECD)			Tourists from North America (OECD)			Tourists from Pacific (OECD)		
	1991	1992	1993	1991	1992	1993	1991	1992	1993	1991	1992	1993
	Average length of stay in tourist accommodation[1]											
Austria	5.2	5.2	5.3	5.5	5.6	5.7	2.5	2.4	2.6	2.2	2.2	2.2
Germany	2.4	2.4	2.4	2.4	2.4	2.4	2.1	2.1	2.1	1.8	1.7	1.7
Italy	4.3	4.1	4.1	4.7	4.6	4.6	2.7	2.6	2.7	2.2	2.1	2.1
Netherlands	2.9	3.0	3.0	3.1	3.1	3.2	2.1	2.1	2.1	2.1	2.1	2.1
Portugal	4.6	4.6	4.6	4.8	4.8	4.8	3.0	2.9	2.8	2.4	2.2	2.2
Spain[2]	6.2	6.0	6.4	6.9	7.0	7.2	2.3	2.3	2.2	1.8	1.9	1.8
Switzerland	3.7	3.6	3.7	4.1	4.1	4.2	2.3	2.2	2.3	1.8	1.7	1.7
Turkey	4.1	4.5	4.2	5.1	5.4	4.9	3.1	2.4	2.4	1.9	1.8	1.6

1. Unless otherwise stated below, the average length of stay in all means of accommodation is obtained by dividing the number of nights recorded in particular means of accommodation by the number of arrivals of tourists at the same means of accommodation (see country tables).
2. Hôtellerie.

	Tourists from all foreign countries			Tourists from Europe (OECD)			Tourists from North America (OECD)			Tourists from Pacific (OECD)		
	1991	1992	1993	1991	1992	1993	1991	1992	1993	1991	1992	1993
	Average length of stay in the country visited[1]											
Canada[4]	5.6	5.4	5.4	12.2	11.9	12.0	4.1	3.9	3.9	7.7	7.6	7.5
Australia	29.0	26.0	23.0	55.0	44.0	40.0	29.0	27.0	28.0	14.0	12.0	11.0
Japan	12.3	11.2	10.2									
New Zealand[2]	20.0	19.0	19.0				16.0	17.0	16.0	14.0		14.0
France	7.2	7.2	7.2	6.8	6.8	6.8	8.9	8.8	8.8	4.7	4.5	4.3
Ireland[3]	9.9	9.5		9.9	9.5		11.4	10.7		16.3	13.5	
Portugal[2]	7.6	7.3	7.0	7.6	7.3	7.0						
Turkey	6.9	8.4	10.0	11.8	12.3	11.4	12.9	13.4	13.8	12.3	18.2	14.3
United Kingdom	11.0	10.0					11.0	10.0		19.0	16.0	

1. Unless otherwise stated below, the average length of stay in the country visited is expressed in number of nights spent.
2. New Zealand and Portugal: number of days.
3. Ireland: visitors on overseas routes.
4. Canada: "Tourists from all foreign countries" : only overseas countries and the United States.

10. Nights spent by foreign and domestic tourists in all means of accommodation[1]

In thousands

	Nights spent by foreign tourists			Nights spent by domestic tourists			Total nights			Proportion spent by foreign tourists (%)	
	1992	1993	% 93/92	1992	1993	% 93/92	1992	1993	% 93/92	1992	1993
Australia	61 444.0	64 931.0	5.7	207 510.0	209 963.0	1.2	268 954.0	274 894.0	2.2	22.8	23.6
Austria	99 757.6	96 823.8	−2.9	30 658.7	30 216.0	−1.4	130 416.3	127 039.8	−2.6	76.5	76.2
Belgium	12 880.0	13 047.4	1.3	14 745.1	14 304.6	−3.0	27 625.1	27 352.0	−1.0	46.6	47.7
Denmark		10 503.5		14 054.9	13 880.9	−1.2		24 384.4			43.1
Finland	2 587.0	2 928.9	13.2	9 286.0	9 737.2	4.9	11 873.0	12 666.2	6.7	21.8	23.1
France	91 864.0	90 665.9	−1.3	155 772.9	155 816.0	0.0	247 636.9	246 481.9	−0.5	37.1	36.8
Germany	38 200.4	34 709.6	−9.1	280 269.5	277 432.2	−1.0	318 469.9	312 141.9	−2.0	12.0	11.1
Greece	36 907.3	37 108.0	0.5	12 421.0	12 536.6	0.9	49 328.3	49 644.6	0.6	74.8	74.7
Italy	83 642.6	83 709.8	0.1	173 720.9	171 484.4	−1.3	257 363.5	255 194.2	−0.8	32.5	32.8
Netherlands	18 023.4	17 177.8	−4.7	40 554.3	38 990.6	−3.9	58 577.7	56 168.4	−4.1	30.8	30.6
Norway	6 487.0	6 881.8	6.1	11 633.1	11 941.4	2.6	18 120.1	18 823.1	3.9	35.8	36.6
Portugal	20 064.5	18 124.1	−9.7	13 659.6	13 998.8	2.5	33 724.1	32 122.9	−4.7	59.5	56.4
Sweden	5 814.5	6 074.6	4.5	23 742.1	24 427.3	2.9	29 556.6	30 501.9	3.2	19.7	19.9
Switzerland	36 999.9	36 728.9	−0.7	39 217.7	38 142.8	−2.7	76 217.5	74 871.7	−1.8	48.5	49.1
Turkey[2]	16 785.5	17 064.1	1.7	9 458.9	9 696.9	2.5	26 244.4	26 761.0	2.0	64.0	63.8

1. For the "Types of accommodation covered by the statistics" see Table C.
2. Turkey: figures based on a monthly sample survey carried out amoung establishments licenced by the Ministry of Tourism.

11. Nights spent by foreign and domestic tourists in hotels and similar establishments[1]

In thousands

	Nights spent by foreign tourists			Nights spent by domestic tourists			Total nights			Proportion spent by foreign tourists (%)	
	1992	1993	% 93/92	1992	1993	% 93/92	1992	1993	% 93/92	1992	1993
Australia	12 967.0	14 763.0	13.9	44 299.0	43 860.0	−1.0	57 266.0	58 623.0	2.4	22.6	25.2
Austria	64 189.0	61 995.9	−3.4	16 162.3	15 953.9	−1.3	80 351.3	77 949.8	−3.0	79.9	79.5
Belgium	7 694.1	7 549.1	−1.9	2 817.6	2 832.1	0.5	10 511.6	10 381.2	−1.2	73.2	72.7
Denmark		5 913.0		5 378.2	5 655.4	5.2		11 568.4			51.1
Finland	2 242.7	2 587.7	15.4	7 539.4	7 984.7	5.9	9 782.1	10 572.4	8.1	22.9	24.5
France[2]	59 635.5	58 261.5	−2.3	91 603.8	90 159.9	−1.6	151 239.3	148 421.4	−1.9	39.4	39.3
Germany	28 377.6	26 069.2	−8.1	146 117.7	142 491.0	−2.5	174 495.3	168 560.2	−3.4	16.3	15.5
Greece	36 260.3	36 475.0	0.6	11 943.1	12 058.9	1.0	48 203.4	48 533.8	0.7	75.2	75.2
Italy	63 415.5	63 215.0	−0.3	129 151.8	120 416.1	−6.8	192 567.3	183 631.1	−4.6	32.9	34.4
Netherlands	8 423.7	7 973.0	−5.4	6 787.2	7 640.0	12.6	15 210.9	15 613.0	2.6	55.4	51.1
Norway	4 275.2	4 556.8	6.6	9 022.5	9 447.2	4.7	13 297.6	14 004.0	5.3	32.1	32.5
Portugal	17 877.0	16 176.0	−9.5	7 437.0	7 423.8	−0.2	25 314.0	23 599.7	−6.8	70.6	68.5
Spain	76 934.3	83 132.2	8.1	54 362.9	54 971.2	1.1	131 297.2	138 103.4	5.2	58.6	60.2
Sweden	2 803.7	2 983.6	6.4	11 344.6	11 890.3	4.8	14 148.3	14 873.9	5.1	19.8	20.1
Switzerland	20 235.9	19 773.9	−2.3	13 204.3	12 821.1	−2.9	33 440.3	32 595.0	−2.5	60.5	60.7
Turkey[3]	13 560.2	14 281.0	5.3	8 542.6	8 583.0	0.5	22 102.8	22 864.0	3.4	61.4	62.5

1. For the "Types of accommodation covered by the statistics" see Table C.
2. France: data covering all France except 2 regions (Pays de la Loire and Champagne-Ardennes in 1991; Champagne-Ardennes and Corse in 1992 and 1993).
3. Turkey: does not include thermal hotels.

12. Nights spent by foreign and domestic tourists in supplementary means of accommodation[1]

In thousands

	Nights spent by foreign tourists			Nights spent by domestic tourists			Total nights			Proportion spent by foreign tourists (%)	
	1992	1993	% 93/92	1992	1993	% 93/92	1992	1993	% 93/92	1992	1993
Australia	48 477.0	50 168.0	3.5	163 211.0	166 103.0	1.8	211 688.0	216 271.0	2.2	22.9	23.2
Austria	35 568.6	34 827.9	−2.1	14 496.4	14 262.1	−1.6	50 065.0	49 090.0	−1.9	71.0	70.9
Belgium	5 185.9	5 498.2	6.0	11 927.5	11 472.5	−3.8	17 113.5	16 970.8	−0.8	30.3	32.4
Denmark		4 590.5		8 676.7	8 225.5	−5.2		12 816.0			35.8
Finland	344.3	341.2	−0.9	1 746.7	1 752.5	0.3	2 091.0	2 093.8	0.1	16.5	16.3
France[2]	32 228.5	35 211.7	9.3	64 169.1	65 656.1	2.3	96 397.6	100 867.9	4.6	33.4	34.9
Germany	9 822.8	8 640.4	−12.0	134 151.8	134 941.3	0.6	143 974.6	143 581.6	−0.3	6.8	6.0
Greece	647.0	633.0	−2.2	477.9	477.7	0.0	1 124.9	1 110.8	−1.3	57.5	57.0
Italy	20 227.1	20 494.8	1.3	44 569.1	51 068.3	14.6	64 796.2	71 563.1	10.4	31.2	28.6
Netherlands	9 599.7	9 204.8	−4.1	33 767.1	31 350.6	−7.2	43 366.8	40 555.4	−6.5	22.1	22.7
Norway	2 211.8	2 325.0	5.1	2 610.6	2 494.1	−4.5	4 822.4	4 819.1	−0.1	45.9	48.2
Portugal	2 187.4	1 948.1	−10.9	6 222.6	6 575.0	5.7	8 410.0	8 523.1	1.3	26.0	22.9
Sweden	3 010.8	3 090.9	2.7	12 397.5	12 537.0	1.1	15 408.3	15 628.0	1.4	19.5	19.8
Switzerland	16 763.9	16 955.0	1.1	26 013.3	25 321.7	−2.7	42 777.3	42 276.7	−1.2	39.2	40.1
Turkey	3 225.3	2 783.1	−13.7	916.3	1 113.9	21.6	4 141.6	3 897.0	−5.9	77.9	71.4
Of which: **on camping sites**											
Australia	1 954.0	1 877.0	−3.9	17 310.0	16 253.0	−6.1	19 264.0	18 130.0	−5.9	10.1	10.4
Austria	5 456.9	4 962.1	−9.1	1 432.8	1 308.1	−8.7	6 889.7	6 270.2	−9.0	79.2	79.1
Belgium	2 079.0	2 002.5	−3.7	4 982.4	4 455.6	−10.6	7 061.4	6 458.1	−8.5	29.4	31.0
Denmark		4 104.5		8 155.6	7 687.7	−5.7		11 792.2			34.8
Finland	344.3	341.2	−0.9	1 746.7	1 752.5	0.3	2 091.0	2 093.8	0.1	16.5	16.3
France[2]	32 228.5	35 211.7	9.3	64 169.1	65 656.1	2.3	96 397.6	100 867.9	4.6	33.4	34.9
Germany	4 380.1	3 640.5	−16.9	20 253.4	19 510.4	−3.7	24 633.5	23 150.9	−6.0	17.8	15.7
Greece	647.0	633.0	−2.2	477.9	477.7	0.0	1 124.9	1 110.8	−1.3	57.5	57.0
Italy	14 806.7			30 574.2			45 380.9			32.6	
Netherlands	4 085.2	3 458.0	−15.4	15 857.5	14 145.8	−10.8	19 942.7	17 603.8	−11.7	20.5	19.6
Norway	2 211.8	2 325.0	5.1	2 610.6	2 494.1	−4.5	4 822.4	4 819.1	−0.1	45.9	48.2
Portugal	2 123.1	1 882.5	−11.3	5 204.0	5 492.1	5.5	7 327.1	7 374.5	0.6	29.0	25.5
Sweden	2 323.8	2 357.0	1.4	9 150.0	9 055.7	−1.0	11 473.8	11 412.7	−0.5	20.3	20.7
Switzerland	2 713.3	2 559.6	−5.7	5 608.9	5 519.9	−1.6	8 322.2	8 079.5	−2.9	32.6	31.7
Turkey	140.4	60.4	−57.0	19.9	30.4	52.3	160.4	90.8	−43.4	87.6	66.5
Of which: **in youth hostels**											
Australia	5 402.0	5 352.0	−0.9	1 641.0	2 192.0	33.6	7 043.0	7 544.0	7.1	76.7	70.9
Austria	866.8	823.8	−5.0	639.5	648.5	1.4	1 506.3	1 472.3	−2.3	57.5	56.0
Denmark		486.0		521.1	537.8	3.2		1 023.8			47.5
Germany	1 194.5	1 100.4	−7.9	12 758.9	12 821.0	0.5	13 953.4	13 921.4	−0.2	8.6	7.9
Italy	586.6			229.4			816.0			71.9	
Netherlands	755.5	731.8	−3.1	320.2	325.4	1.6	1 075.7	1 057.2	−1.7	70.2	69.2
Norway											
Sweden	207.0	211.0	1.9	761.0	794.3	4.4	968.1	1 005.3	3.8	21.4	21.0
Switzerland	543.0	495.7	−8.7	365.3	356.8	−2.3	908.3	852.6	−6.1	59.8	58.1
Of which: **in private rooms, rented apartments and houses**											
Australia	8 083.0	8 789.0	8.7	13 998.0	14 265.0	1.9	22 081.0	23 054.0	4.4	36.6	38.1
Austria	15 574.3	14 474.0	−7.1	4 214.3	3 909.6	−7.2	19 788.6	18 383.6	−7.1	78.7	78.7
Belgium											
Germany	1 628.3	1 433.7	−12.0	26 412.8	26 131.8	−1.1	28 041.1	27 565.6	−1.7	5.8	5.2
Italy	3 504.9			6 283.8			9 788.8			35.8	
Switzerland	11 055.0	11 410.0	3.2	13 500.0	13 120.0	−2.8	24 555.0	24 530.0	−0.1	45.0	46.5

1. For the "Types of accommodatiom covered by the statistics" see Table C.
2. France: data covering all France except 3 regions (Basse Normandie and Corse).

13. Capacity in hotels and similar establishments [1]

In thousands

	Hotels			Motels			Boarding houses			Inns			Others			Total		
	1992	1993	% 93/92	1992	1993	% 93/92	1992	1993	% 93/92	1992	1993	% 93/92	1992	1993	% 93/92	1992	1993	% 93/92
Australia [12]	169.7	175.5	3.4	306.4	302.9	-1.1										476.1	478.4	0.5
Japan	124.2	140.3	13.0							99.0	101.6	2.6						
Austria [2]																653.6	651.0	-0.4
Belgium	101.8	108.2	6.3													101.8	108.2	6.3
Denmark [3]																96.0	107.3	11.7
Finland [4]	94.7	95.0	0.4				12.4	11.4	-8.0							107.0	106.4	-0.6
France [5]	1 198.3	1 178.4	-1.7										211.0	234.0	10.9	1 409.3	1 412.4	0.2
Germany [6]	680.4	703.9	3.4				142.8	142.4	-0.3	231.9	231.1	-0.3	242.5	245.6	1.3	1 297.6	1 323.0	2.0
Greece	389.5	407.0	4.5	3.2	3.1	-2.5	25.1	27.5	9.3	15.7	1.8	-88.7	42.3	48.1	13.6	475.8	487.4	2.4
Netherlands																115.8	133.0	14.8
Norway [7]													120.5	123.1	2.2	120.5	123.1	2.2
Portugal [8]	100.8	103.3	2.5	1.4	1.3	-11.2	44.8	46.5	3.6	4.0	4.5	10.3	39.8	43.4	8.9	190.9	198.9	4.2
Spain [9]	817.3												181.5			998.8		
Sweden [13]	116.3	114.1	-2.0				49.8	47.3	-5.2							166.2	163.3	-1.7
Switzerland [10]	234.9	235.1	0.1	5.1	4.3	-15.8				26.1	25.7	-1.5				266.2	265.1	-0.4
Turkey [11]	164.2	177.9	8.4	3.4	2.9	-16.3	5.9	5.9	0.6	1.2	1.0	-15.8	5.6	5.4	-3.4	180.2	193.0	7.1

Notice : this table contains data on available bed capacity unless otherwise stated in the following notes by country.

1. For the "Types of accommodation covered by the statistics" see Table C.
2. Austria : position at 31st August.
3. Denmark : position at 31st July.
4. Finland : position at 31st December.
5. France : position at 1st January.
6. Germany : position at April; the data relate to the territory of the Federal Republic of Germany prior to 3rd October 1990.
7. Norway : position at 31st December.
8. Portugal : position at 31st July.
9. Spain : position at 31st December.
10. Switzerland : position at 31st December.
11. Turkey : position at 31st December of accommodation establishments approved by Ministry of Culture and Tourism.
12. Australia : position at 31st December.
13. Sweden : position at December.

98

14. Capacity in supplementary means of accommodation[1]

In thousands

	Youth hostels			Camping sites Places			Holiday villages			Rented rooms, houses and flats			Sanatoria and health establishments			Recreational camps			Others			Total		
	1992	1993	% 93/92	1992	1993	% 93/92	1992	1993	% 93/92	1992	1993	% 93/92	1992	1993	% 93/92	1992	1993	% 93/92	1992	1993	% 93/92	1992	1993	% 93/92
Australia[3]	25.4	25.0	-1.7	181.6	188.9	4.1				146.6	154.1	5.1										172.0	179.1	4.1
Japan	24.0	28.7	19.4																			24.0	28.7	19.4
Austria	12.7	13.3	4.4	360.1	365.0	1.3	139.2	147.8	6.2	274.1	257.2	-6.2	15.7	16.6	5.9	26.6	25.7	-3.4	32.0	25.5	-20.3	500.3	494.9	-1.1
Belgium													1.5	1.4	-4.3	31.9	32.9	3.1	103.3	99.8	-3.4	496.9	499.1	0.4
Denmark	10.5	10.2	-2.3																			10.5	10.2	-2.3
France	17.6	18.2	3.4	2 662.2	2 798.7	5.1	234.9	239.5	2.0	450.0	450.0	0.0							206.0	223.5	8.5	3 570.6	3 729.8	4.5
Germany	112.7	112.0	-0.6	579.8	569.7	-1.7	32.2	32.7	1.8	238.2	237.1	-0.5	143.8	148.3	3.1				183.5	183.3	-0.1	183.5	183.3	-0.1
Greece	8.2																							
Italy				1 297.0						153.3									159.7			1 548.1		
Norway																								
Portugal				267.4	267.4	0.0				419.5						9.2	9.3	1.6				276.6	276.7	0.1
Spain				580.8																		1 999.1		
Sweden	15.1	15.1	0.4				46.6	46.7	0.4													61.6	61.9	0.4
Switzerland	8.0	7.3	-8.6	261.7	237.6	-9.2				360.0	360.0	0.0	6.6	6.1	-6.5				224.3	226.3	0.9	860.5	837.3	-2.7
Turkey[2]				6.7	6.6	-2.1	32.7	35.6	8.9				0.0	0.0	0.0							39.7	42.2	6.2

Notice: this table contains data on available bed capacity, unless otherwise stated in the following notes by country.
1. For the "Types of accommodation covered by the statistics" see Table C.
2. Turkey: the total doesn't include licenced yacht bed capacity and beds registered by local municipalities in social tourism establishments.
3. Australia: assuming 3 beds per place.

15. Monthly hotel occupancy rates

		Australia[6] (B)	Japan[7] (R)	Austria (B)	Belgium (B)	Finland[1] (R)	Germany[10] (B)	Italy (B)	Netherlands[11] (B)	Norway[2] (B)	Portugal[8] (B)	Spain (B)	Sweden[3] (B)	Switzerland[9] (B)	Turkey[4] (B)	United Kingdom[5] (B)
1991	January	35.4	62.7	29.0	12.3	38.1	28.9	26.0	16.3	26.5	30.2	38.3	20.5	29.4	21.5	24.0
	February	27.6	78.0	29.0	16.4	45.2	34.3	30.3	20.4	39.3	37.1	41.9	28.0	41.2	22.6	32.0
	March	31.0	79.9	29.0	11.8	45.9	37.3	35.7	28.0	40.1	44.6	45.9	29.0	42.4	25.8	40.0
	April	30.4	76.6	29.0	17.5	44.6	39.0	33.1	41.2	31.3	49.7	46.8	27.2	29.2	29.3	39.0
	May	26.4	77.2	33.9	19.8	43.0	47.1	35.3	45.3	27.8	57.3	49.1	25.1	28.7	31.1	46.0
	June	28.2	75.9	33.9	22.0	48.0	50.4	44.5	42.6	44.6	58.9	53.2	30.6	37.3	36.2	44.0
	July	31.6	75.8	33.9	47.3	48.8	56.7	58.5	47.3	54.8	63.7	62.4	39.9	49.4	46.3	53.0
	August	30.3	81.1	33.9	46.4	46.3	59.4	70.5	54.3	44.9	76.2	77.6	32.2	55.3	59.0	57.0
	September	34.7	76.2	33.9	19.5	44.4	55.7	48.1	46.5	32.5	70.0	64.1	25.3	46.8	54.2	54.0
	October	34.6	82.7	33.9	12.1	41.1	48.7	37.1	36.2	29.1	54.9	52.0	23.6	33.2	41.5	42.0
	November	31.2	82.6		12.8	41.1	33.5	25.0	27.7	28.6	43.1	44.8	22.7	17.6	30.5	31.0
	December	28.8	62.4		13.8	27.8	30.4	25.4	21.5	24.0	29.8	39.2	12.8	23.8	27.3	28.0
1992	January	34.8		29.7	11.2	31.6	29.4		19.7	28.0	29.2		19.4	32.1	24.6	21.0
	February	28.0		29.7	14.2	39.5	34.7		22.1	38.3	35.1		26.0	40.3	30.5	28.0
	March	29.5		29.7	14.2	42.7	35.2		26.7	37.0	42.4		26.1	40.5	26.6	31.0
	April	32.8		29.7	14.5	38.8	40.5		44.7	29.1	50.9		23.1	30.8	39.0	36.0
	May	27.4		33.6	15.2	37.9	46.3		48.7	29.6	55.4		25.2	28.4	55.4	41.0
	June	27.3		33.6	15.0	43.9	50.0		45.5	44.1	50.3		29.7	37.0	65.0	44.0
	July	31.6		33.6	27.9	48.6	55.8		48.7	57.6	51.0		41.5	48.3	63.1	52.0
	August	29.9		33.6	33.0	43.4	57.0		55.1	46.1	67.4		32.0	52.7	70.9	51.0
	September	34.5		33.6	20.0	41.3	54.4		42.9	33.6	58.4		24.9	44.9	64.0	48.0
	October	34.5		33.6	17.5	38.5	46.9		33.4	28.8	48.3		21.7	29.2	54.7	42.0
	November	31.2		29.7	16.9	38.8	32.0		24.2	26.9	30.7		21.1	15.9	30.8	32.0
	December	30.2		29.7	15.0	28.3	29.5		20.1	23.6	28.9		18.5	24.0	29.4	27.0
1993	January	37.4		29.5	12.7	22.4	28.7			28.1	24.3	39.5		32.8	27.1	
	February	29.6		29.5	16.4	30.7	34.6			39.1	30.4	44.8		41.3	29.5	
	March	31.3		29.5	13.7	33.1	34.7			38.0	33.6	47.1		38.1	31.7	
	April	34.0		29.5	14.3	30.1	38.3			31.3	43.3	49.3		30.2	42.6	
	May	28.9		32.3	15.7	26.6	45.4			28.1	43.7	48.7		27.5	53.8	
	June	29.3		32.3	14.0	35.9	48.4			47.7	42.1	53.0		36.6	56.2	
	July	32.7		32.3	27.0	47.3	52.7			59.7	47.6	65.9		46.9	57.6	
	August	31.3		32.3	25.5	36.5	53.5			46.6	62.4	78.7		51.6	60.1	
	September	36.5		32.3	14.1	30.7	50.5			34.3	54.4	66.3		42.6	53.0	
	October	36.7		32.3	17.8	28.4	43.1			29.3	45.5	51.9		27.2	44.3	
	November	33.5		26.4	16.3	28.1	30.5			28.9	32.1	44.9		16.2	33.0	
	December	32.4		26.4	14.3	23.9	27.4			24.6	25.3	40.7		22.8	29.2	

B – Beds.
R – Rooms.
Occupancy rates registered in hotels only, unless otherwise stated.
1. Finland: room occupancy rates in hotels and similar establishment.
2. Norway: Bed occupancy rates covers registered accommodation with 20 beds or more.
3. Sweden: occupancy rates in hotels, motels, resort hotels, holiday villages and youth hostels.
4. Turkey: bed occupancy rates in hotels, motels, boarding houses, inns, holiday villages, thermal resorts and campings.
5. United Kingdom: figures apply to England only.
6. Australia: quarterly figures in bed-places in hotels and motels with facilities in most rooms.
7. Japan: rates concerning hotels which are members of the "Japan Hotel Association".
8. Portugal: bed occupancy rates in hotels, studio-hotels, motels and state-owned inns.
9. Switzerland: bed occupancy rates in hotels, motels and inns.
10. Germany: bed occupancy rates cover registered accommodation with 9 beds or more.
11. Netherlands: bed occupancy rates in all means of accommodation.

16. International fare payments
Rail, air, sea and road transport
In million dollars

	Receipts			Expenditure		
	1991	1992	1993	1991	1992	1993
Canada	923.1	957.0	938.7	2 042.8	2 130.1	2 303.4
Australia	1 552.2	1 409.5	1 630.0	1 768.7	1 794.1	1 644.3
Germany[1]	5 341.2	5 805.0	5 074.2	5 687.3	6 288.4	5 529.6
Finland[2]	532.8	503.8		587.7		
France	10 760.9	11 863.3		3 811.5	4 004.8	
Iceland	92.6	90.9	88.5			
Ireland[2]	442.4	476.6		291.2	318.3	
Portugal	156.3	168.0	607.0	36.5	27.9	217.0
Sweden[3]	816.3	1 137.5	812.3	832.0	1 022.9	804.5
Switzwerland	1 750.8	1 735.8	1 655.0	1 140.5	1 262.7	1 360.6
Turkey[4]	288.2	413.8		1.0	0.6	

1. Germany: air, sea and rail transport.
2. Finland and Ireland: air and sea transport.
3. Sweden: sea and rail transport.
4. Turkey: air, sea and rail transport for receipts; rail transport only for expenditure.

17. Nominal exchange rates of national currencies against the dollar

	Exchange rates (units per dollar)			Per cent changes[1]	
	1991	1992	1993	92/91	93/92
Canada	1.15	1.21	1.29	5.5	6.7
Mexico	3.02	3.10	3.12	2.4	0.6
United States	1.00	1.00	1.00	0.0	0.0
Australia	1.28	1.36	1.47	6.1	8.1
Japan	134.50	126.67	111.18	−5.8	−12.2
New Zealand	1.73	1.86	1.85	7.6	−0.5
Austria	11.67	10.99	11.63	−5.9	5.8
Belgium-Luxembourg	34.16	32.15	34.56	−5.9	7.5
Denmark	6.40	6.04	6.48	−5.6	7.3
Finland	4.04	4.49	5.72	10.9	27.5
France	5.64	5.29	5.66	−6.2	7.0
Germany	1.66	1.56	1.65	−5.8	5.8
Greece	182.06	190.47	229.14	4.6	20.3
Iceland	59.10	57.62	67.64	−2.5	17.4
Ireland	0.62	0.59	0.68	−5.5	16.3
Italy	1 240.65	1 232.03	1 571.66	−0.7	27.6
Netherlands	1.87	1.76	1.86	−6.0	5.6
Norway	6.48	6.21	7.09	−4.1	14.1
Portugal	144.35	134.82	160.65	−6.6	19.2
Spain	103.93	102.40	127.24	−1.5	24.3
Sweden	6.05	5.82	7.79	−3.7	33.7
Switzwerland	1.43	1.41	1.48	−1.9	5.1
Turkey	4 168.91	6 860.59	10 965.58	64.6	59.8
United Kingdom	0.57	0.57	0.67	0.5	16.9

Source: OECD Balance of Payments Division.
1. Minus signs indicate an appreciation of national currencies against the dollar.

18. International tourist receipts (R) and expenditure (E) in dollars

Regional breakdown

In million

	R/E	Europe			North America			Asia and the Pacific		
		1992	1993	% 93/92	1992	1993	% 93/92	1992	1993	% 93/92
Canada[4]	R	1 103.9	1 184.4	7.3	3 498.2	3 689.6	5.5	451.0	433.2	−3.9
	E	1 547.8	1 515.8	−2.1	8 056.0	7 548.5	−6.3	196.5	199.5	1.5
Mexico	R									
	E									
United States	R									
	E									
Australia	R	880.2	860.8	−2.2	488.9	442.0	−9.6	1 348.5	1 247.1	−7.5
	E	1 294.9	1 285.8	−0.7	627.6	591.3	−5.8	364.8	319.8	−12.4
Japan	R									
	E									
New Zealand[5]	R									
	E									
Austria[1]	R	13 035.5	12 068.9	−7.4	852.0	888.3	4.3	127.0	139.9	10.1
	E	6 057.6	5 716.3	−5.6	1 251.8	1 431.3	14.3	60.8	62.1	2.1
Belgium-Luxembourg	R	3 129.0	3 065.4	−2.0	339.6	584.6	72.1	46.8	45.3	−3.3
	E	5 450.7	4 905.5	−10.0	593.4	966.5	62.9	34.4	40.7	18.3
Denmark	R	3 096.7	2 385.8	−23.0	471.5	476.5	1.1	22.9	26.5	16.1
	E	2 886.4	2 327.0	−19.4	657.1	663.8	1.0	7.9	6.6	−16.6
Finland	R	1 063.4			154.3			9.6		
	E	1 731.7			461.7			12.9		
France	R	18 911.5	17 561.8	−7.1	3 449.2	3 445.8	−0.1	803.8	718.6	−10.6
	E	7 706.2	7 085.0	−8.1	3 197.2	3 015.6	−5.7	238.0	218.5	−8.2
Germany	R	8 379.4	7 583.7	−9.5	1 167.8	1 276.3	9.3	478.3	516.6	8.0
	E	27 481.5	28 088.5	2.2	2 566.7	2 674.1	4.2	511.5	529.9	3.6
Greece	R									
	E									
Iceland	R									
	E									
Ireland[2]	R									
	E									
Italy[7]	R									
	E									
Netherlands	R	4 106.8	3 529.6	−14.1	768.5	903.5	17.6	50.6	72.2	42.5
	E	7 370.0	6 929.4	−6.0	1 328.7	1 334.8	0.5	25.0	35.5	42.0
Norway	R									
	E									
Portugal[6]	R	2 770.2			859.2			11.2		
	E	770.8			361.8			4.0		
Spain	R									
	E									
Sweden	R	2 413.3	2 044.5	−15.3	406.1	485.9	19.7	28.3	33.4	17.9
	E	5 239.5	3 388.7	−35.3	1 343.8	809.7	−39.7	46.2	35.5	−23.2
Switzerland	R									
	E									
Turkey	R									
	E									
United Kingdom[3]	R	6 015.7			2 978.9			1 195.4		
	E	12 235.0			2 950.8			639.0		

Important notice: the amounts, excluding those concerning Canada, United States, Ireland, Italy, United Kingdom and Switzerland, refer to receipts and expenditure registered in foreign currency grouped regionally according to the denomination of the currency. Unless otherwice indicated, the data does not include international fare payments.

1. Austria: including international fare payments.
2. Ireland: expenditure include international fare payments.

18. International tourist receipts (R) and expenditure (E) in dollars (Continued)

Regional breakdown

In million

Total OECD countries			Non-Member countries			All countries			
1992	1993	% 93/92	1992	1993	% 93/92	1992	1993	% 93/92	
5 053.1	5 307.2	5.0	610.6	593.1	−2.9	5 663.7	5 849.1	3.3	Canada[4]
9 800.2	9 263.8	−5.5	1 419.5	1 598.2	12.6	11 219.7	10 625.5	−5.3	
						3 866.8	4 072.8	5.3	Mexico
						2 080.5	2 101.3	1.0	
						53 861.0	57 622.0	7.0	United States
						39 872.0	40 564.0	1.7	
2 717.6	2 549.9	−6.2	1 637.0	1 760.4	7.5	4 354.6	4 310.3	−1.0	Australia
2 287.4	2 196.9	−4.0	1 482.1	1 524.8	2.9	3 769.5	3 721.7	−1.3	
						3 589.2	3 544.6	−1.2	Japan
						26 809.7	26 484.5	−1.2	
						1 469.9	1 164.5	−20.8	New Zealand[5]
						1 029.0	1 002.4	−2.6	
14 014.5	13 097.1	−6.5	501.3	462.7	−7.7	14 515.8	13 559.8	−6.6	Austria[1]
7 370.2	7 209.6	−2.2	1 015.0	963.3	−5.1	8 385.2	8 172.9	−2.5	
3 515.5	3 695.3	5.1	532.8	375.0	−29.6	4 047.9	4 069.6	0.5	Belgium-Luxembourg
6 078.5	5 912.6	−2.7	522.8	443.9	−15.1	6 596.8	6 354.7	−3.7	
3 591.1	2 888.9	−19.6	191.3			3 782.4	2 888.9	−23.6	Denmark
3 551.5	2 997.5	−15.6	226.2			3 777.7	2 997.5	−20.7	
1 227.7			42.8			1 313.7	1 199.7	−8.7	Finland
2 222.8			123.7			2 388.9	1 583.9	−33.7	
23 164.5	21 726.2	−6.2	1 888.3	1 680.6	−11.0	25 052.8	23 406.8	−6.6	France
11 141.4	10 319.0	−7.4	2 773.1	2 485.4	−10.4	13 914.6	12 804.4	−8.0	
10 179.7	9 612.4	−5.6	873.3	896.4	2.6	11 053.0	10 508.8	−4.9	Germany
31 033.5	31 701.9	2.2	5 588.6	5 813.9	4.0	36 620.8	37 514.6	2.4	
						3 211.9	3 171.1	−1.3	Greece
						1 156.7	995.2	−14.0	
						128.4	132.2	3.0	Iceland
						287.5	264.9	−7.9	
						1 615.3	1 596.8	−1.1	Ireland[2]
						1 368.5	1 222.1	−10.7	
						21 461.8	22 030.9	2.7	Italy[7]
						16 532.3	14 044.4	−15.0	
4 944.1	4 524.7	−8.5	249.7	122.2	−51.1	5 193.8	4 646.9	−10.5	Netherlands
8 922.3	8 472.1	−5.0	605.2	427.5	−29.4	9 527.5	8 899.7	−6.6	
						1 973.5	1 849.6	−6.3	Norway
						3 867.3	3 532.8	−8.7	
3 642.1			38.0			3 680.1	4 067.5	10.5	Portugal[6]
1 137.1			18.0			1 155.1	1 895.8	64.1	
						22 149.6	19 447.1	−12.2	Spain
						5 526.4	4 710.7	−14.8	
2 851.5	2 568.0	−9.9	203.3	80.8	−60.3	3 054.7	2 648.8	−13.3	Sweden
6 634.0	4 236.9	−36.1	502.4	392.3	−21.9	7 136.4	4 629.2	−35.1	
						7 533.5	7 022.9	−6.8	Switzerland
						6 125.0	5 818.0	−5.0	
						3 701.0	4 040.4	9.2	Turkey
						779.4	944.5	21.2	
10 198.8			3 294.9			13 851.8	13 444.8	−2.9	United Kingdom[3]
15 833.6			3 633.7			19 735.8	17 423.9	−11.7	

3. United Kingdom: including estimates for the Channel Islands receipts and expenditure, and cruise expenditure.
4. Canada: excluding crew spending.
5. New Zealand: includes international airfares payments.
6. Portugal: change of series in 1993 due to a new data collection and statistical production system.
7. Italy : change of methodology in 1990.

19. Foreign tourism by purpose of visit

	1992						1993					
	Business journeys (%)[1]	Private journeys (%)				Total volume in thousands	Business journeys (%)[1]	Private journeys (%)				Total volume in thousands
		Holidays	VFR[2]	Others	Total			Holidays	VFR[2]	Others	Total	
Canada[8]	15.3	55.4	21.6	7.7	84.7	14 741.0	15.2	55.1	21.7	8.1	84.8	15 105.0
Australia[9]	10.3	61.3	18.8	9.6	89.7	2 603.2	10.6	62.3	17.7	9.4	89.4	2 996.2
Japan[11]	26.1	58.7		15.2	73.9	3 581.5	27.4	56.4		16.1	72.6	3 410.4
New zealand[10]	12.3	53.0	24.8	9.8	87.7	1 055.7	12.0	57.1	22.4	8.4	88.0	1 157.0
Greece[3]	9.9	80.5	4.3	5.4	90.1	9 331.4	10.4	80.1	4.2	5.3	89.6	9 412.8
Ireland[4]	14.6	49.9	28.9	6.6	85.4	3 129.0						
Portugal[5]	2.9	91.5	0.9	4.7	97.1	8 884.1						
Spain[6]	17.9	67.0	5.0	10.1	82.1	35 068.0	8.7	63.5	4.6	23.2	91.3	57 263.4
Turkey[12]		79.6		20.4	100.0	7.1						
United Kingdom[7]		54.3	26.3	19.4	100.0	14 413.0						

1. Includes: business, congresses, seminars, on missions, etc.
2. VFR: visits to friends and relatives.
3. Greece: number of tourists. "Others" includes journeys combining visiting relatives and holiday or business and holiday.
4. Ireland: number of visits on overseas routes.
5. Portugal: number of tourists. "Others" includes visits for cultural purposes and journeys for educational reasons.
6. Spain: number of tourists. "Others" includes journeys for educational reasons. Since 1993, also includes shopping, religious and sports purposes.
7. United Kingdom: number of visits. "Others" includes visits for religion, sports, health and visits of more than one purpose where none predominates.
8. Canada: number of tourists.
9. Australia: short-term visitors (less than one year). "Others" includes accompanying business traveller.
10. New Zealand: number of tourists. "Others" includes journeys for educational reasons.
11. Japan: number of visitors. "Others" includes journeys for educational reasons.
12. Turkey: "Others" includes journeys combining shopping and transit and journeys for study, health, religious and sports purposes.

20. Foreign tourism by mode of transport

	1992					1993				
	Breakdown of arrivals (%)				Total volume in thousands	Breakdown of arrivals (%)				Total volume in thousands
	Air	Sea	Rail	Road		Air	Sea	Rail	Road	
Australia[6]	99.5	0.5			2 603.3	99.6	0.4			2 996.2
Japan[7]	97.3	2.7			3 926.3	97.7	2.3			3 747.2
New Zealand[5]	99.0	1.0			1 055.7	99.2	0.8			1 157.0
Belgium[1]	6.0	2.1	92.0		157 659.0					
Iceland	95.0	5.0			142.6	95.2	4.8			157.3
Ireland[8]	58.6	36.2			3 300.0	61.1	38.9			3 330.0
Italy[2]	13.6	2.8	8.2	75.5	50 088.7	14.3	3.3	7.7	74.6	49 909.7
Portugal[2]	90.9	6.1	3.1		4 059.2	91.2	6.3	2.5		3 835.3
Spain[3]	32.8	3.1	4.3	59.8	55 330.7	41.9	4.3	5.0	48.9	46 263.4
Turkey[4]	42.1	10.1	1.1	46.8	7 076.1	54.2	12.0	0.6	33.1	6 500.6
United Kingdom[2]	68.5	31.5			18 179.0					

1. Belgium: air and sea include both arrivals and departures of foreign and domestic visitors. Rail refers to international traffic only.
2. Italy, Portugal and United Kingdom : visitor arrivals.
3. Spain: visitor arrivals, including Spaniards living abroad.
4. Turkey: traveller arrivals.
5. New Zealand: tourist arrivals.
6. Australia: arrivals of short-term visitors (less than one year).
7. Japan: visitor arrivals, including those of returning residents and excluding crew members.
8. Ireland: visitors on overseas routes (average of arrivals and departure).

21. Staff employed in tourism

		1991			1992			1993		
		Total	Men %	Women %	Total	Men %	Women %	Total	Men %	Women %
Canada										
Australia[1]										
	HR	282 500	43.4	56.6	283 100	43.9	56.1	285 100	43.1	56.9
	O	34 700	44.7	55.3	38 600	42.5	57.3	33 200	45.8	54.2
Austria[2]										
	HR	131 240	39.4	60.6	136 543	40.1	59.9	137 963	40.3	59.7
Belgium[3]										
	H	14 666	46.1	53.9	14 777	45.9	54.1			
	R	59 485	48.8	51.2	60 097	49.6	50.4			
	HR	74 151	48.3	51.7						
	V	4 086	33.3	66.7	4 307	33.0	67.0			
	A	10 541	46.3	53.7	10 573	46.2	53.8			
	O	5 727	34.3	65.7	6 065	36.3	63.7			
Finland[4]										
	HR	69 000	23.2	76.8	63 000	23.8	76.2	59 000	25.4	74.6
France[5]										
	H	156 376			156 050					
	R	240 466			242 551					
	HR	487 775			492 584					
	V	24 479			25 120					
	A	6 367			6 919					
	O	17 935			18 179					
Germany										
	HR	774 800	41.0	59.0						
Norway[6]										
	HR	57 000			59 000			60 000		
Sweden										
	HR	98 000	36.7	63.3	91 000	39.6	60.4	88 000	42.0	58.0
Turkey[7]										
	HR	145 530			153 168			171 219		
	V	11 000			17 150			20 000		
	A	1 985	65.4	34.6	1 990	63.4	35.2	2 203	64.4	35.6
	O	2 420			3 874					
United Kingdom[8]										
	H	296 000	39.3	60.7	289 200	40.7	59.3			
	R	291 900	41.0	59.0	295 500	41.6	58.4			
	HR	1 442 700	40.0	60.0	1 442 500	40.7	59.3			
	O	854 800	39.9	60.1	857 800	40.4	59.6			

H: staff employed in hotels.
R: staff employed in restaurants.
HR: staff employed in hotels and restaurants.
V: staff employed in travel agencies.
A: staff employed in national tourism administrations.
O: staff employed in other sectors of tourist industry.
1. Australia: HR = restaurants, hotels and accommodation. O = other services to transport.
2. Austria: weighted average of peak season (August) and low season (November).
3. Belgium: A = tourist offices, libraries, public archives, museums, botanical gardens and zoos. O = sleeper trains and restaurant cars, youth hostels, camping sites, holiday centers and holiday homes, recreation homes for children and furnished appartments.
4. Finland: weighted average of peak season (July) and low season (January).
5. France: data registered at 31 December of each year. A = tourist offfices. HR includes sleeper trains and restaurant cars. O : spas, thalassotherapy and ski lifts.
6. Norway: average of 1st and 4th quarters.
7. Turkey: data registered at 31 December of each year, except for O registered at 31 March and V registered at 31 October. V = total number of persons (new series from 1991) which travel agencies (central and local offices) have to employ. A includes regional tourism administrations and staff working at the Ministry of Tourism. O = tourist guides whose licences have been renewed.
8. United Kingdom: data registered at September. O = ''pubs'', bars, night clubs, clubs, libraries, museums, art galleries, sports and other recreational services.

22. Trends in tourism prices

		%88/87	%89/88	%90/89	%91/90	%92/91	%93/92
Canada[1]	H	7.2	5.3	2.8	2.4	−0.9	0.8
	R	4.6	5.3	4.9	10.9	1.9	1.3
	T	1.4	5.7	7.2	7.6	0.8	2.4
	C	4.0	5.0	4.8	5.6	1.5	1.7
Australia[2]	H	16.6			−10.0	0.3	4.1
	R	7.3			2.2	1.7	1.3
	T	13.5	7.6	7.6	−5.6	−0.5	
	C	7.2	7.6	7.3	3.2	1.0	2.1
Austria	H	3.8	2.2	3.3	4.0		
	R	2.8	2.2	3.3	4.0		
	T	2.5	2.5	3.5	4.1	4.4	4.6
	C	1.9	2.6	3.3	3.3	4.0	3.7
Belgium[3]	H	6.3	3.8	5.7	6.7	10.3	
	R	2.4	3.4	4.7	6.5	8.9	
	T	2.6	3.4	4.1	7.1	7.0	
	C	1.2	3.1	3.4	3.2	2.4	2.7
Finland[4]	H	6.0	6.0	7.0	2.0	7.4	2.9
	R	7.0	8.0	8.0	6.8	2.2	0.1
	T				4.0	0.3	1.1
	C	5.1	6.6	6.1	4.1	2.9	3.0
France	H	7.8	6.3	6.6	6.3	4.5	2.1
	R	5.4	5.0	6.1	4.6	3.0	2.4
	T	5.1	5.7	5.7	5.2	3.9	2.7
	C	2.7	3.5	3.4	3.1	2.4	2.3
Germany	H	4.3	4.4	4.8	5.3	5.8	5.0
	R	1.5	1.9	2.8	3.8	4.2	4.4
	T	1.0	1.8	0.5	1.6	2.5	3.5
	C	1.3	2.8	2.7	3.5	3.8	4.1
Greece	H	10.0					
	R						
	T						
	C	13.5	13.7	20.4	18.9	15.9	14.1
Italy[5]	H	7.3	8.3	7.8	8.6	12.3	8.5
	R	7.2	7.9	7.8	6.6	6.5	5.7
	T	7.1	7.9	7.8	8.0	7.6	6.2
	C	5.0	6.6	6.1	6.5	5.3	4.5
Netherlands[6]	H	2.0	2.0	3.0	3.0	6.6	3.5
	R	1.0	2.0	3.0	3.0	2.9	2.9
	T						
	C	0.7	1.1	2.5	3.9	3.7	2.0
Norway[7]	H	11.5	9.0	6.0	5.0	5.6	4.7
	R	5.7	3.9	3.0	4.7	3.4	3.8
	T						
	C	6.7	4.6	4.1	3.4	2.3	2.3
Portugal[8]	H	12.0	14.0	17.0	15.0	13.0	
	R	17.0	17.0	11.0	12.0	13.0	5.0
	T						
	C	9.7	12.6	13.4	11.4	8.9	6.3
Spain[9]	H	10.9	10.6	13.6	7.5	17.5	6.1
	R	8.7	10.9	10.5	4.9	9.3	3.7
	T	6.9	8.6	9.7	6.9	9.7	6.1
	C	4.8	6.8	6.7	5.9	5.9	4.8
Sweden[10]	H	5.8	6.0	14.4	9.2	2.3	−1.8
	R	9.5	9.3	18.8	6.6	−2.2	−0.3
	T						
	C	5.8	6.4	10.5	9.3	2.3	5.2
Switzerland[11]	H	5.5	6.6	9.2	8.8	6.5	5.9
	R	3.0	4.3	5.1	5.8	4.9	2.1
	T						
	C	1.9	3.2	5.4	5.8	4.0	3.3
Turkey[12]	H						
	R						
	T						
	C	75.4	69.6	60.3	66.0	70.1	71.0
United Kingdom[13]	H	10.9	8.7	11.8	11.6	4.8	
	R	6.8	6.8	8.0	9.6	6.0	
	T	8.1	7.5	8.7	8.5	5.6	
	C	4.9	7.8	9.5	5.9	3.7	3.5

NOTE TO TABLE 22

H: average increase in hotel prices.
R: average increase in restaurant prices.
T: average increase in travel prices.
C: average increase in consumer prices (CPI).
Source: OECD Balance of Payments Division.

1. Canada: H = hotels and motels. R = food purchases for restaurants, T is calculated from domestic tourist spending patterns only.
2. Australia: position every fourth quarter of each year. H = change in the price of a room in hotels, motels, and similar establishments. R = change in the price of meals taken outside home and take-away food (one component of the CPI). C = weighted average of eight State capital cities. T = air, bus and rail fares, hotel, motel and caravan park charges, package tours.
3. Belgium : H = hotels and campings, R = cafés, restaurants and bars, T = hotels, campings, cafés, restaurants, bars and package tours.
4. Finland: H = hotels, R = food and alcoholic beverages, T = transports and communications.
5. Italy: T = hotels, restaurants and public establishments (bars, night club, sea-side resorts....).
6. Netherlands: H = price of a night spent in an hotel, R = price of a certain number of typical expenses made in bars and restaurants (cup of coffee, fruit drinks, beer, jenever, croquette, fried potatoes, several hot meals, ham roll, ice cream).
7. Norway: H = approved hotels and boarding houses, R = restaurants and cafés.
8. Portugal: H = hotels of from 1 to 5 stars, R concerns Lisbon only.
9. Spain: H takes into account the types of accommodation presented in the official guide, R = hotels, restaurants, cafeteria and bars.
10. Sweden: position at December of each year H = hotel room, R = meals not taken at home (lunch, dinner, coffee with bread, hot sausage with bread).
11. Switzerland: H = hotels and similar establishments. R is estimated.
12. Turkey: H = hotels, motels, inns, boarding houses, holiday villages, health resorts. R = 1st and 2nd class restaurants. In 1985 H and R = freely determined prices approved by the Ministry of Culture and Tourism. C concerns the city of Ankara only.
13. United Kingdom: H = all holiday accommodation. R = meals and snacks including take-away. T = accommodation, meals, food, alcohol, tobacco, durable household goods, clothes, footwear, motoring and cycling fares, entertainment and other services.

International tourist flows from main generating countries

Tables 23 to 49 gather data available for the period 1982 to 1993 concerning physical flows to OECD Member countries.

These tables contain data on arrivals at frontiers and arrivals and nights spent at/in accommodation:

-- from all the foreign countries;
-- from the eight main generators of tourism to the OECD area (Canada, France, Germany, Italy, Japan, the Netherlands, the United Kingdom and the United States).

Data used in the synthesis tables are derived from data broken down by country of origin; when these data are not available, the tables are derived from monthly or quarterly statistics.

Methodological notes

These notes present on a country-by-country basis, and where appropriate, the main methodological and statistical changes affecting the series available between 1982 and 1993.

France. Arrivals and nights spent at/in hotels and similar establishments: change of series in 1986. Change of series in 1991; the new frontiers' survey covers car drivers and introduces a better breakdown between visitors, tourists and same-day visitors.

Germany. The data relate to the territory of the Federal Republic of Germany prior to 3rd October 1990. Arrivals and nights spent at/in hotels and similar establishments and in all means of accommodation: changes of series in 1981 and in 1984. Arrivals and nights spent at/in all means of accommodations: from 1988, includes camping sites.

Ireland. Arrivals and nights spent at/in hotels and similar establishments: series available from 1985.

Japan. Arrivals and nights spent at/in hotels and similar establishments: series discontinued from 1986.

Netherlands. Arrivals and nights spent at/in hotels and similar establishments: change of series in 1986. Arrivals and nights spent at/in all means of accommodations: new series from 1988.

Norway. Arrivals of foreign visitors at frontiers: series discontinued from 1984.

Sweden. Nights spent in all means of accommodation: change of series in 1985.

Switzerland. Arrivals of foreign tourists/visitors at frontiers: annual estimates.

United States. Arrivals of foreign tourists at frontiers: change of series in 1984.

Table/Tableau 23

ARRIVALS OF FOREIGN TOURISTS/VISITORS AT FRONTIERS
ARRIVÉES DE TOURISTES/VISITEURS ÉTRANGERS AUX FRONTIÈRES

1988=100

	T/V	Volume 1982	1983	1984	1985	1986	1987	Volume 1988	1989	1990	1991	1992	1993	Volume 1993	T/V	
Canada (R)	T	12 183 300	80.7	83.8	85.1	100.9	97.0	15 484 800	97.9	98.2	96.3	95.2	97.6	15 109 300	T	Canada (R)
Canada (R)	V	34 406 500	87.3	88.8	91.5	103.1	100.9	39 253 100	96.8	96.8	93.8	92.2	92.0	36 114 400	V	Canada (R)
Mexico (R)	T							14 142 100	105.8	76.2	69.2	76.3	69.4	9 815 000	T	Mexique (R)
Mexico (R)	V													65 088 000	V	Mexique (R)
United States (R)	T	21 666 788	78.9	98.1	92.7	89.6	104.9	27 428 569	133.5	144.3	156.5	173.4	166.9	45 778 821	T	États-Unis (R)
Australia (R)	V	954 698	42.0	45.2	50.8	63.5	79.3	2 249 500	92.5	98.5	105.4	115.7	133.2	2 997 000	V	Australie (R)
Japan (N)	T													1 925 496	T	Japon (N)
Japan (N)	V	1 793 164	83.6	89.6	98.8	87.5	91.5	2 355 412	120.4	137.4	150.0	152.1	144.8	3 411 747	V	Japon (N)
New Zealand (R)	V	481 726	58.8	65.6	77.4	84.8	97.6	864 892	104.2	112.8	111.4	122.1	133.8	1 156 978	V	Nouvelle-Zélande (R)
France (R)	T	33 466 000	88.8	92.4	96.0	94.2	96.6	38 288 000	129.4	138.9	143.8	155.9	157.0	60 100 000	T	France (R)
Greece (N)	T	5 032 822	61.4	71.0	84.5	91.2	97.4	7 778 000	103.9	114.1	103.3	120.0	121.0	9 412 923	T	Grèce (N)
Greece (N)	V	5 463 860	63.9	73.2	85.5	89.2	97.2	8 231 000	98.2	107.8	97.6	113.4	114.4	9 412 823	V	Grèce (N)
Iceland (N)	T	72 600	60.2	66.2	75.6	88.1	100.6	128 830	99.6	110.0	111.4	110.7	122.1	157 326	T	Islande (N)
Ireland (R)	V	1 757 000	75.6	79.8	81.4	77.3	87.0	2 346 000	116.5	130.8	127.8	133.7	141.9	3 330 000	V	Irlande (R)
Italy (N)	T	21 885 098	84.6	88.1	95.8	95.7	98.4	26 155 571							T	Italie (N)
Italy (N)	V	48 311 474	83.6	88.3	96.3		94.7	55 690 434	99.0	108.3	92.1	89.9	89.6	49 909 733	V	Italie (N)
Norway (N)	T	468 147													T	Norvège (N)
Norway (N)	V	3 164 262	56.1	62.2	75.3	81.7	92.1	6 623 867	107.4	121.1	130.7	134.1	127.3	8 433 900	V	Portugal (N)
Portugal (N)	V	7 299 293	55.2	61.0	72.7	81.2	100.6	16 076 681	102.5	114.6	122.2	129.0	128.0	20 579 333	V	Portugal (N)
Spain (N)	V	42 011 141	76.2	78.8	79.4	87.5	93.3	54 178 147	99.8	96.1	99.4	102.6	106.9	57 931 161	V	Espagne (N)
Switzerland (R)[1]	T	11 500 000	98.3	101.3	101.7	98.3	100.0	11 700 000	107.7	112.8	107.7	109.4	106.0	12 400 000	T	Suisse (R)[1]
Switzerland (R)[1]	V	89 150 000	84.0	91.4	90.5	99.4	99.6	112 200 000	109.5	115.2	12.2	130.1	115.9	130 000 000	V	Suisse (R)[1]
Turkey (N)	V	1 391 717	38.9	50.7	62.7	57.3	68.4	4 172 727	106.9	129.2	132.2	169.6	155.8	6 500 638	V	Turquie (N)
United Kingdom (R)	T													17 902 000	T	Royaume-Uni (R)
United Kingdom (R)	V	11 635 700	78.9	86.4	91.5	88.0	98.5	15 798 800	109.7	114.0	108.4	117.3	123.4	19 488 000	V	Royaume-Uni (R)

V   Visitors (travellers in Austria, Germany and Turkey)
T   Tourists
(R) Tourist count by country of residence
(N) Tourist count by country of nationality
1.   Estimates

V   Visiteurs (voyageurs en Allemagne, en Autriche et en Turquie)
T   Touristes
(R) Recensement des touristes par pays de résidence
(N) Recensement des touristes par pays de nationalité
1.   Estimations

Table/Tableau 24

ARRIVALS AND NIGHTS OF FOREIGN TOURISTS AT/IN HOTELS
ARRIVÉES ET NUITÉES DE TOURISTES ÉTRANGERS DANS L'HÔTELLERIE

1988=100

Country	AH/NH	Volume 1982	1983	1984	1985	1986	1987	Volume 1988	1989	1990	1991	1992	1993	Volume 1993	Pays
Mexico (R)	NH													19 949 200	Mexique (R)
Mexico (R)	AH													5 230 400	
Australia (R)	NH	5 425 951	41.8	43.5	50.0	62.7	78.1	14 154 400	74.5	88.7	81.3	88.0	100.2	14 178 000	Australie (R)
Japan (N)	NH	2 596 136													Japon (N)
Japan (N)	AH														
Austria (R)	NH	55 954 735	97.6	98.5	96.9	96.8	98.3	56 357 827	109.0	109.8	113.7	113.9	110.0	61 995 886	Autriche (R)
Austria (R)	AH	9 974 119	85.8	91.2	91.8	90.3	95.5	11 921 625	110.3	116.0	114.2	114.6	109.3	13 031 632	
Belgium (R)	NH	4 731 389	90.9	96.9	102.1	98.1	98.0	5 424 140	121.2	126.7	121.2	141.8	138.0	7 484 777	Belgique (R)
Denmark (N)	NH	4 448 100	102.8	105.3	104.9	99.1	102.3	4 377 800	111.6	124.0	136.2	141.1	135.1	5 913 000	Danemark (N)
Finland (R)	NH	2 024 681	89.7	91.9	91.2	88.0	96.0	2 298 300	109.5	107.4	95.8	97.6	112.6	2 587 724	Finlande (R)
Finland (R)	AH													1 487 036	
France (R)[1]	NH	15 978 793	40.1	43.2	43.7	87.7	87.6	41 547 705	124.4	131.3	127.7	141.5	131.4	54 597 773	France (R)[1]
France (R)[1]	AH	6 086 640	31.4	33.4	35.5	87.5	88.0	19 509 178	124.6	129.3	129.4	145.5	134.7	26 269 529	
Germany (R)	NH	18 931 737	75.9	88.2	94.7	93.0	96.7	25 226 141	112.5	118.0	110.1	112.5	103.3	26 069 245	Allemagne (R)
Germany (R)	AH	9 214 569	78.9	91.9	97.9	93.6	97.7	12 061 573	111.7	119.6	108.2	110.2	100.1	12 071 246	
Greece (N)	NH	26 441 887	75.7	87.0	102.1	101.1	101.2	33 341 124	98.8	105.0	89.6	108.7	109.4	36 474 968	Grèce (N)
Greece (N)	AH	5 271 020	83.4	101.5	109.0	98.0	102.7	6 006 759							
Iceland (N)	NH		90.0	89.6	85.4	85.3	89.4	593 149	101.8	70.5	73.0	72.7	111.4	661 035	Islande (N)
Ireland (R)	NH		85.8	90.6	88.3	85.5	90.6	6 184 000	123.4	133.8	152.4	150.9	154.5	9 556 000	Irlande (R)
Ireland (R)	AH							1 235 000	125.2	133.8	138.7	145.6	146.6	1 810 000	
Italy (N)	NH	64 605 580	94.1	91.4	96.2	92.5	100.4	70 406 416	96.8	93.8	93.5	90.1	91.7	64 574 477	Italie (N)
Italy (N)	AH	14 812 017	83.7	84.5	92.2	93.6	97.6	17 436 723	101.4	102.8	96.7	99.6	102.8	17 919 195	
Luxembourg (R)	NH	931 126	88.9	96.7	99.8	105.1	97.2	968 575	105.0	111.1	110.7	104.0	102.8		Luxembourg (R)
Luxembourg (R)	AH	449 581	87.2	96.9	100.2	101.1	95.6	485 345	106.2	108.6	107.2	101.3	105.6		
Netherlands (R)	NH	6 285 412	69.7	103.1	110.6	98.3	104.1	6 761 500	105.0	117.5	118.2	125.7	117.9	7 973 200	Pays-Bas (R)
Netherlands (R)	AH	2 965 088						3 321 700	102.2	105.4	111.0	118.4	115.2	3 828 000	
Norway (N)	NH	2 290 825	74.6	102.4	113.5	96.1	101.0	3 356 255	109.6	114.7	116.7	127.4	135.8	4 556 774	Norvège (N)
Norway (N)	AH	1 212 395						1 703 710	103.1	111.4	124.1	139.4	150.0	2 556 162	
Portugal (N)	NH	9 559 559	65.9	73.5	86.2	95.2	115.2	15 005 318	105.1	113.8	127.2	119.1	107.8	16 175 957	Portugal (N)
Portugal (N)	AH	1 893 268	64.9	74.5	85.6	88.8	104.6	3 192 955	88.6	81.2	122.6	115.0	105.6	3 371 909	
Spain (N)	NH	76 691 027	90.2	100.8	89.3	99.3	96.8	88 350 997	96.7	88.1	84.3	87.1	93.8	82 872 250	Espagne (N)
Spain (N)	AH	11 194 526	84.6	95.4	91.2	99.6	96.2	13 635 765	105.5	100.0	88.4	93.5	95.0	12 949 518	
Sweden (N)	NH	2 744 096	94.8	102.6	111.2	103.7	104.6	3 191 994						2 983 641	Suède (N)
Sweden (N)	AH													1 629 239	
Switzerland (R)	NH	19 982 501	103.9	105.6	106.4	102.4	103.5	19 101 299	107.3	110.2	106.6	105.9	103.5	19 773 898	Suisse (R)
Switzerland (R)	AH	6 808 002	98.2	103.9	104.6	98.2	101.6	7 008 636	109.5	113.6	105.6	107.4	103.1	7 224 502	
Turkey (N)	NH	1 795 545	27.7	36.9	47.2	53.4	69.1	9 427 865	103.3	109.3	86.2	143.8	152.3	14 362 203	Turquie (N)
United Kingdom (R)	NH													9 400 000	Royaume-Uni (R)
United Kingdom (R)	AH	737 530	34.3	43.1	54.2	61.7	77.4	3 100 514	111.8	112.7	71.5	110.0	121.8	3 777 410	

AH   Arrivals at hotels and similar establishments — Arrivées dans les hôtels et les établissements assimilés
NH   Nights in hotels and similar establishments — Nuitées dans les hôtels et établissements assimilés
(R)   Tourist count by country of residence — Recensement des touristes par pays de résidence
(N)   Tourist count by country of nationality — Recensement des touristes par pays de nationalité
1.   Ile de France only — Ile de France seulement

Table/Tableau 25

ARRIVALS AND NIGHTS OF FOREIGN TOURISTS AT/IN ALL MEANS OF ACCOMMODATION
ARRIVÉES ET NUITÉES DE TOURISTES ÉTRANGERS DANS L'ENSEMBLE DES MOYENS D'HÉBERGEMENT

1988=100

	AAA/NAA	Volume 1982	1983	1984	1985	1986	1987	Volume 1988	1989	1990	1991	1992	1993	Volume 1993	AEH/NEH	
Canada (R)	NAA	72 527 500	76.5	83.7	83.9	99.5	92.3	91 911 900	98.0	89.4	90.1	86.4	89.3	82 092 100	NEH	Canada (R)
	AAA	12 183 300	80.7	83.8	85.1	100.9	96.7	15 485 000	97.6	98.2	96.3	95.2	97.5	15 105 100	AEH	
Mexico (R)	AAA													16 440 000	AEH	Mexique (R)
Australia (R)	NAA													35 393 000	NEH	Australie (R)
New Zealand (R)	NAA			68.1	79.5	87.1	98.0	18 519 849	101.8	111.5	104.2	110.7	120.1	22 248 380	NEH	Nouvelle-Zélande (R)
	AAA													793 890	AEH	
Austria (R)	NAA	89 954 002	99.9	99.0	97.1	97.5	97.8	87 575 147	108.4	108.2	113.8	113.9	110.6	96 823 821	NEH	Autriche (R)
	AAA	14 252 624	87.4	91.2	92.0	91.1	95.1	16 571 289	109.8	114.7	115.2	115.3	110.2	18 256 766	AEH	
Belgium (R)	AAA	8 552 707	84.5	88.3	93.0	93.2	95.2	10 577 025	115.0	121.8	115.1	121.8	122.0	12 899 501	AEH	Belgique (R)
Denmark (N)	NAA	9 222 149	117.4	112.2	110.5	104.8	101.0	8 118 706	105.6	115.0	128.5	142.7	128.8	10 460 000	NEH	Danemark (N)
Finland (R)	AAA													1 488 391	AEH	Finlande (R)
France (R)	NAA	298 873 000	100.8	104.8	107.9	108.8	111.3	305 337 000	114.8	126.8	129.7	139.6	140.9	430 300 000	NEH	France (R)
	AAA	33 465 000	88.8	92.4	95.9	94.2	96.5	38 305 000		138.9	143.7	155.5	156.9	60 100 000	AEH	
Germany (R)	NAA	20 865 184	71.6	86.8	93.2	92.3	96.6	30 116 744	111.5	115.7	124.3	126.8	115.3	34 711 411	NEH	Allemagne (R)
	AAA	9 459 714	75.0	71.7	96.7	93.2	97.5	13 113 017	111.7	119.2	119.3	121.4	109.4	14 347 710	AEH	
Greece (N)	NAA	29 954 664	78.6	95.4	102.7	101.9	102.8	34 779 083	98.2	104.4	87.8	106.1	106.7	37 107 985	NEH	Grèce (N)
	AAA	6 073 629													AEH	
Ireland (R)	NAA	17 228 000	71.4	73.5	71.9	72.4	86.4	26 192 000	119.7	128.6	127.1	129.0	134.1	35 130 000	NEH	Irlande (R)
	AAA	1 719 000	70.7	75.8	80.2	77.4		2 425 000	115.6	127.7	124.3	128.5	135.0	3 274 000	AEH	
Italy (N)	NAA	100 759 113	105.4	103.1	104.6	107.6	100.7	92 286 629	94.1	94.0	94.0	90.6	92.6	85 430 773	NEH	Italie (N)
	AAA	18 458 567	89.7	93.5	96.0	92.6	97.9	20 611 025	99.9	98.2	98.2	99.1	102.0	21 025 353	AEH	
Luxembourg (R)	NAA	2 034 327	96.4	114.5	102.5	110.1	101.5	2 139 613	113.0	113.0	119.6	109.1	102.0		NEH	Luxembourg (R)
	AAA		80.4	94.3	94.5	97.6	97.5	728 874	104.2	112.0	113.4	109.1			AEH	
Netherlands (R)	NAA	12 763 461	97.8	110.0	110.0	110.3		12 646 100	112.1	130.1	136.1	143.1	135.8	17 177 800	NEH	Pays-Bas (R)
	AAA	4 531 776	91.4	101.2	102.4	99.0		4 876 100	105.6	118.8	119.8	124.7	117.0	5 706 705	AEH	
Norway (N)	NAA	3 591 000	91.2	95.7	97.5		101.3	5 387 955	102.8	108.4	113.3	120.4	127.7	6 881 760	NEH	Norvège (N)
	AAA														AEH	
Portugal (N)	NAA	11 858 084	67.1	71.7	84.0	93.8	96.2	17 786 568	102.5	108.8	123.4	122.8	101.9	18 124 107	NEH	Portugal (N)
	AAA	2 394 493	64.1	71.9	82.9	89.1	96.0	3 987 962	104.4	111.2	119.6	108.9	99.3	3 961 743	AEH	
Spain (N)	NAA	78 855 059	87.3	96.4	92.3	100.8	103.5	13 635 965	96.7	92.5	78.7	81.8	85.4		NEH	Espagne (N)
	AAA	11 338 616	102.2	103.4	105.2	100.8	99.7	7 112 417	106.6						AEH	
Sweden (N)	NAA	6 145 111				100.8			106.6				85.4	6 074 572	NEH	Suède (N)
	AAA													1 877 296	AEH	
Switzerland (R)	NAA	36 738 300	104.4	101.5	102.1	101.4	100.4	34 447 443	104.4	107.1	107.5	107.4	106.6	36 728 870	NEH	Suisse (R)
	AAA	9 185 900	98.4	101.5	102.0	98.0	99.8	9 346 005	108.0	112.6	108.2	105.9	105.9	9 901 324	AEH	
Turkey (N)	NAA	1 889 028	24.4	31.9	41.9	50.9	71.4	11 655 182	101.8	113.9	83.2	144.0	146.4	17 064 115	NEH	Turquie (N)
	AAA	749 826	32.1	40.1	50.8	58.9	78.0	3 411 983	110.9	113.4	70.3	109.0	120.1	4 097 358	AEH	
United Kingdom (R)	NAA	136 337 000	83.9	89.4	96.6	91.5	103.1	172 899 000	108.4	113.4	107.8	108.2	108.1	186 963 000	NEH	Royaume-Uni (R)
	AAA														AEH	

AAA Arrivals in all means of accommodation
NAA Nights in all means of accommodation
(R) Tourist count by country of residence
(N) Tourist count by country of nationality

AEH Arrivées dans l'ensemble des moyens d'hébergement
NEH Nuitées dans l'ensemble des moyens d'hébergement
(R) Recensement des touristes par pays de résidence
(N) Recensement des touristes par pays de nationalité

Table/Tableau 26

ARRIVALS OF FOREIGN TOURISTS/VISITORS AT FRONTIERS
ARRIVÉES DE TOURISTES/VISITEURS ÉTRANGERS AUX FRONTIÈRES

From Germany / En provenance de l'Allemagne
1988=100

	T/V	Volume 1982	1983	1984	1985	1986	1987	Volume 1988	1989	1990	1991	1992	1993	Volume 1993	T/V	
Canada (R)	T	183 700	62.0	64.6	59.5	75.4	91.1	263 000	102.6	95.6	103.7	110.4	128.8	338 700	T	Canada (R)
	V	219 700	59.4	62.2	56.6	73.3	92.9	321 700	95.9	90.3	97.1	105.7	123.3	396 600	V	
United States (R)	T	665 706	48.8	47.3	44.1	58.1	82.6	1 153 356	93.3	104.3	124.0	146.7	158.4	1 826 757	T	États-Unis (R)
Australia (R)	V	38 901	52.5	51.9	56.6	63.6	80.9	65 900	103.3	112.6	117.9	136.4	160.2	105 600	V	Australie (R)
Japan (N)	T													26 949	T	Japon (N)
	V	41 326	76.2	86.0	85.4	86.3	94.0	56 941	108.1	115.6	107.5	112.3	110.3	62 795	V	
New Zealand (R)	T	8 968	47.4	47.3	53.0	59.9	81.7	20 111	118.2	149.1	170.5	227.3	279.3	56 162	T	Nouvelle-Zélande (R)
France (R)	T	8 403 000	88.4	91.0	95.7	92.4	97.8	9 113 000	116.2	115.9	128.4	139.0	143.1	13 041 000	T	France (R)
	V														V	
Greece (N)	T	606 046	52.7	62.5	76.0	82.9	87.2	1 382 000	119.8	139.1	113.0	140.7	149.7	2 069 379	T	Grèce (N)
Iceland (N)	V	8 518	55.1	60.5	59.3	85.6	88.2	15 894	116.4	129.8	141.4	154.3	197.8	31 443	V	Islande (N)
Ireland (R)	V	81 700	83.0	81.2	85.7	86.6	90.2	112 000	134.8	153.6	173.2	197.3	225.9	253 000	V	Irlande (R)
Italy (N)	V	10 385 238	98.9	103.2	111.8	91.2	91.8	10 479 061	96.7	101.9	87.8	83.8	73.5	7 697 399	V	Italie (N)
Norway (N)	V	84 921	58.9	55.6	69.7	72.2	91.1		106.6	117.3	148.5	153.4	136.6		V	Norvège (N)
Portugal (N)	V	243 142	62.5	60.5	72.6	75.7	92.5	529 569	107.5	119.8	149.8	154.3	139.8	723 600	V	Portugal (N)
		289 514						568 656						794 734		
Spain (N)	V	4 777 817	72.0	76.0	81.7	86.0	95.5	6 904 418	98.3	99.6	111.1	112.4	126.2	8 713 281	V	Espagne (N)
Turkey (N)	V	169 293	22.8	31.5	39.0	50.6	68.2	767 905	116.8	126.8	101.6	151.7	145.7	1 118 750	V	Turquie (N)
														2 200 000		
United Kingdom (R)	V	1 441 600	75.1	81.1	81.1	87.4	89.8	1 830 100	110.8	103.5	116.6	123.9	128.7	2 356 000	V	Royaume-Uni (R)

V Visitors (travellers in Turkey)
T Tourists
(R) Tourist count by country of residence
(N) Tourist count by country of nationality

V Visiteurs (voyageurs en Turquie)
T Touristes
(R) Recensement des touristes par pays de résidence
(N) Recensement des touristes par pays de nationalité

112

Table/Tableau 27

ARRIVALS AND NIGHTS OF FOREIGN TOURISTS AT/IN HOTELS
ARRIVÉES ET NUITÉES DE TOURISTES ÉTRANGERS DANS L'HÔTELLERIE

From Germany / *En provenance de l'Allemagne*
1988=100

Country	AH/NH	Volume 1982	1983	1984	1985	1986	1987	Volume 1988	1989	1990	1991	1992	1993	Volume 1993	AH/NH	
Australia (R)	NH	171 656	49.6	45.7	57.6	63.6	80.9	525 200	97.4	99.0	110.8	144.4	157.3	826 000	NH	Australie (R)
Japan (N)	NH	66 385													NH	Japon (N)
	AH														AH	
Austria (R)	NH	36 419 112	105.7	101.4	98.1	99.3	98.4	33 421 932	106.7	101.8	114.2	115.3	116.2	38 822 504	NH	Autriche (R)
	AH	5 399 329	91.8	90.3	89.2	92.1	95.5	5 947 865	107.0	105.0	116.6	117.3	118.0	7 019 135	AH	
Belgium (R)	NH	706 318	89.9	92.9	93.2	95.0	97.2	801 827	116.3	112.1	120.2	141.0	145.5	1 166 956	NH	Belgique (R)
Denmark (N)	NH	1 235 000	124.4	115.2	104.1	100.2	101.5	929 200	115.5	138.6	170.8	183.4	184.4	1 713 900	NH	Danemark (N)
Finland (R)	NH	269 726	79.3	86.4	85.0	77.8	87.4	321 592	109.9	105.2	109.1	117.1	156.7	504 025	NH	Finlande (R)
	AH													342 585	AH	
France (R)[1]	NH	1 955 399	31.2	29.1	29.4	86.8	92.1	6 704 914	113.2	118.6	126.8	123.9	116.5	7 811 366	NH	France (R)[1]
	AH	764 383	24.2	22.1	23.8	85.3	90.9	3 352 676	113.4	117.6	122.4	123.0	115.5	3 872 626	AH	
Greece (N)	NH	4 833 810	58.2	69.5	87.5	90.6	91.5	7 868 225							NH	Grèce (N)
	AH	835 248	73.5	83.6	96.4	95.7	97.3	1 061 566							AH	
Iceland (N)	NH				62.3	66.7	68.5	50 038	135.7	149.4	184.9	196.2	227.8	113 962	NH	Islande (N)
Ireland (R)	NH		89.5	86.7	74.6	80.6	86.6	514 000	109.7	154.7	158.9	157.2	202.9	1 043 000	NH	Irlande (R)
	AH		79.9	80.6	87.8	94.6	99.7	67 000	129.9	143.3	164.2	186.6	214.9	144 000	AH	
Italy (N)	NH	25 994 770	78.7	84.0	82.5	89.1	97.8	28 396 344	91.5	101.4	92.1	94.7	84.4	24 035 026	NH	Italie (N)
	AH	4 004 186	93.9	82.2	87.9	90.1	99.9	5 046 194	96.7	92.1	101.4	94.7	94.6	4 774 442	AH	
Luxembourg (R)	NH	99 070			87.5	105.5	95.7	123 880							NH	Luxembourg (R)
	AH	60 687			93.4	103.9	106.7	70 804							AH	
Netherlands (R)	NH	1 405 547	88.3	96.1	91.5	110.5	100.2	1 474 200	103.3	112.4	126.0	131.3	140.8	2 076 100	NH	Pays-Bas (R)
	AH	585 976	65.2	92.4	94.6	103.9	93.7	664 800	101.5	110.0	120.1	122.4	136.7	908 600	AH	
Norway (N)	NH	370 205	55.6	60.2	82.7	91.9	99.8	539 333	107.7	107.5	132.2	157.7	192.2	1 036 481	NH	Norvège (N)
Portugal (N)	NH	1 168 562	53.8	57.0	76.8	81.6	98.6	2 056 623	101.2	114.8	157.2	160.4	149.4	3 073 287	NH	Portugal (N)
	AH	187 616			95.8	91.9	105.8	375 576	100.2	111.6	142.2	146.3	134.5	505 221	AH	
Spain (N)	NH	21 683 679	90.9	94.0	92.8	95.8	105.3	24 635 737	88.5	92.3	105.4	107.1	113.9	28 066 058	NH	Espagne (N)
	AH	2 206 423	86.9	90.0	88.4	96.6	89.1	2 692 662	92.2	87.7	108.3	106.7	115.4	3 106 653	AH	
Sweden (N)	NH	384 342	80.2	86.9	96.4	95.2	99.4	475 778	107.3	97.6	94.7	102.2	121.1	575 975	NH	Suède (N)
Switzerland (R)	NH	6 635 171	103.7	97.1	90.9	99.6	97.7	6 223 904	104.3	103.1	111.8	109.9	112.7	7 015 900	NH	Suisse (R)
	AH	1 952 002	96.4	92.3	96.4	95.2	99.4	2 016 032	105.7	104.3	111.3	108.6	109.2	2 202 242	AH	
Turkey (N)	NH	331 835	13.8	19.5	30.1	45.7	64.7	3 519 989	104.8	110.8	98.3	161.9	142.9	5 031 658	NH	Turquie (N)
	AH	122 731	21.3	27.1	39.5	57.9	79.0	896 931	105.9	107.1	62.9	99.2	94.9	851 103	AH	

AH   Arrivals at hotels and similar establishments
NH   Nights in hotels and similar establishments
(R)   Tourist count by country of residence
(N)   Tourist count by country of nationality
1.   Ile de France only

AH   Arrivées dans les hôtels et les établissements assimilés
NH   Nuitées dans les hôtels et établissements assimilés
(R)   Recensement des touristes par pays de résidence
(N)   Recensement des touristes par pays de nationalité
1.   Ile de France seulement

Table/Tableau 28

ARRIVALS AND NIGHTS OF FOREIGN TOURISTS AT/IN ALL MEANS OF ACCOMMODATION
ARRIVÉES ET NUITÉES DE TOURISTES ÉTRANGERS DANS L'ENSEMBLE DES MOYENS D'HÉBERGEMENT

From Germany
En provenance de l'Allemagne
1988=100

Country	AAA/NAA	Volume 1982	1983	1984	1985	1986	1987	Volume 1988	1989	1990	1991	1992	1993	Volume 1993	AEH/NEH	
Canada (R)	NAA	2 821 800	67.9	70.5	63.1	76.2	84.9	3 580 900	90.7	89.8	101.5	100.2	119.6	4 281 000	NEH	Canada (R)
	AAA	183 700	62.0	64.6	59.5	75.4	89.0	263 000	99.9	95.6	103.7	110.4	128.8	338 700	AEH	
Australia (R)	NAA													3 723 000	NEH	Australie (R)
New Zealand (R)	NAA			46.4	51.2	65.6	91.9	625 607	118.3	141.4	181.2	219.9	251.3	1 572 004	NEH	Nouvelle-Zélande (R)
	AAA													56 162	AEH	
Austria (R)	NAA	62 726 773	107.9	102.4	98.9	100.0	98.9	56 058 730	106.9	101.4	114.7	115.4	115.9	64 978 848	NEH	Autriche (R)
	AAA	8 437 218	94.2	92.0	90.5	93.3	95.5	8 996 778	107.4	104.7	118.0	118.5	118.5	10 664 011	AEH	
Belgium (R)	NAA	1 324 760	78.4	83.2	89.7	89.4	92.3	1 691 014	115.9	114.8	122.1	133.8	145.1	2 454 056	NEH	Belgique (R)
Denmark (N)	NAA	4 011 047	146.0	130.5	123.4	116.2	103.6	2 818 399	106.7	119.0	139.4	162.3	160.8	4 530 900	NEH	Danemark (N)
Finland (R)	AAA													405 407	AEH	Finlande (R)
France (R)	NAA	75 072 000	90.5	92.1	95.3	95.3	98.3	80 176 000	85.8	91.4	100.2	107.2	109.1	87 485 000	NEH	France (R)
	AAA	8 403 000	88.5	91.0	95.7	92.4	97.8	9 111 100		115.9	128.5	139.0	143.1	13 041 000	AEH	
Greece (N)	NAA	5 596 571	63.3	74.9	88.5	91.3	92.8	8 315 638							NEH	Grèce (N)
	AAA	1 042 913													AEH	
Ireland (R)	NAA	1 177 200	74.6	69.2	71.5	75.4	86.3	1 766 200	126.3	157.2	182.2	193.6	221.2	3 906 000	NEH	Irlande (R)
	AAA	86 000	81.4	78.8	86.6	88.5		113 000	136.3	157.5	179.6	203.5	234.5	265 000	AEH	
Italy (N)	NAA	43 802 250	108.1	104.7	105.7	113.5	99.4	39 498 355	88.9	104.8	91.4	93.2	85.8	33 883 014	NEH	Italie (N)
	AAA	5 740 886	89.1	89.1	91.7	99.0	98.1	6 487 347	94.3	107.9	100.4	93.2	94.4	6 123 299	AEH	
Luxembourg (R)	NAA	131 377	73.0	93.0	94.0	89.6	100.1	175 801		95.2	117.4	118.6			NEH	Luxembourg (R)
	AAA		73.2	88.7	91.1	90.5	96.2	88 726		96.7	109.7	114.7			AEH	
Netherlands (R)	NAA	6 149 309	108.1	119.2	116.3	122.9		5 638 600	113.1	132.0	148.3	160.8	162.7	9 173 400	NEH	Pays-Bas (R)
	AAA	1 503 041	101.0	106.1	105.2	110.3		1 530 600	107.8	119.2	135.2	140.3	144.8	2 215 900	AEH	
Portugal (N)	NAA	1 784 230	59.8	59.9	80.6	91.1	100.3	2 781 176	99.0	106.6	142.6	137.6	124.8	3 469 750	NEH	Portugal (N)
	AAA	307 257	55.5	57.9	74.9	84.3	99.0	573 400	98.0	104.9	130.8	122.2	107.3	615 187	AEH	
Spain (N)	NAA	22 776 337	106.1	97.3	97.1	93.4	86.7								NEH	Espagne (N)
	AAA	2 354 343	106.4	97.4	98.0	99.9	97.7								AEH	
Sweden (N)	NAA	1 299 747	97.9	92.4	92.2	95.7	96.6	1 377 213	109.9	101.8	95.8	109.8	127.4	1 754 682	NEH	Suède (N)
Switzerland (R)	NAA	15 993 500						14 783 262	101.1	99.6	109.1	108.3	112.3	16 597 783	NEH	Suisse (R)
	AAA	3 057 400						3 127 466	104.0	103.5	112.6	111.6	113.0	3 532 981	AEH	
Turkey (N)	NAA	342 801	12.1	16.0	25.7	44.6	70.6	4 593 089	102.5	118.1	96.9	164.9	145.1	6 663 582	NEH	Turquie (N)
	AAA	124 056	19.2	24.1	35.6	54.4	80.9	1 028 920	105.1	108.2	64.3	100.9	99.6	1 025 263	AEH	
United Kingdom (R)	NAA	15 521 000	81.6	83.0	84.7	95.2	90.9	17 226 000	102.9	101.8	112.9	111.9	108.0	18 612 000	NEH	Royaume-Uni (R)
	AAA														AEH	

AAA Arrivals in all means of accommodation
NAA Nights in all means of accommodation
(R) Tourist count by country of residence
(N) Tourist count by country of nationality

AEH Arrivées dans l'ensemble des moyens d'hébergement
NEH Nuitées dans l'ensemble des moyens d'hébergement
(R) Recensement des touristes par pays de résidence
(N) Recensement des touristes par pays de nationalité

Table/Tableau 29

ARRIVALS OF FOREIGN TOURISTS/VISITORS AT FRONTIERS
ARRIVÉES DE TOURISTES/VISITEURS ÉTRANGERS AUX FRONTIÈRES

From Canada — 1988=100 | En provenance du Canada — 1988=100

From Canada	T/V	Volume 1982	1983	1984	1985	1986	1987	Volume 1988	1989	1990	1991	1992	1993	Volume 1993	T/V	En provenance du Canada
United States (R)	T	10 430 000	86.4	79.3	78.6	79.0	89.7	13 843 106	111.0	124.7	138.1	134.4	124.9	17 293 000	T	États-Unis (R)
Australia (R)	V	32 447	49.5	51.7	61.3	70.5	79.0	66 700	81.3	80.5	80.1	73.3	75.9	50 600	V	Australie (R)
														45 860		
Japan (N)	T	48 288	92.2	91.1	105.0	94.9	100.2	58 164	102.7	109.8	107.1	119.7	124.5	72 395	T	Japon (N)
New Zealand (R)	V	18 008	55.1	62.0	80.3	92.4	95.7	37 137	83.3	91.5	81.5	69.6	74.7	27 755	V	Nouvelle-Zélande (R)
France (R)	T	250 000	82.3	109.6	138.7	112.2	101.5	344 000	144.1	160.5	143.3	171.8	202.6	697 000	T	France (R)
Greece (N)	T	64 891	67.8	76.8	95.8	69.7	85.0	107 000	73.8	69.4	44.0	55.9	48.1	51 472	T	Grèce (N)
Iceland (N)	T	1 003	81.3	78.4	100.7	93.6	100.7	1 277	101.2	89.3	73.8	90.3	115.3	1 473	T	Islande (N)
Ireland (R)	V	16 240	75.0	75.0	89.3	100.0	89.3	28 000	132.1	135.7	107.1	139.3	142.9	40 000	V	Irlande (R)
Italy (N)	V	308 291	93.6	94.9	98.4	95.4	108.5	354 258	119.4	134.1	98.8	101.0	93.0	329 525	V	Italie (N)
		8 202														
Norway (N)	V	37 930	54.5	68.8	90.6	95.0	95.5	76 009	109.3	109.5	82.7	87.2	81.0	61 600	V	Norvège (N)
Portugal (N)	T	41 993	59.2	71.0	88.9	93.4	98.1	79 069	115.2	114.9	87.6	93.5	90.1	71 230	T	Portugal (N)
														103 822		
Spain (N)	V	133 412	82.4	92.6	113.8	105.3	106.4	167 972	102.6	93.9	82.1	87.2	78.3	131 587	T	Espagne (N)
Turkey (N)	V	8 556	49.3	61.8	73.7	44.8	71.3	29 220	108.1	118.3	60.5	90.2	120.3	35 144	V	Turquie (N)
United Kingdom (R)	V	408 800	79.6	87.0	96.9	85.2	91.2	651 400	98.0	106.5	84.0	96.6	90.1	587 000	V	Royaume-Uni (R)

V   Visitors (travellers in Turkey)
T   Tourists
(R)   Tourist count by country of residence
(N)   Tourist count by country of nationality

V   Visiteurs (voyageurs en Turquie)
T   Touristes
(R)   Recensement des touristes par pays de résidence
(N)   Recensement des touristes par pays de nationalité

115

Table/Tableau 30

ARRIVALS AND NIGHTS OF FOREIGN TOURISTS AT/IN HOTELS
ARRIVÉES ET NUITÉES DE TOURISTES ÉTRANGERS DANS L'HÔTELLERIE

From Canada
1988=100

En provenance du Canada
1988=100

Country	AH/NH	Volume 1982	1983	1984	1985	1986	1987	Volume 1988	1989	1990	1991	1992	1993	Volume 1993	AH/NH	
Australia (R)	NH	108 838	63.4	44.2	59.7	70.5	79.0	595 300	65.1	81.5	61.4	47.3	65.0	387 000	NH	Australie (R)
Japan (N)	NH	53 629													NH	Japon (N)
	AH														AH	
Austria (R)	NH	128 198	80.6	97.4	118.9	98.2	108.0	168 266	103.3	115.4	92.2	94.2	93.6	157 433	NH	Autriche (R)
	AH	45 491	79.4	98.6	117.6	91.4	102.4	67 350	107.4	124.3	93.0	97.9	90.7	61 109	AH	
Belgium (R)	NH	49 372	71.7	94.3	116.8	91.6	95.9	79 376	117.8	124.5	96.6	98.1	81.8	64 937	NH	Belgique (R)
Finland (R)	NH	21 369	87.3	90.6	98.3	83.6	95.5	30 427	109.2	105.4	81.8	69.1	80.0	24 335	NH	Finlande (R)
	AH													10 842	AH	
France (R)[1]	NH	330 032	52.7	61.7	74.5	107.3	99.0	753 094	126.9	137.1	100.5	106.2	107.2	807 635	NH	France (R)[1]
	AH	118 153	39.8	49.1	62.9	114.4	99.0	333 415	129.3	141.8	108.2	119.8	114.9	383 051	AH	
Germany (R)	NH	216 057	77.8	101.4	110.1	96.9	93.8	308 906	115.3	122.6	96.5	97.3	87.7	271 059	NH	Allemagne (R)
	AH	113 431	86.1	115.9	123.9	103.1	99.4	148 974	114.8	125.5	94.8	97.9	85.0	126 612	AH	
Greece (N)	NH	189 257	88.7	109.2	153.9	135.7	97.2	236 549							NH	Grèce (N)
	AH	70 334	84.6	110.6	150.9	116.7	97.1	91 304							AH	
Ireland (R)	NH							115 000	220.9	93.9	142.6	181.7	185.2	213 000	NH	Irlande (R)
	AH							24 000	154.2	87.5	120.8	116.7	150.0	36 000	AH	
Italy (N)	NH	446 011	91.9	102.5	116.9	91.2	105.8	573 385	109.7	110.5	84.7	89.1	93.1	533 837	NH	Italie (N)
	AH	167 229	88.9	104.3	115.2	88.3	102.2	231 982	104.9	109.1	81.5	88.9	91.5	212 295	AH	
Luxembourg (R)	NH														NH	Luxembourg (R)
	AH														AH	
Netherlands (R)	NH	119 225	86.1	98.2	110.8	93.7	99.4	175 400	102.7	105.8	76.5	75.3	64.9	113 800	NH	Pays-Bas (R)
	AH	62 826	84.1	96.0	110.6	91.3	96.0	102 900	91.3	89.2	61.3	62.4	55.3	56 900	AH	
Portugal (N)	NH	173 904	69.0	83.0	124.4	116.6	111.2	311 957	109.2	120.5	89.4	69.4	61.2	190 878	NH	Portugal (N)
	AH	51 527	67.0	82.1	107.3	100.7	110.0	91 731	108.6	109.9	69.0	59.4	52.9	48 540	AH	
Spain (N)	NH	290 997	194.4	225.2	264.4	186.8	123.9	182 900	97.2	90.6	67.0	75.3	78.5	143 660	NH	Espagne (N)
	AH	115 133	101.3	126.0	122.8	96.2	112.3	78 264	96.2	113.7	65.2	63.5	66.0	51 688	AH	
Sweden (N)	NH	21 420	110.7	125.6	151.7	124.9	122.9	22 849	109.7	112.2	69.8	69.9	77.0	17 589	NH	Suède (N)
Switzerland (R)	NH	197 857	111.5	134.8	152.4	121.8	114.6	209 480	104.0	116.2	84.7	83.2	79.0	165 567	NH	Suisse (R)
	AH	83 645						93 386	107.1	123.7	82.5	84.1	77.9	72 749	AH	
Turkey (N)	NH	9 662	35.5	46.5	47.2	55.4	64.2	29 606	104.0		65.9	99.8	143.3	42 412	NH	Turquie (N)
	AH	2 817	41.8	47.8	52.7	66.4	72.9	10 546	149.8		75.4	137.9	163.8	17 271	AH	

AH Arrivals at hotels and similar establishments
NH Nights in hotels and similar establishments
(R) Tourist count by country of residence
(N) Tourist count by country of nationality
1. Ile de France only

AH Arrivées dans les hôtels et les établissements assimilés
NH Nuitées dans les hôtels et établissements assimilés
(R) Recensement des touristes par pays de résidence
(N) Recensement des touristes par pays de nationalité
1. Ile de France seulement

116

Table/Tableau 31

ARRIVALS AND NIGHTS OF FOREIGN TOURISTS AT/IN ALL MEANS OF ACCOMMODATION
ARRIVÉES ET NUITÉES DE TOURISTES ÉTRANGERS DANS L'ENSEMBLE DES MOYENS D'HÉBERGEMENT

From Canada
1988=100

En provenance du Canada
1988=100

Country	AAA/NAA	Volume 1982	1983	1984	1985	1986	1987	Volume 1988	1989	1990	1991	1992	1993	Volume 1993	AEH/NEH	Pays
Australia (R)	NAA		108.3	65.0	63.1	70.5	79.0	1 223 900	146.8	218.4	187.0	82.1	99.5	1 218 000	NEH	Australie (R)
New Zealand (R)	NAA													605 501	NEH	Nouvelle-Zélande (R)
	AAA													27 755	AEH	
Austria (R)	NAA	169 310	79.1	93.9	110.0	93.8	101.8	223 492	98.7	111.3	87.8	93.0	91.9	205 374	NEH	Autriche (R)
Belgium (R)	NAA	56 448	76.0	95.4	112.0	90.5	99.8	84 614	106.3	122.7	91.9	97.7	88.8	75 134	NEH	Belgique (R)
	AAA													24 730	AEH	
Finland (R)	NAA	58 914	72.9	94.8	116.8	96.7	94.7	90 735	116.0	125.2	98.8	95.0	79.4	72 085	NEH	Finlande (R)
	AAA													11 088	AEH	
France (R)	NAA	3 555 000	75.0	94.5	116.3	103.4	99.9	5 688 683	95.3	96.9	81.7	95.4	109.8	6 244 000	NEH	France (R)
	AAA	250 000	82.3	109.6	138.7	112.2	101.5	344 000		160.5	143.3	171.8	202.6	697 000	AEH	
Germany (R)	NAA	221 066	70.3	99.9	108.5	96.9	93.4	350 624	115.5	122.3	99.4	100.5	89.8	314 966	NEH	Allemagne (R)
	AAA	114 139	76.0	113.8	120.6	103.4	98.8	169 977	114.9	126.0	98.6	101.8	87.8	149 283	AEH	
Greece (N)	NAA	208 257	94.3	159.9	154.6	84.0	97.6	240 936						555 000	NEH	Grèce (N)
	AAA	78 125	90.9	119.4	151.1	83.8	97.7	93 197							AEH	
Ireland (R)	NAA							34 000	123.5	120.6	102.9	126.5	135.3	46 000	NEH	Irlande (R)
Italy (N)	NAA	617 142	99.9	108.7	119.9	97.4	104.3	675 189	108.9	110.1	88.8	93.6	100.1	675 695	NEH	Italie (N)
	AAA	188 578	88.5	103.1	112.7	89.2	100.8	259 056	104.2	108.4	83.1	90.4	92.5	239 603	AEH	
Luxembourg (R)	NAA														NEH	Luxembourg (R)
	AAA														AEH	
Netherlands (R)	NAA	148 023	87.1	98.7	109.0	88.3		204 400	103.2	108.3	81.0	79.1	68.8	140 700	NEH	Pays-Bas (R)
	AAA	79 267	83.6	95.0	106.7	84.5		122 800	88.5	88.5	64.7	64.6	56.3	69 100	AEH	
Portugal (N)	NAA	184 593	70.1	83.9	124.0	115.7	110.7	323 486	108.7	120.0	89.0	69.4	61.0	197 277	NEH	Portugal (N)
	AAA	54 929	67.9	82.6	107.1	100.2	109.5	95 940	108.6	110.7	69.8	60.3	53.4	51 191	AEH	
Sweden (N)	NAA	24 101	102.2	123.7	121.0	97.5	119.3	25 802	108.9	113.0	71.2	71.6	76.5	19 743	NEH	Suède (N)
Switzerland (R)	NAA	244 700	109.4	123.4	147.1	123.0	114.1	255 652	105.1	111.6	87.3	85.5	80.7	206 362	NEH	Suisse (R)
	AAA	104 500	110.5	130.6	148.4	120.2	110.0	114 140	107.2	114.9	84.7	86.5	78.1	89 117	AEH	
Turkey (N)	NAA	9 708	34.3	45.2	46.0	54.1	64.3	31 074	101.8	94.2	64.9	98.0	139.6	43 370	NEH	Turquie (N)
	AAA	2 827	39.9	45.6	51.0	63.5	71.8	11 162	144.5	120.5	74.2	132.9	157.4	17 572	AEH	
United Kingdom (R)	NAA	7 118 000	91.1	95.2	102.9	96.6	93.0	8 855 000	96.9	104.8	86.1	86.0	86.8	7 690 000	NEH	Royaume-Uni (R)

AAA   Arrivals in all means of accommodation
NAA   Nights in all means of accommodation
(R)   Tourist count by country of residence
(N)   Tourist count by country of nationality

AEH   Arrivées dans l'ensemble des moyens d'hébergement
NEH   Nuitées dans l'ensemble des moyens d'hébergement
(R)   Recensement des touristes par pays de résidence
(N)   Recensement des touristes par pays de nationalité

ARRIVALS OF FOREIGN TOURISTS/VISITORS AT FRONTIERS
ARRIVÉES DE TOURISTES/VISITEURS ÉTRANGERS AUX FRONTIÈRES

From the United States — *En provenance des États-Unis*

1988=100

Country	T/V	Volume 1982	1983	1984	1985	1986	1987	Volume 1988	1989	1990	1991	1992	1993	Volume 1993	T/V	
Canada (R)	T	10 462 300	85.5	88.5	90.6	106.6	99.7	12 763 100	95.5	96.0	94.0	92.6	94.2	12 024 000	T	Canada (R)
	V	32 431 800	89.9	91.2	94.4	105.7	102.2	36 147 100	96.0	96.1	92.9	89.7	90.2	32 622 700	V	
Australia (R)	V	125 400	43.3	49.8	61.0	76.1	95.9	322 300	80.9	77.8	84.3	81.6	87.3	281 300	V	Australie (R)
Japan (N)	T													272 348	T	Japon (N)
New Zealand (R)	T	410 808	89.4	99.0	108.1	107.0	106.6	516 259	103.0	107.5	105.2	108.7	103.3	533 401	V	Nouvelle-Zélande (R)
	V	76 314	51.8	60.3	73.4	91.9	107.7	167 525	82.1	83.4	79.2	78.4	85.7	143 596	T	
France (R)	T	1 355 000	105.1	130.2	142.5	85.5	92.4	1 950 000	111.1	102.7	84.3	103.2	100.9	1 968 000	T	France (R)
	V														V	
Greece (N)	T	333 080	137.9	161.0	158.0	69.4	88.1	295 000	94.6	92.8	61.2	94.6	87.0	256 719	T	Grèce (N)
Iceland (N)	T	20 824	86.7	95.0	110.1	113.8	124.2	28 724	79.9	78.7	78.4	75.6	87.2	25 061	T	Islande (N)
Ireland (R)	V	301 950	71.8	81.2	101.3	79.9	96.0	373 000	101.9	106.2	83.9	98.1	95.7	357 000	T	Irlande (R)
Italy (N)	V	1 602 942	127.1	131.3	135.8	117.8	109.7	1 351 257	100.4	105.2	84.2	95.8	89.6	1 210 390	V	Italie (N)
Norway (N)	V	80 049	59.2	85.2	84.9	58.9	78.1	194 206	96.2	94.7	73.9	80.6	75.2	146 100	V	Norvège (N)
Portugal (N)	T	127 500	83.7	93.8	102.8	67.1	87.4	223 288	105.5	112.9	79.8	98.7	93.0	207 651	T	Portugal (N)
	V	154 200														
Spain (N)	V	758 263	94.5	109.0	116.2	89.6	100.8	858 894	111.0	97.4	76.0	96.1	91.2	783 620	V	Espagne (N)
Turkey (N)	T	104 703	114.2	129.0	118.7	48.1	78.9	165 401	123.6	124.4	47.9	110.3	154.1	254 945	V	Turquie (N)
United Kingdom (R)	V	1 726 100	88.4	105.5	120.8	87.3	106.9	2 620 200	108.5	114.2	88.5	104.9	107.4	2 695 000	T	Royaume-Uni (R)
														2 815 000	V	

V Visitors (travellers in Turkey) — Visiteurs (voyageurs en Turquie)
T Tourists — Touristes
(R) Tourist count by country of residence — Recensement des touristes par pays de résidence
(N) Tourist count by country of nationality — Recensement des touristes par pays de nationalité

Table/Tableau 33

ARRIVALS AND NIGHTS OF FOREIGN TOURISTS AT/IN HOTELS
ARRIVÉES ET NUITÉES DE TOURISTES ÉTRANGERS DANS L'HÔTELLERIE

From the United States — En provenance des États-Unis

1988=100

Country	AH/NH	Volume 1982	1983	1984	1985	1986	1987	Volume 1988	1989	1990	1991	1992	1993	Volume 1993	Pays
Australia (R)	NH	1 481 032	43.9	38.2	58.6	76.1	95.9	2 833 400	72.3	74.0	74.5	67.8	69.9	1 980 000	Australie (R)
Japan (N)	NH	660 243													Japon (N)
Austria (R)	NH	1 296 534	111.0	141.8	152.9	87.8	108.6	1 428 035	107.2	137.2	74.5	95.9	86.3	1 231 701	Autriche (R)
	AH	493 583	113.7	155.9	164.5	81.4	108.8	562 655	109.1	145.0	74.4	100.7	86.9	488 734	
Belgium (R)	NH	543 930	125.4	148.4	166.4	129.4	116.2	463 917	119.4	126.3	104.9	130.0	109.1	506 328	Belgique (R)
	AH	413 500	132.8	140.3	151.5	109.5	117.5	378 200	109.7	105.6	77.1	80.7	77.2	292 000	
Denmark (N)	NH	114 840	73.8	77.5	90.9	78.5	98.3	203 202	99.6	97.1	70.9	74.4	80.7	163 910	Danemark (N)
Finland (R)	NH													88 168	Finlande (R)
	AH														
France (R)[1]	NH	2 079 794	65.5	85.9	97.4	82.5	90.8	3 957 671	132.3	143.3	99.0	125.8	119.9	4 746 255	France (R)[1]
	AH	810 056	54.0	72.9	80.8	80.1	86.8	1 761 455	131.2	140.2	99.6	128.0	120.8	2 128 717	
Germany (R)	NH	2 791 689	94.5	122.5	132.6	98.1	110.5	3 654 158	109.0	121.6	87.0	92.5	82.9	3 030 238	Allemagne (R)
	AH	1 444 170	101.7	134.5	142.2	99.1	110.7	1 785 005	110.0	129.3	86.2	92.8	81.2	1 449 678	
Greece (N)	NH	1 295 056	197.1	235.9	201.7	61.4	95.4	828 553							Grèce (N)
	AH	506 228	183.3	230.1	201.7	52.0	90.7	357 240							
Iceland (N)	NH				100.3	75.7	94.3	50 476	83.7	69.1	70.7	61.0	70.2	35 433	Islande (N)
Ireland (R)	NH				106.1	82.1	100.3	2 133 000	91.3	95.6	84.1	88.6	87.8	1 872 000	Irlande (R)
	AH							380 000	99.5	98.4	75.8	89.7	84.5	321 000	
Italy (N)	NH	4 163 286	113.8	134.0	143.3	73.8	103.7	4 590 961	105.6	79.0	79.0	99.1	107.5	4 933 692	Italie (N)
	AH	1 684 035	117.0	142.5	157.4	68.8	101.1	1 864 011	104.2	76.2	76.2	99.1	104.4	1 946 389	
Luxembourg (R)	NH	51 125	111.4	136.2	173.1	117.7	121.8	63 345	108.4	94.2	70.0	73.8			Luxembourg (R)
	AH	30 048	120.0	145.7	142.4	129.0	134.4	33 264	108.2	99.5	70.4	74.3			
Netherlands (R)	NH	819 716	115.7	141.7	151.3	110.2	110.6	756 100	99.8	120.9	101.1	113.9	105.4	797 300	Pays-Bas (R)
	AH	409 660	119.4	150.8	184.7	110.4	112.0	381 000	104.2	119.6	96.1	107.3	101.7	387 500	
Norway (N)	NH	374 943	128.8	161.2	121.4	118.1	131.4	348 049	106.0	104.7	80.5	101.0	89.5	311 476	Norvège (N)
Portugal (N)	NH	466 180	92.2	109.3	121.8	76.3	96.5	649 983	104.5	103.4	74.7	82.9	71.9	467 286	Portugal (N)
	AH	169 494	94.7	112.5	144.5	71.9	96.7	239 623	106.6	105.2	77.6	84.7	77.5	185 825	
Spain (N)	NH	1 648 986	118.4	140.5	160.1	84.5	108.5	1 756 732	101.8	99.8	73.6	85.9	81.5	1 430 919	Espagne (N)
	AH	652 418	125.1	149.7	148.2	91.6	103.9	775 281	109.1	102.1	74.7	86.8	85.4	662 349	
Sweden (N)	NH	294 185	121.4	127.7	160.0	100.0	107.1	325 521	111.3	100.4	73.3	82.1	87.9	286 293	Suède (N)
Switzerland (R)	NH	2 071 855	117.0	150.7	163.7	102.0	114.4	2 038 856		123.1	77.3	92.7	88.7	1 809 175	Suisse (R)
	AH	934 991	119.5	156.7		96.3	111.8	927 961		129.8	77.1	95.6	88.4	819 975	
Turkey (N)	NH	149 370	60.8	80.8	85.1	69.5	85.0	314 818	121.0	110.8	89.7	122.9	158.7	499 637	Turquie (N)
	AH	49 935	60.5	67.1	74.8	64.5	78.6	118 080	141.9	134.2	77.3	133.8	179.2	211 545	

AH — Arrivals at hotels and similar establishments — Arrivées dans les hôtels et les établissements assimilés
NH — Nights in hotels and similar establishments — Nuitées dans les hôtels et établissements assimilés
(R) — Tourist count by country of residence — Recensement des touristes par pays de résidence
(N) — Tourist count by country of nationality — Recensement des touristes par pays de nationalité
1. — Ile de France only — Ile de France seulement

Table/Tableau 34

ARRIVALS AND NIGHTS OF FOREIGN TOURISTS AT/IN ALL MEANS OF ACCOMMODATION
ARRIVÉES ET NUITÉES DE TOURISTES ÉTRANGERS DANS L'ENSEMBLE DES MOYENS D'HÉBERGEMENT

From the United States
En provenance des États-Unis

1988=100

	AAA/NAA	Volume 1982	1983	1984	1985	1986	1987	Volume 1988	1989	1990	1991	1992	1993	Volume 1993	AEH/NEH	
Canada (R)	NAA	47 324 600	86.0	94.3	95.8	112.7	98.5	56 201 900	95.4	87.6	87.8	82.4	84.5	47 491 100	NEH	Canada (R)
	AAA	10 462 300	85.5	88.5	90.6	106.6	99.7	12 763 100	95.5	96.0	94.0	92.6	94.2	12 024 000	AEH	
Australia (R)	NAA													6 806 000	NEH	Australie (R)
New Zealand (R)	NAA			69.1	87.2	101.2	108.4	2 258 196	89.4	94.2	84.3	87.4	95.4	2 153 334	NEH	Nouvelle-Zélande (R)
	AAA													143 596	AEH	
Austria (R)	NAA	1 438 524	109.4	138.4	149.3	88.5	108.1	1 591 663	106.7	134.4	74.9	95.9	86.2	1 371 261	NEH	Autriche (R)
	AAA	535 365	110.8	150.2	159.3	82.2	108.3	620 078	109.0	142.8	75.6	101.2	87.3	541 570	AEH	
Belgium (R)	NAA	566 231	105.6	129.3	155.8	139.7	127.9	572 837	103.1	110.8	89.0	108.1	91.1	521 734	NEH	Belgique (R)
Denmark (N)	NAA	440 255	131.6	138.8	149.4	109.4	117.2	398 777	109.4	105.6	78.0	81.3	76.8	306 400	NEH	Danemark (N)
Finland (R)	AAA													88 995	AEH	Finlande (R)
France (R)	NAA	15 058 000	86.5	103.9	117.7	88.2	96.9	26 292 000	67.7	65.7	54.3	67.0	66.0	17 343 000	NEH	France (R)
	AAA	1 355 000	105.1	130.2	142.5	85.5	92.4	1 950 000	84.3	102.7	54.3	103.2	100.9	1 968 000	AEH	
Germany (R)	NAA	2 828 951	91.0	121.4	131.4	98.0	110.2	3 874 820	109.2	121.7	88.1	93.9	83.9	3 252 780	NEH	Allemagne (R)
	AAA	1 450 456	97.3	133.0	140.0	98.6	110.3	1 878 557	110.0	129.3	87.1	93.8	82.1	1 542 297	AEH	
Greece (N)	NAA	1 375 398	205.8	248.6	201.3	62.4	95.6	836 244							NEH	Grèce (N)
	AAA	529 374													AEH	
Ireland (R)	NAA	3 082 000	87.0	81.6	99.6	80.1	97.3	4 111 200	110.5	107.9	94.2	103.5	101.7	4 181 000	NEH	Irlande (R)
	AAA	290 000	74.3	82.6	101.8	89.1		385 000	100.0	104.4	83.4	97.1	97.7	376 000	AEH	
Italy (N)	NAA	4 949 304	122.6	140.7	149.3	81.9	103.7	4 923 551	105.0	85.2	80.3	100.3	109.6	5 394 040	NEH	Italie (N)
	AAA	1 759 087	113.5	137.4	151.1	68.0	98.2	1 992 582	101.1	75.5	74.7	96.7	101.6	2 024 735	AEH	
Luxembourg (R)	NAA	52 959	102.6	132.4	151.1	114.7	121.0	70 167	94.8	94.8	74.7	83.4			NEH	Luxembourg (R)
	AAA		105.7	138.5	162.2	123.0	130.2	38 428	96.9	96.9	71.7	77.3			AEH	
Netherlands (R)	NAA	912 860	115.6	139.5	140.4	102.0	102.0	830 800	109.5	123.2	101.6	113.6	105.4	875 700	NEH	Pays-Bas (R)
	AAA	462 897	116.7	144.9	145.1	99.3	99.3	433 000	105.0	117.2	94.6	104.2	97.7	423 000	AEH	
Portugal (N)	NAA	485 442	92.5	108.7	121.0	76.5	97.7	667 041	103.8	103.0	75.0	82.5	71.4	476 378	NEH	Portugal (N)
	AAA	174 729	94.4	111.5	121.0	72.2	96.8	245 967	105.7	105.3	77.7	84.4	77.0	189 447	AEH	
Spain (N)	NAA	1 966 187													NEH	Espagne (N)
	AAA	773 983													AEH	
Sweden (N)	NAA	307 161	120.1	127.1	147.1	100.3	107.2	339 886	102.3	100.7	74.3	82.8	87.5	297 556	NEH	Suède (N)
Switzerland (R)	NAA	2 309 600	114.7	145.6	155.8	102.1	112.8	2 280 122	108.7	122.5	79.1	93.4	90.3	2 059 489	NEH	Suisse (R)
	AAA	1 018 200	118.6	152.9	160.3	96.2	111.1	1 004 952	110.8	128.4	78.0	95.8	88.5	888 981	AEH	
Turkey (N)	NAA	150 790	60.0	80.3	84.2	69.2	85.1	321 917	120.8	111.0	89.3	122.2	157.1	505 813	NEH	Turquie (N)
	AAA	50 464	59.6	66.5	74.1	63.8	78.7	120 858	140.6	133.3	76.5	132.3	176.5	213 374	AEH	
United Kingdom (R)	NAA	19 186 000	90.6	104.5	122.3	96.4	113.4	25 520 000	108.2	110.2	97.7	105.5	108.1	27 587 000	NEH	Royaume-Uni (R)
	AAA														AEH	

AAA Arrivals in all means of accommodation
NAA Nights in all means of accommodation
(R) Tourist count by country of residence
(N) Tourist count by country of nationality

AEH Arrivées dans l'ensemble des moyens d'hébergement
NEH Nuitées dans l'ensemble des moyens d'hébergement
(R) Recensement des touristes par pays de résidence
(N) Recensement des touristes par pays de nationalité

Table/Tableau 35

ARRIVALS OF FOREIGN TOURISTS/VISITORS AT FRONTIERS
ARRIVÉES DE TOURISTES/VISITEURS ÉTRANGERS AUX FRONTIÈRES

From France
1988=100

En provenance de la France
1988=100

Country	T/V	Volume 1982	1983	1984	1985	1986	1987	Volume 1988	1989	1990	1991	1992	1993	Volume 1993	T/V	
Canada (R)	T	118 100	39.5	48.2	46.7	61.1	82.6	229 700	106.5	112.6	133.5	135.0	157.0	360 700	T	Canada (R)
	V	132 500	39.9	48.7	46.8	62.3	84.2	250 400	104.6	110.5	129.8	131.1	153.0	383 200	V	
United States (R)	T	423 379	49.3	53.5	54.3	71.1	88.0	618 439	105.7	115.8	124.5	128.6	136.6	844 644	T	États-Unis (R)
Australia (R)	V	10 248	47.6	53.3	57.1	66.2	81.4	21 000	95.7	100.5	108.1	121.0	147.6	31 000	V	Australie (R)
Japan (N)	T	29 605	71.2	84.3	98.1	87.3	91.9	40 455	116.8	126.1	123.9	120.1	121.6	49 178	T	Japon (N)
	V													21 861	V	
New Zealand (R)	T	1 828	56.1	64.5	70.7	77.1	110.9	3 437	118.5	99.8	135.1	154.9	169.6	5 830	T	Nouvelle-Zélande (R)
Greece (N)	T	335 366	63.9	86.5	94.1	99.9	108.7	469 000	101.9	120.6	100.4	115.6	118.3	554 644	T	Grèce (N)
Iceland (N)	T	4 429	63.9	78.9	73.0	91.5	86.5	6 141	133.3	163.2	164.0	129.1	122.5	7 522	T	Islande (N)
Ireland (R)	V	93 810	75.7	75.7	86.9	80.4	103.7	107 000	127.1	183.2	204.7	202.8	222.4	238 000	V	Irlande (R)
Italy (N)	V	8 476 179	87.9	94.3	97.0	95.5	100.7	8 975 273	104.6	102.7	101.6	98.0	92.0	8 254 589	V	Italie (N)
Norway (N)	V	29 138													V	Norvège (N)
Portugal (N)	T	279 415	55.8	55.3	56.6	60.2	73.2	565 440	108.0	109.3	118.0	114.6	96.6	546 000	T	Portugal (N)
	V	288 414	55.3	55.0	58.5	59.0	73.3	593 422	109.0	110.9	119.9	115.5	99.5	590 711	V	
Spain (N)	V	10 871 872	85.5	82.6	91.0	93.3	96.6	12 085 584	99.2	96.2	99.7	97.6	99.9	12 070 214	V	Espagne (N)
Turkey (N)	V	99 366	35.7	41.9	60.8	58.3	68.3	246 784	114.9	125.9	47.4	100.3	122.0	301 009	V	Turquie (N)
United Kingdom (R)	V													1 995 000	V	Royaume-Uni (R)
		1 518 500	77.0	82.8	82.3	89.2	102.0	1 969 500	114.8	116.6	116.3	126.1	127.6	2 513 000		

V	Visitors (travellers in Turkey)	Visiteurs (voyageurs en Turquie)
T	Tourists	Touristes
(R)	Tourist count by country of residence	Recensement des touristes par pays de résidence
(N)	Tourist count by country of nationality	Recensement des touristes par pays de nationalité

Table/Tableau 36

ARRIVALS AND NIGHTS OF FOREIGN TOURISTS AT/IN HOTELS
ARRIVÉES ET NUITÉES DE TOURISTES ÉTRANGERS DANS L'HÔTELLERIE

From France / En provenance de la France
1988=100

Country	AH/NH	Volume 1982	1983	1984	1985	1986	1987	Volume 1988	1989	1990	1991	1992	1993	Volume 1993	AH/NH	(French)
Australia (R)	NH	143 960	55.6	70.5	65.1	66.2		128 400							NH	Australie (R)
Japan (N)	NH	53 364													NH	Japon (N)
Japan (N)	AH														AH	Japon (N)
Austria (R)	NH	1 576 823	66.9	86.3	92.1	102.3	100.6	2 074 545	109.4	114.4	119.3	105.6	97.4	2 020 623	NH	Autriche (R)
Austria (R)	AH	455 110	70.2	89.1	93.9	102.6	99.0	560 006	110.8	117.1	119.0	103.0	94.7	530 126	AH	Autriche (R)
Belgium (R)	NH	569 032	73.5	80.6	87.8	90.2	92.2	657 214	119.3	125.4	125.9	153.6	153.3	1 007 518	NH	Belgique (R)
Denmark (N)	NH	89 900	95.3	106.7	111.1	101.1	101.2	75 800	104.2	108.8	112.4	107.1	110.7	83 900	NH	Danemark (N)
Finland (R)	NH	50 753	70.0	88.6	87.1	81.9	93.2	66 433	107.3	126.0	121.7	126.0	142.7	94 809	NH	Finlande (R)
Finland (R)	AH													55 390	AH	Finlande (R)
Germany (R)	NH	1 070 319	76.1	86.0	91.2	95.1	97.1	1 222 269	114.0	120.0	114.8	113.4	108.5	1 326 007	NH	Allemagne (R)
Germany (R)	AH	574 758	78.2	88.1	92.9	95.8	97.3	639 893	113.4	118.9	114.0	112.6	106.9	683 740	AH	Allemagne (R)
Greece (N)	NH	2 032 020	69.5	94.8	107.8	98.8	104.3	2 445 075							NH	Grèce (N)
Greece (N)	AH	682 807	76.8	105.2	111.4	105.7	107.8	722 049							AH	Grèce (N)
Iceland (N)	NH				80.5		79.0	15 841	164.2	174.9	208.0	167.6	163.1	25 842	NH	Islande (N)
Ireland (R)	NH				83.6		103.0	447 000		211.0	199.6	199.1	215.7	964 000	NH	Irlande (R)
Ireland (R)	AH							67 000		194.0	206.0	207.5	216.4	145 000	AH	Irlande (R)
Italy (N)	NH	5 886 342	86.3	91.4	95.1	101.1	103.8	5 530 553	105.1	92.2	92.2	82.5	84.7	4 684 913	NH	Italie (N)
Italy (N)	AH	1 791 932	81.6	90.6	92.0	96.5	100.4	1 795 569	114.9	95.4	95.4	88.3	90.9	1 631 733	AH	Italie (N)
Luxembourg (R)	NH	68 354	64.4	69.9	78.1	80.8	89.3	85 034	92.8	127.1	116.8	112.8			NH	Luxembourg (R)
Luxembourg (R)	AH	43 475	63.8	68.4	75.0	80.8	87.9	48 057	98.0	114.1	106.5	105.0			AH	Luxembourg (R)
Netherlands (R)	NH	443 407	77.5	88.9	90.4	100.2	103.4	444 800	104.5	122.7	111.4	123.6	105.4	468 900	NH	Pays-Bas (R)
Netherlands (R)	AH	249 831	77.5	90.3	85.0	99.3	102.4	257 700	100.5	118.1	100.8	111.7	95.9	247 100	AH	Pays-Bas (R)
Norway (N)	NH	89 491	61.4	85.3	90.8	91.5	99.7	119 897	116.7	142.4	173.8	202.2	223.1	267 487	NH	Norvège (N)
Portugal (N)	NH	583 942	69.6	88.1	78.6	101.1	91.6	740 838	107.9	111.4	132.3	105.9	96.9	717 623	NH	Portugal (N)
Portugal (N)	AH	187 846	60.4	75.9	84.2	89.4	90.5	280 101	106.1	110.7	125.1	107.8	98.4	275 583	AH	Portugal (N)
Spain (N)	NH	6 214 031	84.6	89.4	78.0	87.2	95.7	7 115 042	99.1	87.7	94.6	90.9	91.5	6 508 506	NH	Espagne (N)
Spain (N)	AH	1 386 126	80.3	79.7	92.9	90.2	96.9	1 728 250	101.0	108.1	91.6	85.7	87.3	1 508 506	AH	Espagne (N)
Sweden (N)	NH	84 292	80.4	91.6	103.5	97.1	92.7	90 889	105.8	98.5	101.8	101.9	104.8	95 208	NH	Suède (N)
Switzerland (R)	NH	1 737 594	96.7	103.4	104.5	108.8	103.4	1 558 541	101.2	104.1	99.2	92.5	89.4	1 393 278	NH	Suisse (R)
Switzerland (R)	AH	582 924	89.8	98.5		104.5	101.0	539 767	103.9	103.5	103.5	97.8	93.9	506 586	AH	Suisse (R)
Turkey (N)	NH	254 382	27.1	31.3	48.4	56.2	75.6	1 120 980	101.2	107.4	41.7	91.9	138.1	1 547 885	NH	Turquie (N)
Turkey (N)	AH	129 970	30.0	35.4	54.9	63.7	83.9	542 400	120.9	116.5	33.9	80.1	113.4	614 975	AH	Turquie (N)

AH Arrivals at hotels and similar establishments
NH Nights in hotels and similar establishments
(R) Tourist count by country of residence
(N) Tourist count by country of nationality

AH Arrivées dans les hôtels et les établissements assimilés
NH Nuitées dans les hôtels et établissements assimilés
(R) Recensement des touristes par pays de résidence
(N) Recensement des touristes par pays de nationalité

Table/Tableau 37

ARRIVALS AND NIGHTS OF FOREIGN TOURISTS AT/IN ALL MEANS OF ACCOMMODATION
ARRIVÉES ET NUITÉES DE TOURISTES ÉTRANGERS DANS L'ENSEMBLE DES MOYENS D'HÉBERGEMENT

From France — 1988=100
En provenance de la France — 1988=100

	AAA/NAA	Volume 1982	1983	1984	1985	1986	1987	Volume 1988	1989	1990	1991	1992	1993	Volume 1993	AEH/NEH	
Canada (R)	NAA	1 510 200	42.5	49.9	48.3	63.6	81.7	2 841 800	102.8	108.1	133.4	134.4	150.4	4 273 400	NEH	Canada (R)
	AAA	118 100	39.5	48.2	46.7	61.1	81.7	229 700	105.7	112.6	133.5	135.0	157.0	360 700	AEH	
Australia (R)	NAA													132 927	NEH	Australie (R)
New Zealand (R)	NAA													5 830	NEH	Nouvelle-Zélande (R)
	AAA														AEH	
Austria (R)	NAA	2 150 667	69.2	89.1	93.5	101.9	100.6	2 651 607	109.3	116.0	119.5	107.3	99.4	2 636 429	NEH	Autriche (R)
	AAA	590 168	70.1	91.1	94.8	103.1	98.8	701 455	111.0	119.4	120.5	105.2	96.6	677 626	AEH	
Belgium (R)	NAA	1 005 085	88.6	94.6	93.5	96.2	96.2	1 010 799	119.7	124.9	120.0	129.4	131.6	1 329 829	NEH	Belgique (R)
Denmark (N)	NAA	154 108	82.0	107.6	103.6	94.7	98.7	138 810	103.1	106.9	109.7	108.3	102.7	142 600	NEH	Danemark (N)
Finland (R)	AAA													67 474	AEH	Finlande (R)
Germany (R)	NAA	1 126 622	66.9	82.5	88.2	91.7	95.2	1 466 820	113.0	119.5	124.1	123.0	115.5	1 694 449	NEH	Allemagne (R)
	AAA	583 716	71.2	86.5	91.2	94.2	96.3	714 545	113.1	118.9	123.1	121.8	114.1	815 212	AEH	
Greece (N)	NAA	2 536 954	81.5	107.1	107.8	99.5	105.2	2 594 230							NEH	Grèce (N)
	AAA	815 038													AEH	
Ireland (R)	NAA	1 096 000	68.8	55.4	69.7	66.9	92.7	1 566 300	137.8	199.2	193.4	212.2	207.5	3 250 000	NEH	Irlande (R)
	AAA	93 000	73.0	78.4	85.6	81.1		111 000	124.3	178.4	198.2	198.2	218.0	242 000	AEH	
Italy (N)	NAA	8 413 204	98.5	102.6	105.8	111.0	104.7	6 838 470	92.2	96.8	91.5	81.5	83.4	5 703 287	NEH	Italie (N)
	AAA	2 152 289	84.4	93.3	95.1	98.9	100.9	2 085 589	97.5	95.6	94.2	86.4	88.4	1 844 590	AEH	
Luxembourg (R)	NAA	86 797	61.8	76.1	80.1	81.4	88.3	108 482	123.0	115.5	120.8	112.0			NEH	Luxembourg (R)
	AAA		60.7	72.8	76.6	81.1	86.8	55 450	109.4	123.0	109.4	106.2			AEH	
Netherlands (R)	NAA	617 116	79.4	94.2	91.6	94.3		618 700	108.7	128.6	123.4	127.9	109.0	674 500	NEH	Pays-Bas (R)
	AAA	343 568	76.0	89.9	87.8	91.2		363 500	96.1	112.4	102.0	108.9	91.9	333 900	AEH	
Portugal (N)	NAA	1 084 823	74.7	79.6	81.6	94.8	90.5	1 254 330	106.0	105.0	118.4	95.3	90.0	1 129 071	NEH	Portugal (N)
	AAA	319 187	61.7	72.0	73.7	90.3	92.0	457 459	105.5	107.6	117.0	100.4	93.8	429 079	AEH	
Spain (N)	NAA	7 117 715													NEH	Espagne (N)
	AAA	1 527 796													AEH	
Sweden (N)	NAA	145 302	78.5	99.6	94.3	103.6	97.0	151 345	110.1	120.5	108.8	110.4	101.9	154 235	NEH	Suède (N)
Switzerland (R)	NAA	2 901 100	97.8	100.2	100.6	106.9	104.6	2 491 589	99.2	98.0	100.1	93.7	92.3	2 298 802	NEH	Suisse (R)
	AAA	776 600	89.3	97.4	97.0	103.8	100.8	719 238	102.8	104.4	104.7	99.3	95.7	688 006	AEH	
Turkey (N)	NAA	288 855	24.4	28.0	42.8	54.1	71.4	1 529 027	96.6	103.7	41.3	94.7	124.4	1 902 332	NEH	Turquie (N)
	AAA	134 382	28.9	33.9	53.2	62.7	82.7	594 487	119.4	116.8	34.7	81.9	112.5	668 665	AEH	
United Kingdom (R)	NAA	11 171 000	80.3	92.9	91.1	86.9	119.0	14 045 000	115.5	120.5	105.3	106.1	105.6	14 827 000	NEH	Royaume-Uni (R)
	AAA														AEH	

AAA Arrivals in all means of accommodation
NAA Nights in all means of accommodation
(R) Tourist count by country of residence
(N) Tourist count by country of nationality

AEH Arrivées dans l'ensemble des moyens d'hébergement
NEH Nuitées dans l'ensemble des moyens d'hébergement
(R) Recensement des touristes par pays de résidence
(N) Recensement des touristes par pays de nationalité

Table/Tableau 38

ARRIVALS OF FOREIGN TOURISTS/VISITORS AT FRONTIERS
ARRIVÉES DE TOURISTES/VISITEURS ÉTRANGERS AUX FRONTIÈRES

From Italy
1988=100

En provenance de l'Italie
1988=100

	T/V	Volume 1982	1983	1984	1985	1986	1987	Volume 1988	1989	1990	1991	1992	1993	Volume 1993	T/V	
Canada (R)	T	47 100	53.0	61.6	64.0	75.6	89.3	86 300	107.5	105.3	101.2	109.8	111.9	96 600	T	Canada (R)
	V	62 200	53.5	61.0	60.6	74.8	96.2	107 600	99.8	94.0	92.9	103.3	103.3	111 000	V	
United States (R)	T	232 446	55.7	61.3	61.8	75.2	89.4	356 528	99.5	111.1	134.3	165.4	155.9	555 785	T	États-Unis (R)
Australia (R)	V	12 092	47.6	53.2	57.5	68.7	76.6	25 200	81.3	96.8	96.4	108.7	125.4	31 600	V	Australie (R)
Japan (N)	T													10 883	T	Japon (N)
New Zealand (R)	V	13 690	60.7	66.9	92.0	80.2	89.0	23 462	117.9	127.0	128.7	114.5	107.8	25 283	V	Nouvelle-Zélande (R)
	T	916	30.7	34.0	44.8	60.8	92.8	2 815	93.4	112.0	127.2	133.8	145.4	4 092	T	
France (R)	T	2 000 000	63.7	73.9	76.9	81.3	91.7	3 441 000	152.3	164.4	171.4	210.1	188.1	6 473 000	T	France (R)
	V														V	
Greece (N)	T	223 922	60.2	60.4	66.9	80.9	85.5	544 000	104.6	114.1	95.1	114.5	115.0	625 509	T	Grèce (N)
Iceland (N)	T	903	37.3	36.7	41.5	75.1	95.6	2 822	105.6	128.1	170.4	147.3	128.2	3 617	T	Islande (N)
Norway (N)	V	6 830													V	Norvège (N)
Portugal (N)	T	54 543	38.9	42.8	59.6	65.3	86.7	138 798	120.4	136.5	180.5	186.2	169.7	235 500	T	Portugal (N)
	V	72 492	42.7	46.4	60.4	70.2	86.9	154 684	119.7	142.9	188.1	183.0	171.5	265 263	V	
Spain (N)	T	657 766	50.2	61.1	76.7	81.8	89.5	1 333 055	113.4	124.3	132.6	139.0	151.4	1 828 766	T	Espagne (N)
	V													2 018 506	V	
Turkey (N)	V	44 560	39.9	45.6	51.8	60.7	70.9	144 322	106.8	108.3	44.4	109.6	93.3	134 669	V	Turquie (N)
United Kingdom (R)	V	397 700	69.3	71.9	74.8	74.7	103.3	660 900	107.1	107.9	109.2	118.6	120.0	793 000	V	Royaume-Uni (R)

V   Visitors (travellers in Turkey)
T   Tourists
(R)   Tourist count by country of residence
(N)   Tourist count by country of nationality

V   Visiteurs (voyageurs en Turquie)
T   Touristes
(R)   Recensement des touristes par pays de résidence
(N)   Recensement des touristes par pays de nationalité

Table/Tableau 39

ARRIVALS AND NIGHTS OF FOREIGN TOURISTS AT/IN HOTELS
ARRIVÉES ET NUITÉES DE TOURISTES ÉTRANGERS DANS L'HÔTELLERIE

From Italy — En provenance de l'Italie
1988=100

Country	AH/NH	Volume 1982	1983	1984	1985	1986	1987	Volume 1988	1989	1990	1991	1992	1993	Volume 1993
Australia (R) / Australie (R)	NH	71 271												
Japan (N) / Japon (N)	NH	23 578												
	AH		25.1	37.8	49.2	68.7	76.6	189 900						
Austria (R) / Autriche (R)	NH	785 305	46.0	55.2	58.8	71.6	79.3	1 844 312	132.3	145.8	152.2	164.7	123.9	2 285 194
	AH	350 708	47.9	57.5	60.3	73.2	80.8	784 077	126.8	136.0	133.2	137.0	106.9	838 092
Belgium (R) / Belgique (R)	NH	185 070	74.9	78.4	82.6	81.8	90.0	266 212	120.9	129.4	127.4	147.5	128.3	341 618
Denmark (N) / Danemark (N)	NH	84 200	79.0	78.2	75.6	75.5	85.3	103 900	104.7	122.3	137.0	151.8	123.0	127 800
Finland (R) / Finlande (R)	NH	37 803	48.5	54.9	57.5	61.8	82.2	81 838	106.2	96.9	100.0	93.5	93.9	76 861
	AH													44 252
France (R)[1] / France (R)[1]	NH	1 248 568	24.4	26.0	25.4	68.8	75.2	5 260 731	129.5	133.2	133.1	159.3	134.3	7 067 733
	AH	448 180	20.2	21.7	22.2	73.3	80.2	2 201 293	134.4	141.4	142.5	169.1	141.7	3 119 247
Germany (R) / Allemagne (R)	NH	833 763	65.6	71.9	75.6	82.7	88.4	1 330 648	118.4	126.9	130.5	127.5	104.8	1 394 018
	AH	433 279	65.0	71.6	75.4	81.5	87.8	695 591	117.7	126.2	129.2	124.5	99.8	693 898
Greece (N) / Grèce (N)	NH	907 684	59.8	68.2	83.8	81.6	84.0	1 649 934						
	AH	304 760	70.1	78.1	88.9	87.3	100.4	497 727						
Ireland (R) / Irlande (R)	NH	13 983												596 000
	AH	8 297												78 000
Luxembourg (R) / Luxembourg (R)	NH													
	AH													
Netherlands (R) / Pays-Bas (R)	NH	211 083	53.1	58.7	61.6	74.4	86.1	361 600	113.7	168.6	148.9	143.0	112.9	408 200
	AH	94 604	54.3	61.1	66.1	76.1	86.5	164 900	126.7	181.4	149.7	148.1	124.0	204 400
Norway (N) / Norvège (N)	NH													129 071
Portugal (N) / Portugal (N)	NH	147 967	43.1	48.1	60.6	70.2	86.6	350 827	108.0	131.1	170.7	163.3	138.3	485 141
	AH	52 434	42.6	47.7	60.1	70.3	88.0	134 794	109.3	130.1	172.4	172.4	148.3	199 837
Spain (N) / Espagne (N)	NH	1 821 841	51.0	77.1	88.0	83.7	92.7	4 650 705	98.6	92.0	99.6	113.3	122.5	5 697 259
	AH	565 951	60.7	84.6	94.6	98.2	96.5	1 125 665	106.4	93.8	99.3	99.0	101.4	1 141 264
Sweden (N) / Suède (N)	NH	65 657	65.4	73.1	79.3	82.3	99.9	95 907	122.9	128.7	123.4	120.6	113.2	108 575
Switzerland (R) / Suisse (R)	NH	866 027	76.7	81.3	83.2	89.1	94.6	1 096 670	115.6	124.5	128.4	127.4	98.7	1 082 949
	AH	419 113	77.9	82.7	84.7	90.9	95.5	535 132	114.8	119.1	123.2	121.7	95.0	508 403
Turkey (N) / Turquie (N)	NH	105 876	45.5	48.6	55.5	61.3	80.3	391 230	96.8	102.5	74.9	129.8	105.1	411 303
	AH	50 002	43.7	47.8	56.7	61.1	81.5	187 249	105.5	110.7	61.5	116.0	92.1	172 484

AH   Arrivals at hotels and similar establishments
NH   Nights in hotels and similar establishments
(R)   Tourist count by country of residence
(N)   Tourist count by country of nationality

AH   Arrivées dans les hôtels et les établissements assimilés
NH   Nuitées dans les hôtels et établissements assimilés
(R)   Recensement des touristes par pays de résidence
(N)   Recensement des touristes par pays de nationalité

Table/Tableau 40

ARRIVALS AND NIGHTS OF FOREIGN TOURISTS AT/IN ALL MEANS OF ACCOMMODATION
ARRIVÉES ET NUITÉES DE TOURISTES ÉTRANGERS DANS L'ENSEMBLE DES MOYENS D'HÉBERGEMENT

From Italy
1988=100

En provenance de l'Italie
1988=100

Country	AAA/NAA	Volume 1982	1983	1984	1985	1986	1987	Volume 1988	1989	1990	1991	1992	1993	Volume 1993	AEH/NEH	
Canada (R)	NAA	734 300	50.7	68.3	70.6	78.1	93.4	1 070 600	94.0	83.6	83.0	84.7	92.6	991 300	NEH	Canada (R)
Australia (R)	NAA		30.2	30.1	32.6	68.7	76.6	439 900						72 498	NEH	Australie (R)
New Zealand (R)	NAA													4 092	NEH	Nouvelle-Zélande (R)
	AAA														AEH	
Austria (R)	NAA	928 790	50.3	59.6	60.5	72.6	80.9	2 091 245	133.3	147.8	158.2	172.6	133.1	2 783 211	NEH	Autriche (R)
Belgium (R)	AAA	398 093	50.1	62.4	61.7	74.0	81.7	866 122	127.2	136.8	137.0	140.8	111.2	962 753	AEH	Belgique (R)
Denmark (N)	NAA	212 985	74.9	78.7	82.1	81.4	88.6	304 331	118.7	127.3	123.0	141.3	123.2	374 917	NEH	Danemark (N)
Finland (R)	NAA	118 666	78.8	78.2	78.7	76.7	89.8	153 449	108.6	122.3	142.7	152.0	119.6	183 600	NEH	Finlande (R)
	AAA													86 527	AEH	
France (R)	NAA	16 888 000	64.1	71.8	73.5	82.1	94.5	28 200 990	103.8	108.1	125.4	151.6	134.0	37 790 000	NEH	France (R)
	AAA	2 000 000	63.7	73.9	76.9	81.3	91.7	3 441 000	117.8	164.4	171.4	210.1	188.1	6 473 000	AEH	
Germany (R)	NAA	851 333	62.9	70.6	74.9	82.4	88.2	1 413 465	126.1	126.1	137.4	134.2	109.6	1 549 361	NEH	Allemagne (R)
	AAA	435 793	62.7	70.8	74.8	81.3	87.8	724 486	117.3	125.9	136.9	131.9	104.5	757 367	AEH	
Greece (N)	NAA	1 155 783	68.0	82.0	87.7	84.6	98.0	1 792 673						1 800 000	NEH	Grèce (N)
	AAA	383 310	79.0	87.4	92.8	90.4	65.4	548 002							AEH	
Ireland (R)	NAA							21 000	176.2	347.6	457.1	481.0	552.4	116 000	NEH	Irlande (R)
Luxembourg (R)	NAA	15 944												50 497	NEH	Luxembourg (R)
Netherlands (R)	NAA	276 528	58.0	64.5	64.4	72.4		462 200	115.5	166.1	149.7	139.4	110.1	509 100	NEH	Pays-Bas (R)
	AAA	125 416	57.6	65.6	68.2	73.5		213 800	121.3	170.0	144.7	141.2	114.6	245 000	AEH	
Portugal (N)	NAA	215 324	46.4	47.4	63.0	75.4	87.2	426 693	108.7	125.5	166.2	151.4	130.0	554 829	NEH	Portugal (N)
	AAA	65 727	44.1	47.2	63.0	75.6	88.9	161 651	110.1	125.8	167.3	161.2	140.8	227 565	AEH	
Spain (N)	NAA	1 821 841	62.8	71.1	75.3	79.5	98.1		123.2	127.8	121.7	118.1	107.3		NEH	Espagne (N)
	AAA	565 951													AEH	
Sweden (N)	NAA	71 375	75.2	79.5	81.0	87.2	93.0	110 245	114.0	125.5	130.5	132.6	110.1	118 338	NEH	Suède (N)
Switzerland (R)	NAA	1 136 900	77.5	82.5	84.6	90.9	95.0	1 515 685	113.6	119.3	123.8	122.9	99.0	1 669 470	NEH	Suisse (R)
	AAA	481 900						626 569						620 005	AEH	
Turkey (N)	NAA	108 997	38.8	42.0	48.0	53.7	77.0	491 999	99.6	108.5	74.6	130.5	102.2	502 666	NEH	Turquie (N)
	AAA	50 442	39.0	43.1	50.9	54.8	80.7	213 460	105.6	110.2	58.5	109.6	86.5	184 564	AEH	
United Kingdom (R)	NAA	5 225 000	74.8	73.0	81.9	72.0	108.6	8 507 000	97.3	98.3	106.7	104.1	103.5	8 802 000	NEH	Royaume-Uni (R)

AAA Arrivals in all means of accommodation
NAA Nights in all means of accommodation
(R) Tourist count by country of residence
(N) Tourist count by country of nationality

AEH Arrivées dans l'ensemble des moyens d'hébergement
NEH Nuitées dans l'ensemble des moyens d'hébergement
(R) Recensement des touristes par pays de résidence
(N) Recensement des touristes par pays de nationalité

Table/Tableau 41

ARRIVALS OF FOREIGN TOURISTS/VISITORS AT FRONTIERS
ARRIVÉES DE TOURISTES/VISITEURS ÉTRANGERS AUX FRONTIÈRES

From Japan — 1988=100 · En provenance du Japon — 1988=100

	T/V	Volume 1982	1983	1984	1985	1986	1987	Volume 1988	1989	1990	1991	1992	1993	Volume 1993	T/V	
Canada (R)	T	114 900	36.0	41.7	45.0	60.8	76.9	324 100	120.2	126.7	121.3	121.0	126.0	408 500	T	Canada (R)
	V	139 500	34.3	40.1	43.1	58.1	77.0	404 600	114.4	117.2	118.7	122.5	125.0	505 800	V	
United States (R)	T	1 436 238	50.6	55.8	59.0	66.3	84.0	2 534 084	121.6	127.5	131.0	144.1	139.8	3 542 546	T	États-Unis (R)
Australia (R)	V	60 389	20.4	25.0	30.5	41.3	61.2	352 300	99.2	136.2	150.0	178.8	190.4	670 800	V	Australie (R)
New Zealand (R)	T	27 333	34.6	44.7	53.6	66.8	81.2	93 789	103.8	115.0	122.3	137.5	144.9	135 934	T	Nouvelle-Zélande (R)
France (R)	T			77.0	79.8	76.7	86.4	662 000	116.5	113.3	63.7	67.8	49.1	325 000	T	France (R)
	V														V	
Greece (N)	T	74 802	78.1	82.4	88.4	81.0	87.6	105 000	99.0	102.6	55.1	104.5	85.6	89 907	T	Grèce (N)
Iceland (N)	T	386	45.6	54.3	72.1	86.3	100.7	993	126.3	117.2	126.3	144.1	184.2	1 829	T	Islande (N)
Ireland (R)	V													18 000	V	Irlande (R)
Italy (N)	V	303 485	85.0	88.4	87.1	104.3	100.0	384 850	118.7	165.5	145.4	192.8	190.2	731 880	V	Italie (N)
Norway (N)	V	8 294	46.6	57.1	65.3	78.1	97.8	28 189	106.8	115.9	94.3	90.7	115.3	32 500	V	Norvège (N)
Portugal (N)	T	11 767	48.4	65.8	67.4	78.4	96.4	29 661	108.3	119.5	95.8	91.8	115.4	34 229	T	Portugal (N)
	V	13 835													V	
Spain (N)	V	80 228	55.8	63.8	74.4	71.1	76.6	170 281	127.2	143.2	109.5	130.5	141.1	240 260	V	Espagne (N)
Turkey (N)	V	6 275	27.8	46.6	60.0	59.8	75.2	28 008	115.3	126.2	66.0	130.0	168.9	47 317	V	Turquie (N)
United Kingdom (R)	V	159 500	43.9	51.7	54.3	52.9	76.6	388 200	130.0	145.0	118.0	142.7	126.5	491 000	V	Royaume-Uni (R)

V   Visitors (travellers in Austria, Germany and Turkey)
T   Tourists
(R)   Tourist count by country of residence
(N)   Tourist count by country of nationality
1.   Estimates

V   Visiteurs (voyageurs en Allemagne, en Autriche et en Turquie)
T   Touristes
(R)   Recensement des touristes par pays de résidence
(N)   Recensement des touristes par pays de nationalité
1.   Estimations

Table/Tableau 42

ARRIVALS AND NIGHTS OF FOREIGN TOURISTS AT/IN HOTELS
ARRIVÉES ET NUITÉES DE TOURISTES ÉTRANGERS DANS L'HÔTELLERIE

From Japan — 1988=100 / En provenance du Japon — 1988=100

	AH/NH	Volume 1982	1983	1984	1985	1986	1987	Volume 1988	1989	1990	1991	1992	1993	Volume 1993	AH/NH	
Australia (R)	NH		21.5	31.1	36.2	41.3	61.2	1 754 500	107.7	144.9	152.5	180.0	194.2	3 407 000	NH	Australie (R)
Austria (R)	NH	166 088	56.7	61.7	73.0	71.8	96.2	320 548	115.6	146.2	128.9	141.4	137.6	441 187	NH	Autriche (R)
	AH	84 051	54.6	64.0	75.6	71.3	98.1	166 215	115.5	141.8	114.4	132.0	127.5	211 996	AH	
Belgium (R)	NH	79 160	60.0	70.6	78.1	79.1	88.3	120 540	138.9	128.7	127.1	190.4	158.3	190 823	NH	Belgique (R)
Denmark (N)	NH	74 300	76.2	73.8	72.4	65.1	77.0	107 700	109.0	100.3	86.7	103.0	92.9	100 000	NH	Danemark (N)
Finland (R)	NH	24 070	66.0	75.1	79.2	69.1	92.0	55 766	109.1	114.2	102.7	102.5	128.3	71 522	NH	Finlande (R)
	AH													41 863	AH	
France (R)[1]	NH	1 123 107	67.1	62.9	60.4	70.0	80.2	1 706 111	168.4	156.8	128.4	205.3	192.4	3 283 295	NH	France (R)[1]
	AH	469 581	59.1	57.9	60.8	70.2	79.1	774 039	162.4	163.4	131.4	200.4	194.7	1 506 951	AH	
Germany (R)	NH	630 280	63.2	68.9	81.8	83.1	93.1	1 009 960	120.4	130.9	110.1	118.3	108.9	1 099 530	NH	Allemagne (R)
	AH	347 547	59.1	66.4	79.2	80.0	95.1	598 784	122.9	134.5	106.8	119.3	109.8	657 742	AH	
Greece (N)	NH	215 179	84.0	90.8	98.4	79.3	91.2	261 343							NH	Grèce (N)
	AH	88 298	76.8	82.3	92.8	76.7	88.1	119 831							AH	
Italy (N)	NH	540 817	50.3	51.5	50.7	57.0	81.9	1 149 702	125.2	136.7	119.0	161.2	180.8	2 078 561	NH	Italie (N)
	AH	249 151	45.9	49.3	48.5	56.4	82.7	572 236	123.6	132.6	114.9	158.3	180.0	1 030 209	AH	
Luxembourg (R)	NH														NH	Luxembourg (R)
	AH														AH	
Netherlands (R)	NH	149 287	83.2	79.0	95.7	97.3	92.9	160 100	101.6	116.1	108.9	137.1	110.9	177 600	NH	Pays-Bas (R)
	AH	77 208	78.9	84.4	91.8	87.8	94.4	83 900	100.6	114.2	104.1	133.1	106.7	89 500	AH	
Norway (N)	NH	41 622	79.4	94.4	96.5	69.0	112.6	66 715	120.1	126.7	127.4	149.7	181.2	120 868	NH	Norvège (N)
Portugal (N)	NH	33 096	50.0	69.3	68.7	73.7	89.6	72 195	101.5	106.4	100.7	103.5	141.9	102 419	NH	Portugal (N)
	AH	13 741	49.2	71.2	71.5	76.0	94.2	32 309	102.7	105.8	98.7	107.3	153.6	49 639	AH	
Spain (N)	NH	308 430	49.0	53.0	61.1	66.0	92.4	639 230	134.1	137.3	96.5	111.1	91.8	586 836	NH	Espagne (N)
	AH	135 128	40.1	47.9	57.6	65.2	91.9	356 506	132.3	139.7	95.9	104.0	91.3	325 493	AH	
Sweden (N)	NH	55 680	70.2	78.7	77.8	71.9	83.7	74 298	109.8	127.0	113.2	109.7	130.9	97 261	NH	Suède (N)
Switzerland (R)	NH	450 148	74.5	76.1	79.0	82.2	95.6	652 954	119.8	125.1	111.0	124.9	122.2	797 828	NH	Suisse (R)
	AH	244 432	67.3	70.6	74.1	78.8	92.8	397 739	118.7	125.1	104.3	126.4	122.8	488 594	AH	
Turkey (N)	NH	32 652	40.2	38.2	61.2	76.2	84.0	117 035	115.1	114.7	77.7	183.3	185.1	216 589	NH	Turquie (N)
	AH	13 933	36.2	35.0	52.3	68.3	82.7	63 043	117.6	122.2	78.7	195.7	217.6	137 162	AH	

AH Arrivals at hotels and similar establishments — Arrivées dans les hôtels et les établissements assimilés
NH Nights in hotels and similar establishments — Nuitées dans les hôtels et établissements assimilés
(R) Tourist count by country of residence — Recensement des touristes par pays de résidence
(N) Tourist count by country of nationality — Recensement des touristes par pays de nationalité
1. Ile de France only — Ile de France seulement

Table/Tableau 43

ARRIVALS AND NIGHTS OF FOREIGN TOURISTS AT/IN ALL MEANS OF ACCOMMODATION
ARRIVÉES ET NUITÉES DE TOURISTES ÉTRANGERS DANS L'ENSEMBLE DES MOYENS D'HÉBERGEMENT

From Japan / *En provenance du Japon*
1988=100

	AAA/NAA	Volume 1982	1983	1984	1985	1986	1987	Volume 1988	1989	1990	1991	1992	1993	Volume 1993	AEH/NEH	
Canada (R)	NAA	857 200	33.2	45.5	41.7	68.5	79.0	2 229 000	113.9	110.0	118.3	112.0	129.2	2 879 300	NEH	Canada (R)
Australia (R)	NAA		21.5	28.0	39.6	41.3	61.2	2 314 700	185.6	252.1	184.1	183.5	186.1	4 307 000	NEH	Australie (R)
New Zealand (R)	NAA													1 699 407	NEH	Nouvelle-Zélande (R)
	AAA													135 934	AEH	
Austria (R)	NAA	166 088	56.7	61.7	73.0	71.8	96.2	320 548	115.6	146.2	128.9	141.4	137.6	441 187	NEH	Autriche (R)
	AAA	84 051	54.6	64.0	75.6	71.3	98.1	166 215	115.5	141.8	114.4	132.0	127.5	211 996	AEH	
Belgium (R)	NAA	80 959	59.7	70.7	78.3	78.9	87.9	125 375	138.1	129.4	126.0	186.1	155.3	194 675	NEH	Belgique (R)
Denmark (N)	NAA							107 700	109.0	100.3	86.7	103.0	92.9	100 000	NEH	Danemark (N)
Finland (R)	NAA													71 846	NEH	Finlande (R)
	AAA													42 032	AEH	
France (R)	NAA	634 172	61.1	113.7	117.1	116.5	134.0	3 170 000	141.8	88.2	62.3	63.8	44.3	1 405 000	NEH	France (R)
	AAA			77.0	79.8	76.7	86.4	662 000		113.3	63.7	67.8	49.1	325 000	AEH	
Germany (R)	NAA	348 346	57.0	68.5	80.9	82.3	92.6	1 054 941	119.9	130.9	109.9	118.7	109.6	1 156 533	NEH	Allemagne (R)
	AAA	222 309	85.3	65.9	78.5	79.4	94.5	622 770	122.4	135.1	107.0	119.9	110.0	684 856	AEH	
Greece (N)	NAA	90 490	77.7	92.0	98.5	79.4	91.2	261 527	124.3	136.0	119.0	160.7			NEH	Grèce (N)
	AAA			83.5	92.8	76.7	88.1	119 921	123.3	132.5	114.9	158.0			AEH	
Ireland (R)	AAA													18 000	NEH	Irlande (R)
Italy (N)	NAA	587 458	52.0	53.4	52.8	59.8	82.2	1 189 552	101.6	117.3	109.0	138.4	181.6	2 160 524	NEH	Italie (N)
	AAA	254 608	46.0	49.5	48.9	56.9	82.8	583 158	99.4	113.9	103.4	132.5	179.5	1 047 006	AEH	
Luxembourg (R)	NAA														NEH	Luxembourg (R)
	AAA														AEH	
Netherlands (R)	NAA	153 729	84.7	80.3	95.8	90.3		165 000	101.3	107.5	100.5	102.4	111.4	183 800	NEH	Pays-Bas (R)
	AAA	80 381	79.2	85.1	91.7	81.5		87 600	101.9	106.8	98.1	105.8	105.5	92 400	AEH	
Portugal (N)	NAA	34 489	50.2	68.9	68.6	73.2	89.0	73 801					141.6	104 518	NEH	Portugal (N)
	AAA	14 183	49.1	70.5	70.8	75.1	93.0	33 190					152.3	50 532	AEH	
Spain (N)	NAA	308 430													NEH	Espagne (N)
	AAA	135 128													AEH	
Sweden (N)	NAA	57 011	71.0	78.6	78.3	71.4	84.0	76 564	109.5	126.9	117.3	112.2	131.3	100 560	NEH	Suède (N)
Switzerland (R)	NAA	467 700	74.2	76.0	79.2	82.7	95.9	679 601	119.7	125.1	111.1	124.8	121.7	827 153	NEH	Suisse (R)
	AAA	253 100	67.1	70.6	74.3	79.0	92.7	412 924	118.6	124.8	104.0	125.8	121.9	503 537	AEH	
Turkey (N)	NAA	32 760	40.1	38.3	61.2	76.1	85.3	117 549	115.1	114.9	77.5	182.7	186.4	219 055	NEH	Turquie (N)
	AAA	13 970	36.2	35.0	52.4	68.4	83.9	63 212	117.7	122.5	78.6	195.4	220.1	139 146	AEH	
United Kingdom (R)	NAA	1 099 000	33.5	52.1	81.5	59.6	79.2	2 944 000	111.8	132.4	143.2	143.0	138.4	4 075 000	NEH	Royaume-Uni (R)

AAA Arrivals in all means of accommodation
NAA Nights in all means of accommodation
(R) Tourist count by country of residence
(N) Tourist count by country of nationality

AEH Arrivées dans l'ensemble des moyens d'hébergement
NEH Nuitées dans l'ensemble des moyens d'hébergement
(R) Recensement des touristes par pays de résidence
(N) Recensement des touristes par pays de nationalité

129

ARRIVALS OF FOREIGN TOURISTS/VISITORS AT FRONTIERS
ARRIVÉES DE TOURISTES/VISITEURS ÉTRANGERS AUX FRONTIÈRES

From the Netherlands
1988=100

En provenance des Pays-Bas
1988=100

	T/V	Volume 1982	1983	1984	1985	1986	1987	Volume 1988	1989	1990	1991	1992	1993	Volume 1993	T/V	
Canada (R)	T	71 600	71.9	69.1	66.4	78.0	88.5	88 000	101.9	96.5	99.7	96.8	95.7	84 200	T	Canada (R)
	V	79 200	69.8	67.5	64.6	76.5	89.5	98 900	97.9	94.3	96.3	93.1	92.3	91 300	V	
United States (R)	T	189 846	58.5	54.1	53.0	65.7	81.4	247 843	105.2	114.6	127.7	138.0	152.9	378 904	T	États-Unis (R)
Australia (R)	V	16 758	66.5	62.9	68.7	71.0	77.2	22 400	89.7	94.2	95.5	104.9	122.8	27 500	V	Australie (R)
Japan (N)	T	11 456	80.8	89.3	97.2	91.4	100.3	15 852	103.7	110.9	113.8	115.1	112.7	17 872	T	Japon (N)
New Zealand (R)	V	5 147	68.3	73.1	76.6	81.9	89.5	7 063	100.9	110.2	107.4	137.8	152.2	10 750	T	Nouvelle-Zélande (R)
	V													6 746		
France (R)	T	3 888 000	94.0	93.1	90.3	99.1	97.3	4 047 000	98.5	98.7	146.6	155.6	176.5	7 141 000	T	France (R)
	V														V	
Greece (N)	T	139 286	39.5	49.6	72.1	84.8	88.7	389 000	110.0	127.4	115.7	140.4	131.3	510 872	T	Grèce (N)
Iceland (N)	T	1 707	53.2	56.9	58.4	81.5	85.4	2 832	88.8	105.7	104.2	134.5	187.6	5 314	T	Islande (N)
Italy (N)	V	1 774 385	94.6	97.8	92.1	96.7	77.0	1 802 684	102.1	117.7	85.1	66.9	59.0	1 063 798	V	Italie (N)
Norway (N)	V	38 021													V	Norvège (N)
Portugal (N)	T	114 119	53.1	51.8	55.0	59.3	74.5	275 420	115.0	108.5	118.2	122.5	119.1	327 900	T	Portugal (N)
	V	124 745	54.8	53.3	57.4	60.2	75.1	285 199	116.7	115.5	126.4	128.6	129.4	369 014		
Spain (N)	V	1 355 536	65.6	69.1	70.7	77.7	84.0	2 004 455	101.5	97.5	107.6	105.6	102.9	2 062 024	T	Espagne (N)
	V													1 800 147		
Turkey (N)	V	22 271	32.4	33.4	38.5	48.7	61.6	81 039	131.7	185.5	132.1	252.7	266.8	216 182	V	Turquie (N)
United Kingdom (R)	V	701 400	83.4	84.1	86.5	87.3	97.1	880 800	106.8	113.1	126.9	113.1	137.7	1 213 000	V	Royaume-Uni (R)

V   Visitors (travellers in Turkey)
T   Tourists
(R) Tourist count by country of residence
(N) Tourist count by country of nationality

V   Visiteurs (voyageurs en Turquie)
T   Touristes
(R) Recensement des touristes par pays de résidence
(N) Recensement des touristes par pays de nationalité

Table/Tableau 45

ARRIVALS AND NIGHTS OF FOREIGN TOURISTS AT/IN HOTELS
ARRIVÉES ET NUITÉES DE TOURISTES ÉTRANGERS DANS L'HÔTELLERIE

From the Netherlands / En provenance des Pays-Bas
1988=100

Country	AH/NH	Volume 1982	1983	1984	1985	1986	1987	Volume 1988	1989	1990	1991	1992	1993	Volume 1993
Australia (R)	NH	48 718	64.2	62.7	85.1	71.0	77.3	85 500						
Japan (N)	NH	16 821												
	AH													
Austria (R)	NH	5 552 614	103.4	106.2	101.6	100.7	102.2	4 999 132	105.1	99.9	103.1	100.0	94.0	4 699 376
	AH	769 553	94.5	97.2	95.1	94.4	98.4	776 351	105.4	102.5	102.5	99.9	96.5	748 839
Belgium (R)	NH	521 146	82.4	89.3	88.9	91.3	96.3	740 873	124.5	127.7	125.9	136.4	140.5	1 041 195
Denmark (N)	NH	114 900	118.0	106.1	96.0	91.9	98.4	102 100	105.7	111.5	153.5	190.7	179.7	183 500
Finland (R)	NH	36 049	79.5	95.4	87.3	79.9	90.2	46 266	112.8	119.2	114.2	133.7	141.7	65 581
	AH													36 608
France (R)[1]	NH	809 381	35.0	37.0	33.2	84.9	89.9	2 279 008	106.4	102.4	106.2	106.4	106.2	2 420 524
	AH	323 910	25.0	24.7	23.5	81.7	87.3	1 266 311	100.1	99.0	105.6	102.2	103.3	1 308 447
Germany (R)	NH	3 228 876	87.1	90.9	91.7	96.5	100.2	3 436 766	105.4	102.8	101.7	96.2	90.6	3 113 119
	AH	1 436 512	88.0	92.2	92.7	93.9	98.7	1 557 603	103.2	102.6	99.6	96.4	92.6	1 442 874
Greece (N)	NH	982 881	54.8	76.9	113.8	117.6	99.5	1 657 731						
	AH	173 615	63.5	83.0	109.4	106.5	100.6	257 698						
Ireland (R)	NH							125 000	160.0	174.4	241.6	218.4	196.8	246 000
	AH							25 000	132.0	160.0	200.0	180.0	176.0	44 000
Italy (N)	NH	1 404 392	84.7	69.0	74.9	85.2	80.0	1 506 585	91.6	90.3	93.5	84.0	94.9	1 429 112
	AH	286 531	79.5	70.7	77.0	81.5	122.2	340 605	98.1	101.3	101.1	94.6	104.5	355 994
Luxembourg (R)	NH	176 228	56.0	60.6	123.2		90.3	107 853	109.7	116.9	139.4	161.6	174.4	188 057
	AH	68 246	102.7	117.9	62.4		111.9							
Norway (N)	NH	117 433	93.4	96.6	62.8		73.3	1 195 354	107.9	119.5	141.6	125.0	96.0	1 147 844
Portugal (N)	NH	767 704	173.9	121.1	103.1	117.2	76.4	169 588	108.3	122.3	134.4	120.7	91.9	155 815
	AH	94 843												
Spain (N)	NH	3 618 235	117.7	102.7	97.7	64.9	102.0	3 324 088	84.5	62.9	73.2	73.7	88.8	2 953 346
	AH	431 741			111.2	68.2	100.2	445 589	92.0	72.9	80.1	81.1	91.7	408 528
Sweden (N)	NH	103 375				105.8	101.1	69 273	109.8	112.5	99.3	121.0	123.2	85 370
Switzerland (R)	NH	1 039 242	111.7	100.6	99.9	105.7	103.1	801 212	107.3	107.6	111.4	110.0	112.4	900 232
	AH	296 455			96.5	102.4	100.4	247 410	107.8	106.8	110.4	106.9	110.3	272 900

AH Arrivals at hotels and similar establishments
NH Nights in hotels and similar establishments
(R) Tourist count by country of residence
(N) Tourist count by country of nationality
1. Ile de France only

AH Arrivées dans les hôtels et les établissements assimilés
NH Nuitées dans les hôtels et établissements assimilés
(R) Recensement des touristes par pays de résidence
(N) Recensement des touristes par pays de nationalié
1. Ile de France seulement

Table/Tableau 46

ARRIVALS AND NIGHTS OF FOREIGN TOURISTS AT/IN ALL MEANS OF ACCOMMODATION
ARRIVÉES ET NUITÉES DE TOURISTES ÉTRANGERS DANS L'ENSEMBLE DES MOYENS D'HÉBERGEMENT

From the Netherlands
1988=100

En provenance des Pays-Bas
1988=100

	AAA/NAA	Volume 1982	1983	1984	1985	1986	1987	Volume 1988	1989	1990	1991	1992	1993	Volume 1993	AEH/NEH	
Canada (R)	NAA	1 158 800	83.4	79.6	76.0	80.3	91.0	1 206 600	95.2	92.8	87.7	87.7	96.0	1 158 200	NEH	Canada (R)
Australia (R)	NAA		112.0	77.4	70.3	71.0	77.2	209 200						371 688	NEH	Australie (R)
New Zealand (R)	NAA													10 750	NEH	Nouvelle-Zélande (R)
	AAA														AEH	
Austria (R)	NAA	9 723 867	97.6	100.9	99.0	99.0	100.6	9 268 514	104.2	98.3	99.7	97.1	91.1	8 442 757	NEH	Autriche (R)
	AAA	1 267 168	90.4	94.0	93.7	93.4	97.6	1 331 165	105.4	101.0	99.4	97.0	93.1	1 238 886	AEH	
Belgium (R)	NAA	2 786 314	75.6	75.7	77.8	81.7	88.3	4 069 115	110.2	118.1	107.6	103.7	108.3	4 408 044	NEH	Belgique (R)
Denmark (N)	NAA	772 579	174.4	142.3	131.7	117.5	106.1	509 366	103.4	100.2	123.8	197.0	134.7	685 900	NEH	Danemark (N)
Finland (R)	NAA													88 325	NEH	Finlande (R)
	AAA													49 085	AEH	
France (R)	NAA	33 509 000	98.4	100.4	93.6	103.5	98.5	33 416 845	104.0	100.6	167.2	180.5	208.1	69 556 000	NEH	France (R)
	AAA	3 888 000	94.0	93.1	90.3	99.1	97.3	4 047 000		98.7	146.6	155.6	176.5	7 141 000	AEH	
Germany (R)	NAA	4 423 492	78.6	87.6	88.8	93.8	99.1	5 690 235	104.8	101.2	146.5	142.4	128.7	7 324 284	NEH	Allemagne (R)
	AAA	1 573 835	83.0	90.5	90.9	93.1	98.8	1 878 699	104.0	102.0	131.3	130.2	122.4	2 299 550	AEH	
Greece (N)	NAA	1 176 670	61.3	88.1	114.4	117.6	100.3	1 752 071							NEH	Grèce (N)
	AAA	222 005	70.2	93.0	110.5	108.0	101.1	288 995							AEH	
Ireland (R)	NAA							38 000	121.1	189.5	218.4	192.1	181.6	792 000	NEH	Irlande (R)
	AAA													69 000	AEH	
Italy (N)	NAA	4 340 381	100.2	86.6	93.4	102.9	95.7	3 556 767	90.8	86.0	90.2	80.5	81.5	2 898 305	NEH	Italie (N)
	AAA	550 107	83.5	75.9	82.4	89.4	94.4	587 287	95.5	94.1	97.4	89.8	93.0	546 084	AEH	
Luxembourg (R)	NAA	912 921													NEH	Luxembourg (R)
	AAA														AEH	
Portugal (N)	NAA	1 052 957	53.3	57.6	61.4	68.6	74.0	1 649 848	105.7	112.1	130.5	111.8	86.9	1 432 960	NEH	Portugal (N)
	AAA	151 215	51.8	55.0	63.1	70.0	78.0	279 737	105.6	110.7	122.3	104.1	79.9	223 466	AEH	
Sweden (N)	NAA	473 226	208.4	151.4	137.0	109.9	109.0	343 965	116.1	110.6	93.4	98.2	98.8	339 674	NEH	Suède (N)
Switzerland (R)	NAA	3 685 600	112.3	99.3	93.1	102.5	99.8	2 982 780	105.9	112.1	113.8	114.4	113.6	3 388 149	NEH	Suisse (R)
	AAA	617 600	111.0	100.2	91.7	100.2	98.7	518 555	107.2	111.2	114.4	114.6	114.5	593 802	AEH	
United Kingdom (R)	NAA	4 415 000	85.2	82.0	96.6	78.6	92.7	5 566 000	93.2	100.6	116.6	103.8	109.0	6 065 000	NEH	Royaume-Uni (R)

AAA   Arrivals in all means of accommodation
NAA   Nights in all means of accommodation
(R)   Tourist count by country of residence
(N)   Tourist count by country of nationality

AEH   Arrivées dans l'ensemble des moyens d'hébergement
NEH   Nuitées dans l'ensemble des moyens d'hébergement
(R)   Recensement des touristes par pays de résidence
(N)   Recensement des touristes par pays de nationalité

132

Table/Tableau 47

ARRIVALS OF FOREIGN TOURISTS/VISITORS AT FRONTIERS
ARRIVÉES DE TOURISTES/VISITEURS ÉTRANGERS AUX FRONTIÈRES

From the United Kingdom
1988=100

En provenance du Royaume-Uni
1988=100

Country	T/V	Volume 1982	1983	1984	1985	1986	1987	Volume 1988	1989	1990	1991	1992	1993	Volume 1993	T/V	
Canada (R)	T	425 700	68.9	66.4	59.6	75.8	84.7	527 200	108.1	104.9	100.6	101.7	106.5	561 600	T	Canada (R)
	V	474 100	68.4	65.8	58.9	75.0	86.5	585 800	105.0	102.8	99.1	101.7	107.4	629 200	V	
United States (R)	T	1 293 860	55.9	51.0	47.4	62.4	74.9	1 818 029	122.2	123.4	137.3	155.3	165.0	2 999 301	T	États-Unis (R)
Australia (R)	V	173 137	56.7	55.9	58.9	67.6	76.4	260 300	104.8	106.8	101.3	111.4	119.2	310 300	V	Australie (R)
Japan (N)	T													128 919	T	Japon (N)
	V	152 703	112.9	108.1	118.3	91.9	95.9	154 582	114.7	138.7	141.9	156.5	146.0	225 737	V	
New Zealand (R)	T	37 931	53.8	55.3	60.0	68.3	84.0	72 704	102.2	120.0	121.0	132.8	142.2	103 387	T	Nouvelle-Zélande (R)
France (R)	T	6 018 000	89.3	82.5	88.2	94.8	95.8	6 645 000	106.7	121.8	121.9	124.8	122.6	8 148 000	T	France (R)
Greece (N)	T	1 022 692	49.7	58.3	74.3	95.5	110.6	1 790 000	91.2	92.0	93.6	120.4	122.4	2 191 347	T	Grèce (N)
Iceland (N)	T	7 276	84.3	89.3	92.4	97.5	100.5	10 525	113.9	130.6	139.3	132.1	147.2	15 498	T	Islande (N)
Ireland (R)	V	1 076 920	77.1	81.1	75.4	74.0	82.5	1 465 000	113.9	121.9	118.0	120.0	128.6	1 884 000	V	Irlande (R)
Italy (N)	V	1 844 837	103.9	98.3	97.3	112.6	109.9	1 819 232	104.8	112.6	94.1	88.7	95.5	1 737 737	V	Italie (N)
Norway (N)	V	135 599													V	Norvège (N)
Portugal (N)	T	508 848	52.0	60.0	71.0	93.2	106.9	1 064 571	96.5	99.7	109.1	119.9	114.8	1 221 900	T	Portugal (N)
	V	570 599	55.2	62.3	77.2	93.8	105.7	1 139 693	99.8	105.5	114.7	125.9	120.1	1 368 356	V	
Spain (N)	V	4 850 439	67.9	78.8	65.9	84.1	98.8	7 645 598	96.1	82.2	80.4	85.2	97.9	7 485 129	V	Espagne (N)
Turkey (N)	V	59 582	18.2	19.3	26.8	33.2	57.4	465 142	87.3	75.6	43.2	67.6	95.0	441 817	V	Turquie (N)

V   Visitors (travellers in Turkey)
T   Tourists
(R)   Tourist count by country of residence
(N)   Tourist count by country of nationality

V   Visiteurs (voyageurs en Turquie)
T   Touristes
(R)   Recensement des touristes par pays de résidence
(N)   Recensement des touristes par pays de nationalité

Table/Tableau 48

ARRIVALS AND NIGHTS OF FOREIGN TOURISTS AT/IN HOTELS
ARRIVÉES ET NUITÉES DE TOURISTES ÉTRANGERS DANS L'HÔTELLERIE

From the United Kingdom 1988=100 — En provenance du Royaume-Uni 1988=100

Country	AH/NH	Volume 1982	1983	1984	1985	1986	1987	Volume 1988	1989	1990	1991	1992	1993	Volume 1993	AH/NH	Pays
Australia (R)	NH	258 782	35.7	35.7	45.3	67.6	76.4	1 652 200	86.8	133.0	81.7	90.5	90.8	1 500 000	NH	Australie (R)
Japan (N)	NH	92 501													NH	Japon (N)
	AH														AH	
Austria (R)	NH	3 171 933	97.0	105.0	100.6	102.7	101.4	3 722 901	112.2	117.9	98.4	95.7	86.9	3 234 309	NH	Autriche (R)
	AH	597 971	101.0	111.7	106.4	102.8	101.9	655 460	114.7	125.3	103.0	99.5	91.6	600 515	AH	
Belgium (R)	NH	963 657	123.9	122.7	122.7	114.0	105.8	856 412	123.2	140.1	129.5	155.0	137.9	1 181 260	NH	Belgique (R)
Denmark (N)	NH	363 300	117.5	103.6	114.9	107.5	105.0	290 000	105.3	115.0	109.1	110.5	113.2	328 300	NH	Danemark (N)
Finland (R)	NH	96 078	79.0	82.1	82.2	78.5	88.5	131 711	107.3	107.9	100.0	96.3	106.8	140 677	NH	Finlande (R)
	AH													74 513	AH	
France (R)[1]	NH	1 875 927	28.7	31.1	32.2	87.4	84.7	6 753 189	131.8	162.3	150.6	164.7	139.9	9 449 566	NH	France (R)[1]
	AH	782 742	22.6	23.2	25.1	88.6	87.9	3 501 519	131.9	139.2	146.7	158.7	135.8	4 756 106	AH	
Germany (R)	NH	1 885 554	82.3	94.1	98.2	102.5	98.7	2 320 020	116.4	130.0	116.9	118.3	113.7	2 637 683	NH	Allemagne (R)
	AH	950 080	86.0	96.6	99.5	100.5	98.4	1 116 501	114.3	129.4	109.4	112.0	103.8	1 158 558	AH	
Greece (N)	NH	6 234 066	71.6	86.3	104.5	119.1	116.6	7 222 144	122.8	139.7	130.3	128.4			NH	Grèce (N)
	AH	801 763	76.6	88.6	105.0	112.2	112.4	876 995	138.3	125.9	169.8	158.1			AH	
Iceland (N)	NH				78.2	90.3	87.9	35 478	128.2	134.8	150.3	149.1	116.8	41 453	NH	Islande (N)
Ireland (R)	NH				77.3	83.9	80.9	2 098 000					159.1	3 338 000	NH	Irlande (R)
	AH					80.9		529 000					154.1	815 000	AH	
Italy (N)	NH	5 821 011	113.6	99.0	94.7	112.0	106.8	5 183 734	107.6	87.7	87.7	88.2	89.6	4 643 868	NH	Italie (N)
	AH	1 156 448	101.2	93.2	90.8	100.6	101.6	1 162 034	108.9	94.5	94.5	99.1	101.3	1 176 980	AH	
Luxembourg (R)	NH		79.8	76.6	82.1	96.9	92.5	55 672							NH	Luxembourg (R)
	AH		86.5	80.8	93.3	95.4	91.0	28 181							AH	
Netherlands (R)	NH	1 232 097	90.8	98.7	105.1	108.6	101.7	1 229 800	110.5	113.8	113.1	132.8	115.0	1 414 500	NH	Pays-Bas (R)
	AH	565 984	86.4	92.7	98.3	102.6	99.5	603 800	107.5	113.6	113.4	123.5	112.8	681 300	AH	
Norway (N)	NH	321 890	89.7	128.4	135.0	109.6	104.1	333 142	101.3	123.5	116.5	128.7	123.6	411 925	NH	Norvège (N)
Portugal (N)	NH	3 289 334	67.9	74.3	94.0	110.7	105.7	5 268 854	96.7	99.8	102.3	108.1	102.1	5 377 624	NH	Portugal (N)
	AH	391 190	68.5	78.0	98.4	108.1	105.6	654 178	99.0	106.3	106.6	107.4	103.2	675 326	AH	
Spain (N)	NH	28 001 763	95.9	112.4	80.0	108.1	107.9	31 291 489	80.7	62.5	60.9	62.2	71.3	22 301 851	NH	Espagne (N)
	AH	3 136 299	93.9	107.3	80.4	108.6	108.2	3 458 626	86.3	64.0	67.6	68.7	76.6	2 647 783	AH	
Sweden (N)	NH	245 566	106.3	106.8	106.8	103.0	94.3	239 379	111.1	113.1	95.3	99.7	100.3	240 007	NH	Suède (N)
Switzerland (R)	NH	1 968 906	113.7	110.1	108.9	113.6	102.5	1 775 380	108.4	114.0	104.0	104.1	96.1	1 706 670	NH	Suisse (R)
	AH	544 442	104.8	104.7	101.4	102.9	99.2	524 254	107.8	115.3	102.3	104.5	97.4	510 477	AH	
Turkey (N)	NH	86 227	16.9	18.6	28.5	36.8	57.1	890 987	86.9	71.3	42.5	88.4	159.5	1 421 321	NH	Turquie (N)
	AH	34 411	23.6	28.9	38.4	46.8	64.6	220 537	92.4	79.2	42.7	71.9	110.7	244 103	AH	

AH Arrivals at hotels and similar establishments
NH Nights in hotels and similar establishments
(R) Tourist count by country of residence
(N) Tourist count by country of nationality
1. Ile de France only

AH Arrivées dans les hôtels et les établissements assimilés
NH Nuitées dans les hôtels et établissements assimilés
(R) Recensement des touristes par pays de résidence
(N) Recensement des touristes par pays de nationalité
1. Ile de France seulement

Table/Tableau 49

ARRIVALS AND NIGHTS OF FOREIGN TOURISTS AT/IN ALL MEANS OF ACCOMMODATION
ARRIVÉES ET NUITÉES DE TOURISTES ÉTRANGERS DANS L'ENSEMBLE DES MOYENS D'HÉBERGEMENT

From the United Kingdom
En provenance du Royaume-Uni

1988=100

	AAA/NAA	Volume 1982	1983	1984	1985	1986	1987	Volume 1988	1989	1990	1991	1992	1993	Volume 1993	AEH/NEH	
Canada (R)	NAA	6 184 400	78.8	76.1	67.6	84.2	83.6	6 813 500	100.3	97.1	92.7	89.8	94.9	6 468 600	NEH	Canada (R)
	AAA	425 700	68.9	66.4	59.6	75.8	83.3	527 200	106.3	104.9	100.6	101.7	106.5	561 600	AEH	
Australia (R)	NAA													12 151 000	NEH	Australie (R)
New Zealand (R)	NAA	2 909 375		59.8	65.0	73.5	88.3	2 909 375	98.3	109.7	107.8	108.9	108.6	3 160 339	NEH	Nouvelle-Zélande (R)
	AAA													5 071	AEH	
Austria (R)	NAA	3 559 289	96.4	103.0	100.5	102.0	100.9	4 213 101	112.0	117.0	99.8	96.6	87.4	3 680 327	NEH	Autriche (R)
	AAA	679 834	100.3	109.1	105.7	102.6	101.6	753 230	114.6	124.2	104.4	100.0	90.8	683 730	AEH	
Belgium (R)	NAA	1 163 387	129.7	129.0	126.7	118.0	110.9	974 784	121.4	138.5	128.6	154.5	139.7	1 361 911	NEH	Belgique (R)
Denmark (N)	NAA	452 951	123.5	109.4	117.0	107.8	103.0	347 978	103.6	113.7	105.4	109.7	107.9	375 300	NEH	Danemark (N)
Finland (R)	AAA													76 701	AEH	Finlande (R)
France (R)	NAA	51 551 000	121.5	116.8	123.9	136.9	141.5	42 808 000	118.4	142.0	141.1	143.4	140.0	59 920 000	NEH	France (R)
	AAA	6 018 000	89.3	82.5	88.2	94.8	95.8	6 645 000	115.8	121.8	121.9	124.8	122.6	8 148 000	AEH	
Germany (R)	NAA	1 939 651	77.0	92.2	96.9	100.7	99.5	2 558 954	115.8	127.5	129.0	129.3	123.2	3 152 468	NEH	Allemagne (R)
	AAA	958 099	81.7	96.3	99.4	99.9	99.0	1 186 131	114.3	128.7	119.4	120.7	110.9	1 315 046	AEH	
Greece (N)	NAA	6 589 703	75.5	93.4	104.7	119.3	116.8	7 284 895							NEH	Grèce (N)
	AAA	862 762													AEH	
Ireland (R)	NAA	9 425 300	72.8	78.5	69.4	70.6	87.3	13 803 000	116.9	112.9	106.7	104.1	109.2	15 066 000	NEH	Irlande (R)
	AAA	1 031 000	69.6	74.3	74.2	74.7		1 508 000	113.8	118.4	113.4	113.2	118.2	1 783 000	AEH	
Italy (N)	NAA	7 179 420	117.7	101.4	97.7	116.1	144.4	6 131 890	106.0	92.1	84.6	88.0	89.5	5 488 110	NEH	Italie (N)
	AAA	1 320 243	101.2	92.9	90.2	101.4	101.4	1 322 377	108.0	95.8	94.3	97.7	98.9	1 307 553	AEH	
Luxembourg (R)	NAA		83.9	91.4	87.4	93.5	94.1	77 481	115.9	115.9	112.2	129.7			NEH	Luxembourg (R)
	AAA		89.7	93.5	92.9	94.2	93.3	37 235	117.8	117.8	116.1	122.3			AEH	
Netherlands (R)	NAA	1 521 345	91.4	100.9	104.7	101.6		1 510 800	111.9	127.6	128.5	136.4	113.5	1 715 200	NEH	Pays-Bas (R)
	AAA	686 851	88.8	96.1	99.8	95.9		711 200	105.6	116.5	117.0	122.5	109.0	775 400	AEH	
Portugal (N)	NAA	3 453 778	68.9	74.7	93.9	110.7	106.0	5 414 867	96.8	100.2	106.8	107.6	101.6	5 501 385	NEH	Portugal (N)
	AAA	421 339	69.6	78.5	98.4	108.3	106.1	683 221	99.2	106.4	109.8	106.7	102.4	699 478	AEH	
Spain (N)	NAA	28 390 332													NEH	Espagne (N)
	AAA	3 191 925													AEH	
Sweden (N)	NAA	355 519	113.3	111.7	111.0	106.9	96.7	311 699	109.5	108.3	88.6	92.5	90.3	281 397	NEH	Suède (N)
Switzerland (R)	NAA	2 668 100	108.5	105.7	105.7	112.1	103.1	2 587 370	105.3	108.3	98.6	100.3	94.3	2 440 935	NEH	Suisse (R)
	AAA	700 200	106.8	105.5	102.0	104.7	100.8	662 574	108.0	113.2	101.2	102.8	95.7	634 086	AEH	
Turkey (N)	NAA	88 406	16.1	17.3	27.1	36.0	60.6	980 484	85.8	68.9	42.8	88.8	151.3	1 483 606	NEH	Turquie (N)
	AAA	34 719	22.8	27.9	37.2	46.1	65.6	231 857	92.3	78.5	44.2	72.8	108.6	251 748	AEH	

AAA Arrivals in all means of accommodation
NAA Nights in all means of accommodation
(R) Tourist count by country of residence
(N) Tourist count by country of nationality

AEH Arrivées dans l'ensemble des moyens d'hébergement
NEH Nuitées dans l'ensemble des moyens d'hébergement
(R) Recensement des touristes par pays de résidence
(N) Recensement des touristes par pays de nationalité

AUSTRALIA

ARRIVALS OF FOREIGN VISITORS AT FRONTIERS[1]

(by country of residence)

	1992	Relative share	1993	Relative share	% Variation over 1992
Canada	48 900	1.9	50 600	1.7	3.5
Mexico	1 900	0.1	2 100	0.1	10.5
United States	262 900	10.1	281 300	9.4	7.0
Total North America	313 700	12.1	334 000	11.1	6.5
Australia	..	..	..	..	
Japan	629 900	24.2	670 800	22.4	6.5
New Zealand	447 500	17.2	499 300	16.7	11.6
Total Asia and the Pacific	1 077 400	41.4	1 170 100	39.0	8.6
Austria	10 800	0.4	13 200	0.4	22.2
Belgium	4 200	0.2	5 300	0.2	26.2
Denmark	10 300	0.4	11 600	0.4	12.6
Finland	5 100	0.2	4 700	0.2	–7.8
France	25 400	1.0	31 000	1.0	22.0
Germany [2]	89 900	3.5	105 600	3.5	17.5
Greece	6 100	0.2	6 700	0.2	9.8
Iceland	100	0.0	300	0.0	200.0
Ireland	8 800	0.3	11 000	0.4	25.0
Italy	27 400	1.1	31 600	1.1	15.3
Luxembourg	500	0.0	400	0.0	–20.0
Netherlands	23 500	0.9	27 500	0.9	17.0
Norway	4 500	0.2	4 600	0.2	2.2
Portugal	1 600	0.1	1 900	0.1	18.8
Spain	4 900	0.2	5 400	0.2	10.2
Sweden	19 100	0.7	17 600	0.6	–7.9
Switzerland	29 000	1.1	30 600	1.0	5.5
Turkey	1 400	0.1	1 700	0.1	21.4
United Kingdom	289 900	11.1	310 300	10.4	7.0
Other OECD-Europe	..	..	..	..	..
Total Europe	562 500	21.6	621 000	20.7	10.4
Total OECD Countries	**1 953 600**	**75.1**	**2 125 100**	**70.9**	**8.8**
Other European countries	15 900	0.6	17 500	0.6	10.1
Bulgaria	200	0.0	200	0.0	0.0
Ex-Czechoslovakia	1 500	0.1	1 400	0.0	–6.7
Hungary	1 700	0.1	1 900	0.1	11.8
Poland	2 000	0.1	2 400	0.1	20.0
Rumania	400	0.0	500	0.0	25.0
Ex-USSR	4 500	0.2	4 900	0.2	8.9
Ex-Yugoslavia	3 200	0.1	3 500	0.1	9.4
Latin America	9 700	0.4	11 100	0.4	14.4
Argentina	3 100	0.1	3 900	0.1	25.8
Brazil	2 500	0.1	2 700	0.1	8.0
Chile	1 400	0.1	1 600	0.1	14.3
Colombia	500	0.0	600	0.0	20.0
Venezuela	400	0.0	400	0.0	0.0
Asia-Oceania	594 200	22.8	798 700	26.6	34.4
China	18 700	0.7	22 300	0.7	19.3
Hong Kong	74 700	2.9	92 000	3.1	23.2
India	9 600	0.4	9 800	0.3	2.1
Iran	1 200	0.0	1 100	0.0	–8.3
Israel	4 600	0.2	5 500	0.2	19.6
Republic of Korea	33 600	1.3	62 200	2.1	85.1
Lebanon	1 800	0.1	2 700	0.1	50.0
Malaysia	60 400	2.3	80 400	2.7	33.1
Pakistan	1 600	0.1	1 400	0.0	–12.5
Philippines	16 100	0.6	17 900	0.6	11.2
Saudi Arabia	2 600	0.1	3 400	0.1	30.8
Singapore	116 800	4.5	154 900	5.2	32.6
Taiwan	63 500	2.4	108 700	3.6	71.2
Thailand	33 600	1.3	46 500	1.6	38.4
Africa	24 300	0.9	38 200	1.3	57.2
Egypt	1 000	0.0	900	0.0	–10.0
South Africa	15 300	0.6	26 400	0.9	72.5
Origin country undetermined	5 300	0.2	6 400	0.2	20.8
Total non-OECD Countries	**649 400**	**24.9**	**871 900**	**29.1**	**34.3**
TOTAL	**2 603 000**	**100.0**	**2 997 000**	**100.0**	**15.1**

1. Includes a small number of "in transit" passengers who leave the port or airport, but do not necessarily stay overnight in Australia.
2. Germany includes Federal and Democratic Republics.

AUSTRALIA

NIGHTS SPENT BY FOREIGN TOURISTS IN HOTELS[1]

(by country of residence)

	1992	Relative share	1993	Relative share	% Variation over 1992
Canada	281 500	2.3	387 000	2.7	37.5
Mexico	..	..	..	..	..
United States	1 920 100	15.4	1 980 000	14.0	3.1
Total North America	2 201 600	17.7	2 367 000	16.7	7.5
Australia	..	..	..	..	..
Japan	3 158 900	25.4	3 407 000	24.0	7.9
New Zealand	1 314 300	10.5	1 483 000	10.5	12.8
Total Asia and the Pacific	4 473 200	35.9	4 890 000	34.5	9.3
Austria	..	..	..	..	..
Belgium	..	..	..	..	..
Denmark	..	..	..	..	..
Finland	..	..	..	..	..
France	..	..	..	..	..
Germany	758 300	6.1	826 000	5.8	8.9
Greece	..	..	..	..	..
Iceland	..	..	..	..	..
Ireland[2]	..	..	..	..	..
Italy	..	..	..	..	..
Luxembourg	..	..	..	..	..
Netherlands	..	..	..	..	..
Norway	..	..	..	..	..
Portugal	..	..	..	..	..
Spain	..	..	..	..	..
Sweden	..	..	..	..	..
Switzerland	..	..	..	..	..
Turkey	..	..	..	..	..
United Kingdom[2]	1 494 700	12.0	1 500 000	10.6	0.4
Other OECD-Europe	1 178 200	9.5	1 416 000	10.0	20.2
Total Europe	3 431 200	27.5	3 742 000	26.4	9.1
Total OECD Countries	**10 106 000**	**81.1**	**10 999 000**	**77.6**	**8.8**
Origin country indetermined	2 354 800	18.9	3 179 000	22.4	35.0
Total non-OECD Countries	**2 354 800**	**18.9**	**3 179 000**	**22.4**	**35.0**
TOTAL	**12 460 800**	**100.0**	**14 178 000**	**100.0**	**13.8**

1.   Includes nights spent by tourists aged 15 years and above.
2.   United Kingdom includes Ireland.

AUSTRALIA

NIGHTS SPENT BY FOREIGN TOURISTS IN REGISTERED TOURIST ACCOMMODATION[1]

(by country of residence)

	1992	Relative share	1993	Relative share	% Variation over 1992
Canada	1 004 700	3.1	1 218 000	3.4	21.2
Mexico	..	..	..	..	..
United States	3 819 200	11.8	4 825 000	13.6	26.3
Total North America	4 823 900	14.9	6 043 000	17.1	25.3
Australia	..	..	..	..	..
Japan	4 247 200	13.1	4 307 000	12.2	1.4
New Zealand	3 402 200	10.5	3 506 000	9.9	3.1
Total Asia and the Pacific	7 649 400	23.6	7 813 000	22.1	2.1
Austria	..	..	..	..	..
Belgium	..	..	..	..	..
Denmark	..	..	..	..	..
Finland	..	..	..	..	..
France	..	..	..	..	..
Germany	2 154 100	6.6	2 286 000	6.5	6.1
Greece	..	..	..	..	..
Iceland	..	..	..	..	..
Ireland[2]	..	..	..	..	..
Italy	..	..	..	..	..
Luxembourg	..	..	..	..	..
Netherlands	..	..	..	..	..
Norway	..	..	..	..	..
Portugal	..	..	..	..	..
Spain	..	..	..	..	..
Sweden	..	..	..	..	..
Switzerland	..	..	..	..	..
Turkey	..	..	..	..	..
United Kingdom[2]	5 721 900	17.6	4 807 000	13.6	−16.0
Other OECD-Europe	3 769 800	11.6	4 296 000	12.1	14.0
Total Europe	11 645 800	35.9	11 389 000	32.2	−2.2
Total OECD Countries	**24 119 100**	**74.4**	**25 245 000**	**71.3**	**4.7**
Origin country indetermined	8 320 500	25.6	10 147 000	28.7	22.0
Total non-OECD Countries	**8 320 500**	**25.6**	**10 147 000**	**28.7**	**22.0**
TOTAL	**32 439 600**	**100.0**	**35 392 000**	**100.0**	**9.1**

1. Covers only commercial accommodation (ie excluding stays with friends/relatives).
2. United Kingdom includes Ireland.

AUSTRIA

ARRIVALS OF FOREIGN TOURISTS AT HOTELS

(by country of residence)

	1992	Relative share	1993	Relative share	% Variation over 1992
Canada	65 933	0.5	61 109	0.5	–7.3
Mexico	..	..	..	..	..
United States	566 756	4.1	488 734	3.8	–13.8
Total North America	632 689	4.6	549 843	4.2	–13.1
Australia [1]	79 867	0.6	68 850	0.5	–13.8
Japan	219 337	1.6	211 996	1.6	–3.3
New Zealand [1]	..	..	..	..	..
Total Asia and the Pacific	299 204	2.2	280 846	2.2	–6.1
Austria	..	..	..	..	..
Belgium [2]	337 970	2.5	325 356	2.5	–3.7
Denmark	117 530	0.9	107 276	0.8	–8.7
Finland	45 777	0.3	31 454	0.2	–31.3
France	576 589	4.2	530 126	4.1	–8.1
Germany	6 978 329	51.1	7 019 135	53.9	0.6
Greece	38 791	0.3	34 402	0.3	–11.3
Iceland [3]	169	0.0	2 836	0.0	1578.1
Ireland	12 704	0.1	11 093	0.1	–12.7
Italy	1 074 544	7.9	838 092	6.4	–22.0
Luxembourg [2]	..	..	..	..	..
Netherlands	775 249	5.7	748 839	5.7	–3.4
Norway	47 396	0.3	38 071	0.3	–19.7
Portugal	18 390	0.1	16 293	0.1	–11.4
Spain	221 717	1.6	180 045	1.4	–18.8
Sweden	231 818	1.7	177 266	1.4	–23.5
Switzerland	644 493	4.7	615 667	4.7	–4.5
Turkey	21 462	0.2	20 900	0.2	–2.6
United Kingdom	652 332	4.8	600 515	4.6	–7.9
Other OECD-Europe	..	..	..	..	..
Total Europe	11 795 260	86.3	11 297 366	86.7	–4.2
Total OECD Countries	**12 727 153**	**93.1**	**12 128 055**	**93.1**	**–4.7**
Other European countries [3]	526 962	3.9	473 178	3.6	–10.2
Bulgaria	14 704	0.1	21 649	0.2	47.2
Ex-Czechoslovakia	93 571	0.7	62 954	0.5	–32.7
Hungary	157 377	1.2	154 650	1.2	–1.7
Poland	65 737	0.5	59 933	0.5	–8.8
Rumania	18 461	0.1	18 210	0.1	–1.4
Ex-USSR	40 388	0.3	44 534	0.3	10.3
Ex-Yugoslavia	136 724	1.0	111 248	0.9	–18.6
Latin America	91 865	0.7	80 872	0.6	–12.0
Asia-Oceania	191 929	1.4	205 177	1.6	6.9
Africa	27 503	0.2	26 852	0.2	–2.4
Origin country undetermined	98 368	0.7	117 498	0.9	19.4
Total non-OECD Countries	**936 627**	**6.9**	**903 577**	**6.9**	**–3.5**
TOTAL	**13 663 780**	**100.0**	**13 031 632**	**100.0**	**–4.6**

Australia includes New Zealand.
Belgium includes Luxembourg.
"Other European countries" includes Iceland.

AUSTRIA

ARRIVALS OF FOREIGN TOURISTS AT REGISTERED TOURIST ACCOMMODATION

(by country of residence)

	1992	Relative share	1993	Relative share	% Variation over 1992
Canada	82 638	0.4	75 134	0.4	–9.1
Mexico	..	..	..	..	..
United States	627 632	3.3	541 570	3.0	–13.7
Total North America	710 270	3.7	616 704	3.4	–13.2
Australia [1]	79 867	0.4	68 850	0.4	–13.8
Japan	219 337	1.1	211 996	1.2	–3.3
New Zealand [1]	..	..	..	..	..
Total Asia and the Pacific	299 204	1.6	280 846	1.5	–6.1
Austria	..	..	..	..	..
Belgium [2]	468 264	2.5	444 847	2.4	–5.0
Denmark	181 519	1.0	164 791	0.9	–9.2
Finland	45 777	0.2	31 454	0.2	–31.3
France	737 709	3.9	677 626	3.7	–8.1
Germany	10 664 269	55.8	10 664 011	58.4	–0.0
Greece	41 696	0.2	37 193	0.2	–10.8
Iceland [3]	169	0.0	2 836	0.0	1578.1
Ireland	12 704	0.1	11 093	0.1	–12.7
Italy	1 219 512	6.4	962 753	5.3	–21.1
Luxembourg [2]	..	..	..	..	..
Netherlands	1 291 134	6.8	1 238 886	6.8	–4.0
Norway	47 396	0.2	38 071	0.2	–19.7
Portugal	18 390	0.1	16 293	0.1	–11.4
Spain	221 717	1.2	180 045	1.0	–18.8
Sweden	301 331	1.6	227 305	1.2	–24.6
Switzerland	752 532	3.9	718 038	3.9	–4.6
Turkey	21 462	0.1	20 900	0.1	–2.6
United Kingdom	752 918	3.9	683 730	3.7	–9.2
Other OECD-Europe	..	..	..	..	..
Total Europe	16 778 499	87.9	16 119 872	88.3	–3.9
Total OECD Countries	**17 787 973**	**93.1**	**17 017 422**	**93.2**	**–4.3**
Other European countries [3]	732 428	3.8	657 142	3.6	–10.3
Bulgaria	16 875	0.1	27 598	0.2	63.5
Ex-Czechoslovakia	153 291	0.8	103 696	0.6	–32.4
Hungary	227 681	1.2	223 268	1.2	–1.9
Poland	111 528	0.6	97 616	0.5	–12.5
Rumania	21 191	0.1	20 971	0.1	–1.0
Ex-USSR	46 935	0.2	51 239	0.3	9.2
Ex-Yugoslavia	154 927	0.8	132 754	0.7	–14.3
Latin America	91 865	0.5	80 872	0.4	–12.0
Asia-Oceania	198 907	1.0	210 864	1.2	6.0
Africa	27 503	0.1	26 852	0.1	–2.4
Origin country undetermined	259 802	1.4	263 614	1.4	1.5
Total non-OECD Countries	**1 310 505**	**6.9**	**1 239 344**	**6.8**	**–5.4**
TOTAL	**19 098 478**	**100.0**	**18 256 766**	**100.0**	**–4.4**

1. Australia includes New Zealand.
2. Belgium includes Luxembourg.
3. "Other European countries" includes Iceland.

AUSTRIA

NIGHTS SPENT BY FOREIGN TOURISTS IN HOTELS

(by country of residence)

	1992	Relative share	1993	Relative share	% Variation over 1992
Canada	158 559	0.2	157 433	0.3	–0.7
Mexico	..	..	..	..	..
United States	1 369 969	2.1	1 231 701	2.0	–10.1
Total North America	1 528 528	2.4	1 389 134	2.2	–9.1
Australia [1]	194 135	0.3	166 754	0.3	–14.1
Japan	453 099	0.7	441 187	0.7	–2.6
New Zealand [1]	..	..	..	..	..
Total Asia and the Pacific	647 234	1.0	607 941	1.0	–6.1
Austria	..	..	..	..	..
Belgium [2]	2 065 705	3.2	1 970 636	3.2	–4.6
Denmark	597 917	0.9	543 236	0.9	–9.1
Finland	196 307	0.3	132 134	0.2	–32.7
France	2 189 896	3.4	2 020 623	3.3	–7.7
Germany	38 519 615	60.0	38 822 504	62.6	0.8
Greece	122 300	0.2	107 415	0.2	–12.2
Iceland [3]	998	0.0	10 300	0.0	932.1
Ireland	64 335	0.1	59 903	0.1	–6.9
Italy	3 037 178	4.7	2 285 194	3.7	–24.8
Luxembourg [2]	..	..	..	..	..
Netherlands	4 998 214	7.8	4 699 376	7.6	–6.0
Norway	168 305	0.3	134 518	0.2	–20.1
Portugal	40 236	0.1	37 359	0.1	–7.2
Spain	466 291	0.7	400 424	0.6	–14.1
Sweden	1 016 497	1.6	788 214	1.3	–22.5
Switzerland	2 520 498	3.9	2 352 419	3.8	–6.7
Turkey	60 597	0.1	64 620	0.1	6.6
United Kingdom	3 563 269	5.6	3 234 309	5.2	–9.2
Other OECD-Europe	..	..	..	..	..
Total Europe	59 628 158	92.9	57 663 184	93.0	–3.3
Total OECD Countries	**61 803 920**	**96.3**	**59 660 259**	**96.2**	**–3.5**
Other European countries [3]	1 393 132	2.2	1 284 823	2.1	–7.8
Bulgaria	38 555	0.1	52 403	0.1	35.9
Ex-Czechoslovakia	214 195	0.3	136 973	0.2	–36.1
Hungary	384 010	0.6	393 415	0.6	2.4
Poland	176 046	0.3	164 310	0.3	–6.7
Rumania	55 190	0.1	48 177	0.1	–12.7
Ex-USSR	150 692	0.2	176 713	0.3	17.3
Ex-Yugoslavia	374 444	0.6	312 832	0.5	–16.5
Latin America	175 084	0.3	157 832	0.3	–9.9
Asia-Oceania	451 067	0.7	485 575	0.8	7.7
Africa	102 551	0.2	102 845	0.2	0.3
Origin country undetermined	263 222	0.4	304 552	0.5	15.7
Total non-OECD Countries	**2 385 056**	**3.7**	**2 335 627**	**3.8**	**–2.1**
TOTAL	**64 188 976**	**100.0**	**61 995 886**	**100.0**	**–3.4**

1. Australia includes New Zealand.
2. Belgium includes Luxembourg.
3. "Other European countries" includes Iceland.

AUSTRIA

NIGHTS SPENT BY FOREIGN TOURISTS IN REGISTERED TOURIST ACCOMMODATION
(by country of residence)

	1992	Relative share	1993	Relative share	% Variation over 1992
Canada	207 787	0.2	205 374	0.2	−1.2
Mexico	..	..	..	..	..
United States	1 526 478	1.5	1 371 261	1.4	−10.2
Total North America	1 734 265	1.7	1 576 635	1.6	−9.1
Australia [1]	194 135	0.2	166 754	0.2	−14.1
Japan	453 099	0.5	441 187	0.5	−2.6
New Zealand [1]	..	..	..	..	..
Total Asia and the Pacific	647 234	0.6	607 941	0.6	−6.1
Austria	..	..	..	..	..
Belgium [2]	3 010 297	3.0	2 851 528	2.9	−5.3
Denmark	928 020	0.9	851 336	0.9	−8.3
Finland	196 307	0.2	132 134	0.1	−32.7
France	2 845 545	2.9	2 636 429	2.7	−7.3
Germany	64 715 088	64.9	64 978 848	67.1	0.4
Greece	135 223	0.1	119 423	0.1	−11.7
Iceland [3]	998	0.0	10 300	0.0	932.1
Ireland	64 335	0.1	59 903	0.1	−6.9
Italy	3 609 209	3.6	2 783 211	2.9	−22.9
Luxembourg [2]	..	..	..	..	..
Netherlands	8 998 720	9.0	8 442 757	8.7	−6.2
Norway	168 305	0.2	134 518	0.1	−20.1
Portugal	40 236	0.0	37 359	0.0	−7.2
Spain	466 291	0.5	400 424	0.4	−14.1
Sweden	1 355 865	1.4	1 047 052	1.1	−22.8
Switzerland	3 121 254	3.1	2 925 647	3.0	−6.3
Turkey	60 597	0.1	64 620	0.1	6.6
United Kingdom	4 068 302	4.1	3 680 327	3.8	−9.5
Other OECD-Europe	..	..	..	..	..
Total Europe	93 784 592	94.0	91 155 816	94.1	−2.8
Total OECD Countries	**96 166 091**	**96.4**	**93 340 392**	**96.4**	**−2.9**
Other European countries [3]	2 101 494	2.1	1 966 263	2.0	−6.4
Bulgaria	48 651	0.0	72 059	0.1	48.1
Ex-Czechoslovakia	373 006	0.4	240 375	0.2	−35.6
Hungary	625 314	0.6	649 077	0.7	3.8
Poland	302 638	0.3	287 345	0.3	−5.1
Rumania	68 555	0.1	59 431	0.1	−13.3
Ex-USSR	195 082	0.2	221 323	0.2	13.5
Ex-Yugoslavia	488 248	0.5	436 653	0.5	−10.6
Latin America	175 084	0.2	157 832	0.2	−9.9
Asia-Oceania	479 661	0.5	511 680	0.5	6.7
Africa	102 551	0.1	102 845	0.1	0.3
Origin country undetermined	732 714	0.7	744 809	0.8	1.7
Total non-OECD Countries	**3 591 504**	**3.6**	**3 483 429**	**3.6**	**−3.0**
TOTAL	**99 757 595**	**100.0**	**96 823 821**	**100.0**	**−2.9**

1. Australia includes New Zealand.
2. Belgium includes Luxembourg.
3. "Other European countries" includes Iceland.

BELGIUM

NIGHTS SPENT BY FOREIGN TOURISTS IN HOTELS

(by country of residence)

	1992	Relative share	1993	Relative share	% Variation over 1992
Canada	77 901	1.0	64 937	0.9	−16.6
Mexico[1]	19 962	0.3	24 294	0.3	21.7
United States	602 921	7.8	506 328	6.8	−16.0
Total North America	700 784	9.1	595 559	8.0	−15.0
Australia[2]	..	..	..	..	..
Japan	229 517	3.0	190 823	2.5	−16.9
New Zealand[2]	..	..	..	..	..
Total Asia and the Pacific	229 517	3.0	190 823	2.5	−16.9
Austria	66 858	0.9	106 811	1.4	59.8
Belgium	..	..	..	..	..
Denmark	95 270	1.2	129 950	1.7	36.4
Finland[3]	..	..	..	..	..
France	1 009 516	13.1	1 007 518	13.5	−0.2
Germany	1 130 757	14.7	1 166 956	15.6	3.2
Greece	85 994	1.1	109 829	1.5	27.7
Iceland[3]	..	..	..	..	..
Ireland	39 757	0.5	42 277	0.6	6.3
Italy	392 560	5.1	341 618	4.6	−13.0
Luxembourg	110 447	1.4	132 928	1.8	20.4
Netherlands	1 010 282	13.1	1 041 195	13.9	3.1
Norway	50 011	0.6	51 923	0.7	3.8
Portugal	99 667	1.3	155 270	2.1	55.8
Spain	271 205	3.5	209 617	2.8	−22.7
Sweden	147 254	1.9	125 397	1.7	−14.8
Switzerland	106 543	1.4	103 588	1.4	−2.8
Turkey	22 664	0.3	27 928	0.4	23.2
United Kingdom	1 327 547	17.3	1 181 260	15.8	−11.0
Other OECD-Europe	..	..	..	..	..
Total Europe	5 966 332	77.5	5 934 065	79.3	−0.5
Total OECD Countries	**6 896 633**	**89.6**	**6 720 447**	**89.8**	**−2.6**
Other European countries[3]	234 001	3.0	234 810	3.1	0.3
Ex-USSR	47 836	0.6	64 343	0.9	34.5
Latin America	30 487	0.4	69 953	0.9	129.5
Asia-Oceania[2]	183 318	2.4	193 551	2.6	5.6
Africa	149 108	1.9	126 449	1.7	−15.2
Origin country undetermined	200 508	2.6	139 567	1.9	−30.4
Total non-OECD Countries	**797 422**	**10.4**	**764 330**	**10.2**	**−4.1**
TOTAL	**7 694 055**	**100.0**	**7 484 777**	**100.0**	**−2.7**

1. Mexico includes Central America.
2. ''Asia-Oceania'' includes Australia and New Zealand.
3. ''Other European countries'' includes Finland and Iceland.

BELGIUM

NIGHTS SPENT BY FOREIGN TOURISTS IN REGISTERED TOURIST ACCOMMODATION

(by country of residence)

	1992	Relative share	1993	Relative share	% Variation over 1992
Canada [1]	86 204	0.7	72 085	0.6	−16.4
Mexico [1]	22 004	0.2	26 015	0.2	18.2
United States	619 092	4.8	521 734	4.0	−15.7
Total North America	727 300	5.6	619 834	4.8	−14.8
Australia [2]	..	..	..	..	..
Japan	233 368	1.8	194 675	1.5	−16.6
New Zealand [2]	..	..	..	..	..
Total Asia and the Pacific	233 368	1.8	194 675	1.5	−16.6
Austria	72 216	0.6	112 145	0.9	55.3
Belgium	..	..	..	..	..
Denmark	136 864	1.1	158 219	1.2	15.6
Finland [3]	..	..	..	..	..
France	1 307 776	10.2	1 329 829	10.3	1.7
Germany	2 263 102	17.6	2 454 056	19.0	8.4
Greece	88 904	0.7	112 703	0.9	26.8
Iceland [3]	..	..	..	..	..
Ireland	44 699	0.3	46 264	0.4	3.5
Italy	430 160	3.3	374 917	2.9	−12.8
Luxembourg	153 534	1.2	188 788	1.5	23.0
Netherlands	4 220 802	32.8	4 408 044	34.2	4.4
Norway	53 378	0.4	54 996	0.4	3.0
Portugal	112 106	0.9	159 670	1.2	42.4
Spain	322 096	2.5	238 168	1.8	−26.1
Sweden	160 060	1.2	135 146	1.0	−15.6
Switzerland	114 678	0.9	111 787	0.9	−2.5
Turkey	23 558	0.2	28 880	0.2	22.6
United Kingdom	1 506 260	11.7	1 361 911	10.6	−9.6
Other OECD-Europe	..	..	..	..	..
Total Europe	11 010 193	85.5	11 275 523	87.4	2.4
Total OECD Countries	**11 970 861**	**92.9**	**12 090 032**	**93.7**	**1.0**
Other European countries [3]	293 721	2.3	242 469	1.9	−17.4
Ex-USSR	54 795	0.4	71 847	0.6	31.1
Latin America	34 859	0.3	55 277	0.4	58.6
Asia-Oceania [2]	202 944	1.6	244 822	1.9	20.6
Africa	161 313	1.3	136 674	1.1	−15.3
Origin country undetermined	216 284	1.7	130 227	1.0	−39.8
Total non-OECD Countries	**909 121**	**7.1**	**809 469**	**6.3**	**−11.0**
TOTAL	**12 879 982**	**100.0**	**12 899 501**	**100.0**	**0.2**

1. Mexico includes Central America.
2. "Asia-Oceania" includes Australia and New Zealand.
3. "Other European countries" includes Finland and Iceland.

CANADA

ARRIVALS OF FOREIGN TOURISTS AT FRONTIERS

(by country of residence)

	1992	Relative share	1993	Relative share	% Variation over 1992
Canada	..	..	..	..	..
Mexico	65 100	0.4	73 700	0.5	13.2
United States	11 818 700	80.2	12 024 000	79.6	1.7
Total North America	11 883 800	80.6	12 097 700	80.1	1.8
Australia [1]	103 200	0.7	96 000	0.6	-7.0
Japan	392 300	2.7	408 500	2.7	4.1
New Zealand	28 400	0.2	28 500	0.2	0.4
Total Asia and the Pacific	523 900	3.6	533 000	3.5	1.7
Austria	26 500	0.2	28 700	0.2	8.3
Belgium [2]	34 800	0.2	38 000	0.3	9.2
Denmark	17 900	0.1	18 600	0.1	3.9
Finland	12 400	0.1	11 700	0.1	-5.6
France [3]	310 000	2.1	360 700	2.4	16.4
Germany	290 300	2.0	338 700	2.2	16.7
Greece	14 300	0.1	14 600	0.1	2.1
Iceland	1 400	0.0	1 100	0.0	-21.4
Ireland	17 500	0.1	19 300	0.1	10.3
Italy	94 800	0.6	96 600	0.6	1.9
Luxembourg [2]	..	..	..	..	..
Netherlands	85 200	0.6	84 200	0.6	-1.2
Norway	13 300	0.1	12 900	0.1	-3.0
Portugal	15 400	0.1	15 600	0.1	1.3
Spain	27 700	0.2	27 000	0.2	-2.5
Sweden	25 900	0.2	23 600	0.2	-8.9
Switzerland	79 100	0.5	83 100	0.5	5.1
Turkey	3 400	0.0	3 800	0.0	11.8
United Kingdom	536 400	3.6	561 600	3.7	4.7
Other OECD-Europe	..	..	..	..	..
Total Europe	1 606 300	10.9	1 739 800	11.5	8.3
Total OECD Countries	**14 014 000**	**95.1**	**14 370 500**	**95.1**	**2.5**
Other European countries	67 400	0.5	71 700	0.5	6.4
Bulgaria [2]	4 100	0.0	4 800	0.0	17.1
Ex-Czechoslovakia	10 100	0.1	11 300	0.1	11.9
Hungary	7 500	0.1	8 300	0.1	10.7
Poland	20 200	0.1	19 600	0.1	-3.0
Ex-USSR	17 600	0.1	17 800	0.1	1.1
Ex-Yugoslavia	7 900	0.1	8 000	0.1	1.3
Latin America	58 600	0.4	61 600	0.4	5.1
Argentina	15 800	0.1	17 600	0.1	11.4
Brazil	26 300	0.2	25 900	0.2	-1.5
Colombia	5 300	0.0	6 900	0.0	30.2
Venezuela	11 200	0.1	12 200	0.1	8.9
Asia-Oceania	385 600	2.6	385 400	2.6	-0.1
China [4]	27 600	0.2	30 700	0.2	11.2
Hong Kong	119 400	0.8	116 400	0.8	-2.5
India [2]	47 400	0.3	46 100	0.3	-2.7
Israel	48 800	0.3	47 600	0.3	-2.5
Republic of Korea [2]	37 600	0.3	39 900	0.3	6.1
Malaysia [2]	14 500	0.1	14 300	0.1	-1.4
Philippines [2]	18 300	0.1	17 800	0.1	-2.7
Singapore [2]	18 900	0.1	18 300	0.1	-3.2
Taiwan	40 900	0.3	44 800	0.3	9.5
Thailand [2]	12 200	0.1	10 800	0.1	-11.5
Africa	13 900	0.1	18 800	0.1	35.3
South Africa	13 900	0.1	16 900	0.1	21.6
Origin country undetermined [5]	201 300	1.4	201 300	1.3	0.0
Total non-OECD Countries	**726 800**	**4.9**	**738 800**	**4.9**	**1.7**
TOTAL [2]	14 740 800	100.0	15 109 300	100.0	2.5

Australia includes Papua New Guinea, Solomon, Caroline and Christmas islands.
Estimate.
France includes Andorra and Monaco.
China includes Mongolia and Tibet.
"Origin country undetermined" includes Bermuda, Caribbean, Central America, Greenland and St. Pierre and Miquelon.

145

CANADA

ARRIVALS OF FOREIGN VISITORS AT FRONTIERS

(by country of residence)

	1992	Relative share	1993	Relative share	% Variation over 1992
Canada	..	..	..	..	..
Mexico	75 500	0.2	84 500	0.2	11.9
United States	32 427 300	89.6	32 622 700	90.3	0.6
Total North America	32 502 800	89.8	32 707 200	90.6	0.6
Australia [1]	113 300	0.3	102 700	0.3	−9.4
Japan	495 800	1.4	505 800	1.4	2.0
New Zealand	30 800	0.1	31 200	0.1	1.3
Total Asia and the Pacific	639 900	1.8	639 700	1.8	−0.0
Austria	28 400	0.1	30 800	0.1	8.5
Belgium [2]	36 700	0.1	38 800	0.1	5.7
Denmark	20 400	0.1	21 100	0.1	3.4
Finland	13 600	0.0	13 100	0.0	−3.7
France [3]	328 300	0.9	383 200	1.1	16.7
Germany	339 900	0.9	396 600	1.1	16.7
Greece	16 000	0.0	18 200	0.1	13.8
Iceland	1 500	0.0	1 300	0.0	−13.3
Ireland	18 800	0.1	20 900	0.1	11.2
Italy	111 100	0.3	111 000	0.3	−0.1
Luxembourg [2]	..	..	..	..	..
Netherlands	92 100	0.3	91 300	0.3	−0.9
Norway	14 500	0.0	14 000	0.0	−3.4
Portugal	15 800	0.0	18 100	0.1	14.6
Spain	31 000	0.1	30 300	0.1	−2.3
Sweden	28 100	0.1	26 000	0.1	−7.5
Switzerland	85 500	0.2	88 700	0.2	3.7
Turkey	3 800	0.0	4 200	0.0	10.5
United Kingdom	595 600	1.6	629 200	1.7	5.6
Other OECD-Europe	..	..	..	..	..
Total Europe	1 781 100	4.9	1 936 800	5.4	8.7
Total OECD Countries	**34 923 800**	**96.5**	**35 283 700**	**97.7**	**1.0**
Other European countries	71 700	0.2	76 900	0.2	7.3
Bulgaria [2]	4 300	0.0	5 200	0.0	20.9
Ex-Czechoslovakia	11 000	0.0	12 400	0.0	12.7
Hungary	7 900	0.0	8 900	0.0	12.7
Poland	21 600	0.1	21 000	0.1	−2.8
Ex-USSR	18 000	0.0	18 200	0.1	1.1
Ex-Yugoslavia	8 900	0.0	9 100	0.0	2.2
Latin America	66 600	0.2	79 500	0.2	19.4
Argentina	19 100	0.1	20 000	0.1	4.7
Brazil	28 600	0.1	29 000	0.1	1.4
Colombia	6 200	0.0	7 000	0.0	12.9
Venezuela	12 700	0.0	13 500	0.0	6.3
Asia-Oceania	440 400	1.2	440 800	1.2	0.1
China [4]	32 200	0.1	34 600	0.1	7.5
Hong Kong	126 400	0.3	123 100	0.3	−2.6
India [2]	60 100	0.2	57 600	0.2	−4.2
Israel	59 100	0.2	57 000	0.2	−3.6
Republic of Korea [2]	46 200	0.1	48 400	0.1	4.8
Malaysia [2]	16 900	0.0	18 400	0.1	8.9
Philippines [2]	20 700	0.1	20 900	0.1	1.0
Singapore [2]	21 900	0.1	20 200	0.1	−7.8
Taiwan	43 600	0.1	48 300	0.1	10.8
Thailand [2]	13 300	0.0	12 700	0.0	−4.5
Africa	14 800	0.0	17 500	0.0	18.2
South Africa	14 800	0.0	17 600	0.0	18.9
Origin country undetermined [5]	669 000	1.8	216 000	0.6	−67.7
Total non-OECD Countries	**1 262 500**	**3.5**	**830 700**	**2.3**	**−34.2**
TOTAL [2]	36 186 300	100.0	36 114 400	100.0	−0.2

1. Australia includes Papua New Guinea, Solomon, Caroline and Christmas islands.
2. Estimate.
3. France includes Andorra and Monaco.
4. China includes Mongolia and Tibet.
5. "Origin country undetermined" includes Bermuda, Caribbean, Central America, Greenland and St. Pierre and Miquelon.

CANADA

NIGHTS SPENT BY FOREIGN TOURISTS IN TOURIST ACCOMMODATION[1]

(by country of residence)

	1992	Relative share	1993	Relative share	% Variation over 1992
Canada	..	..	..	..	..
Mexico	564 500	0.7	650 200	0.8	15.2
United States	46 289 400	58.3	47 491 100	57.9	2.6
Total North America	46 853 900	59.0	48 141 300	58.6	2.7
Australia	1 171 900	1.5	974 600	1.2	−16.8
Japan	2 495 400	3.1	2 879 300	3.5	15.4
New Zealand	310 800	0.4	287 700	0.4	−7.4
Total Asia and the Pacific	3 978 100	5.0	4 141 600	5.0	4.1
Austria	305 000	0.4	373 000	0.5	22.3
Belgium	442 500	0.6	406 600	0.5	−8.1
Denmark	195 900	0.2	217 800	0.3	11.2
Finland	103 500	0.1	125 300	0.2	21.1
France	3 819 600	4.8	4 273 400	5.2	11.9
Germany	3 589 400	4.5	4 281 000	5.2	19.3
Greece	279 600	0.4	270 000	0.3	−3.4
Iceland	5 600	0.0	4 600	0.0	−17.9
Ireland	201 800	0.3	202 900	0.2	0.5
Italy	907 000	1.1	991 300	1.2	9.3
Luxembourg	..	..	..	..	..
Netherlands	1 058 700	1.3	1 158 200	1.4	9.4
Norway	144 700	0.2	119 200	0.1	−17.6
Portugal	236 800	0.3	198 300	0.2	−16.3
Spain	302 800	0.4	338 600	0.4	11.8
Sweden	222 100	0.3	209 000	0.3	−5.9
Switzerland	1 115 300	1.4	1 096 000	1.3	−1.7
Turkey	44 700	0.1	40 200	0.0	−10.1
United Kingdom	6 118 700	7.7	6 468 600	7.9	5.7
Other OECD-Europe	..	..	..	..	..
Total Europe	19 093 700	24.0	20 774 000	25.3	8.8
Total OECD Countries	**69 925 700**	**88.0**	**73 056 900**	**89.0**	**4.5**
Other European countries	1 792 300	2.3	1 442 800	1.8	−19.5
Bulgaria	151 000	0.2	175 400	0.2	16.2
Ex-Czechoslovakia	204 300	0.3	182 200	0.2	−10.8
Hungary	204 600	0.3	114 300	0.1	−44.1
Poland	631 800	0.8	476 900	0.6	−24.5
Ex-USSR	451 900	0.6	298 000	0.4	−34.1
Ex-Yugoslavia	148 700	0.2	164 000	0.2	10.3
Latin America	620 000	0.8	598 100	0.7	−3.5
Argentina	209 900	0.3	262 600	0.3	25.1
Brazil	273 300	0.3	249 800	0.3	−8.6
Colombia	41 600	0.1	47 000	0.1	13.0
Venezuela	95 200	0.1	147 000	0.2	54.4
Asia-Oceania	3 908 900	4.9	3 936 100	4.8	0.7
China	407 000	0.5	518 700	0.6	27.4
Hong Kong	407 000	0.5	1 167 400	1.4	186.8
India	443 100	0.6	633 500	0.8	43.0
Israel	398 600	0.5	437 900	0.5	9.9
Republic of Korea	237 100	0.3	308 000	0.4	29.9
Malaysia	151 900	0.2	134 400	0.2	−11.5
Philippines	296 000	0.4	159 000	0.2	−46.3
Singapore	203 900	0.3	168 400	0.2	−17.4
Taiwan	450 600	0.6	412 700	0.5	−8.4
Thailand	114 600	0.1	122 100	0.1	6.5
Africa	173 000	0.2	204 800	0.2	18.4
South Africa	173 000	0.2	204 800	0.2	18.4
Origin country undetermined	3 003 600	3.8	2 853 400	3.5	−5.0
Total non-OECD Countries	**9 497 800**	**12.0**	**9 035 200**	**11.0**	**−4.9**
TOTAL	**79 423 500**	**100.0**	**82 092 100**	**100.0**	**3.4**

1. Covers all forms of accommodation, including homes of friends or relatives.

DENMARK

NIGHTS SPENT BY FOREIGN TOURISTS IN HOTELS

(by country of nationality)

	1992	Relative share	1993	Relative share	% Variation over 1992
Canada [1]	..	..	..	..	..
Mexico	..	..	..	..	..
United States	305 200	4.9	292 000	4.9	−4.3
Total North America	305 200	4.9	292 000	4.9	−4.3
Australia [1]	..	..	..	..	..
Japan	110 900	1.8	100 000	1.7	−9.8
New Zealand [1]	..	..	..	..	..
Total Asia and the Pacific	110 900	1.8	100 000	1.7	−9.8
Austria [2]	..	..	..	..	..
Belgium [2]	..	..	..	..	..
Denmark	..	..	..	..	..
Finland	104 000	1.7	78 700	1.3	−24.3
France	81 200	1.3	83 900	1.4	3.3
Germany	1 703 900	27.6	1 713 900	29.0	0.6
Greece [2]	..	..	..	..	..
Iceland [2]	..	..	..	..	..
Ireland [2]	..	..	..	..	..
Italy	157 700	2.6	127 800	2.2	−19.0
Luxembourg [2]	..	..	..	..	..
Netherlands	194 700	3.2	183 500	3.1	−5.8
Norway	793 800	12.8	813 100	13.8	2.4
Portugal [2]	..	..	..	..	..
Spain [2]	..	..	..	..	..
Sweden	1 724 900	27.9	1 430 300	24.2	−17.1
Switzerland [2]	..	..	..	..	..
Turkey [2]	..	..	..	..	..
United Kingdom	320 400	5.2	328 300	5.6	2.5
Other OECD-Europe [2]	317 600	5.1	359 900	6.1	13.3
Total Europe	5 398 200	87.4	5 119 400	86.6	−5.2
Total OECD Countries	**5 814 300**	**94.1**	**5 511 400**	**93.2**	**−5.2**
Origin country undetermined [1]	363 400	5.9	401 600	6.8	10.5
Total non-OECD Countries	**363 400**	**5.9**	**401 600**	**6.8**	**10.5**
TOTAL	**6 177 700**	**100.0**	**5 913 000**	**100.0**	**−4.3**

1. ''Origin country undetermined'' includes Australia, Canada and New Zealand.
2. ''Other OECD-Europe'' includes Austria, Belgium, Greece,Iceland, Ireland, Luxembourg, Portugal, Spain, Switzerland, Turkey as well as European non-member countries.

DENMARK

NIGHTS SPENT BY FOREIGN TOURISTS IN REGISTERED TOURIST ACCOMMODATION

(by country of nationality)

	1992	Relative share	1993	Relative share	% Variation over 1992
Canada [1]	..	..	..	..	..
Mexico	..	..	..	..	..
United States	324 200	2.8	306 400	2.9	−5.5
Total North America	324 200	2.8	306 400	2.9	−5.5
Australia [1]	..	..	..	..	..
Japan [2]	110 900	1.0	100 000	1.0	−9.8
New Zealand [1]	..	..	..	..	..
Total Asia and the Pacific	110 900	1.0	100 000	1.0	−9.8
Austria [3]	..	..	..	..	..
Belgium [3]	..	..	..	..	..
Denmark	..	..	..	..	..
Finland	191 600	1.7	130 000	1.2	−32.2
France	150 400	1.3	142 600	1.4	−5.2
Germany	4 573 000	39.5	4 530 900	43.3	−0.9
Greece [3]	..	..	..	..	..
Iceland [3]	..	..	..	..	..
Ireland [3]	..	..	..	..	..
Italy	233 300	2.0	183 600	1.8	−21.3
Luxembourg [3]	..	..	..	..	..
Netherlands	1 003 300	8.7	685 900	6.6	−31.6
Norway	1 140 200	9.8	1 110 300	10.6	−2.6
Portugal [3]	..	..	..	..	..
Spain [3]	..	..	..	..	..
Sweden	2 614 500	22.6	1 959 100	18.7	−25.1
Switzerland [3]	..	..	..	..	..
Turkey [3]	..	..	..	..	..
United Kingdom	381 800	3.3	375 300	3.6	−1.7
Other OECD-Europe [3]	442 400	3.8	475 300	4.5	7.4
Total Europe	10 730 500	92.6	9 593 000	91.7	−10.6
Total OECD Countries	**11 165 600**	**96.4**	**9 999 400**	**95.6**	**−10.4**
Origin country undetermined [1]	422 500	3.6	460 600	4.4	9.0
Total non-OECD Countries	**422 500**	**3.6**	**460 600**	**4.4**	**9.0**
TOTAL	**11 588 100**	**100.0**	**10 460 000**	**100.0**	**−9.7**

1. "Origin country undetermined" includes Australia, Canada and New Zealand.
2. Japan includes only nights spent in hotels.
3. "Other OECD-Europe" includes Austria, Belgium, Greece, Iceland, Ireland, Luxembourg, Portugal, Spain, Switzerland, Turkey as well as European non-member countries.

FINLAND

ARRIVALS OF FOREIGN TOURISTS AT HOTELS

(by country of residence)

	1992	Relative share	1993	Relative share	% Variation over 1992
Canada	..	..	10 842	0.7	..
Mexico	..	..	630	0.0	..
United States	..	..	88 168	5.9	..
Total North America	..	..	99 640	6.7	..
Australia	..	..	5 335	0.4	..
Japan	..	..	41 863	2.8	..
New Zealand	..	..	764	0.1	..
Total Asia and the Pacific	..	..	47 962	3.2	..
Austria	..	..	12 251	0.8	..
Belgium	..	..	11 919	0.8	..
Denmark	..	..	34 018	2.3	..
Finland	..	..	..	..	..
France	..	..	55 390	3.7	..
Germany	..	..	342 585	23.0	..
Greece	..	..	5 743	0.4	..
Iceland	..	..	2 994	0.2	..
Ireland [1]	..	..	1 240	0.1	..
Italy	..	..	44 252	3.0	..
Luxembourg	..	..	435	0.0	..
Netherlands	..	..	36 608	2.5	..
Norway	..	..	68 874	4.6	..
Portugal [2]	..	..	5 255	0.4	..
Spain [2]	..	..	26 787	1.8	..
Sweden	..	..	336 217	22.6	..
Switzerland	..	..	39 320	2.6	..
Turkey	..	..	2 495	0.2	..
United Kingdom [1]	..	..	74 513	5.0	..
Other OECD-Europe	..	..	..	..	..
Total Europe	..	..	1 100 896	74.0	..
Total OECD Countries	..	..	**1 248 498**	**84.0**	..
Bulgaria	..	..	881	0.1	..
Hungary	..	..	4 848	0.3	..
Poland	..	..	8 020	0.5	..
Rumania	..	..	1 820	0.1	..
Ex-USSR	..	..	93 924	6.3	..
Ex-Yugoslavia	..	..	230	0.0	..
Argentina	..	..	367	0.0	..
Brazil	..	..	1 566	0.1	..
Chile	..	..	360	0.0	..
Colombia	..	..	117	0.0	..
Venezuela	..	..	873	0.1	..
China	..	..	6 568	0.4	..
Hong Kong	..	..	1 185	0.1	..
India	..	..	1 130	0.1	..
Iran	..	..	772	0.1	..
Israel	..	..	3 596	0.2	..
Republic of Korea	..	..	2 438	0.2	..
Lebanon	..	..	62	0.0	..
Malaysia	..	..	494	0.0	..
Pakistan	..	..	141	0.0	..
Philippines	..	..	253	0.0	..
Saudi Arabia	..	..	401	0.0	..
Singapore	..	..	1 292	0.1	..
Taiwan	..	..	3 043	0.2	..
Thailand	..	..	2 553	0.2	..
Algeria	..	..	82	0.0	..
Egypt	..	..	489	0.0	..
Morocco	..	..	211	0.0	..
South Africa	..	..	491	0.0	..
Origin country undetermined [3]	..	..	238 538	16.0	..
Total non-OECD Countries	..	..	**238 538**	**16.0**	..
TOTAL	..	..	**1 487 036**	**100.0**	..

1. United Kingdom includes Ireland.
2. Spain includes Portugal.
3. "Origin country undetermined" includes all non-OECD countries.

FINLAND

NIGHTS SPENT BY FOREIGN TOURISTS IN HOTELS

(by country of residence)

	1992	Relative share	1993	Relative share	% Variation over 1992
Canada	21 033	0.9	24 335	0.9	15.7
Mexico	..	..	1 130	0.0	..
United States	151 137	6.7	163 910	6.3	8.5
Total North America	172 170	7.7	189 375	7.3	10.0
Australia	..	..	10 282	0.4	..
Japan	57 170	2.5	71 522	2.8	25.1
New Zealand	..	..	1 594	0.1	..
Total Asia and the Pacific	57 170	2.5	83 398	3.2	45.9
Austria	23 164	1.0	21 558	0.8	–6.9
Belgium	16 427	0.7	20 999	0.8	27.8
Denmark	64 155	2.9	60 340	2.3	–5.9
Finland	..	..	..	..	..
France	83 679	3.7	94 809	3.7	13.3
Germany	376 700	16.8	504 025	19.5	33.8
Greece	..	..	10 088	0.4	..
Iceland	7 806	0.3	6 402	0.2	–18.0
Ireland [1]	..	..	2 408	0.1	..
Italy	76 557	3.4	76 861	3.0	0.4
Luxembourg	..	..	793	0.0	..
Netherlands	61 863	2.8	65 581	2.5	6.0
Norway	99 759	4.4	118 907	4.6	19.2
Portugal [2]	..	..	9 186	0.4	..
Spain [2]	32 966	1.5	47 465	1.8	44.0
Sweden	510 089	22.7	542 150	21.0	6.3
Switzerland	59 327	2.6	68 078	2.6	14.8
Turkey	..	..	4 858	0.2	..
United Kingdom [1]	126 885	5.7	140 677	5.4	10.9
Other OECD-Europe	..	..	..	..	..
Total Europe	1 539 377	68.6	1 795 185	69.4	16.6
Total OECD Countries	**1 768 717**	**78.9**	**2 067 958**	**79.9**	**16.9**
Bulgaria [3]	9 163	0.4	3 571	0.1	–61.0
Ex-Czechoslovakia	10 976	0.5	..	..	..
Hungary	13 383	0.6	13 792	0.5	3.1
Poland	19 342	0.9	20 662	0.8	6.8
Rumania [3]	..	..	5 050	0.2	..
Ex-USSR	171 349	7.6	203 474	7.9	18.7
Ex-Yugoslavia	..	..	1 012	0.0	..
Argentina	..	..	662	0.0	..
Brazil	..	..	3 950	0.2	..
Chile	..	..	803	0.0	..
Colombia	..	..	207	0.0	..
Venezuela	..	..	2 126	0.1	..
China	..	..	20 103	0.8	..
Hong Kong	..	..	1 993	0.1	..
India	..	..	2 988	0.1	..
Iran	..	..	2 802	0.1	..
Israel	..	..	5 934	0.2	..
Republic of Korea	..	..	4 102	0.2	..
Lebanon	..	..	148	0.0	..
Malaysia	..	..	1 436	0.1	..
Pakistan	..	..	374	0.0	..
Philippines	..	..	965	0.0	..
Saudi Arabia	..	..	1 187	0.0	..
Singapore	..	..	2 132	0.1	..
Taiwan	..	..	3 921	0.2	..
Thailand	..	..	4 847	0.2	..
Algeria	..	..	289	0.0	..
Egypt	..	..	1 292	0.0	..
Morocco	..	..	569	0.0	..
South Africa	..	..	1 127	0.0	..
Origin country undetermined [4]	474 024	21.1	519 766	20.1	9.6
Total non-OECD Countries	**474 024**	**21.1**	**519 766**	**20.1**	**9.6**
TOTAL	**2 242 741**	**100.0**	**2 587 724**	**100.0**	**15.4**

1. United Kingdom includes Ireland.
2. Spain includes Portugal.
3. For Bulgaria includes Rumania.
4. ''Origin country undetermined'' includes all non-OECD countries.

FRANCE

ARRIVALS OF FOREIGN TOURISTS AT FRONTIERS[1]

(by country of residence)

	1992	Relative share	1993	Relative share	% Variation over 1992
Canada	591 000	1.0	697 000	1.2	17.9
Mexico	..	..	..	..	..
United States	2 013 000	3.4	1 968 000	3.3	-2.2
Total North America	2 604 000	4.4	2 665 000	4.4	2.3
Australia	..	..	..	..	..
Japan	449 000	0.8	325 000	0.5	-27.6
New Zealand	..	..	..	..	..
Total Asia and the Pacific	449 000	0.8	325 000	0.5	-27.6
Austria	460 000	0.8	332 000	0.6	-27.8
Belgium	7 307 000	12.2	7 939 000	13.2	8.6
Denmark	728 000	1.2	708 000	1.2	-2.7
Finland	88 000	0.1	109 000	0.2	23.9
France	..	..	..	..	..
Germany	12 663 000	21.2	13 041 000	21.7	3.0
Greece	303 000	0.5	341 000	0.6	12.5
Iceland	24 000	0.0	14 000	0.0	-41.7
Ireland	425 000	0.7	449 000	0.7	5.6
Italy	7 229 000	12.1	6 473 000	10.8	-10.5
Luxembourg	322 000	0.5	350 000	0.6	8.7
Netherlands	6 298 000	10.5	7 141 000	11.9	13.4
Norway	332 000	0.6	316 000	0.5	-4.8
Portugal	1 358 000	2.3	1 686 000	2.8	24.2
Spain	3 432 000	5.7	3 062 000	5.1	-10.8
Sweden	850 000	1.4	912 000	1.5	7.3
Switzerland	2 396 000	4.0	1 967 000	3.3	-17.9
Turkey	..	..	..	..	..
United Kingdom	8 292 000	13.9	8 148 000	13.6	-1.7
Other OECD-Europe	..	..	..	..	..
Total Europe	52 507 000	87.9	52 988 000	88.2	0.9
Total OECD Countries	**55 560 000**	**93.0**	**55 978 000**	**93.1**	**0.8**
Origin country indetermined	4 150 000	7.0	4 122 000	6.9	-0.7
Total non-OECD Countries	**4 150 000**	**7.0**	**4 122 000**	**6.9**	**-0.7**
TOTAL	**59 710 000**	**100.0**	**60 100 000**	**100.0**	**0.7**

1. Estimates of number of "trips", the same person coming perhaps several times in one year.

152

FRANCE[1]

ARRIVALS OF FOREIGN TOURISTS AT HOTELS

(by country of residence)

	1992	Relative share	1993	Relative share	% Variation over 1992
Canada	399 387	1.4	383 051	1.5	–4.1
Mexico	..	..	..	..	..
United States	2 254 545	7.9	2 128 717	8.1	–5.6
Total North America	2 653 932	9.3	2 511 768	9.6	–5.4
Australia	..	..	..	..	..
Japan	1 551 074	5.5	1 506 951	5.7	–2.8
New Zealand	..	..	..	..	..
Total Asia and the Pacific	1 551 074	5.5	1 506 951	5.7	–2.8
Austria [2]	..	..	..	..	..
Belgium [3]	1 764 431	6.2	1 781 358	6.8	1.0
Denmark	221 305	0.8	228 988	0.9	3.5
Finland [2]	..	..	..	..	..
France	..	..	..	..	..
Germany	4 124 757	14.5	3 872 626	14.7	–6.1
Greece [4]	..	..	..	..	..
Iceland [2]	..	..	..	..	..
Ireland [5]	..	..	..	..	..
Italy [4]	3 722 894	13.1	3 119 247	11.9	–16.2
Luxembourg [3]	..	..	..	..	..
Netherlands	1 293 800	4.6	1 308 447	5.0	1.1
Norway [2]	..	..	..	..	..
Portugal [6]	..	..	..	..	..
Spain [6]	1 933 124	6.8	1 699 163	6.5	–12.1
Sweden [2]	..	..	..	..	..
Switzerland	1 199 975	4.2	1 209 437	4.6	0.8
Turkey	..	..	..	..	..
United Kingdom [5]	5 556 868	19.6	4 756 106	18.1	–14.4
Other OECD-Europe [2]	1 173 360	4.1	1 092 171	4.2	–6.9
Total Europe	20 990 514	73.9	19 067 543	72.6	–9.2
Total OECD Countries	**25 195 520**	**88.7**	**23 086 262**	**87.9**	**–8.4**
Latin America [7]	376 648	1.3	362 107	1.4	–3.9
Asia-Oceania [8]	923 326	3.3	1 057 451	4.0	14.5
Africa	371 572	1.3	320 060	1.2	–13.9
Origin country undetermined	1 523 394	5.4	1 443 649	5.5	–5.2
Total non-OECD Countries	**3 194 940**	**11.3**	**3 183 267**	**12.1**	**–0.4**
TOTAL	**28 390 460**	**100.0**	**26 269 529**	**100.0**	**–7.5**

. Data covering all France except 2 regions (Champagne-Ardenne and Corse).
. "Other OECD-Europe" includes Austria, Iceland, Finland, Norway and Sweden.
. Belgium includes Luxembourg.
. Italy includes Greece.
. United Kingdom includes Ireland.
. Spain includes Portugal.
. Latin America includes Central and South America.
. Asia only.

FRANCE[1]

NIGHTS SPENT BY FOREIGN TOURISTS IN HOTELS

(by country of residence)

	1992	Relative share	1993	Relative share	% Variation over 1992
Canada	799 555	1.4	807 635	1.5	1.0
Mexico	..	..	..	..	..
United States	4 976 852	8.5	4 746 255	8.7	−4.6
Total North America	5 776 407	9.8	5 553 890	10.2	−3.9
Australia	..	..	..	..	..
Japan	3 501 848	6.0	3 283 295	6.0	−6.2
New Zealand	..	..	..	..	..
Total Asia and the Pacific	3 501 848	6.0	3 283 295	6.0	−6.2
Austria[2]	..	..	..	..	..
Belgium[3]	3 795 877	6.5	3 801 169	7.0	0.1
Denmark	510 814	0.9	513 077	0.9	0.4
Finland[2]	..	..	..	..	..
France	..	..	..	..	..
Germany	8 308 398	14.1	7 811 366	14.3	−6.0
Greece[4]	..	..	..	..	..
Iceland[2]	..	..	..	..	..
Ireland[5]	..	..	..	..	..
Italy[4]	8 380 527	14.3	7 067 733	12.9	−15.7
Luxembourg[3]	..	..	..	..	..
Netherlands	2 424 585	4.1	2 420 524	4.4	−0.2
Norway[2]	..	..	..	..	..
Portugal[6]	..	..	..	..	..
Spain[6]	3 906 144	6.6	3 522 577	6.5	−9.8
Sweden[2]	..	..	..	..	..
Switzerland	2 483 674	4.2	2 477 014	4.5	−0.3
Turkey	..	..	..	..	..
United Kingdom[5]	11 123 432	18.9	9 449 566	17.3	−15.0
Other OECD-Europe[2]	2 717 209	4.6	2 654 798	4.9	−2.3
Total Europe	43 650 660	74.2	39 717 824	72.7	−9.0
Total OECD Countries	**52 928 915**	**90.0**	**48 555 009**	**88.9**	**−8.3**
Latin America[7]	880 968	1.5	890 623	1.6	1.1
Asia-Oceania[8]	1 205 025	2.0	1 456 162	2.7	20.8
Africa	984 027	1.7	792 989	1.5	−19.4
Origin country undetermined	2 795 949	4.8	2 902 990	5.3	3.8
Total non-OECD Countries	**5 865 969**	**10.0**	**6 042 764**	**11.1**	**3.0**
TOTAL	**58 794 884**	**100.0**	**54 597 773**	**100.0**	**−7.1**

1. Data covering all France except 2 regions (Champagne-Ardenne and Corse).
2. "Other OECD-Europe" includes Austria, Iceland, Finland, Norway and Sweden.
3. Belgium includes Luxembourg.
4. Italy includes Greece.
5. United Kingdom includes Ireland.
6. Spain includes Portugal.
7. Latin America includes Central and South America.
8. Asia only.

FRANCE

NIGHTS SPENT BY FOREIGN TOURISTS IN TOURIST ACCOMMODATION [1]

(by country of residence)

	1992	Relative share	1993	Relative share	% Variation over 1992
Canada	5 429 000	1.3	6 244 000	1.5	15.0
Mexico	..	..	..	..	..
United States	17 606 000	4.1	17 343 000	4.0	−1.5
Total North America	23 035 000	5.4	23 587 000	5.5	2.4
Australia	..	..	..	..	..
Japan	2 022 000	0.5	1 405 000	0.3	−30.5
New Zealand	..	..	..	..	..
Total Asia and the Pacific	2 022 000	0.5	1 405 000	0.3	−30.5
Austria	2 495 000	0.6	1 734 000	0.4	−30.5
Belgium	45 748 000	10.7	48 582 000	11.3	6.2
Denmark	6 170 000	1.4	6 052 000	1.4	−1.9
Finland	1 810 000	0.4	2 508 000	0.6	38.6
France	..	..	..	..	..
Germany	85 916 000	20.2	87 485 000	20.3	1.8
Greece	1 726 000	0.4	1 837 000	0.4	6.4
Iceland	172 000	0.0	99 000	0.0	−42.4
Ireland	3 141 000	0.7	3 296 000	0.8	4.9
Italy	42 766 000	10.0	37 790 000	8.8	−11.6
Luxembourg	2 010 000	0.5	2 134 000	0.5	6.2
Netherlands	60 318 000	14.1	69 556 000	16.2	15.3
Norway	2 467 000	0.6	2 321 000	0.5	−5.9
Portugal	6 540 000	1.5	7 972 000	1.9	21.9
Spain	15 130 000	3.5	13 306 000	3.1	−12.1
Sweden	6 083 000	1.4	6 358 000	1.5	4.5
Switzerland	12 557 000	2.9	10 388 000	2.4	−17.3
Turkey	..	..	..	..	..
United Kingdom	61 405 000	14.4	59 920 000	13.9	−2.4
Other OECD-Europe	..	..	..	..	..
Total Europe	356 454 000	83.6	361 338 000	84.0	1.4
Total OECD Countries	**381 511 000**	**89.5**	**386 330 000**	**89.8**	**1.3**
Origin country indetermined	44 770 000	10.5	43 970 000	10.2	−1.8
Total non-OECD Countries	**44 770 000**	**10.5**	**43 970 000**	**10.2**	**−1.8**
TOTAL	**426 281 000**	**100.0**	**430 300 000**	**100.0**	**0.9**

1. The figures are based on an update of the findings of the 1991 frontier survey.

GERMANY [1]

ARRIVALS OF FOREIGN TOURISTS AT HOTELS [2]

(by country of residence)

	1992	Relative share	1993	Relative share	% Variation over 1992
Canada	145 804	1.1	126 612	1.0	−13.2
Mexico	32 911	0.2	28 953	0.2	−12.0
United States	1 655 826	12.5	1 449 678	12.0	−12.4
Total North America	1 834 541	13.8	1 605 243	13.3	−12.5
Australia	91 054	0.7	77 677	0.6	−14.7
Japan	714 370	5.4	657 742	5.4	−7.9
New Zealand	10 957	0.1	10 719	0.1	−2.2
Total Asia and the Pacific	816 381	6.1	746 138	6.2	−8.6
Austria	570 146	4.3	561 751	4.7	−1.5
Belgium	501 025	3.8	480 741	4.0	−4.0
Denmark	550 155	4.1	493 099	4.1	−10.4
Finland	140 101	1.1	103 499	0.9	−26.1
France	720 259	5.4	683 740	5.7	−5.1
Germany	..	..	..	..	..
Greece	101 051	0.8	88 529	0.7	−12.4
Iceland	17 852	0.1	17 832	0.1	−0.1
Ireland	32 454	0.2	31 954	0.3	−1.5
Italy	865 776	6.5	693 898	5.7	−19.9
Luxembourg	71 121	0.5	70 811	0.6	−0.4
Netherlands	1 501 341	11.3	1 442 874	12.0	−3.9
Norway	247 721	1.9	202 301	1.7	−18.3
Portugal	46 531	0.4	47 387	0.4	1.8
Spain	270 659	2.0	239 599	2.0	−11.5
Sweden	900 390	6.8	620 254	5.1	−31.1
Switzerland	722 702	5.4	710 829	5.9	−1.6
Turkey	91 805	0.7	97 577	0.8	6.3
United Kingdom	1 250 436	9.4	1 158 558	9.6	−7.3
Other OECD-Europe	..	..	..	..	..
Total Europe	8 601 525	64.7	7 745 233	64.2	−10.0
Total OECD Countries	**11 252 447**	**84.7**	**10 096 614**	**83.6**	**−10.3**
Other European countries	810 745	6.1	805 061	6.7	−0.7
Bulgaria	23 575	0.2	22 966	0.2	−2.6
Ex-Czechoslovakia	150 022	1.1	141 514	1.2	−5.7
Hungary	117 725	0.9	115 621	1.0	−1.8
Poland	190 316	1.4	187 026	1.5	−1.7
Rumania	30 548	0.2	28 630	0.2	−6.3
Ex-USSR	132 825	1.0	167 584	1.4	26.2
Ex-Yugoslavia	165 734	1.2	141 720	1.2	−14.5
Latin America	100 751	0.8	94 740	0.8	−6.0
Argentina	28 471	0.2	24 293	0.2	−14.7
Brazil	62 608	0.5	60 993	0.5	−2.6
Chile	9 672	0.1	9 454	0.1	−2.3
Asia-Oceania	102 738	0.8	91 421	0.8	−11.0
Israel	102 738	0.8	91 421	0.8	−11.0
Africa	39 537	0.3	38 416	0.3	−2.8
South Africa	39 537	0.3	38 416	0.3	−2.8
Origin country undetermined	986 180	7.4	944 994	7.8	−4.2
Total non-OECD Countries	**2 039 951**	**15.3**	**1 974 632**	**16.4**	**−3.2**
TOTAL	**13 292 398**	**100.0**	**12 071 246**	**100.0**	**−9.2**

1. The data relate to the whole of Germany.
2. Arrivals at hotels (including "bed and breakfast"), boarding houses and inns.

GERMANY [1]

ARRIVALS OF FOREIGN TOURISTS AT REGISTERED TOURIST ACCOMMODATION [2]

(by country of residence)

	1992	Relative share	1993	Relative share	% Variation over 1992
Canada	172 968	1.1	149 283	1.0	−13.7
Mexico	36 367	0.2	32 141	0.2	−11.6
United States	1 762 595	11.1	1 542 297	10.7	−12.5
Total North America	1 971 930	12.4	1 723 721	12.0	−12.6
Australia	140 298	0.9	121 621	0.8	−13.3
Japan	746 681	4.7	684 856	4.8	−8.3
New Zealand	26 646	0.2	23 778	0.2	−10.8
Total Asia and the Pacific	913 625	5.7	830 255	5.8	−9.1
Austria	624 860	3.9	609 801	4.3	−2.4
Belgium	596 069	3.7	565 807	3.9	−5.1
Denmark	752 422	4.7	657 425	4.6	−12.6
Finland	192 109	1.2	134 693	0.9	−29.9
France	870 660	5.5	815 212	5.7	−6.4
Germany	..	..	..	..	..
Greece	105 810	0.7	92 094	0.6	−13.0
Iceland	20 551	0.1	19 614	0.1	−4.6
Ireland	49 516	0.3	44 393	0.3	−10.3
Italy	955 851	6.0	757 367	5.3	−20.8
Luxembourg	80 366	0.5	80 497	0.6	0.2
Netherlands	2 446 314	15.4	2 299 550	16.0	−6.0
Norway	285 652	1.8	231 737	1.6	−18.9
Portugal	52 071	0.3	54 096	0.4	3.9
Spain	311 593	2.0	270 253	1.9	−13.3
Sweden	1 042 374	6.6	707 686	4.9	−32.1
Switzerland	790 651	5.0	776 302	5.4	−1.8
Turkey	98 115	0.6	105 352	0.7	7.4
United Kingdom	1 431 827	9.0	1 315 046	9.2	−8.2
Other OECD-Europe	..	..	..	..	..
Total Europe	10 706 811	67.3	9 536 925	66.5	−10.9
Total OECD Countries	**13 592 366**	**85.4**	**12 090 901**	**84.3**	**−11.0**
Other European countries	982 299	6.2	967 484	6.7	−1.5
Bulgaria	26 100	0.2	25 655	0.2	−1.7
Ex-Czechoslovakia	184 620	1.2	171 917	1.2	−6.9
Hungary	142 668	0.9	138 645	1.0	−2.8
Poland	256 852	1.6	242 977	1.7	−5.4
Rumania	34 062	0.2	32 835	0.2	−3.6
Ex-USSR	161 487	1.0	202 881	1.4	25.6
Ex-Yugoslavia	176 510	1.1	152 574	1.1	−13.6
Latin America	117 577	0.7	108 569	0.8	−7.7
Argentina	34 040	0.2	28 620	0.2	−15.9
Brazil	70 938	0.4	67 952	0.5	−4.2
Chile	12 599	0.1	11 997	0.1	−4.8
Asia-Oceania	110 038	0.7	97 236	0.7	−11.6
Israel	110 038	0.7	97 236	0.7	−11.6
Africa	47 778	0.3	48 088	0.3	0.6
South Africa	47 778	0.3	48 088	0.3	0.6
Origin country undetermined	1 063 156	6.7	1 035 432	7.2	−2.6
Total non-OECD Countries	**2 320 848**	**14.6**	**2 256 809**	**15.7**	**−2.8**
TOTAL	**15 913 214**	**100.0**	**14 347 710**	**100.0**	**−9.8**

1. The data relate to the whole of Germany. Since 1992, includes camping sites.
2. Arrivals at hotels and similar establishments, holiday villages, sanatoria and recreation and holiday homes.

GERMANY[1]

NIGHTS SPENT BY FOREIGN TOURISTS IN HOTELS[2]

(by country of residence)

	1992	Relative share	1993	Relative share	% Variation over 1992
Canada	300 434	1.1	271 059	1.0	−9.8
Mexico	77 226	0.3	65 550	0.3	−15.1
United States	3 379 703	11.9	3 030 238	11.6	−10.3
Total North America	3 757 363	13.2	3 366 847	12.9	−10.4
Australia	183 868	0.6	164 525	0.6	−10.5
Japan	1 194 905	4.2	1 099 530	4.2	−8.0
New Zealand	24 424	0.1	24 287	0.1	−0.6
Total Asia and the Pacific	1 403 197	4.9	1 288 342	4.9	−8.2
Austria	1 187 839	4.2	1 167 024	4.5	−1.8
Belgium	1 168 754	4.1	1 137 061	4.4	−2.7
Denmark	1 039 490	3.7	954 003	3.7	−8.2
Finland	258 888	0.9	207 014	0.8	−20.0
France	1 386 205	4.9	1 326 007	5.1	−4.3
Germany	..	..	..	..	..
Greece	257 560	0.9	229 308	0.9	−11.0
Iceland	40 696	0.1	40 813	0.2	0.3
Ireland	80 138	0.3	90 707	0.3	13.2
Italy	1 696 316	6.0	1 394 018	5.3	−17.8
Luxembourg	200 146	0.7	195 988	0.8	−2.1
Netherlands	3 305 991	11.6	3 113 119	11.9	−5.8
Norway	419 189	1.5	356 322	1.4	−15.0
Portugal	121 478	0.4	133 215	0.5	9.7
Spain	582 002	2.1	501 269	1.9	−13.9
Sweden	1 444 087	5.1	1 021 570	3.9	−29.3
Switzerland	1 484 355	5.2	1 430 634	5.5	−3.6
Turkey	233 353	0.8	247 091	0.9	5.9
United Kingdom	2 745 668	9.7	2 637 683	10.1	−3.9
Other OECD-Europe	..	..	..	..	..
Total Europe	17 652 155	62.2	16 182 846	62.1	−8.3
Total OECD Countries	**22 812 715**	**80.4**	**20 838 035**	**79.9**	**−8.7**
Other European countries	2 652 614	9.3	2 416 762	9.3	−8.9
Bulgaria	81 010	0.3	66 319	0.3	−18.1
Ex-Czechoslovakia	438 389	1.5	362 301	1.4	−17.4
Hungary	340 305	1.2	311 540	1.2	−8.5
Poland	704 383	2.5	555 976	2.1	−21.1
Rumania	97 009	0.3	92 393	0.4	−4.8
Ex-USSR	443 028	1.6	541 580	2.1	22.2
Ex-Yugoslavia	548 490	1.9	486 653	1.9	−11.3
Latin America	239 920	0.8	224 947	0.9	−6.2
Argentina	67 915	0.2	59 513	0.2	−12.4
Brazil	148 289	0.5	141 710	0.5	−4.4
Chile	23 716	0.1	23 724	0.1	0.0
Asia-Oceania	282 519	1.0	232 970	0.9	−17.5
Israel	282 519	1.0	232 970	0.9	−17.5
Africa	95 282	0.3	93 756	0.4	−1.6
South Africa	95 282	0.3	93 756	0.4	−1.6
Origin country undetermined	2 294 557	8.1	2 262 775	8.7	−1.4
Total non-OECD Countries	**5 564 892**	**19.6**	**5 231 210**	**20.1**	**−6.0**
TOTAL	**28 377 607**	**100.0**	**26 069 245**	**100.0**	**−8.1**

1. The data relate to the whole of Germany.
2. Nights spent in hotels (including "bed and breakfast"), boarding houses and inns.

GERMANY [1]

NIGHTS SPENT BY FOREIGN TOURISTS IN REGISTERED TOURIST ACCOMMODATION [2]

(by country of residence)

	1992	Relative share	1993	Relative share	% Variation over 1992
Canada	352 442	0.9	314 966	0.9	−10.6
Mexico	85 164	0.2	72 897	0.2	−14.4
United States	3 637 657	9.5	3 252 780	9.4	−10.6
Total North America	4 075 263	10.7	3 640 643	10.5	−10.7
Australia	262 940	0.7	236 329	0.7	−10.1
Japan	1 252 052	3.3	1 156 533	3.3	−7.6
New Zealand	50 323	0.1	45 643	0.1	−9.3
Total Asia and the Pacific	1 565 315	4.1	1 438 505	4.1	−8.1
Austria	1 345 342	3.5	1 301 729	3.8	−3.2
Belgium	1 562 168	4.1	1 476 035	4.3	−5.5
Denmark	1 614 339	4.2	1 412 675	4.1	−12.5
Finland	348 823	0.9	262 775	0.8	−24.7
France	1 804 103	4.7	1 694 449	4.9	−6.1
Germany	..	..	..	..	..
Greece	277 463	0.7	246 212	0.7	−11.3
Iceland	50 062	0.1	45 987	0.1	−8.1
Ireland	130 995	0.3	128 577	0.4	−1.8
Italy	1 897 022	5.0	1 549 361	4.5	−18.3
Luxembourg	254 624	0.7	238 744	0.7	−6.2
Netherlands	8 101 892	21.2	7 324 284	21.1	−9.6
Norway	495 102	1.3	415 587	1.2	−16.1
Portugal	147 709	0.4	159 869	0.5	8.2
Spain	690 394	1.8	579 689	1.7	−16.0
Sweden	1 740 201	4.6	1 203 394	3.5	−30.8
Switzerland	1 701 230	4.5	1 633 075	4.7	−4.0
Turkey	255 616	0.7	274 593	0.8	7.4
United Kingdom	3 309 460	8.7	3 152 468	9.1	−4.7
Other OECD-Europe	..	..	..	..	..
Total Europe	25 726 545	67.3	23 099 503	66.5	−10.2
Total OECD Countries	**31 367 123**	**82.1**	**28 178 651**	**81.2**	**−10.2**
Other European countries	3 582 242	9.4	3 292 209	9.5	−8.1
Bulgaria	93 416	0.2	79 121	0.2	−15.3
Ex-Czechoslovakia	537 752	1.4	459 539	1.3	−14.5
Hungary	415 385	1.1	381 305	1.1	−8.2
Poland	1 129 437	3.0	912 157	2.6	−19.2
Rumania	112 810	0.3	107 993	0.3	−4.3
Ex-USSR	693 132	1.8	804 764	2.3	16.1
Ex-Yugoslavia	600 310	1.6	547 330	1.6	−8.8
Latin America	277 271	0.7	257 498	0.7	−7.1
Argentina	79 330	0.2	67 899	0.2	−14.4
Brazil	166 521	0.4	157 840	0.5	−5.2
Chile	31 420	0.1	31 759	0.1	1.1
Asia-Oceania	314 515	0.8	256 280	0.7	−18.5
Israel	314 515	0.8	256 280	0.7	−18.5
Africa	113 607	0.3	113 474	0.3	−0.1
South Africa	113 607	0.3	113 474	0.3	−0.1
Origin country undetermined	2 545 672	6.7	2 613 299	7.5	2.7
Total non-OECD Countries	**6 833 307**	**17.9**	**6 532 760**	**18.8**	**−4.4**
TOTAL	**38 200 430**	**100.0**	**34 711 411**	**100.0**	**−9.1**

. The data relate to the whole of Germany. Since 1992, includes camping sites.
. Nights spent in hotels and similar establishments, holiday villages, sanatoria, and recreation and holiday homes.

GREECE

ARRIVALS OF FOREIGN TOURISTS AT FRONTIERS[1]

(by country of nationality)

	1992	Relative share	1993	Relative share	% Variation over 1992
Canada	59 807	0.6	51 472	0.5	−13.9
Mexico	6 535	0.1	5 336	0.1	−18.3
United States	278 941	3.0	256 719	2.7	−8.0
Total North America	345 283	3.7	313 527	3.3	−9.2
Australia	69 658	0.7	56 064	0.6	−19.5
Japan	109 680	1.2	89 907	1.0	−18.0
New Zealand	8 035	0.1	6 930	0.1	−13.8
Total Asia and the Pacific	187 373	2.0	152 901	1.6	−18.4
Austria	345 259	3.7	288 636	3.1	−16.4
Belgium[2]	225 099	2.4	224 036	2.4	−0.5
Denmark	281 235	3.0	253 622	2.7	−9.8
Finland	172 099	1.8	116 518	1.2	−32.3
France	542 222	5.8	554 644	5.9	2.3
Germany	1 944 704	20.8	2 069 379	22.0	6.4
Greece	..	..	..	..	..
Iceland	..	..	..	..	..
Ireland	57 885	0.6	62 780	0.7	8.5
Italy	622 619	6.7	625 509	6.6	0.5
Luxembourg[2]	..	..	..	..	..
Netherlands	546 187	5.9	510 872	5.4	−6.5
Norway	95 898	1.0	102 452	1.1	6.8
Portugal	26 245	0.3	20 919	0.2	−20.3
Spain	119 964	1.3	118 967	1.3	−0.8
Sweden	314 251	3.4	317 030	3.4	0.9
Switzerland	163 126	1.7	164 999	1.8	1.1
Turkey	73 650	0.8	149 390	1.6	102.8
United Kingdom	2 154 850	23.1	2 191 347	23.3	1.7
Other OECD-Europe	..	..	..	..	..
Total Europe	7 685 293	82.4	7 771 100	82.6	1.1
Total OECD Countries	**8 217 949**	**88.1**	**8 237 528**	**87.5**	**0.2**
Bulgaria	140 725	1.5	144 534	1.5	2.7
Ex-Czechoslovakia	191 585	2.1	89 642	1.0	−53.2
Hungary	107 403	1.2	73 999	0.8	−31.1
Poland	43 788	0.5	34 292	0.4	−21.7
Rumania	19 683	0.2	18 862	0.2	−4.2
Ex-USSR	100 058	1.1	117 160	1.2	17.1
Ex-Yugoslavia	93 413	1.0	191 792	2.0	105.3
Argentina	8 655	0.1	8 794	0.1	1.6
Brazil	8 999	0.1	8 555	0.1	−4.9
Iran	6 794	0.1	7 615	0.1	12.1
Israel	35 065	0.4	45 815	0.5	30.7
Lebanon	15 922	0.2	14 924	0.2	−6.3
Egypt	19 525	0.2	19 609	0.2	0.4
South Africa	16 944	0.2	14 687	0.2	−13.3
Origin country undetermined	1 113 411	11.9	1 175 395	12.5	5.6
Total non-OECD Countries	**1 113 411**	**11.9**	**1 175 395**	**12.5**	**5.6**
TOTAL	**9 331 360**	**100.0**	**9 412 923**	**100.0**	**0.9**

1. Excluding Greek nationals residing abroad and cruise passengers.
2. Belgium includes Luxembourg.

ICELAND

ARRIVALS OF FOREIGN TOURISTS AT FRONTIERS[1]

(by country of nationality)

	1992	Relative share	1993	Relative share	% Variation over 1992
Canada	1 153	0.8	1 473	0.9	27.8
Mexico	140	0.1	149	0.1	6.4
United States	21 706	15.2	25 061	15.9	15.5
Total North America	22 999	16.1	26 683	17.0	16.0
Australia	436	0.3	513	0.3	17.7
Japan	1 431	1.0	1 829	1.2	27.8
New Zealand	178	0.1	154	0.1	−13.5
Total Asia and the Pacific	2 045	1.4	2 496	1.6	22.1
Austria	3 123	2.2	3 102	2.0	−0.7
Belgium	1 223	0.9	1 204	0.8	−1.6
Denmark	14 396	10.1	15 207	9.7	5.6
Finland	4 866	3.4	2 669	1.7	−45.2
France	7 925	5.6	7 522	4.8	−5.1
Germany	24 520	17.2	31 443	20.0	28.2
Greece	181	0.1	155	0.1	−14.4
Iceland	..	..	..	..	
Ireland	542	0.4	685	0.4	26.4
Italy	4 158	2.9	3 617	2.3	−13.0
Luxembourg	332	0.2	489	0.3	47.3
Netherlands	3 808	2.7	5 314	3.4	39.5
Norway	11 218	7.9	12 628	8.0	12.6
Portugal	361	0.3	281	0.2	−22.2
Spain	1 154	0.8	1 533	1.0	32.8
Sweden	16 050	11.3	15 533	9.9	−3.2
Switzerland	5 852	4.1	5 191	3.3	−11.3
Turkey	55	0.0	49	0.0	−10.9
United Kingdom	13 900	9.8	15 498	9.9	11.5
Other OECD-Europe	..	..	1 056	0.7	..
Total Europe	113 664	79.7	123 176	78.3	8.4
Total OECD Countries	**138 708**	**97.3**	**152 355**	**96.8**	**9.8**
Other European countries	1 675	1.2	2 351	1.5	40.4
Bulgaria	35	0.0	77	0.0	120.0
Ex-Czechoslovakia	220	0.2	231	0.1	5.0
Hungary	157	0.1	319	0.2	103.2
Poland	396	0.3	462	0.3	16.7
Rumania	11	0.0	41	0.0	272.7
Ex-USSR	583	0.4	558	0.4	−4.3
Ex-Yugoslavia	221	0.2	104	0.1	−52.9
Latin America	321	0.2	357	0.2	11.2
Argentina	38	0.0	40	0.0	5.3
Brazil	68	0.0	68	0.0	0.0
Chile	34	0.0	53	0.0	55.9
Colombia	14	0.0	19	0.0	35.7
Venezuela	16	0.0	21	0.0	31.3
Asia-Oceania	1 527	1.1	1 949	1.2	27.6
China	129	0.1	156	0.1	20.9
Hong Kong	8	0.0	20	0.0	150.0
India	85	0.1	108	0.1	27.1
Iran	21	0.0	29	0.0	38.1
Israel	249	0.2	235	0.1	−5.6
Republic of Korea	71	0.0	124	0.1	74.6
Lebanon	18	0.0	13	0.0	−27.8
Malaysia	23	0.0	36	0.0	56.5
Pakistan	11	0.0	19	0.0	72.7
Philippines	120	0.1	164	0.1	36.7
Saudi Arabia	8	0.0	6	0.0	−25.0
Singapore	23	0.0	38	0.0	65.2
Taiwan	453	0.3	716	0.5	58.1
Thailand	138	0.1	136	0.1	−1.4
Africa	328	0.2	314	0.2	−4.3
Algeria	8	0.0	14	0.0	75.0
Egypt	31	0.0	20	0.0	−35.5
Morocco	19	0.0	22	0.0	15.8
South Africa	115	0.1	95	0.1	−17.4
Total non-OECD Countries	**3 851**	**2.7**	**4 971**	**3.2**	**29.1**
TOTAL	**142 559**	**100.0**	**157 326**	**100.0**	**10.4**

. Excluding shore excursionists.

161

IRELAND

ARRIVALS OF FOREIGN VISITORS AT FRONTIERS[1]

(by country of residence)

	1992	Relative share	1993	Relative share	% Variation over 1992
Canada	39 000	1.2	40 000	1.2	2.6
Mexico	..	..	..	..	..
United States	366 000	11.7	357 000	10.7	-2.5
Total North America	405 000	12.9	397 000	11.9	-2.0
Australia[2]	53 000	1.7	55 000	1.7	3.8
Japan	13 000	0.4	18 000	0.5	38.5
New Zealand[2]	..	..	..	..	..
Total Asia and the Pacific	66 000	2.1	73 000	2.2	10.6
Austria[3]	..	..	..	..	..
Belgium[3]	..	..	..	..	..
Denmark[3]	..	..	..	..	..
Finland[3]	..	..	..	..	..
France	217 000	6.9	238 000	7.1	9.7
Germany	221 000	7.0	253 000	7.6	14.5
Greece[3]	..	..	..	..	..
Iceland[3]	..	..	..	..	..
Ireland	..	..	..	..	..
Italy[3]	..	..	..	..	..
Luxembourg[3]	..	..	..	..	..
Netherlands[3]	..	..	..	..	..
Norway[3]	..	..	..	..	..
Portugal[3]	..	..	..	..	..
Spain[3]	..	..	..	..	..
Sweden[3]	..	..	..	..	..
Switzerland[3]	..	..	..	..	..
Turkey[3]	..	..	..	..	..
United Kingdom	1 758 000	56.0	1 884 000	56.6	7.2
Other OECD-Europe[3]	417 000	13.3	433 000	13.0	3.8
Total Europe	2 613 000	83.3	2 808 000	84.3	7.5
Total OECD Countries	**3 084 000**	**98.3**	**3 278 000**	**98.4**	**6.3**
Origin country indetermined	53 000	1.7	52 000	1.6	-1.9
Total non-OECD Countries	**53 000**	**1.7**	**52 000**	**1.6**	**-1.9**
TOTAL	**3 137 000**	**100.0**	**3 330 000**	**100.0**	**6.2**

1. Visitors arrivals on overseas routes only.
2. Australia includes New Zealand.
3. Included in "Other OECD-Europe".

IRELAND

ARRIVALS OF FOREIGN TOURISTS AT HOTELS

(by country of residence)

	1992	Relative share	1993	Relative share	% Variation over 1992
Canada	28 000	1.6	36 000	2.0	28.6
Mexico	..	..	..	..	..
United States	341 000	19.0	321 000	17.7	−5.9
Total North America	369 000	20.5	357 000	19.7	−3.3
Australia [1]	35 000	1.9	38 000	2.1	8.6
Japan	..	..	..	..	..
New Zealand [1]	..	..	..	..	..
Total Asia and the Pacific	35 000	1.9	38 000	2.1	8.6
Austria	..	..	..	..	..
Belgium [2]	26 000	1.4	25 000	1.4	−3.8
Denmark	..	..	..	..	..
Finland	..	..	..	..	..
France	139 000	7.7	145 000	8.0	4.3
Germany	125 000	7.0	144 000	8.0	15.2
Greece	..	..	..	..	..
Iceland	..	..	..	..	..
Ireland	..	..	..	..	..
Italy	80 000	4.4	78 000	4.3	−2.5
Luxembourg [2]	..	..	..	..	..
Netherlands	45 000	2.5	44 000	2.4	−2.2
Norway	..	..	..	..	..
Portugal	..	..	..	..	..
Spain	..	..	..	..	..
Sweden	..	..	..	..	..
Switzerland	38 000	2.1	21 000	1.2	−44.7
Turkey	..	..	..	..	..
United Kingdom [3]	789 000	43.9	815 000	45.0	3.3
Other OECD-Europe	100 000	5.6	100 000	5.5	0.0
Total Europe	1 342 000	74.6	1 372 000	75.8	2.2
Total OECD Countries	**1 746 000**	**97.1**	**1 767 000**	**97.6**	**1.2**
Origin country indetermined	52 000	2.9	43 000	2.4	−17.3
Total non-OECD Countries	**52 000**	**2.9**	**43 000**	**2.4**	**−17.3**
TOTAL	**1 798 000**	**100.0**	**1 810 000**	**100.0**	**0.7**

1. Australia includes New Zealand.
2. Belgium includes Luxembourg.
3. The United Kingdom exclude Northern Ireland.

IRELAND

ARRIVALS OF FOREIGN TOURISTS IN TOURIST ACCOMMODATION

(by country of residence)

	1992	Relative share	1993	Relative share	% Variation over 1992
Canada	43 000	1.4	46 000	1.4	7.0
Mexico	..	..	..	..	..
United States	374 000	12.0	376 000	11.5	0.5
Total North America	417 000	13.4	422 000	12.9	1.2
Australia [2]	..	..	..	..	..
Japan	14 000	0.4	18 000	0.5	28.6
New Zealand [1]	57 000	1.8	56 000	1.7	−1.8
Total Asia and the Pacific	71 000	2.3	74 000	2.3	4.2
Austria	..	..	..	..	..
Belgium [2]	40 000	1.3	41 000	1.3	2.5
Denmark	18 000	0.6	17 000	0.5	−5.6
Finland	..	..	..	..	..
France	220 000	7.1	242 000	7.4	10.0
Germany	230 000	7.4	265 000	8.1	15.2
Greece	..	..	..	..	..
Iceland	..	..	..	..	..
Ireland	..	..	..	..	..
Italy	101 000	3.2	116 000	3.5	14.9
Luxembourg [2]	..	..	..	..	..
Netherlands	73 000	2.3	69 000	2.1	−5.5
Norway [3]	26 000	0.8	32 000	1.0	23.1
Portugal	..	..	..	..	..
Spain	56 000	1.8	57 000	1.7	1.8
Sweden [3]	..	..	..	..	..
Switzerland	52 000	1.7	40 000	1.2	−23.1
Turkey	..	..	..	..	..
United Kingdom [4]	1 707 000	54.8	1 783 000	54.5	4.5
Other OECD-Europe	..	..	..	..	..
Total Europe	2 523 000	81.0	2 662 000	81.3	5.5
Total OECD Countries	**3 011 000**	**96.6**	**3 158 000**	**96.5**	**4.9**
Origin country indetermined	105 000	3.4	116 000	3.5	10.5
Total non-OECD Countries	**105 000**	**3.4**	**116 000**	**3.5**	**10.5**
TOTAL	**3 116 000**	**100.0**	**3 274 000**	**100.0**	**5.1**

1. New Zealand includes Australia.
2. Belgium includes Luxembourg.
3. Norway includes Sweden.
4. The United Kingdom exclude Northern Ireland.

IRELAND

NIGHTS SPENT BY FOREIGN TOURISTS IN HOTELS

(by country of residence)

	1992	Relative share	1993	Relative share	% Variation over 1992
Canada	209 000	2.2	213 000	2.2	1.9
Mexico	..	..	..	..	..
United States	1 890 000	20.3	1 872 000	19.6	-1.0
Total North America	2 099 000	22.5	2 085 000	21.8	-0.7
Australia[1]	167 000	1.8	204 000	2.1	22.2
Japan	..	..	..	..	..
New Zealand[1]	..	..	..	..	..
Total Asia and the Pacific	167 000	1.8	204 000	2.1	22.2
Austria	..	..	..	..	..
Belgium[2]	176 000	1.9	182 000	1.9	3.4
Denmark	..	..	..	..	..
Finland	..	..	..	..	..
France	890 000	9.5	964 000	10.1	8.3
Germany	808 000	8.7	1 043 000	10.9	29.1
Greece	..	..	..	..	..
Iceland	..	..	..	..	..
Ireland	..	..	..	..	..
Italy	509 000	5.5	596 000	6.2	17.1
Luxembourg[2]	..	..	..	..	..
Netherlands	273 000	2.9	246 000	2.6	-9.9
Norway	..	..	..	..	..
Portugal	..	..	..	..	..
Spain	..	..	..	..	..
Sweden	..	..	..	..	..
Switzerland	312 000	3.3	133 000	1.4	-57.4
Turkey	..	..	..	..	..
United Kingdom[3]	3 316 000	35.5	3 338 000	34.9	0.7
Other OECD-Europe	..	..	620 000	6.5	..
Total Europe	6 284 000	67.3	7 122 000	74.5	13.3
Total OECD Countries	**8 550 000**	**91.6**	**9 411 000**	**98.5**	**10.1**
Origin country indetermined	783 000	8.4	145 000	1.5	-81.5
Total non-OECD Countries	**783 000**	**8.4**	**145 000**	**1.5**	**-81.5**
TOTAL	**9 333 000**	**100.0**	**9 556 000**	**100.0**	**2.4**

1. Australia includes New Zealand.
2. Belgium includes Luxembourg.
3. The United Kingdom exclude Northern Ireland.

IRELAND

NIGHTS SPENT BY FOREIGN TOURISTS IN TOURIST ACCOMMODATION

(by country of residence)

	1992	Relative share	1993	Relative share	% Variation over 1992
Canada	569 000	1.7	555 000	1.6	−2.5
Mexico	..	..	..	..	..
United States	4 256 000	12.6	4 181 000	11.9	−1.8
Total North America	4 825 000	14.3	4 736 000	13.5	−1.8
Australia[1]	..	..	..	..	..
Japan	..	..	..	..	..
New Zealand[1]	566 000	1.7	528 000	1.5	−6.7
Total Asia and the Pacific	566 000	1.7	528 000	1.5	−6.7
Austria	..	..	..	..	..
Belgium[2]	472 000	1.4	547 000	1.6	15.9
Denmark	..	..	..	..	..
Finland	..	..	..	..	..
France	3 324 000	9.8	3 250 000	9.3	−2.2
Germany	3 420 000	10.1	3 906 000	11.1	14.2
Greece	..	..	..	..	..
Iceland	..	..	..	..	..
Ireland	..	..	..	..	..
Italy	1 340 000	4.0	1 800 000	5.1	34.3
Luxembourg[2]	..	..	..	..	..
Netherlands	827 000	2.4	792 000	2.3	−4.2
Norway	..	..	..	..	..
Portugal	..	..	..	..	..
Spain	..	..	..	..	..
Sweden	..	..	..	..	..
Switzerland	689 000	2.0	618 000	1.8	−10.3
Turkey	..	..	..	..	..
United Kingdom[3]	14 373 000	42.6	15 066 000	42.9	4.8
Other OECD-Europe	..	..	2 761 000	7.9	..
Total Europe	24 445 000	72.4	28 740 000	81.8	17.6
Total OECD Countries	**29 836 000**	**88.3**	**34 004 000**	**96.8**	**14.0**
Origin country indetermined	3 941 000	11.7	1 126 000	3.2	−71.4
Total non-OECD Countries	**3 941 000**	**11.7**	**1 126 000**	**3.2**	**−71.4**
TOTAL	**33 777 000**	**100.0**	**35 130 000**	**100.0**	**4.0**

1. New Zealand includes Australia.
2. Belgium includes Luxembourg.
3. The United Kingdom exclude Northern Ireland.

ITALY

ARRIVALS OF FOREIGN VISITORS AT FRONTIERS[1]

(by country of nationality)

	1992	Relative share	1993	Relative share	% Variation over 1992
Canada	357 692	0.7	329 525	0.7	−7.9
Mexico	127 397	0.3	111 536	0.2	−12.5
United States	1 294 423	2.6	1 210 390	2.4	−6.5
Total North America	1 779 512	3.6	1 651 451	3.3	−7.2
Australia	215 637	0.4	200 685	0.4	−6.9
Japan	741 984	1.5	731 880	1.5	−1.4
New Zealand	..	..	..	..	..
Total Asia and the Pacific	957 621	1.9	932 565	1.9	−2.6
Austria	5 325 611	10.6	5 067 417	10.2	−4.8
Belgium	781 892	1.6	791 186	1.6	1.2
Denmark	371 260	0.7	320 488	0.6	−13.7
Finland	210 170	0.4	194 114	0.4	−7.6
France	8 798 740	17.6	8 254 589	16.5	−6.2
Germany	8 782 614	17.5	7 697 399	15.4	−12.4
Greece	509 582	1.0	541 379	1.1	6.2
Iceland [2]					
Ireland	143 520	0.3	139 930	0.3	−2.5
Italy	..	..	..	..	..
Luxembourg	184 889	0.4	193 000	0.4	4.4
Netherlands	1 205 676	2.4	1 063 798	2.1	−11.8
Norway	218 539	0.4	201 091	0.4	−8.0
Portugal	201 986	0.4	277 518	0.6	37.4
Spain	606 680	1.2	647 066	1.3	6.7
Sweden	417 465	0.8	404 134	0.8	−3.2
Switzerland	10 083 072	20.1	8 456 025	16.9	−16.1
Turkey	198 678	0.4	223 944	0.4	12.7
United Kingdom	1 612 803	3.2	1 737 737	3.5	7.7
Other OECD-Europe	..	..	..	..	..
Total Europe	39 653 177	79.2	36 210 815	72.6	−8.7
Total OECD Countries	**42 390 310**	**84.6**	**38 794 831**	**77.7**	**−8.5**
Other European countries [2]	6 290 364	12.6	9 514 264	19.1	51.3
Ex-USSR	91 709	0.2	158 221	0.3	72.5
Ex-Yugoslavia	4 100 526	8.2	6 788 554	13.6	65.6
Latin America	543 422	1.1	593 798	1.2	9.3
Argentina	144 412	0.3	160 394	0.3	11.1
Brazil	147 613	0.3	157 027	0.3	6.4
Venezuela	99 861	0.2	102 400	0.2	2.5
Asia-Oceania	178 877	0.4	204 989	0.4	14.6
Israel	74 495	0.1	78 059	0.2	4.8
Africa	121 895	0.2	141 867	0.3	16.4
Egypt	60 816	0.1	65 477	0.1	7.7
South Africa	61 079	0.1	76 390	0.2	25.1
Origin country undetermined	563 842	1.1	659 984	1.3	17.1
Total non-OECD Countries	**7 698 400**	**15.4**	**11 114 902**	**22.3**	**44.4**
TOTAL	**50 088 710**	**100.0**	**49 909 733**	**100.0**	**−0.4**

1. Includes about 53% of excursionists.
2. "Other European countries" includes Iceland.

ITALY

ARRIVALS OF FOREIGN TOURISTS AT HOTELS

(by country of nationality)

	1992	Relative share	1993	Relative share	% Variation over 1992
Canada	206 297	1.2	212 295	1.2	2.9
Mexico	101 245	0.6	102 653	0.6	1.4
United States	1 846 323	10.6	1 946 389	10.9	5.4
Total North America	2 153 865	12.4	2 261 337	12.6	5.0
Australia	233 194	1.3	245 504	1.4	5.3
Japan	905 784	5.2	1 030 209	5.7	13.7
New Zealand	..	..	..	..	..
Total Asia and the Pacific	1 138 978	6.6	1 275 713	7.1	12.0
Austria	822 974	4.7	890 417	5.0	8.2
Belgium	410 883	2.4	414 845	2.3	1.0
Denmark	113 115	0.7	112 442	0.6	−0.6
Finland	64 860	0.4	53 970	0.3	−16.8
France	1 585 031	9.1	1 631 733	9.1	2.9
Germany	4 780 006	27.5	4 774 442	26.6	−0.1
Greece	193 263	1.1	190 399	1.1	−1.5
Iceland [1]	..	..	..	..	..
Ireland	58 404	0.3	58 837	0.3	0.7
Italy	..	..	..	..	..
Luxembourg	25 215	0.1	25 170	0.1	−0.2
Netherlands	322 190	1.9	355 994	2.0	10.5
Norway	63 130	0.4	59 549	0.3	−5.7
Portugal	94 024	0.5	104 936	0.6	11.6
Spain	800 370	4.6	740 318	4.1	−7.5
Sweden	200 073	1.2	179 502	1.0	−10.3
Switzerland	875 383	5.0	881 085	4.9	0.7
Turkey	60 451	0.3	80 517	0.4	33.2
United Kingdom	1 151 684	6.6	1 176 980	6.6	2.2
Other OECD-Europe	..	..	..	..	..
Total Europe	11 621 056	66.9	11 731 136	65.5	0.9
Total OECD Countries	**14 913 899**	**85.9**	**15 268 186**	**85.2**	**2.4**
Other European countries [1]	821 061	4.7	928 921	5.2	13.1
Ex-USSR	185 302	1.1	111 225	0.6	−40.0
Ex-Yugoslavia	185 302	1.1	189 363	1.1	2.2
Latin America	502 291	2.9	518 558	2.9	3.2
Argentina	157 491	0.9	153 781	0.9	−2.4
Brazil	180 256	1.0	188 038	1.0	4.3
Venezuela	35 044	0.2	30 618	0.2	−12.6
Asia-Oceania	196 471	1.1	220 061	1.2	12.0
Israel	121 322	0.7	136 136	0.8	12.2
Africa	52 361	0.3	58 966	0.3	12.6
Egypt	18 394	0.1	19 326	0.1	5.1
South Africa	33 967	0.2	39 640	0.2	16.7
Origin country undetermined	879 766	5.1	924 503	5.2	5.1
Total non-OECD Countries	**2 451 950**	**14.1**	**2 651 009**	**14.8**	**8.1**
TOTAL	**17 365 849**	**100.0**	**17 919 195**	**100.0**	**3.2**

1. "Other European countries" includes Iceland.

ITALY

ARRIVALS OF FOREIGN TOURISTS AT REGISTERED TOURIST ACCOMMODATION

(by country of nationality)

	1992	Relative share	1993	Relative share	% Variation over 1992
Canada	234 163	1.1	239 603	1.1	2.3
Mexico	106 988	0.5	108 190	0.5	1.1
United States	1 926 351	9.4	2 024 735	9.6	5.1
Total North America	2 267 502	11.1	2 372 528	11.3	4.6
Australia	279 787	1.4	297 336	1.4	6.3
Japan	921 431	4.5	1 047 006	5.0	13.6
New Zealand	..	..	..	..	..
Total Asia and the Pacific	1 201 218	5.9	1 344 342	6.4	11.9
Austria	1 036 988	5.1	1 107 826	5.3	6.8
Belgium	478 458	2.3	476 369	2.3	−0.4
Denmark	173 001	0.8	169 784	0.8	−1.9
Finland	75 882	0.4	62 159	0.3	−18.1
France	1 801 753	8.8	1 844 590	8.8	2.4
Germany	6 046 075	29.6	6 123 299	29.1	1.3
Greece	199 127	1.0	195 194	0.9	−2.0
Iceland [1]	..	..	..	..	..
Ireland	67 044	0.3	66 665	0.3	−0.6
Italy		..	..	..	..
Luxembourg	28 105	0.1	28 022	0.1	−0.3
Netherlands	527 305	2.6	546 084	2.6	3.6
Norway	75 201	0.4	69 983	0.3	−6.9
Portugal	105 674	0.5	118 217	0.6	11.9
Spain	854 644	4.2	789 838	3.8	−7.6
Sweden	244 406	1.2	215 190	1.0	−12.0
Switzerland	1 022 621	5.0	1 029 230	4.9	0.6
Turkey	64 001	0.3	83 320	0.4	30.2
United Kingdom	1 292 347	6.3	1 307 553	6.2	1.2
Other OECD-Europe	..	..	..	..	..
Total Europe	14 092 632	69.0	14 233 323	67.7	1.0
Total OECD Countries	**17 561 352**	**86.0**	**17 950 193**	**85.4**	**2.2**
Other European countries [1]	1 131 920	5.5	1 249 291	5.9	10.4
Ex-USSR	96 619	0.5	117 189	0.6	21.3
Ex-Yugoslavia	196 928	1.0	201 238	1.0	2.2
Latin America	543 256	2.7	558 435	2.7	2.8
Argentina	171 730	0.8	167 808	0.8	−2.3
Brazil	194 864	1.0	202 463	1.0	3.9
Venezuela	36 114	0.2	31 681	0.2	−12.3
Asia-Oceania	205 367	1.0	229 218	1.1	11.6
Israel	126 230	0.6	141 401	0.7	12.0
Africa	58 841	0.3	66 289	0.3	12.7
Egypt	18 883	0.1	19 751	0.1	4.6
South Africa	39 958	0.2	46 538	0.2	16.5
Origin country undetermined	924 246	4.5	971 927	4.6	5.2
Total non-OECD Countries	**2 863 630**	**14.0**	**3 075 160**	**14.6**	**7.4**
TOTAL	**20 424 982**	**100.0**	**21 025 353**	**100.0**	**2.9**

1. "Other European countries" includes Iceland.

ITALY

NIGHTS SPENT BY FOREIGN TOURISTS IN HOTELS

(by country of nationality)

	1992	Relative share	1993	Relative share	% Variation over 1992
Canada	510 908	0.8	533 837	0.8	4.5
Mexico	241 534	0.4	251 410	0.4	4.1
United States	4 550 965	7.2	4 933 692	7.6	8.4
Total North America	5 303 407	8.4	5 718 939	8.9	7.8
Australia	538 195	0.8	546 676	0.8	1.6
Japan	1 853 210	2.9	2 078 561	3.2	12.2
New Zealand	..	..	..	..	..
Total Asia and the Pacific	2 391 405	3.8	2 625 237	4.1	9.8
Austria	3 418 193	5.4	3 618 522	5.6	5.9
Belgium	1 846 198	2.9	1 868 352	2.9	1.2
Denmark	520 445	0.8	513 008	0.8	−1.4
Finland	312 815	0.5	245 468	0.4	−21.5
France	4 564 715	7.2	4 684 913	7.3	2.6
Germany	23 979 885	37.8	24 035 026	37.2	0.2
Greece	453 007	0.7	440 731	0.7	−2.7
Iceland [1]	..	..	..	..	..
Ireland	209 070	0.3	205 415	0.3	−1.7
Italy	..	..	..	..	..
Luxembourg	165 189	0.3	157 752	0.2	−4.5
Netherlands	1 265 965	2.0	1 429 112	2.2	12.9
Norway	232 738	0.4	217 975	0.3	−6.3
Portugal	252 257	0.4	258 164	0.4	2.3
Spain	1 787 743	2.8	1 684 333	2.6	−5.8
Sweden	744 496	1.2	650 559	1.0	−12.6
Switzerland	3 579 837	5.6	3 598 988	5.6	0.5
Turkey	169 939	0.3	213 982	0.3	25.9
United Kingdom	4 571 866	7.2	4 643 868	7.2	1.6
Other OECD-Europe	..	..	..	..	..
Total Europe	48 074 358	75.8	48 466 168	75.1	0.8
Total OECD Countries	**55 769 170**	**87.9**	**56 810 344**	**88.0**	**1.9**
Other European countries [1]	2 984 940	4.7	3 160 530	4.9	5.9
Ex-USSR	373 101	0.6	439 206	0.7	17.7
Ex-Yugoslavia	761 428	1.2	706 610	1.1	−7.2
Latin America	1 434 717	2.3	1 441 037	2.2	0.4
Argentina	429 295	0.7	415 036	0.6	−3.3
Brazil	490 633	0.8	503 718	0.8	2.7
Venezuela	95 923	0.2	85 729	0.1	−10.6
Asia-Oceania	534 587	0.8	564 097	0.9	5.5
Israel	270 943	0.4	292 175	0.5	7.8
Africa	177 497	0.3	176 984	0.3	−0.3
Egypt	76 265	0.1	75 998	0.1	−0.4
South Africa	101 232	0.2	100 986	0.2	−0.2
Origin country undetermined	2 514 548	4.0	2 421 485	3.7	−3.7
Total non-OECD Countries	**7 646 289**	**12.1**	**7 764 133**	**12.0**	**1.5**
TOTAL	**63 415 459**	**100.0**	**64 574 477**	**100.0**	**1.8**

1. "Other European countries" includes Iceland.

ITALY

NIGHTS SPENT BY FOREIGN TOURISTS IN REGISTERED TOURIST ACCOMMODATION

(by country of nationality)

	1992	Relative share	1993	Relative share	% Variation over 1992
Canada	632 043	0.8	675 695	0.8	6.9
Mexico	264 284	0.3	274 312	0.3	3.8
United States	4 936 644	5.9	5 394 040	6.3	9.3
Total North America	5 832 971	7.0	6 344 047	7.4	8.8
Australia	653 397	0.8	700 683	0.8	7.2
Japan	1 911 799	2.3	2 160 524	2.5	13.0
New Zealand	..	..	..	..	..
Total Asia and the Pacific	2 565 196	3.1	2 861 207	3.3	11.5
Austria	4 902 375	5.9	5 106 291	6.0	4.2
Belgium	2 415 602	2.9	2 390 885	2.8	−1.0
Denmark	971 774	1.2	955 890	1.1	−1.6
Finland	378 392	0.5	290 257	0.3	−23.3
France	5 571 214	6.7	5 703 287	6.7	2.4
Germany	33 205 307	39.7	33 883 014	39.7	2.0
Greece	490 056	0.6	494 443	0.6	0.9
Iceland[1]	..		..		
Ireland	244 192	0.3	242 378	0.3	−0.7
Italy	..		..		
Luxembourg	191 200	0.2	181 482	0.2	−5.1
Netherlands	2 864 264	3.4	2 898 305	3.4	1.2
Norway	315 519	0.4	291 839	0.3	−7.5
Portugal	286 292	0.3	296 480	0.3	3.6
Spain	1 979 930	2.4	1 859 011	2.2	−6.1
Sweden	1 059 458	1.3	903 614	1.1	−14.7
Switzerland	4 775 053	5.7	4 817 148	5.6	0.9
Turkey	197 552	0.2	231 069	0.3	17.0
United Kingdom	5 398 815	6.5	5 488 110	6.4	1.7
Other OECD-Europe	..	..	..	..	..
Total Europe	65 246 995	78.0	66 033 503	77.3	1.2
Total OECD Countries	**73 645 162**	**88.0**	**75 238 757**	**88.1**	**2.2**
Other European countries[1]	4 757 525	5.7	4 967 926	5.8	4.4
Ex-USSR	432 823	0.5	477 820	0.6	10.4
Ex-Yugoslavia	904 299	1.1	834 259	1.0	−7.7
Latin America	1 621 896	1.9	1 624 475	1.9	0.2
Argentina	485 126	0.6	496 737	0.6	2.4
Brazil	655 774	0.8	574 229	0.7	−12.4
Venezuela	107 666	0.1	95 346	0.1	−11.4
Asia-Oceania	601 935	0.7	637 605	0.7	5.9
Israel	291 172	0.3	323 808	0.4	11.2
Africa	211 472	0.3	208 075	0.2	−1.6
Egypt	89 057	0.1	83 009	0.1	−6.8
South Africa	122 415	0.1	125 066	0.1	2.2
Origin country undetermined	2 804 577	3.4	2 753 935	3.2	−1.8
Total non-OECD Countries	**9 997 405**	**12.0**	**10 192 016**	**11.9**	**1.9**
TOTAL	**83 642 567**	**100.0**	**85 430 773**	**100.0**	**2.1**

1. "Other European countries" includes Iceland.

171

JAPAN

ARRIVALS OF FOREIGN TOURISTS AT FRONTIERS

(by country of nationality)

	1992	Relative share	1993	Relative share	% Variation over 1992
Canada	43 661	2.1	45 860	2.4	5.0
Mexico	7 161	0.3	6 787	0.4	−5.2
United States	298 049	14.2	272 348	14.1	−8.6
Total North America	348 871	16.6	324 995	16.9	−6.8
Australia	28 412	1.4	30 390	1.6	7.0
Japan	..	..	..	..	..
New Zealand	10 936	0.5	10 492	0.5	−4.1
Total Asia and the Pacific	39 348	1.9	40 882	2.1	3.9
Austria	3 746	0.2	3 746	0.2	0.0
Belgium	3 282	0.2	3 289	0.2	0.2
Denmark	4 136	0.2	3 459	0.2	−16.4
Finland	3 348	0.2	3 029	0.2	−9.5
France	20 490	1.0	21 861	1.1	6.7
Germany	27 640	1.3	26 949	1.4	−2.5
Greece	2 066	0.1	1 899	0.1	−8.1
Iceland	..	..	..	..	..
Ireland	1 718	0.1	1 873	0.1	9.0
Italy	11 038	0.5	10 883	0.6	−1.4
Luxembourg	..	..	..	..	..
Netherlands	6 229	0.3	6 746	0.4	8.3
Norway	1 862	0.1	2 234	0.1	20.0
Portugal	4 374	0.2	4 558	0.2	4.2
Spain	7 085	0.3	5 173	0.3	−27.0
Sweden	6 273	0.3	5 567	0.3	−11.3
Switzerland	7 169	0.3	7 032	0.4	−1.9
Turkey	1 604	0.1	1 785	0.1	11.3
United Kingdom	143 341	6.8	128 919	6.7	−10.1
Other OECD-Europe	..	..	..	..	..
Total Europe	255 401	12.1	239 002	12.4	−6.4
Total OECD Countries	**643 620**	**30.6**	**604 879**	**31.4**	**−6.0**
Other European countries	17 065	0.8	20 230	1.1	18.5
Ex-Czechoslovakia	..	..	698	0.0	..
Poland	724	0.0	797	0.0	10.1
Ex-USSR	14 848	0.7	17 420	0.9	17.3
Ex-Yugoslavia	524	0.0	715	0.0	36.5
Latin America	62 454	3.0	49 424	2.6	−20.9
Argentina	3 330	0.2	3 124	0.2	−6.2
Brazil	36 325	1.7	27 786	1.4	−23.5
Chile	877	0.0	937	0.0	6.8
Colombia	2 092	0.1	2 376	0.1	13.6
Venezuela	839	0.0	952	0.0	13.5
Asia-Oceania	1 375 727	65.4	1 245 915	64.7	−9.4
China	29 147	1.4	26 454	1.4	−9.2
Hong Kong	28 619	1.4	23 683	1.2	−17.2
India	5 801	0.3	5 705	0.3	−1.7
Iran	10 597	0.5	1 229	0.1	−88.4
Israel	5 788	0.3	5 482	0.3	−5.3
Republic of Korea	502 871	23.9	473 318	24.6	−5.9
Lebanon	91	0.0	96	0.0	5.5
Malaysia	35 670	1.7	23 698	1.2	−33.6
Pakistan	1 873	0.1	1 374	0.1	−26.6
Philippines	20 734	1.0	19 937	1.0	−3.8
Singapore	25 433	1.2	23 289	1.2	−8.4
Taiwan	622 707	29.6	581 958	30.2	−6.5
Thailand	58 583	2.8	35 298	1.8	−39.7
Africa	3 896	0.2	4 274	0.2	9.7
Egypt	573	0.0	664	0.0	15.9
South Africa	1 107	0.1	1 101	0.1	−0.5
Origin country undetermined	808	0.0	774	0.0	−4.2
Total non-OECD Countries	**1 459 950**	**69.4**	**1 320 617**	**68.6**	**−9.5**
TOTAL	**2 103 570**	**100.0**	**1 925 496**	**100.0**	**−8.5**

JAPAN

ARRIVALS OF FOREIGN VISITORS AT FRONTIERS

(by country of nationality)

	1992	Relative share	1993	Relative share	% Variation over 1992
Canada	69 620	1.9	72 395	2.1	4.0
Mexico	10 045	0.3	9 934	0.3	−1.1
United States	560 940	15.7	533 401	15.6	−4.9
Total North America	640 605	17.9	615 730	18.0	−3.9
Australia	59 844	1.7	69 439	2.0	16.0
Japan	..	..	..	..	..
New Zealand	21 014	0.6	21 014	0.6	0.0
Total Asia and the Pacific	80 858	2.3	90 453	2.7	11.9
Austria	8 024	0.2	8 054	0.2	0.4
Belgium	7 812	0.2	7 790	0.2	−0.3
Denmark	9 254	0.3	8 511	0.2	−8.0
Finland	7 901	0.2	7 734	0.2	−2.1
France	48 605	1.4	49 178	1.4	1.2
Germany	63 930	1.8	62 795	1.8	−1.8
Greece	3 578	0.1	3 409	0.1	−4.7
Iceland	342	0.0	376	0.0	9.9
Ireland	5 176	0.1	5 607	0.2	8.3
Italy	26 866	0.8	25 283	0.7	−5.9
Luxembourg	396	0.0	336	0.0	−15.2
Netherlands	18 253	0.5	17 872	0.5	−2.1
Norway	5 316	0.1	5 820	0.2	9.5
Portugal	6 180	0.2	6 667	0.2	7.9
Spain	13 580	0.4	9 443	0.3	−30.5
Sweden	14 888	0.4	14 040	0.4	−5.7
Switzerland	15 237	0.4	15 346	0.4	0.7
Turkey	3 511	0.1	3 739	0.1	6.5
United Kingdom	241 893	6.8	225 737	6.6	−6.7
Other OECD-Europe	..	..	..	..	..
Total Europe	500 742	14.0	477 737	14.0	−4.6
Total OECD Countries	**1 222 205**	**34.1**	**1 183 920**	**34.7**	**−3.1**
Other European countries	33 964	0.9	39 600	1.2	16.6
Bulgaria	579	0.0	708	0.0	22.3
Ex-Czechoslovakia	..	..	2 106	0.1	..
Hungary	2 456	0.1	2 450	0.1	−0.2
Poland	2 196	0.1	2 131	0.1	−3.0
Rumania	719	0.0	746	0.0	3.8
Ex-USSR	26 765	0.7	32 183	0.9	20.2
Ex-Yugoslavia	1 225	0.0	1 300	0.0	6.1
Latin America	77 157	2.2	64 699	1.9	−16.1
Argentina	4 980	0.1	4 818	0.1	−3.3
Brazil	41 487	1.2	33 444	1.0	−19.4
Chile	1 935	0.1	1 954	0.1	1.0
Colombia	2 772	0.1	3 233	0.1	16.6
Venezuela	1 428	0.0	1 531	0.0	7.2
Asia-Oceania	2 234 931	62.4	2 108 480	61.8	−5.7
China	183 220	5.1	206 743	6.1	12.8
Hong Kong	40 174	1.1	34 203	1.0	−14.9
India	26 159	0.7	23 847	0.7	−8.8
Iran	14 999	0.4	3 978	0.1	−73.5
Israel	8 411	0.2	8 155	0.2	−3.0
Republic of Korea	864 052	24.1	845 423	24.8	−2.2
Lebanon	479	0.0	425	0.0	−11.3
Malaysia	60 894	1.7	46 165	1.4	−24.2
Pakistan	6 711	0.2	5 495	0.2	−18.1
Philippines	105 195	2.9	91 199	2.7	−13.3
Saudi Arabia	1 217	0.0	1 118	0.0	−8.1
Singapore	40 956	1.1	38 446	1.1	−6.1
Taiwan	715 487	20.0	668 581	19.6	−6.6
Thailand	97 234	2.7	70 946	2.1	−27.0
Africa	12 677	0.4	13 174	0.4	3.9
Algeria	334	0.0	355	0.0	6.3
Egypt	1 861	0.1	2 078	0.1	11.7
Morocco	427	0.0	437	0.0	2.3
South Africa	3 016	0.1	2 973	0.1	−1.4
Origin country undetermined	1 106	0.0	1 874	0.1	69.4
Total non-OECD Countries	**2 359 835**	**65.9**	**2 227 827**	**65.3**	**−5.6**
TOTAL	**3 582 040**	**100.0**	**3 411 747**	**100.0**	**−4.8**

NETHERLANDS

ARRIVALS OF FOREIGN TOURISTS AT HOTELS

(by country of residence)

	1992	Relative share	1993	Relative share	% Variation over 1992
Canada	64 200	1.6	56 900	1.5	−11.4
Mexico	..	..	..	..	..
United States	408 800	10.4	387 500	10.1	−5.2
Total North America	473 000	12.0	444 400	11.6	−6.0
Australia [1]	53 000	1.3	39 600	1.0	−25.3
Japan	111 700	2.8	89 500	2.3	−19.9
New Zealand [1]	..	..	..	..	..
Total Asia and the Pacific	164 700	4.2	129 100	3.4	−21.6
Austria [2]	..	..	..	..	..
Belgium	170 000	4.3	185 700	4.9	9.2
Denmark	63 100	1.6	58 700	1.5	−7.0
Finland	26 900	0.7	21 000	0.5	−21.9
France	287 800	7.3	247 100	6.5	−14.1
Germany	813 900	20.7	908 600	23.7	11.6
Greece [2]	..	..	..	..	..
Iceland [2]	..	..	..	..	..
Ireland	25 900	0.7	26 500	0.7	2.3
Italy	244 200	6.2	204 400	5.3	−16.3
Luxembourg	14 600	0.4	12 200	0.3	−16.4
Netherlands	..	..	..	..	..
Norway	49 800	1.3	45 700	1.2	−8.2
Portugal [3]	..	..	..	..	..
Spain [3]	146 800	3.7	123 000	3.2	−16.2
Sweden	118 800	3.0	89 700	2.3	−24.5
Switzerland	92 500	2.4	85 600	2.2	−7.5
Turkey [2]	..	..	..	..	..
United Kingdom	745 500	19.0	681 300	17.8	−8.6
Other OECD-Europe [2]	229 400	5.8	290 200	7.6	26.5
Total Europe	3 029 200	77.0	2 979 700	77.8	−1.6
Total OECD Countries	**3 666 900**	**93.3**	**3 553 200**	**92.8**	**−3.1**
Latin America	64 900	1.7	62 400	1.6	−3.9
Asia-Oceania	157 200	4.0	170 500	4.5	8.5
Africa	42 900	1.1	41 900	1.1	−2.3
Total non-OECD Countries	**265 000**	**6.7**	**274 800**	**7.2**	**3.7**
TOTAL	**3 931 900**	**100.0**	**3 828 000**	**100.0**	**−2.6**

1. Australia includes New Zealand.
2. "Other OECD-Europe" includes Austria, Greece, Iceland, Turkey and all non-OECD European countries.
3. Spain includes Portugal.

NETHERLANDS

ARRIVALS OF FOREIGN TOURISTS AT REGISTERED TOURIST ACCOMMODATION

(by country of residence)

	1992	Relative share	1993	Relative share	% Variation over 1992
Canada	79 300	1.3	69 100	1.2	−12.9
Mexico	..	..	..	..	..
United States	451 200	7.4	423 000	7.4	−6.3
Total North America	530 500	8.7	492 100	8.6	−7.2
Australia [1]	81 100	1.3	63 000	1.1	−22.3
Japan	116 100	1.9	92 400	1.6	−20.4
New Zealand [1]	..	..	..	..	..
Total Asia and the Pacific	197 200	3.2	155 400	2.7	−21.2
Austria [2]	..	..	..	..	..
Belgium	342 500	5.6	370 400	6.5	8.1
Denmark	96 700	1.6	85 800	1.5	−11.3
Finland	34 700	0.6	25 500	0.4	−26.5
France	396 000	6.5	333 900	5.9	−15.7
Germany	2 146 700	35.3	2 215 900	38.8	3.2
Greece [2]	..	..	..	..	..
Iceland [2]	..	..	..	..	..
Ireland	32 400	0.5	31 600	0.6	−2.5
Italy	301 800	5.0	245 000	4.3	−18.8
Luxembourg	16 000	0.3	13 400	0.2	−16.3
Netherlands	..	..	..	..	..
Norway	59 700	1.0	52 300	0.9	−12.4
Portugal [3]	..	..	..	..	..
Spain [3]	187 400	3.1	153 400	2.7	−18.1
Sweden	146 400	2.4	106 100	1.9	−27.5
Switzerland	122 000	2.0	107 200	1.9	−12.1
Turkey [2]	..	..	..	..	..
United Kingdom	871 200	14.3	775 400	13.6	−11.0
Other OECD-Europe [2]	299 600	4.9	285 900	5.0	−4.6
Total Europe	5 053 100	83.1	4 801 800	84.1	−5.0
Total OECD Countries	**5 780 800**	**95.0**	**5 449 300**	**95.5**	**−5.7**
Latin America	75 200	1.2	72 000	1.3	−4.3
Asia-Oceania	174 200	2.9	184 900	3.2	6.1
Africa	52 700	0.9	505	0.0	−99.0
Total non-OECD Countries	**302 100**	**5.0**	**257 405**	**4.5**	**−14.8**
TOTAL	**6 082 900**	**100.0**	**5 706 705**	**100.0**	**−6.2**

1. Australia includes New Zealand.
2. "Other OECD-Europe" includes Austria, Greece, Iceland, Turkey and non-OECD European countries.
3. Spain includes Portugal.

NETHERLANDS

NIGHTS SPENT BY FOREIGN TOURISTS IN HOTELS

(by country of residence)

	1992	Relative share	1993	Relative share	% Variation over 1992
Canada	132 000	1.6	113 800	1.4	−13.8
Mexico	..	..	..	..	..
United States	861 200	10.1	797 300	10.0	−7.4
Total North America	993 200	11.7	911 100	11.4	−8.3
Australia [1]	112 600	1.3	84 900	1.1	−24.6
Japan	220 500	2.6	177 600	2.2	−19.5
New Zealand [1]	..	..	..	..	..
Total Asia and the Pacific	333 100	3.9	262 500	3.3	−21.2
Austria [2]	..	..	..	..	..
Belgium	322 400	3.8	352 200	4.4	9.2
Denmark	129 200	1.5	117 600	1.5	−9.0
Finland	56 400	0.7	42 500	0.5	−24.6
France	549 900	6.5	468 900	5.9	−14.7
Germany	1 935 200	22.8	2 076 100	26.0	7.3
Greece [2]	..	..	..	..	..
Iceland [2]	..	..	..	..	..
Ireland	55 300	0.7	59 400	0.7	7.4
Italy	517 100	6.1	408 200	5.1	−21.1
Luxembourg	29 100	0.3	25 800	0.3	−11.3
Netherlands	..	..	..	..	..
Norway	101 200	1.2	90 300	1.1	−10.8
Portugal [3]	..	..	..	..	..
Spain [3]	311 700	3.7	262 800	3.3	−15.7
Sweden	234 800	2.8	179 900	2.3	−23.4
Switzerland	199 500	2.3	181 900	2.3	−8.8
Turkey [2]	..	..	..	..	..
United Kingdom	1 633 300	19.2	1 414 500	17.7	−13.4
Other OECD-Europe [2]	492 600	5.8	496 400	6.2	0.8
Total Europe	6 567 700	77.3	6 176 500	77.5	−6.0
Total OECD Countries	**7 894 000**	**92.9**	**7 350 100**	**92.2**	**−6.9**
Latin America	143 900	1.7	138 400	1.7	−3.8
Asia-Oceania	356 100	4.2	382 200	4.8	7.3
Africa	102 000	1.2	102 500	1.3	0.5
Total non-OECD Countries	**602 000**	**7.1**	**623 100**	**7.8**	**3.5**
TOTAL	**8 496 000**	**100.0**	**7 973 200**	**100.0**	**−6.2**

1. Australia includes New Zealand.
2. "Other OECD-Europe" includes Austria, Greece, Iceland, Turkey and all non-OECD European countries.
3. Spain includes Portugal.

176

NETHERLANDS

NIGHTS SPENT BY FOREIGN TOURISTS IN REGISTERED TOURIST ACCOMMODATION

(by country of residence)

	1992	Relative share	1993	Relative share	% Variation over 1992
Canada	161 700	0.9	140 700	0.8	−13.0
Mexico	..	..	..	..	..
United States	944 000	5.2	875 700	5.1	−7.2
Total North America	1 105 700	6.1	1 016 400	5.9	−8.1
Australia [1]	176 900	1.0	139 300	0.8	−21.3
Japan	228 400	1.3	183 800	1.1	−19.5
New Zealand [1]	..	..	..	..	..
Total Asia and the Pacific	405 300	2.2	323 100	1.9	−20.3
Austria [2]	..	..	..	..	..
Belgium	1 130 700	6.2	1 167 100	6.8	3.2
Denmark	237 100	1.3	208 400	1.2	−12.1
Finland	73 300	0.4	53 100	0.3	−27.6
France	791 600	4.4	674 500	3.9	−14.8
Germany	9 067 700	50.1	9 173 400	53.4	1.2
Greece [2]	..	..	..	..	..
Iceland [2]	..	..	..	..	..
Ireland	74 900	0.4	73 900	0.4	−1.3
Italy	644 500	3.6	509 100	3.0	−21.0
Luxembourg	34 400	0.2	30 600	0.2	−11.0
Netherlands					
Norway	124 100	0.7	106 300	0.6	−14.3
Portugal [3]	..	..	..	..	..
Spain [3]	408 200	2.3	341 500	2.0	−16.3
Sweden	296 700	1.6	219 300	1.3	−26.1
Switzerland	299 900	1.7	251 500	1.5	−16.1
Turkey [2]	..	..	..	..	..
United Kingdom	2 061 200	11.4	1 715 200	10.0	−16.8
Other OECD-Europe [2]	666 500	3.7	616 900	3.6	−7.4
Total Europe	15 910 800	87.9	15 140 800	88.1	−4.8
Total OECD Countries	**17 421 800**	**96.3**	**16 480 300**	**95.9**	**−5.4**
Latin America	163 000	0.9	158 500	0.9	−2.8
Asia-Oceania	390 700	2.2	414 500	2.4	6.1
Africa	123 500	0.7	124 500	0.7	0.8
Total non-OECD Countries	**677 200**	**3.7**	**697 500**	**4.1**	**3.0**
TOTAL	**18 099 000**	**100.0**	**17 177 800**	**100.0**	**−5.1**

Australia includes New Zealand.
"Other OECD-Europe" includes Austria, Greece, Iceland, Turkey and all non-OECD European countries.
Spain includes Portugal.

NEW ZEALAND

ARRIVALS OF FOREIGN TOURISTS AT FRONTIERS

(by country of residence)

	1992	Relative share	1993	Relative share	% Variation over 1992
Canada	25 849	2.4	27 755	2.4	7.4
Mexico	1 099	0.1	1 468	0.1	33.6
United States	131 357	12.4	143 596	12.4	9.3
Total North America	158 305	15.0	172 819	14.9	9.2
Australia	363 642	34.4	358 975	31.0	−1.3
Japan	128 962	12.2	135 934	11.7	5.4
New Zealand [1]	6 484	0.6	6 441	0.6	−0.7
Total Asia and the Pacific	499 088	47.3	501 350	43.3	0.5
Austria	3 507	0.3	5 202	0.4	48.3
Belgium	1 135	0.1	1 226	0.1	8.0
Denmark	4 174	0.4	4 026	0.3	−3.5
Finland	1 388	0.1	1 379	0.1	−0.6
France	5 325	0.5	5 830	0.5	9.5
Germany	45 705	4.3	56 162	4.9	22.9
Greece	303	0.0	248	0.0	−18.2
Iceland	..	..	198	0.0	..
Ireland	1 724	0.2	2 285	0.2	32.5
Italy	3 766	0.4	4 092	0.4	8.7
Luxembourg	153	0.0	332	0.0	117.0
Netherlands	9 734	0.9	10 750	0.9	10.4
Norway	1 962	0.2	2 021	0.2	3.0
Portugal	205	0.0	370	0.0	80.5
Spain	1 528	0.1	1 802	0.2	17.9
Sweden	6 700	0.6	6 535	0.6	−2.5
Switzerland	12 457	1.2	13 109	1.1	5.2
Turkey	379	0.0	310	0.0	−18.2
United Kingdom	96 523	9.1	103 387	8.9	7.1
Other OECD-Europe	..	..	..	..	..
Total Europe	196 668	18.6	219 264	19.0	11.5
Total OECD Countries	**854 061**	**80.9**	**893 433**	**77.2**	**4.6**
Bulgaria	..	..	92	0.0	..
Ex-Czechoslovakia	142	0.0	84	0.0	−40.8
Hungary	216	0.0	237	0.0	9.7
Poland	393	0.0	456	0.0	16.0
Rumania	68	0.0	12	0.0	−82.4
Ex-USSR	2 830	0.3	..	..	..
Ex-Yugoslavia	219	0.0	..	..	..
Argentina	2 320	0.2	3 217	0.3	38.7
Brazil	1 046	0.1	1 277	0.1	22.1
Chile	344	0.0	615	0.1	78.8
Colombia	283	0.0	271	0.0	−4.2
Venezuela	160	0.0	166	0.0	3.8
China	3 612	0.3	4 301	0.4	19.1
Hong Kong	19 327	1.8	23 388	2.0	21.0
India	1 810	0.2	1 665	0.1	−8.0
Iran	143	0.0	114	0.0	−20.3
Israel	1 047	0.1	1 420	0.1	35.6
Republic of Korea	12 757	1.2	27 340	2.4	114.3
Lebanon	..	..	13	0.0	..
Malaysia	10 110	1.0	12 638	1.1	25.0
Pakistan	305	0.0	194	0.0	−36.4
Philippines	2 370	0.2	2 820	0.2	19.0
Saudi Arabia	944	0.1	1 342	0.1	42.2
Singapore	19 044	1.8	23 883	2.1	25.4
Taiwan	25 060	2.4	44 815	3.9	78.8
Thailand	9 905	0.9	16 427	1.4	65.8
Algeria	..	..	618	0.1	..
Egypt	66	0.0	76	0.0	15.2
Morocco	..	..	22	0.0	..
South Africa	3 586	0.3	6 648	0.6	85.4
Origin country undetermined	201 620	19.1	263 545	22.8	30.7
Total non-OECD Countries	**201 620**	**19.1**	**263 545**	**22.8**	**30.7**
TOTAL	**1 055 681**	**100.0**	**1 156 978**	**100.0**	**9.6**

1. New Zealanders who have lived abroad for less than 12 months and who return for a short stay.

NEW ZEALAND

NIGHTS SPENT BY FOREIGN TOURISTS IN REGISTERED TOURIST ACCOMMODATION

(by country of residence)

	1992	Relative share	1993	Relative share	% Variation over 1992
Canada	620 000	3.0	605 501	2.7	−2.3
Mexico	..	..	16 970	0.1	..
United States	1 973 664	9.6	2 153 334	9.7	9.1
Total North America	2 593 664	12.6	2 775 805	12.5	7.0
Australia	5 357 289	26.1	5 188 357	23.3	−3.2
Japan	1 456 413	7.1	1 699 407	7.6	16.7
New Zealand [1]	192 501	0.9	266 622	1.2	38.5
Total Asia and the Pacific	7 006 203	34.2	7 154 386	32.2	2.1
Austria	94 295	0.5	138 380	0.6	46.8
Belgium	24 079	0.1	27 423	0.1	13.9
Denmark	170 025	0.8	158 138	0.7	−7.0
Finland	27 547	0.1	28 100	0.1	2.0
France	103 560	0.5	132 927	0.6	28.4
Germany	1 375 924	6.7	1 572 004	7.1	14.3
Greece	..	..	5 683	0.0	..
Iceland	..	..	3 572	0.0	..
Ireland	45 489	0.2	69 036	0.3	51.8
Italy	57 817	0.3	72 498	0.3	25.4
Luxembourg	..	..	5 963	0.0	..
Netherlands	367 003	1.8	371 688	1.7	1.3
Norway	..	..	665	0.0	..
Portugal	..	..	3 674	0.0	..
Spain	31 194	0.2	49 081	0.2	57.3
Sweden	163 173	0.8	156 188	0.7	−4.3
Switzerland	484 951	2.4	494 356	2.2	1.9
Turkey	5 138	0.0	12 507	0.1	143.4
United Kingdom	3 169 126	15.5	3 160 339	14.2	−0.3
Other OECD-Europe	..	..	..	..	..
Total Europe	6 119 321	29.8	6 462 222	29.0	5.6
Total OECD Countries	**15 719 188**	**76.6**	**16 392 413**	**73.7**	**4.3**
Bulgaria	..	..	2 382	0.0	..
Ex-Czechoslovakia	..	..	948	0.0	..
Hungary	..	..	5 365	0.0	..
Poland	..	..	59 744	0.3	..
Rumania	..	..	24	0.0	..
Ex-USSR	431 372	2.1	420 720	1.9	−2.5
Ex-Yugoslavia	8 999	0.0	12 246	0.1	36.1
Argentina	31 856	0.2	45 043	0.2	41.4
Brazil	18 531	0.1	20 641	0.1	11.4
Chile	..	..	18 312	0.1	..
Colombia	..	..	3 081	0.0	..
Venezuela	..	..	4 897	0.0	..
China	129 209	0.6	130 358	0.6	0.9
Hong Kong	290 215	1.4	343 053	1.5	18.2
India	66 310	0.3	61 057	0.3	−7.9
Iran	..	..	2 498	0.0	..
Israel	39 159	0.2	59 348	0.3	51.6
Republic of Korea	160 941	0.8	260 838	1.2	62.1
Lebanon	..	..	182	0.0	..
Malaysia	224 344	1.1	259 409	1.2	15.6
Pakistan	..	..	4 896	0.0	..
Philippines	..	..	63 895	0.3	..
Saudi Arabia	..	..	28 246	0.1	..
Singapore	..	..	339 932	1.5	..
Taiwan	350 894	1.7	502 134	2.3	43.1
Thailand	153 912	0.8	244 121	1.1	58.6
Egypt	..	..	2 808	0.0	..
Morocco	..	..	220	0.0	..
South Africa	..	..	196 749	0.9	..
Origin country undetermined	4 789 096	23.4	5 855 967	26.3	22.3
Total non-OECD Countries	**4 789 096**	**23.4**	**5 855 967**	**26.3**	**22.3**
TOTAL	**20 508 284**	**100.0**	**22 248 380**	**100.0**	**8.5**

. New Zealanders who have lived abroad for less than 12 months and who return for a short stay.

NORWAY

NIGHTS SPENT BY FOREIGN TOURISTS IN HOTELS

(by country of nationality)

	1992	Relative share	1993	Relative share	% Variation over 1992
Canada [1]	..	..	..	..	..
Mexico	..	..	..	..	..
United States	351 528	8.2	311 476	6.8	−11.4
Total North America	351 528	8.2	311 476	6.8	−11.4
Australia [1]	..	..	..	..	..
Japan	99 840	2.3	120 868	2.7	21.1
New Zealand [1]	..	..	..	..	..
Total Asia and the Pacific	99 840	2.3	120 868	2.7	21.1
Austria [1]	..	..	..	..	..
Belgium [1]	..	..	..	..	..
Denmark	714 750	16.7	748 323	16.4	4.7
Finland	95 414	2.2	94 191	2.1	−1.3
France	242 475	5.7	267 487	5.9	10.3
Germany	850 587	19.9	1 036 481	22.7	21.9
Greece [1]	..	..	..	..	..
Iceland [1]	..	..	..	..	..
Ireland [1]	..	..	..	..	..
Italy	157 252	3.7	129 071	2.8	−17.9
Luxembourg [1]	..	..	..	..	..
Netherlands	174 272	4.1	188 057	4.1	7.9
Norway	..	..	..	..	..
Portugal [1]	..	..	..	..	..
Spain	42 775	1.0	50 772	1.1	18.7
Sweden	661 670	15.5	641 914	14.1	−3.0
Switzerland	50 970	1.2	59 074	1.3	15.9
Turkey [1]	..	..	..	..	..
United Kingdom	428 593	10.0	411 925	9.0	−3.9
Other OECD-Europe	152 268	3.6	180 543	4.0	18.6
Total Europe	3 571 026	83.5	3 807 838	83.6	6.6
Total OECD Countries	**4 022 394**	**94.1**	**4 240 182**	**93.1**	**5.4**
Origin country undetermined [1]	252 769	5.9	316 592	6.9	25.2
Total non-OECD Countries	**252 769**	**5.9**	**316 592**	**6.9**	**25.2**
TOTAL	**4 275 163**	**100.0**	**4 556 774**	**100.0**	**6.6**

1. Included in "Origin country undetermined".

PORTUGAL

ARRIVALS OF FOREIGN TOURISTS AT FRONTIERS

(by country of nationality)

	1992	Relative share	1993	Relative share	% Variation over 1992
Canada	66 276	0.7	61 600	0.7	−7.1
Mexico	..	..	..	..	..
United States	156 583	1.8	146 100	1.7	−6.7
Total North America	222 859	2.5	207 700	2.5	−6.8
Australia[1]	19 908	0.2	..	..	..
Japan	25 569	0.3	32 500	0.4	27.1
New-Zealand[1]	..	..	..	..	..
Total Asia and the Pacific	45 477	0.5	32 500	0.4	−28.5
Austria	42 706	0.5	44 900	0.5	5.1
Belgium	191 122	2.2	169 000	2.0	−11.6
Denmark	115 768	1.3	102 800	1.2	−11.2
Finland	83 661	0.9	46 100	0.5	−44.9
France	647 807	7.3	546 000	6.5	−15.7
Germany	812 310	9.1	723 600	8.6	−10.9
Greece[2]	..	..	..	..	..
Iceland[2]	..	..	..	..	..
Ireland	88 877	1.0	84 400	1.0	−5.0
Italy	258 443	2.9	235 500	2.8	−8.9
Luxembourg	17 615	0.2	24 300	0.3	38.0
Netherlands	337 427	3.8	327 900	3.9	−2.8
Norway	29 480	0.3	27 900	0.3	−5.4
Portugal	..	..	..	..	..
Spain	4 225 764	47.6	4 187 500	49.7	−0.9
Sweden	101 158	1.1	86 700	1.0	−14.3
Switzerland	64 257	0.7	71 200	0.8	10.8
Turkey[2]	..	..	..	..	..
United Kingdom	1 276 001	14.4	1 221 900	14.5	−4.2
Other OECD-Europe	..	..	..	..	..
Total Europe	8 292 396	93.3	7 899 700	93.7	−4.7
Total OECD Countries	**8 560 732**	**96.4**	**8 139 900**	**96.5**	**−4.9**
Other European countries[2]	59 883	0.7	..	..	..
Africa	94 834	1.1	..	..	..
Origin country undetermined	168 694	1.9	294 000	3.5	74.3
Total non-OECD Countries	**323 411**	**3.6**	**294 000**	**3.5**	**−9.1**
TOTAL	**8 884 143**	**100.0**	**8 433 900**	**100.0**	**−5.1**

1. Australia includes New Zealand.
2. "Other European countries" includes Greece, Iceland, Turkey.

PORTUGAL

ARRIVALS OF FOREIGN VISITORS AT FRONTIERS

(by country of nationality)

	1992	Relative share	1993	Relative share	% Variation over 1992
Canada	73 955	0.4	71 230	0.3	−3.7
Mexico	7 314	0.0	4 518	0.0	−38.2
United States	220 452	1.1	207 651	1.0	−5.8
Total North America	301 721	1.5	283 399	1.4	−6.1
Australia	17 498	0.1	13 523	0.1	−22.7
Japan	27 234	0.1	34 229	0.2	25.7
New Zealand	4 711	0.0	3 356	0.0	−28.8
Total Asia and the Pacific	49 443	0.2	51 108	0.2	3.4
Austria	45 220	0.2	48 165	0.2	6.5
Belgium	207 272	1.0	196 554	1.0	−5.2
Denmark	119 587	0.6	108 751	0.5	−9.1
Finland	85 682	0.4	47 275	0.2	−44.8
France	685 682	3.3	590 711	2.9	−13.9
Germany	877 456	4.2	794 734	3.9	−9.4
Greece	17 645	0.1	17 564	0.1	−0.5
Iceland	5 197	0.0	4 175	0.0	−19.7
Ireland	92 864	0.4	87 578	0.4	−5.7
Italy	283 063	1.4	265 263	1.3	−6.3
Luxembourg	18 840	0.1	27 243	0.1	44.6
Netherlands	366 674	1.8	369 014	1.8	0.6
Norway	33 589	0.2	29 430	0.1	−12.4
Portugal	..		..		
Spain	15 553 444	75.0	15 776 374	76.7	1.4
Sweden	108 417	0.5	93 361	0.5	−13.9
Switzerland	72 534	0.3	82 582	0.4	13.9
Turkey	3 207	0.0	2 871	0.0	−10.5
United Kingdom	1 435 346	6.9	1 368 356	6.6	−4.7
Other OECD-Europe	..		..		..
Total Europe	20 011 719	96.5	19 910 001	96.7	−0.5
Total OECD Countries	**20 362 883**	**98.2**	**20 244 508**	**98.4**	**−0.6**
Other European countries	67 412	0.3	59 528	0.3	−11.7
Bulgaria	2 445	0.0	2 933	0.0	20.0
Ex-Czechoslovakia	10 329	0.0	7 301	0.0	−29.3
Hungary	5 880	0.0	5 619	0.0	−4.4
Poland	11 326	0.1	11 827	0.1	4.4
Rumania	1 483	0.0	1 158	0.0	−21.9
Ex-USSR	25 155	0.1	21 219	0.1	−15.6
Ex-Yugoslavia	8 450	0.0	7 216	0.0	−14.6
Latin America	155 215	0.7	126 204	0.6	−18.7
Argentina	10 497	0.1	7 737	0.0	−26.3
Brazil	106 080	0.5	85 142	0.4	−19.7
Chile	3 214	0.0	1 865	0.0	−42.0
Colombia	2 583	0.0	2 325	0.0	−10.0
Venezuela	22 745	0.1	19 128	0.1	−15.9
Asia-Oceania	55 626	0.3	52 310	0.3	−6.0
China	2 397	0.0	1 603	0.0	−33.1
Hong Kong	767	0.0	883	0.0	15.1
India	6 993	0.0	6 537	0.0	−6.5
Iran	937	0.0	824	0.0	−12.1
Israel	8 049	0.0	10 217	0.0	26.9
Republic of Korea	5 000	0.0	3 797	0.0	−24.1
Lebanon	486	0.0	439	0.0	−9.7
Malaysia	1 453	0.0	1 382	0.0	−4.9
Pakistan	1 406	0.0	1 476	0.0	5.0
Philippines	20 010	0.1	17 064	0.1	−14.7
Saudi Arabia	317	0.0	432	0.0	36.3
Singapore	1 180	0.0	1 182	0.0	0.2
Thailand	1 728	0.0	1 215	0.0	−29.7
Africa	98 876	0.5	96 503	0.5	−2.4
Algeria	1 164	0.0	890	0.0	−23.5
Egypt	800	0.0	857	0.0	7.1
Morocco	4 413	0.0	5 118	0.0	16.0
South Africa	14 925	0.1	15 658	0.1	4.9
Origin country undetermined	1 867	0.0	280	0.0	−85.0
Total non-OECD Countries	**378 996**	**1.8**	**334 825**	**1.6**	**−11.7**
TOTAL	**20 741 879**	**100.0**	**20 579 333**	**100.0**	**−0.8**

PORTUGAL

ARRIVALS OF FOREIGN TOURISTS AT HOTELS[1]

(by country of residence)

	1992	Relative share	1993	Relative share	% Variation over 1992
Canada	54 444	1.5	48 540	1.4	−10.8
Mexico	5 075	0.1	3 601	0.1	−29.0
United States	202 938	5.5	185 825	5.5	−8.4
Total North America	262 457	7.1	237 966	7.1	−9.3
Australia	9 987	0.3	10 329	0.3	3.4
Japan	34 663	0.9	49 639	1.5	43.2
New Zealand	1 365	0.0	1 326	0.0	−2.9
Total Asia and the Pacific	46 015	1.3	61 294	1.8	33.2
Austria	42 794	1.2	47 867	1.4	11.9
Belgium	94 596	2.6	89 053	2.6	−5.9
Denmark	58 518	1.6	42 924	1.3	−26.6
Finland	67 377	1.8	30 939	0.9	−54.1
France	301 913	8.2	275 583	8.2	−8.7
Germany	549 600	15.0	502 221	14.9	−8.6
Greece	9 470	0.3	9 780	0.3	3.3
Iceland	3 337	0.1	1 682	0.0	−49.6
Ireland	53 028	1.4	45 282	1.3	−14.6
Italy	232 420	6.3	199 837	5.9	−14.0
Luxembourg	5 577	0.2	4 848	0.1	−13.1
Netherlands	204 772	5.6	155 815	4.6	−23.9
Norway	26 981	0.7	25 310	0.8	−6.2
Portugal	..	..	..	..	..
Spain	651 846	17.8	633 149	18.8	−2.9
Sweden	90 424	2.5	65 863	2.0	−27.2
Switzerland	81 240	2.2	78 438	2.3	−3.4
Turkey	1 488	0.0	1 669	0.0	12.2
United Kingdom	702 502	19.1	675 326	20.0	−3.9
Other OECD-Europe	..	..	..	..	..
Total Europe	3 177 883	86.6	2 885 586	85.6	−9.2
Total OECD Countries	**3 486 355**	**95.0**	**3 184 846**	**94.5**	**−8.6**
Other European countries	15 422	0.4	21 558	0.6	39.8
Bulgaria	1 087	0.0	1 722	0.1	58.4
Ex-Czechoslovakia	2 080	0.1	..	..	..
Hungary	1 635	0.0	3 199	0.1	95.7
Poland	1 903	0.1	2 898	0.1	52.3
Rumania	550	0.0	1 379	0.0	150.7
Ex-USSR	4 718	0.1	5 928	0.2	25.6
Ex-Yugoslavia	1 620	0.0	..	..	..
Latin America	99 580	2.7	87 581	2.6	−12.0
Argentina	6 856	0.2	6 329	0.2	−7.7
Brazil	76 955	2.1	68 073	2.0	−11.5
Chile	1 646	0.0	1 453	0.0	−11.7
Colombia	1 070	0.0	1 035	0.0	−3.3
Venezuela	9 582	0.3	7 629	0.2	−20.4
Asia-Oceania	18 168	0.5	24 478	0.7	34.7
China	1 601	0.0	1 990	0.1	24.3
Iran	83	0.0	401	0.0	383.1
Israel	7 585	0.2	13 819	0.4	82.2
Lebanon	177	0.0	196	0.0	10.7
Philippines	1 428	0.0	1 237	0.0	−13.4
Saudi Arabia	614	0.0	753	0.0	22.6
Africa	52 014	1.4	53 446	1.6	2.8
Egypt	488	0.0	439	0.0	−10.0
Morocco	3 341	0.1	3 853	0.1	15.3
South Africa	11 852	0.3	15 759	0.5	33.0
Total non-OECD Countries	**185 184**	**5.0**	**187 063**	**5.5**	**1.0**
TOTAL	**3 671 539**	**100.0**	**3 371 909**	**100.0**	**−8.2**

1. Includes arrivals at hotels, studio-hotels, holiday-flats, villages, motels, inns and boarding-houses.

PORTUGAL

ARRIVALS OF FOREIGN TOURISTS AT REGISTERED TOURIST ACCOMMODATION[1]

(by country of residence)

	1992	Relative share	1993	Relative share	% Variation over 1992
Canada	57 814	1.3	51 191	1.3	−11.5
Mexico	5 231	0.1	3 713	0.1	−29.0
United States	207 664	4.8	189 447	4.8	−8.8
Total North America	270 709	6.2	244 351	6.2	−9.7
Australia	15 564	0.4	14 267	0.4	−8.3
Japan	35 127	0.8	50 532	1.3	43.9
New Zealand	4 494	0.1	3 651	0.1	−18.8
Total Asia and the Pacific	55 185	1.3	68 450	1.7	24.0
Austria	53 174	1.2	55 466	1.4	4.3
Belgium	127 118	2.9	118 952	3.0	−6.4
Denmark	67 071	1.5	49 937	1.3	−25.5
Finland	68 818	1.6	32 799	0.8	−52.3
France	459 327	10.6	429 079	10.8	−6.6
Germany	700 490	16.1	615 187	15.5	−12.2
Greece	9 729	0.2	10 158	0.3	4.4
Iceland	3 355	0.1	1 694	0.0	−49.5
Ireland	54 931	1.3	47 068	1.2	−14.3
Italy	260 621	6.0	227 565	5.7	−12.7
Luxembourg	6 118	0.1	5 425	0.1	−11.3
Netherlands	291 256	6.7	223 466	5.6	−23.3
Norway	27 924	0.6	26 070	0.7	−6.6
Portugal	..	..	..	..	..
Spain	777 190	17.9	753 046	19.0	−3.1
Sweden	92 906	2.1	67 388	1.7	−27.5
Switzerland	89 606	2.1	85 288	2.2	−4.8
Turkey	1 598	0.0	1 754	0.0	9.8
United Kingdom	729 221	16.8	699 478	17.7	−4.1
Other OECD-Europe	..	..	..	..	..
Total Europe	3 820 453	87.9	3 449 820	87.1	−9.7
Total OECD Countries	**4 146 347**	**95.4**	**3 762 621**	**95.0**	**−9.3**
Other European countries	20 254	0.5	26 062	0.7	28.7
Bulgaria	1 115	0.0	1 789	0.0	60.4
Ex-Czechoslovakia	2 878	0.1	..	..	..
Hungary	2 928	0.1	4 041	0.1	38.0
Poland	3 950	0.1	4 639	0.1	17.4
Rumania	657	0.0	1 466	0.0	123.1
Ex-USSR	4 809	0.1	6 172	0.2	28.3
Ex-Yugoslavia	2 054	0.0	..	..	..
Latin America	104 396	2.4	92 119	2.3	−11.8
Argentina	7 344	0.2	6 689	0.2	−8.9
Brazil	80 260	1.8	71 340	1.8	−11.1
Chile	1 865	0.0	1 625	0.0	−12.9
Colombia	1 135	0.0	1 089	0.0	−4.1
Venezuela	9 864	0.2	7 918	0.2	−19.7
Asia-Oceania	18 740	0.4	25 013	0.6	33.5
China	1 652	0.0	2 013	0.1	21.9
Iran	141	0.0	444	0.0	214.9
Israel	7 736	0.2	13 913	0.4	79.8
Lebanon	186	0.0	196	0.0	5.4
Philippines	1 437	0.0	1 261	0.0	−12.2
Saudi Arabia	614	0.0	753	0.0	22.6
Africa	54 810	1.3	55 928	1.4	2.0
Egypt	494	0.0	459	0.0	−7.1
Morocco	4 301	0.1	4 910	0.1	14.2
South Africa	12 669	0.3	16 509	0.4	30.3
Total non-OECD Countries	**198 200**	**4.6**	**199 122**	**5.0**	**0.5**
TOTAL	**4 344 547**	**100.0**	**3 961 743**	**100.0**	**−8.8**

1. Includes arrivals at hotels, studio-hotels, holiday-flats, villages, motels, inns, boarding-houses, recreation centres for children and camping-sites.

PORTUGAL

NIGHTS SPENT BY FOREIGN TOURISTS IN HOTELS[1]

(by country of residence)

	1992	Relative share	1993	Relative share	% Variation over 1992
Canada	216 555	1.2	190 878	1.2	−11.9
Mexico	13 597	0.1	8 667	0.1	−36.3
United States	538 840	3.0	467 286	2.9	−13.3
Total North America	768 992	4.3	666 831	4.1	−13.3
Australia	24 322	0.1	26 796	0.2	10.2
Japan	74 686	0.4	102 419	0.6	37.1
New Zealand	3 161	0.0	3 117	0.0	−1.4
Total Asia and the Pacific	102 169	0.6	132 332	0.8	29.5
Austria	176 477	1.0	202 253	1.3	14.6
Belgium	419 049	2.3	393 046	2.4	−6.2
Denmark	371 470	2.1	242 843	1.5	−34.6
Finland	399 973	2.2	208 017	1.3	−48.0
France	784 594	4.4	717 623	4.4	−8.5
Germany	3 297 973	18.4	3 073 287	19.0	−6.8
Greece	27 458	0.2	29 246	0.2	6.5
Iceland	32 514	0.2	16 581	0.1	−49.0
Ireland	416 055	2.3	391 325	2.4	−5.9
Italy	573 061	3.2	485 141	3.0	−15.3
Luxembourg	30 624	0.2	21 758	0.1	−29.0
Netherlands	1 494 667	8.4	1 147 844	7.1	−23.2
Norway	184 159	1.0	167 836	1.0	−8.9
Portugal	..	..	..	..	
Spain	1 625 356	9.1	1 530 663	9.5	−5.8
Sweden	593 717	3.3	404 737	2.5	−31.8
Switzerland	291 886	1.6	279 682	1.7	−4.2
Turkey	4 585	0.0	5 337	0.0	16.4
United Kingdom	5 696 672	31.9	5 377 624	33.2	−5.6
Other OECD-Europe	..	..	..	..	
Total Europe	16 420 290	91.9	14 694 843	90.8	−10.5
Total OECD Countries	**17 291 451**	**96.7**	**15 494 006**	**95.8**	**−10.4**
Other European countries	59 067	0.3	123 853	0.8	109.7
Bulgaria	3 133	0.0	3 761	0.0	20.0
Ex-Czechoslovakia	6 522	0.0	..	..	..
Hungary	6 728	0.0	15 992	0.1	137.7
Poland	6 446	0.0	12 011	0.1	86.3
Rumania	5 093	0.0	44 352	0.3	770.8
Ex-USSR	17 368	0.1	22 185	0.1	27.7
Ex-Yugoslavia	8 229	0.0	..	..	..
Latin America	241 264	1.3	219 633	1.4	−9.0
Argentina	16 459	0.1	15 583	0.1	−5.3
Brazil	188 284	1.1	170 208	1.1	−9.6
Chile	4 413	0.0	4 266	0.0	−3.3
Colombia	2 305	0.0	2 458	0.0	6.6
Venezuela	19 912	0.1	17 615	0.1	−11.5
Asia-Oceania	50 397	0.3	64 580	0.4	28.1
China	5 172	0.0	5 611	0.0	8.5
Iran	369	0.0	1 541	0.0	317.6
Israel	17 048	0.1	30 926	0.2	81.4
Lebanon	723	0.0	633	0.0	−12.4
Philippines	3 185	0.0	2 708	0.0	−15.0
Saudi Arabia	1 858	0.0	2 279	0.0	22.7
Africa	234 852	1.3	273 885	1.7	16.6
Egypt	1 652	0.0	1 333	0.0	−19.3
Morocco	10 623	0.1	13 565	0.1	27.7
South Africa	41 750	0.2	37 939	0.2	−9.1
Total non-OECD Countries	**585 580**	**3.3**	**681 951**	**4.2**	**16.5**
TOTAL	**17 877 031**	**100.0**	**16 175 957**	**100.0**	**−9.5**

1. Includes nights spent at hotels, studio-hotels, holiday-flats, villages, motels, inns and boarding-houses.

PORTUGAL

NIGHTS SPENT BY FOREIGN TOURISTS IN REGISTERED TOURIST ACCOMMODATION[1]
(by country of residence)

	1992	Relative share	1993	Relative share	% Variation over 1992
Canada	224 440	1.1	197 277	1.1	−12.1
Mexico	13 888	0.1	8 875	0.0	−36.1
United States	550 449	2.7	476 378	2.6	−13.5
Total North America	788 777	3.9	682 530	3.8	−13.5
Australia	37 947	0.2	36 454	0.2	−3.9
Japan	75 595	0.4	104 518	0.6	38.3
New Zealand	10 267	0.1	8 284	0.0	−19.3
Total Asia and the Pacific	123 809	0.6	149 256	0.8	20.6
Austria	205 135	1.0	222 267	1.2	8.4
Belgium	527 174	2.6	493 927	2.7	−6.3
Denmark	403 841	2.0	268 531	1.5	−33.5
Finland	408 088	2.0	217 129	1.2	−46.8
France	1 195 064	6.0	1 129 071	6.2	−5.5
Germany	3 825 534	19.1	3 469 750	19.1	−9.3
Greece	27 996	0.1	30 200	0.2	7.9
Iceland	32 561	0.2	16 599	0.1	−49.0
Ireland	422 616	2.1	397 748	2.2	−5.9
Italy	646 027	3.2	554 829	3.1	−14.1
Luxembourg	32 189	0.2	23 296	0.1	−27.6
Netherlands	1 844 244	9.2	1 432 960	7.9	−22.3
Norway	188 416	0.9	171 289	0.9	−9.1
Portugal	..	..	..	..	..
Spain	2 012 404	10.0	1 919 247	10.6	−4.6
Sweden	603 733	3.0	412 397	2.3	−31.7
Switzerland	316 002	1.6	300 821	1.7	−4.8
Turkey	5 322	0.0	5 532	0.0	3.9
United Kingdom	5 824 570	29.0	5 501 385	30.4	−5.5
Other OECD-Europe	..	..	..	..	..
Total Europe	18 520 916	92.3	16 566 978	91.4	−10.5
Total OECD Countries	**19 433 502**	**96.9**	**17 398 764**	**96.0**	**−10.5**
Other European countries	70 746	0.4	136 181	0.8	92.5
Bulgaria	3 188	0.0	4 156	0.0	30.4
Ex-Czechoslovakia	8 495	0.0	..	..	..
Hungary	10 127	0.1	17 966	0.1	77.4
Poland	10 657	0.1	15 725	0.1	47.6
Rumania	5 671	0.0	44 711	0.2	688.4
Ex-USSR	17 608	0.1	24 648	0.1	40.0
Ex-Yugoslavia	9 377	0.0	..	..	..
Latin America	257 833	1.3	239 393	1.3	−7.2
Argentina	17 536	0.1	16 337	0.1	−6.8
Brazil	201 004	1.0	187 009	1.0	−7.0
Chile	5 067	0.0	4 738	0.0	−6.5
Colombia	2 515	0.0	2 531	0.0	0.6
Venezuela	20 577	0.1	18 305	0.1	−11.0
Asia-Oceania	51 682	0.3	65 611	0.4	27.0
China	5 315	0.0	5 646	0.0	6.2
Iran	565	0.0	1 641	0.0	190.4
Israel	17 348	0.1	31 081	0.2	79.2
Lebanon	752	0.0	635	0.0	−15.6
Philippines	3 198	0.0	2 757	0.0	−13.8
Saudi Arabia	1 858	0.0	2 279	0.0	22.7
Africa	250 702	1.2	284 158	1.6	13.3
Egypt	1 661	0.0	1 450	0.0	−12.7
Morocco	15 369	0.1	18 174	0.1	18.3
South Africa	43 616	0.2	39 827	0.2	−8.7
Total non-OECD Countries	**630 963**	**3.1**	**725 343**	**4.0**	**15.0**
TOTAL	**20 064 465**	**100.0**	**18 124 107**	**100.0**	**−9.7**

1. Includes nights spent at hotels, studio-hotels, holiday-flats, villages, motels, inns, boarding-houses, recreation centres for children and camping-sites.

SPAIN

ARRIVALS OF FOREIGN VISITORS AT FRONTIERS[1]

(by country of nationality)

	1992	Relative share	1993	Relative share	% Variation over 1992
Canada	146 429	0.3	131 587	0.2	−10.1
Mexico	89 882	0.2	84 821	0.1	−5.6
United States	825 387	1.5	783 620	1.4	−5.1
Total North America	1 061 698	1.9	1 000 028	1.7	−5.8
Australia	52 247	0.1	53 553	0.1	2.5
Japan	222 243	0.4	240 260	0.4	8.1
New Zealand	21 605	0.0	19 505	0.0	−9.7
Total Asia and the Pacific	296 095	0.5	313 318	0.5	5.8
Austria	325 961	0.6	367 796	0.6	12.8
Belgium	1 361 774	2.4	1 470 020	2.5	7.9
Denmark	437 037	0.8	428 039	0.7	−2.1
Finland	289 764	0.5	256 556	0.4	−11.5
France	11 792 108	21.2	12 070 214	20.8	2.4
Germany	7 762 127	14.0	8 713 281	15.0	12.3
Greece	95 096	0.2	91 183	0.2	−4.1
Iceland	15 786	0.0	18 402	0.0	16.6
Ireland	207 899	0.4	236 657	0.4	13.8
Italy	1 852 567	3.3	2 018 506	3.5	9.0
Luxembourg	90 683	0.2	87 254	0.2	−3.8
Netherlands	2 117 030	3.8	2 062 024	3.6	−2.6
Norway	285 696	0.5	287 585	0.5	0.7
Portugal	11 567 533	20.8	11 358 655	19.6	−1.8
Spain[2]	3 700 095	6.7	3 413 931	5.9	−7.7
Sweden	745 491	1.3	657 972	1.1	−11.7
Switzerland	1 109 871	2.0	1 169 610	2.0	5.4
Turkey	17 370	0.0	20 507	0.0	18.1
United Kingdom	6 515 540	11.7	7 485 129	12.9	14.9
Other OECD-Europe[3]	285 007	0.5	650 737	1.1	128.3
Total Europe	50 574 435	90.9	52 864 058	91.3	4.5
Total OECD Countries	**51 932 228**	**93.4**	**54 177 404**	**93.5**	**4.3**
Other European countries	322 117	0.6	663 370	1.1	105.9
Bulgaria	24 287	0.0	10 251	0.0	−57.8
Ex-Czechoslovakia	61 120	0.1	62 413	0.1	2.1
Hungary	28 747	0.1	26 508	0.0	−7.8
Poland	35 456	0.1	37 515	0.1	5.8
Rumania	100 635	0.2	9 157	0.0	−90.9
Ex-USSR	110 487	0.2	102 422	0.2	−7.3
Ex-Yugoslavia	37 110	0.1	22 472	0.0	−39.4
Latin America	490 536	0.9	457 860	0.8	−6.7
Argentina	128 713	0.2	123 780	0.2	−3.8
Brazil	107 135	0.2	90 762	0.2	−15.3
Chile	30 536	0.1	29 617	0.1	−3.0
Colombia	37 764	0.1	35 393	0.1	−6.3
Venezuela	60 869	0.1	45 210	0.1	−25.7
Asia-Oceania	534 632	1.0	240 846	0.4	−55.0
China	17 499	0.0	12 929	0.0	−26.1
Hong Kong	..	..	1 383	0.0	
India	24 587	0.0	29 882	0.1	21.5
Iran	3 717	0.0	3 563	0.0	−4.1
Israel	30 454	0.1	34 428	0.1	13.0
Republic of Korea	22 916	0.0	22 546	0.0	−1.6
Lebanon	4 134	0.0	4 575	0.0	10.7
Malaysia	4 362	0.0	4 196	0.0	−3.8
Pakistan	4 367	0.0	5 033	0.0	15.3
Philippines	66 839	0.1	77 488	0.1	15.9
Saudi Arabia	4 525	0.0	3 800	0.0	−16.0
Singapore	3 607	0.0	3 873	0.0	7.4
Taiwan	647	0.0	6 160	0.0	852.1
Thailand	4 459	0.0	4 756	0.0	6.7
Africa	2 262 340	4.1	2 391 681	4.1	5.7
Algeria	148 726	0.3	183 594	0.3	23.4
Egypt	9 800	0.0	10 747	0.0	9.7
Morocco	2 034 737	3.7	2 130 442	3.7	4.7
South Africa	..	..	9 379	0.0	..
Origin country undetermined	68 877	0.1	..	..	..
Total non-OECD Countries	**3 678 502**	**6.6**	**3 753 757**	**6.5**	**2.0**
TOTAL	**55 610 730**	**100.0**	**57 931 161**	**100.0**	**4.2**

1. Includes about 34% of arrivals of excursionists.
2. Spanish nationals residing abroad.
3. "Other OECD-Europe" includes Andorra, Cyprus, Malta, Monaco, and the Vatican States.

SPAIN

ARRIVALS OF FOREIGN TOURISTS AT HOTELS[1]

(by country of nationality)

	1992	Relative share	1993	Relative share	% Variation over 1992
Canada	49 673	0.4	51 688	0.4	4.1
Mexico	111 617	0.9	80 596	0.6	−27.8
United States	673 242	5.3	662 349	5.1	−1.6
Total North America	834 532	6.5	794 633	6.1	−4.8
Australia	..	..	..	..	..
Japan	370 754	2.9	325 493	2.5	−12.2
New Zealand	..	..	..	..	..
Total Asia and the Pacific	370 754	2.9	325 493	2.5	−12.2
Austria	120 336	0.9	..	..	..
Belgium	482 147	3.8	546 932	4.2	13.4
Denmark	124 662	1.0	105 089	0.8	−15.7
Finland	59 924	0.5	..	..	..
France	1 571 202	12.3	1 508 506	11.6	−4.0
Germany	2 873 735	22.5	3 106 653	24.0	8.1
Greece	33 146	0.3	50 765	0.4	53.2
Iceland	..	..	..	..	..
Ireland	55 536	0.4	53 377	0.4	−3.9
Italy	1 114 641	8.7	1 141 264	8.8	2.4
Luxembourg	38 226	0.3	30 360	0.2	−20.6
Netherlands	361 176	2.8	408 528	3.2	13.1
Norway	85 386	0.7	70 126	0.5	−17.9
Portugal	326 142	2.6	357 049	2.8	9.5
Spain	..	..	..	..	..
Sweden	236 441	1.9	184 422	1.4	−22.0
Switzerland	305 317	2.4	331 990	2.6	8.7
Turkey	..	..	..	..	..
United Kingdom	2 375 488	18.6	2 647 783	20.4	11.5
Other OECD-Europe	235 782	1.8	433 297	3.3	83.8
Total Europe	10 399 287	81.5	10 976 141	84.8	5.5
Total OECD Countries	**11 604 573**	**91.0**	**12 096 267**	**93.4**	**4.2**
Other European countries	234 672	1.8	..	..	..
Argentina	147 788	1.2	117 218	0.9	−20.7
Venezuela	388 001	3.0	23 873	0.2	−93.8
Origin country undetermined	915 225	7.2	853 251	6.6	−6.8
Total non-OECD Countries	**1 149 897**	**9.0**	**853 251**	**6.6**	**−25.8**
TOTAL	**12 754 470**	**100.0**	**12 949 518**	**100.0**	**1.5**

1. Arrivals recorded in hotels with "estrellas de oro" (golden stars) and "estrellas de plata" (silver stars).

SPAIN

NIGHTS SPENT BY FOREIGN TOURISTS IN HOTELS[1]

(by country of nationality)

	1992	Relative share	1993	Relative share	% Variation over 1992
Canada	137 742	0.2	143 660	0.2	4.3
Mexico	266 440	0.3	189 415	0.2	−28.9
United States	1 508 424	2.0	1 430 919	1.7	−5.1
Total North America	1 912 606	2.5	1 763 994	2.1	−7.8
Australia	..	..	..	..	..
Japan	710 206	0.9	586 836	0.7	−17.4
New Zealand	..	..	..	..	..
Total Asia and the Pacific	710 206	0.9	586 836	0.7	−17.4
Austria	917 146	1.2	..	..	..
Belgium	3 467 490	4.5	4 226 345	5.1	21.9
Denmark	781 483	1.0	649 369	0.8	−16.9
Finland	506 554	0.7	..	..	..
France	6 100 873	7.9	6 508 506	7.9	6.7
Germany	26 394 973	34.3	28 066 058	33.9	6.3
Greece	93 810	0.1	152 568	0.2	62.6
Iceland	..	..	..	..	..
Ireland	509 373	0.7	501 665	0.6	−1.5
Italy	5 267 608	6.8	5 697 259	6.9	8.2
Luxembourg	292 449	0.4	233 434	0.3	−20.2
Netherlands	2 448 593	3.2	2 953 346	3.6	20.6
Norway	641 129	0.8	562 828	0.7	−12.2
Portugal	828 366	1.1	900 568	1.1	8.7
Spain	..	..	..	..	..
Sweden	1 762 208	2.3	1 399 253	1.7	−20.6
Switzerland	2 116 680	2.8	2 175 110	2.6	2.8
Turkey	..	..	..	..	..
United Kingdom	19 451 447	25.3	22 301 851	26.9	14.7
Other OECD-Europe	1 056 586	1.4	2 632 258	3.2	149.1
Total Europe	72 636 768	94.4	78 960 418	95.3	8.7
Total OECD Countries	**75 259 580**	**97.8**	**81 311 248**	**98.1**	**8.0**
Other European countries	1 053 177	1.4	..	..	..
Argentina	318 697	0.4	216 876	0.3	−31.9
Venezuela	91 166	0.1	59 218	0.1	−35.0
Origin country undetermined	621 461	0.8	1 561 002	1.9	151.2
Total non-OECD Countries	**1 674 638**	**2.2**	**1 561 002**	**1.9**	**−6.8**
TOTAL	**76 934 218**	**100.0**	**82 872 250**	**100.0**	**7.7**

1. Nights recorded in hotels with "estrellas de oro" (golden stars) and "estrellas de plata" (silver stars).

SWEDEN

NIGHTS SPENT BY FOREIGN TOURISTS IN HOTELS

(by country of nationality)

	1992	Relative share	1993	Relative share	% Variation over 1992
Canada	15 967	0.6	17 589	0.6	10.2
Mexico	..	..	..	..	..
United States	267 328	9.5	286 293	9.6	7.1
Total North America	283 295	10.1	303 882	10.2	7.3
Australia [1]	..	..	..	..	..
Japan	81 528	2.9	97 261	3.3	19.3
New Zealand [1]	..	..	..	..	..
Total Asia and the Pacific	81 528	2.9	97 261	3.3	19.3
Austria [2]	..	..	..	..	..
Belgium [2]	..	..	..	..	..
Denmark	184 603	6.6	176 409	5.9	−4.4
Finland	278 589	9.9	241 486	8.1	−13.3
France	92 599	3.3	95 208	3.2	2.8
Germany	486 464	17.4	575 975	19.3	18.4
Greece [2]	..	..	..	..	..
Iceland [2]	..	..	..	..	..
Ireland [2]	..	..	..	..	..
Italy	115 680	4.1	108 575	3.6	−6.1
Luxembourg [2]	..	..	..	..	..
Netherlands	83 804	3.0	85 370	2.9	1.9
Norway	356 298	12.7	371 646	12.5	4.3
Portugal [2]	..	..	..	..	..
Spain [2]	..	..	..	..	..
Sweden					
Switzerland	56 358	2.0	60 929	2.0	8.1
Turkey [2]	..	..	..	..	..
United Kingdom	238 579	8.5	240 007	8.0	0.6
Other OECD-Europe	..	..	..	..	..
Total Europe	1 892 974	67.5	1 955 605	65.5	3.3
Total OECD Countries	**2 257 797**	**80.5**	**2 356 748**	**79.0**	**4.4**
Other European countries [2]	252 599	9.0	254 736	8.5	0.8
Origin country undetermined [1]	293 315	10.5	372 157	12.5	26.9
Total non-OECD Countries	**545 914**	**19.5**	**626 893**	**21.0**	**14.8**
TOTAL	**2 803 711**	**100.0**	**2 983 641**	**100.0**	**6.4**

1. Included in "Origin country undetermined".
2. Included in "Other European countries".

SWEDEN

NIGHTS SPENT BY FOREIGN TOURISTS IN REGISTERED TOURIST ACCOMMODATION

(by country of nationality)

	1992	Relative share	1993	Relative share	% Variation over 1992
Canada	18 463	0.3	19 743	0.3	6.9
Mexico	..	..	..	..	..
United States	281 476	4.8	297 556	4.9	5.7
Total North America	299 939	5.2	317 299	5.2	5.8
Australia [1]	..	..	..	..	..
Japan	85 901	1.5	100 560	1.7	17.1
New Zealand [1]	..	..	..	..	..
Total Asia and the Pacific	85 901	1.5	100 560	1.7	17.1
Austria [2]	..	..	..	..	..
Belgium [2]	..	..	..	..	..
Denmark	537 121	9.2	602 238	9.9	12.1
Finland	440 486	7.6	355 937	5.9	−19.2
France	167 108	2.9	154 235	2.5	−7.7
Germany	1 512 494	26.0	1 754 682	28.9	16.0
Greece [2]	..	..	..	..	..
Iceland [2]	..	..	..	..	..
Ireland [2]	..	..	..	..	..
Italy	130 178	2.2	118 338	1.9	−9.1
Luxembourg [2]	..	..	..	..	..
Netherlands	337 636	5.8	339 674	5.6	0.6
Norway	1 134 597	19.5	1 130 478	18.6	−0.4
Portugal [2]	..	..	..	..	..
Spain [2]	..	..	..	..	..
Sweden					
Switzerland	69 767	1.2	74 765	1.2	7.2
Turkey [2]	..	..	..	..	..
United Kingdom	288 183	5.0	281 397	4.6	−2.4
Other OECD-Europe	..	..	..	..	..
Total Europe	4 617 570	79.4	4 811 744	79.2	4.2
Total OECD Countries	**5 003 410**	**86.1**	**5 229 603**	**86.1**	**4.5**
Other European countries [2]	434 473	7.5	409 597	6.7	−5.7
Origin country undetermined [1]	376 639	6.5	435 372	7.2	15.6
Total non-OECD Countries	**811 112**	**13.9**	**844 969**	**13.9**	**4.2**
TOTAL	**5 814 522**	**100.0**	**6 074 572**	**100.0**	**4.5**

1. Included in "Origin country undetermined".
2. Included in "Other European countries".

SWITZERLAND

ARRIVALS OF FOREIGN TOURISTS AT HOTELS

(by country of residence)

	1992	Relative share	1993	Relative share	% Variation over 1992
Canada	78 549	1.0	72 749	1.0	−7.4
Mexico	19 523	0.3	16 750	0.2	−14.2
United States	887 431	11.8	819 975	11.3	−7.6
Total North America	985 503	13.1	909 474	12.6	−7.7
Australia [1]	72 794	1.0	66 941	0.9	−8.0
Japan	502 796	6.7	488 594	6.8	−2.8
New Zealand [1]	..	..	..	..	..
Total Asia and the Pacific	575 590	7.6	555 535	7.7	−3.5
Austria	157 632	2.1	160 370	2.2	1.7
Belgium	231 039	3.1	235 871	3.3	2.1
Denmark	41 016	0.5	38 945	0.5	−5.0
Finland	29 090	0.4	24 739	0.3	−15.0
France	527 755	7.0	506 586	7.0	−4.0
Germany	2 190 223	29.1	2 202 242	30.5	0.5
Greece	54 245	0.7	46 511	0.6	−14.3
Iceland [2]	..	..	..	..	..
Ireland	14 338	0.2	14 517	0.2	1.2
Italy	651 364	8.7	508 403	7.0	−21.9
Luxembourg	32 144	0.4	32 290	0.4	0.5
Netherlands	264 555	3.5	272 900	3.8	3.2
Norway	29 443	0.4	26 379	0.4	−10.4
Portugal	33 758	0.4	31 442	0.4	−6.9
Spain	217 446	2.9	190 205	2.6	−12.5
Sweden	104 507	1.4	84 456	1.2	−19.2
Switzerland					
Turkey	29 365	0.4	30 940	0.4	5.4
United Kingdom	548 076	7.3	510 477	7.1	−6.9
Other OECD-Europe	..	..	..	..	..
Total Europe	5 155 996	68.5	4 917 273	68.1	−4.6
Total OECD Countries	**6 717 089**	**89.2**	**6 382 282**	**88.3**	**−5.0**
Other European countries [2]	165 386	2.2	180 395	2.5	9.1
Ex-USSR	27 151	0.4	37 141	0.5	36.8
Ex-Yugoslavia	30 598	0.4	24 161	0.3	−21.0
Latin America	121 118	1.6	105 996	1.5	−12.5
Argentina	24 927	0.3	23 650	0.3	−5.1
Brazil	46 919	0.6	43 585	0.6	−7.1
Asia-Oceania	417 959	5.6	451 468	6.2	8.0
India	28 833	0.4	30 456	0.4	5.6
Iran	8 629	0.1	7 956	0.1	−7.8
Israel	104 454	1.4	109 483	1.5	4.8
Africa	106 446	1.4	104 361	1.4	−2.0
Egypt	17 810	0.2	16 604	0.2	−6.8
South Africa	24 064	0.3	23 850	0.3	−0.9
Total non-OECD Countries	**810 909**	**10.8**	**842 220**	**11.7**	**3.9**
TOTAL	**7 527 998**	**100.0**	**7 224 502**	**100.0**	**−4.0**

1. Australia includes New Zealand.
2. "Other European countries" includes Iceland.

SWITZERLAND

ARRIVALS OF FOREIGN TOURISTS AT REGISTERED TOURIST ACCOMMODATION

(by country of residence)

	1992	Relative share	1993	Relative share	% Variation over 1992
Canada	98 744	1.0	89 117	0.9	−9.7
Mexico	22 245	0.2	18 954	0.2	−14.8
United States	962 581	9.4	888 981	9.0	−7.6
Total North America	1 083 570	10.6	997 052	10.1	−8.0
Australia [1]	114 501	1.1	101 306	1.0	−11.5
Japan	519 624	5.1	503 537	5.1	−3.1
New Zealand [1]	..	..	..	..	..
Total Asia and the Pacific	634 125	6.2	604 843	6.1	−4.6
Austria	202 944	2.0	203 917	2.1	0.5
Belgium	374 182	3.6	377 073	3.8	0.8
Denmark	60 895	0.6	55 975	0.6	−8.1
Finland	37 340	0.4	29 616	0.3	−20.7
France	714 371	7.0	688 006	6.9	−3.7
Germany	3 488 693	34.0	3 532 981	35.7	1.3
Greece	56 673	0.6	48 470	0.5	−14.5
Iceland [2]	..	..	..	..	..
Ireland	18 393	0.2	18 326	0.2	−0.4
Italy	770 366	7.5	620 005	6.3	−19.5
Luxembourg	41 943	0.4	42 375	0.4	1.0
Netherlands	594 490	5.8	593 802	6.0	−0.1
Norway	35 279	0.3	30 780	0.3	−12.8
Portugal	40 091	0.4	38 103	0.4	−5.0
Spain	284 860	2.8	246 137	2.5	−13.6
Sweden	126 807	1.2	98 215	1.0	−22.5
Switzerland	..	..	..	..	..
Turkey	30 544	0.3	32 263	0.3	5.6
United Kingdom	680 834	6.6	634 086	6.4	−6.9
Other OECD-Europe	..	..	..	..	..
Total Europe	7 558 705	73.6	7 290 130	73.6	−3.6
Total OECD Countries	**9 276 400**	**90.4**	**8 892 025**	**89.8**	**−4.1**
Other European countries [2]	269 997	2.6	281 265	2.8	4.2
Ex-Yugoslavia	33 976	0.3	27 457	0.3	−19.2
Latin America	137 039	1.3	120 424	1.2	−12.1
Argentina	29 406	0.3	27 364	0.3	−6.9
Brazil	52 957	0.5	48 742	0.5	−8.0
Asia-Oceania	461 277	4.5	491 272	5.0	6.5
India	30 735	0.3	32 221	0.3	4.8
Iran	9 204	0.1	8 313	0.1	−9.7
Israel	114 981	1.1	118 723	1.2	3.3
Africa	120 080	1.2	116 338	1.2	−3.1
Egypt	18 645	0.2	17 158	0.2	−8.0
South Africa	31 628	0.3	30 812	0.3	−2.6
Total non-OECD Countries	**988 393**	**9.6**	**1 009 299**	**10.2**	**2.1**
TOTAL	**10 264 793**	**100.0**	**9 901 324**	**100.0**	**−3.5**

1. Australia includes New Zealand.
2. "Other European countries" includes Iceland.

SWITZERLAND

NIGHTS SPENT BY FOREIGN TOURISTS IN HOTELS

(by country of residence)

	1992	Relative share	1993	Relative share	% Variation over 1992
Canada	174 388	0.9	165 567	0.8	−5.1
Mexico	41 519	0.2	37 579	0.2	−9.5
United States	1 889 289	9.3	1 809 175	9.1	−4.2
Total North America	2 105 196	10.4	2 012 321	10.2	−4.4
Australia [1]	158 401	0.8	145 660	0.7	−8.0
Japan	815 392	4.0	797 828	4.0	−2.2
New Zealand [1]	..	..	..	..	..
Total Asia and the Pacific	973 793	4.8	943 488	4.8	−3.1
Austria	364 379	1.8	370 391	1.9	1.6
Belgium	970 615	4.8	1 013 782	5.1	4.4
Denmark	100 347	0.5	94 174	0.5	−6.2
Finland	65 051	0.3	55 905	0.3	−14.1
France	1 442 258	7.1	1 393 278	7.0	−3.4
Germany	6 838 980	33.8	7 015 900	35.5	2.6
Greece	126 809	0.6	112 486	0.6	−11.3
Iceland [2]	..	..	..	..	..
Ireland	34 268	0.2	35 645	0.2	4.0
Italy	1 397 301	6.9	1 082 949	5.5	−22.5
Luxembourg	124 845	0.6	128 054	0.6	2.6
Netherlands	881 383	4.4	900 232	4.6	2.1
Norway	65 161	0.3	57 624	0.3	−11.6
Portugal	72 647	0.4	67 147	0.3	−7.6
Spain	410 304	2.0	360 150	1.8	−12.2
Sweden	233 927	1.2	187 389	0.9	−19.9
Switzerland	..	..	..	..	..
Turkey	81 712	0.4	80 650	0.4	−1.3
United Kingdom	1 847 948	9.1	1 706 670	8.6	−7.6
Other OECD-Europe	..	..	..	..	..
Total Europe	15 057 935	74.4	14 662 426	74.2	−2.6
Total OECD Countries	**18 136 924**	**89.6**	**17 618 235**	**89.1**	**−2.9**
Other European countries [2]	455 808	2.3	488 240	2.5	7.1
Ex-USSR	92 170	0.5	126 964	0.6	37.7
Ex-Yugoslavia	99 814	0.5	59 589	0.3	−40.3
Latin America	284 509	1.4	253 981	1.3	−10.7
Argentina	56 905	0.3	53 476	0.3	−6.0
Brazil	108 474	0.5	100 368	0.5	−7.5
Asia-Oceania	1 006 384	5.0	1 083 780	5.5	7.7
India	67 067	0.3	71 129	0.4	6.1
Iran	29 174	0.1	25 592	0.1	−12.3
Israel	268 654	1.3	276 668	1.4	3.0
Africa	352 313	1.7	329 662	1.7	−6.4
Egypt	61 289	0.3	55 619	0.3	−9.3
South Africa	62 254	0.3	61 514	0.3	−1.2
Total non-OECD Countries	**2 099 014**	**10.4**	**2 155 663**	**10.9**	**2.7**
TOTAL	**20 235 938**	**100.0**	**19 773 898**	**100.0**	**−2.3**

1. Australia includes New Zealand.
2. "Other European countries" includes Iceland.

SWITZERLAND

NIGHTS SPENT BY FOREIGN TOURISTS IN REGISTERED TOURIST ACCOMMODATION

(by country of residence)

	1992	Relative share	1993	Relative share	% Variation over 1992
Canada	218 582	0.6	206 362	0.6	−5.6
Mexico	46 946	0.1	41 465	0.1	−11.7
United States	2 129 373	5.8	2 059 489	5.6	−3.3
Total North America	2 394 901	6.5	2 307 316	6.3	−3.7
Australia [1]	240 265	0.6	216 767	0.6	−9.8
Japan	848 175	2.3	827 153	2.3	−2.5
New Zealand [1]	..	..	..	..	..
Total Asia and the Pacific	1 088 440	2.9	1 043 920	2.8	−4.1
Austria	531 927	1.4	531 236	1.4	−0.1
Belgium	2 125 508	5.7	2 158 799	5.9	1.6
Denmark	195 461	0.5	180 645	0.5	−7.6
Finland	88 374	0.2	70 223	0.2	−20.5
France	2 335 034	6.3	2 298 802	6.3	−1.6
Germany	16 012 468	43.3	16 597 783	45.2	3.7
Greece	135 993	0.4	120 633	0.3	−11.3
Iceland [2]	..	..	..	..	..
Ireland	46 798	0.1	46 487	0.1	−0.7
Italy	2 009 734	5.4	1 669 470	4.5	−16.9
Luxembourg	209 984	0.6	211 799	0.6	0.9
Netherlands	3 412 578	9.2	3 388 149	9.2	−0.7
Norway	85 578	0.2	73 836	0.2	−13.7
Portugal	89 367	0.2	85 492	0.2	−4.3
Spain	626 541	1.7	542 845	1.5	−13.4
Sweden	339 089	0.9	257 616	0.7	−24.0
Switzerland	..	..	..	..	..
Turkey	87 532	0.2	87 418	0.2	−0.1
United Kingdom	2 595 708	7.0	2 440 935	6.6	−6.0
Other OECD-Europe	..	..	..	..	..
Total Europe	30 927 674	83.6	30 762 168	83.8	−0.5
Total OECD Countries	**34 411 015**	**93.0**	**34 113 404**	**92.9**	**−0.9**
Other European countries [2]	699 139	1.9	724 709	2.0	3.7
Ex-Yugoslavia	116 609	0.3	73 215	0.2	−37.2
Latin America	324 529	0.9	291 114	0.8	−10.3
Argentina	64 699	0.2	60 317	0.2	−6.8
Brazil	122 778	0.3	111 861	0.3	−8.9
Asia-Oceania	1 149 470	3.1	1 217 775	3.3	5.9
India	72 660	0.2	78 177	0.2	7.6
Iran	31 547	0.1	27 316	0.1	−13.4
Israel	333 567	0.9	337 967	0.9	1.3
Africa	415 721	1.1	381 868	1.0	−8.1
Egypt	69 297	0.2	60 834	0.2	−12.2
South Africa	89 396	0.2	86 524	0.2	−3.2
Total non-OECD Countries	**2 588 859**	**7.0**	**2 615 466**	**7.1**	**1.0**
TOTAL	**36 999 874**	**100.0**	**36 728 870**	**100.0**	**−0.7**

. Australia includes New Zealand.
.. "Other European countries" includes Iceland.

TURKEY

ARRIVALS OF FOREIGN TRAVELLERS AT FRONTIERS

(by country of nationality)

	1992	Relative share	1993	Relative share	% Variation over 1992
Canada	26 355	0.4	35 144	0.5	33.3
Mexico	5 260	0.1	7 110	0.1	35.2
United States	182 429	2.6	254 945	3.9	39.8
Total North America	214 044	3.0	297 199	4.6	38.8
Australia	30 907	0.4	30 585	0.5	–1.0
Japan	36 398	0.5	47 317	0.7	30.0
New Zealand	7 337	0.1	7 629	0.1	4.0
Total Asia and the Pacific	74 642	1.1	85 531	1.3	14.6
Austria	204 662	2.9	211 337	3.3	3.3
Belgium	75 071	1.1	88 120	1.4	17.4
Denmark	64 016	0.9	79 369	1.2	24.0
Finland	104 190	1.5	96 359	1.5	–7.5
France	247 603	3.5	301 009	4.6	21.6
Germany	1 165 164	16.5	1 118 750	17.2	–4.0
Greece	147 174	2.1	148 198	2.3	0.7
Iceland [1]	2 470	0.0	2 980	0.0	20.6
Ireland [1]	22 997	0.3	26 608	0.4	15.7
Italy	158 185	2.2	134 669	2.1	–14.9
Luxembourg [1]	1 743	0.0	2 076	0.0	19.1
Netherlands	204 802	2.9	216 182	3.3	5.6
Norway	42 482	0.6	54 332	0.8	27.9
Portugal [1]	5 811	0.1	10 125	0.2	74.2
Spain	47 318	0.7	63 120	1.0	33.4
Sweden	120 248	1.7	87 021	1.3	–27.6
Switzerland	78 735	1.1	82 853	1.3	5.2
Turkey	..	..	..	..	..
United Kingdom	314 608	4.4	441 817	6.8	40.4
Other OECD-Europe [1]	..	..	..	..	..
Total Europe	3 007 279	42.5	3 164 925	48.7	5.2
Total OECD Countries	**3 295 965**	**46.6**	**3 547 655**	**54.6**	**7.6**
Other European countries	3 182 649	45.0	2 269 809	34.9	–28.7
Bulgaria	818 895	11.6	368 813	5.7	–55.0
Ex-Czechoslovakia	126 773	1.8	75 176	1.2	–40.7
Hungary	148 131	2.1	98 921	1.5	–33.2
Poland	111 931	1.6	51 562	0.8	–53.9
Rumania	566 665	8.0	311 235	4.8	–45.1
Ex-USSR	1 241 010	17.5	1 167 044	18.0	–6.0
Ex-Yugoslavia	155 559	2.2	169 854	2.6	9.2
Latin America	21 015	0.3	31 294	0.5	48.9
Argentina	5 053	0.1	8 514	0.1	68.5
Brazil	4 838	0.1	8 971	0.1	85.4
Chile	2 109	0.0	1 931	0.0	–8.4
Colombia	1 852	0.0	2 431	0.0	31.3
Venezuela	1 318	0.0	1 515	0.0	14.9
Asia-Oceania	503 547	7.1	563 959	8.7	12.0
China	5 500	0.1	6 952	0.1	26.4
India	4 431	0.1	8 734	0.1	97.1
Iran	150 168	2.1	119 692	1.8	–20.3
Israel	49 858	0.7	100 748	1.5	102.1
Republic of Korea	3 959	0.1	5 095	0.1	28.7
Lebanon	14 776	0.2	19 373	0.3	31.1
Malaysia	1 711	0.0	2 952	0.0	72.5
Pakistan	10 223	0.1	11 864	0.2	16.1
Philippines	3 966	0.1	7 366	0.1	85.7
Saudi Arabia	19 423	0.3	21 077	0.3	8.5
Singapore	2 279	0.0	2 959	0.0	29.8
Africa	69 320	1.0	75 509	1.2	8.9
Algeria	5 735	0.1	5 711	0.1	–0.4
Egypt	11 181	0.2	12 673	0.2	13.3
Morocco	5 165	0.1	6 743	0.1	30.6
Origin country undetermined [2]	3 600	0.1	12 412	0.2	244.8
Total non-OECD Countries	**3 780 131**	**53.4**	**2 952 983**	**45.4**	**–21.9**
TOTAL	**7 076 096**	**100.0**	**6 500 638**	**100.0**	**–8.1**

1. "Other OECD-Europe" includes Iceland, Ireland, Luxembourg and Portugal.
2. "Origin country undetermined" includes Other North America and Stateless persons.

TURKEY

ARRIVALS OF FOREIGN TOURISTS AT HOTELS

(by country of nationality)

	1992	Relative share	1993	Relative share	% Variation over 1992
Canada	14 544	0.4	17 271	0.5	18.8
Mexico	..	..	..	..	..
United States	158 048	4.6	211 545	5.6	33.8
Total North America	172 592	5.1	228 816	6.1	32.6
Australia	12 082	0.4	15 653	0.4	29.6
Japan	123 402	3.6	137 162	3.6	11.2
New Zealand	..	..	..	..	..
Total Asia and the Pacific	135 484	4.0	152 815	4.0	12.8
Austria	87 597	2.6	92 679	2.5	5.8
Belgium [1]	231 348	6.8	246 921	6.5	6.7
Denmark [2]	154 180	4.5	106 121	2.8	−31.2
Finland [2]	..	..	..	..	..
France	434 260	12.7	614 975	16.3	41.6
Germany	889 630	26.1	851 103	22.5	−4.3
Greece	25 877	0.8	21 451	0.6	−17.1
Iceland	..	..	..	..	..
Ireland	..	..	..	..	..
Italy	217 119	6.4	172 484	4.6	−20.6
Luxembourg [1]	..	..	..	..	..
Netherlands [1]	..	..	..	..	..
Norway [2]	..	..	..	..	..
Portugal	..	..	..	..	..
Spain	133 396	3.9	160 571	4.3	20.4
Sweden [2]	..	..	..	..	..
Switzerland	41 725	1.2	45 564	1.2	9.2
Turkey	..	..	..	..	..
United Kingdom	158 533	4.6	244 103	6.5	54.0
Other OECD-Europe	..	..	..	..	..
Total Europe	2 373 665	69.6	2 555 972	67.7	7.7
Total OECD Countries	**2 681 741**	**78.6**	**2 937 603**	**77.8**	**9.5**
Other European countries	356 241	10.4	360 162	9.5	1.1
Bulgaria	49 741	1.5	56 000	1.5	12.6
Hungary	45 826	1.3	35 632	0.9	−22.2
Poland	34 703	1.0	16 593	0.4	−52.2
Rumania	56 555	1.7	33 335	0.9	−41.1
Ex-USSR	133 238	3.9	184 922	4.9	38.8
Ex-Yugoslavia	36 178	1.1	33 680	0.9	−6.9
Asia-Oceania [3]	100 576	2.9	120 530	3.2	19.8
Iran	23 070	0.7	24 652	0.7	6.9
Lebanon	5 610	0.2	7 227	0.2	28.8
Pakistan	8 384	0.2	10 074	0.3	20.2
Saudi Arabia	25 673	0.8	29 240	0.8	13.9
Africa	14 816	0.4	17 313	0.5	16.9
Egypt	7 476	0.2	10 742	0.3	43.7
Origin country undetermined	256 815	7.5	341 802	9.0	33.1
Total non-OECD Countries	**728 448**	**21.4**	**839 807**	**22.2**	**15.3**
TOTAL	**3 410 189**	**100.0**	**3 777 410**	**100.0**	**10.8**

.   Belgium includes Luxembourg and Netherlands.
.   Denmark includes Finland, Norway and Sweden.
.   Asia-Oceania includes Iraq, Kuwait, Lebanon, Syria, Saudi Arabia, Jordan, Iran and Pakistan.

TURKEY

ARRIVALS OF FOREIGN TOURISTS AT REGISTERED TOURIST ACCOMMODATION

(by country of nationality)

	1992	Relative share	1993	Relative share	% Variation over 1992
Canada	14 829	0.4	17 572	0.4	18.5
Mexico	..	..	..	..	..
United States	159 848	4.3	213 374	5.2	33.5
Total North America	174 677	4.7	230 946	5.6	32.2
Australia	12 842	0.3	17 423	0.4	35.7
Japan	123 504	3.3	139 146	3.4	12.7
New Zealand	..	..	..	..	..
Total Asia and the Pacific	136 346	3.7	156 569	3.8	14.8
Austria	115 891	3.1	112 744	2.8	−2.7
Belgium[1]	247 473	6.7	262 721	6.4	6.2
Denmark[2]	160 964	4.3	113 699	2.8	−29.4
Finland[2]	..	..	..	..	..
France	487 120	13.1	668 665	16.3	37.3
Germany	1 038 062	27.9	1 025 263	25.0	−1.2
Greece	26 100	0.7	21 654	0.5	−17.0
Iceland	..	..	..	..	..
Ireland	..	..	..	..	..
Italy	233 962	6.3	184 564	4.5	−21.1
Luxembourg[1]	..	..	..	..	..
Netherlands[1]	..	..	..	..	..
Norway[2]	..	..	..	..	..
Portugal	..	..	..	..	..
Spain	133 859	3.6	162 427	4.0	21.3
Sweden[2]	..	..	..	..	..
Switzerland	51 581	1.4	51 854	1.3	0.5
Turkey	..	..	..	..	..
United Kingdom	168 803	4.5	251 748	6.1	49.1
Other OECD-Europe	..	..	..	..	..
Total Europe	2 663 815	71.6	2 855 339	69.7	7.2
Total OECD Countries	**2 974 838**	**80.0**	**3 242 854**	**79.1**	**9.0**
Other European countries	360 948	9.7	363 566	8.9	0.7
Bulgaria	50 059	1.3	56 272	1.4	12.4
Hungary	46 901	1.3	36 455	0.9	−22.3
Poland	35 608	1.0	17 124	0.4	−51.9
Rumania	56 923	1.5	33 540	0.8	−41.1
Ex-USSR	134 834	3.6	186 205	4.5	38.1
Ex-Yugoslavia	36 633	1.0	33 970	0.8	−7.3
Asia-Oceania[3]	103 653	2.8	122 168	3.0	17.9
Iran	23 879	0.6	25 216	0.6	5.6
Lebanon	5 863	0.2	7 327	0.2	25.0
Pakistan	8 485	0.2	10 125	0.2	19.3
Saudi Arabia	26 284	0.7	29 742	0.7	13.2
Africa	14 936	0.4	17 375	0.4	16.3
Egypt	7 533	0.2	10 722	0.3	42.3
Origin country undetermined	266 252	7.2	351 395	8.6	32.0
Total non-OECD Countries	**745 789**	**20.0**	**854 504**	**20.9**	**14.6**
TOTAL	**3 720 627**	**100.0**	**4 097 358**	**100.0**	**10.1**

1. Belgium includes Luxembourg and Netherlands.
2. Denmark includes Finland, Norway and Sweden.
3. Asia-Oceania includes Iraq, Kuwait, Lebanon, Syria, Saudi Arabia, Jordan, Iran and Pakistan.

TURKEY

NIGHTS SPENT BY FOREIGN TOURISTS IN HOTELS

(by country of nationality)

	1992	Relative share	1993	Relative share	% Variation over 1992
Canada	29 546	0.2	42 412	0.3	43.5
Mexico	..	..	..	..	..
United States	386 880	2.9	499 637	3.5	29.1
Total North America	416 426	3.1	542 049	3.8	30.2
Australia	28 861	0.2	33 742	0.2	16.9
Japan	214 535	1.6	216 589	1.5	1.0
New Zealand	..	..	..	..	..
Total Asia and the Pacific	243 396	1.8	250 331	1.7	2.8
Austria	596 726	4.4	584 440	4.1	−2.1
Belgium [1]	971 027	7.2	1 073 470	7.5	10.5
Denmark [2]	940 934	6.9	627 838	4.4	−33.3
Finland [2]	..	..	..	..	..
France	1 030 526	7.6	1 547 885	10.8	50.2
Germany	5 699 323	42.0	5 031 658	35.0	−11.7
Greece	84 255	0.6	50 158	0.3	−40.5
Iceland	..	..	..	..	..
Ireland	..	..	..	..	..
Italy	507 873	3.7	411 303	2.9	−19.0
Luxembourg [1]	..	..	..	..	..
Netherlands [1]	..	..	..	..	..
Norway [2]	..	..	..	..	..
Portugal	..	..	..	..	..
Spain	284 740	2.1	379 571	2.6	33.3
Sweden [2]	..	..	..	..	..
Switzerland	257 867	1.9	198 900	1.4	−22.9
Turkey	..	..	..	..	..
United Kingdom	787 486	5.8	1 421 321	9.9	80.5
Other OECD-Europe	..	..	..	..	..
Total Europe	11 160 757	82.3	11 326 544	78.9	1.5
Total OECD Countries	**11 820 579**	**87.2**	**12 118 924**	**84.4**	**2.5**
Other European countries	771 543	5.7	929 266	6.5	20.4
Bulgaria	76 830	0.6	85 207	0.6	10.9
Hungary	97 743	0.7	91 318	0.6	−6.6
Poland	107 743	0.8	51 393	0.4	−52.3
Rumania	112 886	0.8	73 961	0.5	−34.5
Ex-USSR	304 112	2.2	559 463	3.9	84.0
Ex-Yugoslavia	72 765	0.5	67 922	0.5	−6.7
Asia-Oceania [3]	259 602	1.9	333 816	2.3	28.6
Iran	72 444	0.5	75 870	0.5	4.7
Lebanon	13 474	0.1	20 120	0.1	49.3
Pakistan	17 237	0.1	25 195	0.2	46.2
Saudi Arabia	65 438	0.5	80 987	0.6	23.8
Africa	46 592	0.3	57 180	0.4	22.7
Egypt	24 682	0.2	34 265	0.2	38.8
Origin country undetermined	661 843	4.9	923 017	6.4	39.5
Total non-OECD Countries	**1 739 580**	**12.8**	**2 243 279**	**15.6**	**29.0**
TOTAL	**13 560 159**	**100.0**	**14 362 203**	**100.0**	**5.9**

1. Belgium includes Luxembourg and Netherlands.
2. Denmark includes Finland, Norway and Sweden.
3. Asia-Oceania includes Iraq, Kuwait, Lebanon, Syria, Saudi Arabia, Jordan, Iran and Pakistan.

TURKEY

NIGHTS SPENT BY FOREIGN TOURISTS IN REGISTERED TOURIST ACCOMMODATION

(by country of nationality)

	1992	Relative share	1993	Relative share	% Variation over 1992
Canada	30 466	0.2	43 370	0.3	42.4
Mexico	..	..	..	..	..
United States	393 281	2.3	505 813	3.0	28.6
Total North America	423 747	2.5	549 183	3.2	29.6
Australia	30 792	0.2	38 973	0.2	26.6
Japan	214 770	1.3	219 055	1.3	2.0
New Zealand	..	..	..	..	..
Total Asia and the Pacific	245 562	1.5	258 028	1.5	5.1
Austria	921 678	5.5	796 924	4.7	−13.5
Belgium [1]	1 118 657	6.7	1 218 490	7.1	8.9
Denmark [2]	985 526	5.9	693 578	4.1	−29.6
Finland [2]	..	..	..	..	..
France	1 447 251	8.6	1 902 332	11.1	31.4
Germany	7 573 318	45.1	6 663 582	39.1	−12.0
Greece	85 033	0.5	50 836	0.3	−40.2
Iceland	..	..	..	..	..
Ireland	..	..	..	..	..
Italy	642 069	3.8	502 666	2.9	−21.7
Luxembourg [1]	..	..	..	..	..
Netherlands [1]	..	..	..	..	..
Norway [2]	..	..	..	..	..
Portugal	..	..	..	..	..
Spain	288 342	1.7	384 797	2.3	33.5
Sweden [2]	..	..	..	..	..
Switzerland	368 719	2.2	255 590	1.5	−30.7
Turkey	..	..	..	..	..
United Kingdom	870 592	5.2	1 483 606	8.7	70.4
Other OECD-Europe	..	..	..	..	..
Total Europe	14 301 185	85.2	13 952 401	81.8	−2.4
Total OECD Countries	**14 970 494**	**89.2**	**14 759 612**	**86.5**	**−1.4**
Other European countries	788 479	4.7	945 833	5.5	20.0
Bulgaria	77 743	0.5	85 725	0.5	10.3
Hungary	99 285	0.6	93 510	0.5	−5.8
Poland	111 123	0.7	53 593	0.3	−51.8
Rumania	114 100	0.7	74 642	0.4	−34.6
Ex-USSR	312 558	1.9	569 642	3.3	82.3
Ex-Yugoslavia	73 670	0.4	68 721	0.4	−6.7
Asia-Oceania [3]	266 725	1.6	339 284	2.0	27.2
Iran	74 260	0.4	77 659	0.5	4.6
Lebanon	14 418	0.1	20 441	0.1	41.8
Pakistan	17 586	0.1	25 339	0.1	44.1
Saudi Arabia	67 284	0.4	82 609	0.5	22.8
Africa	46 971	0.3	57 630	0.3	22.7
Egypt	24 951	0.1	34 469	0.2	38.1
Origin country undetermined	712 786	4.2	961 756	5.6	34.9
Total non-OECD Countries	**1 814 961**	**10.8**	**2 304 503**	**13.5**	**27.0**
TOTAL	**16 785 455**	**100.0**	**17 064 115**	**100.0**	**1.7**

1. Belgium includes Luxembourg and Netherlands.
2. Denmark includes Finland, Norway and Sweden.
3. Asia-Oceania includes Iraq, Kuwait, Lebanon, Syria, Saudi Arabia, Jordan, Iran and Pakistan.

UNITED KINGDOM

ARRIVALS OF FOREIGN VISITORS AT FRONTIERS

(by country of residence)

	1992	Relative share	1993	Relative share	% Variation over 1992
Canada	629 000	3.4	587 000	3.0	-6.7
Mexico	..	..	..	..	..
United States	2 748 000	14.8	2 815 000	14.4	2.4
Total North America	3 377 000	18.2	3 402 000	17.5	0.7
Australia	507 000	2.7	499 000	2.6	-1.6
Japan	554 000	3.0	491 000	2.5	-11.4
New Zealand	113 000	0.6	86 000	0.4	-23.9
Total Asia and the Pacific	1 174 000	6.3	1 076 000	5.5	-8.3
Austria	180 000	1.0	194 000	1.0	7.8
Belgium	771 000	4.2	883 000	4.5	14.5
Denmark	315 000	1.7	345 000	1.8	9.5
Finland	98 000	0.5	89 000	0.5	-9.2
France	2 483 000	13.4	2 513 000	12.9	1.2
Germany	2 268 000	12.2	2 356 000	12.1	3.9
Greece	128 000	0.7	140 000	0.7	9.4
Iceland	52 000	0.3	29 000	0.1	-44.2
Ireland	1 416 000	7.6	1 554 000	8.0	9.7
Italy	784 000	4.2	793 000	4.1	1.1
Luxembourg	31 000	0.2	54 000	0.3	74.2
Netherlands	996 000	5.4	1 213 000	6.2	21.8
Norway	297 000	1.6	308 000	1.6	3.7
Portugal	102 000	0.6	130 000	0.7	27.5
Spain	684 000	3.7	707 000	3.6	3.4
Sweden	507 000	2.7	489 000	2.5	-3.6
Switzerland	433 000	2.3	501 000	2.6	15.7
Turkey	42 000	0.2	53 000	0.3	26.2
United Kingdom	..	..	..	..	..
Other OECD-Europe	..	..	..	..	..
Total Europe	11 587 000	62.5	12 351 000	63.4	6.6
Total OECD Countries	**16 138 000**	**87.1**	**16 829 000**	**86.4**	**4.3**
Other European countries	447 000	2.4	566 000	2.9	26.6
Ex-Yugoslavia	26 000	0.1	23 000	0.1	-11.5
Latin America	234 000	1.3	216 000	1.1	-7.7
Asia-Oceania	1 126 000	6.1	1 270 000	6.5	12.8
Africa	536 000	2.9	553 000	2.8	3.2
Origin country undetermined	53 000	0.3	54 000	0.3	1.9
Total non-OECD Countries	**2 396 000**	**12.9**	**2 659 000**	**13.6**	**11.0**
TOTAL	**18 534 000**	**100.0**	**19 488 000**	**100.0**	**5.1**

UNITED KINGDOM

NIGHTS SPENT BY FOREIGN TOURISTS IN TOURIST ACCOMMODATION [1]

(by country of residence)

	1992	Relative share	1993	Relative share	% Variation over 1992
Canada	7 611 000	4.1	7 690 000	4.1	1.0
Mexico	..	..	..	..	..
United States	26 930 000	14.4	27 587 000	14.8	2.4
Total North America	34 541 000	18.5	35 277 000	18.9	2.1
Australia	11 712 000	6.3	9 780 000	5.2	−16.5
Japan	4 210 000	2.2	4 075 000	2.2	−3.2
New Zealand	2 463 000	1.3	2 064 000	1.1	−16.2
Total Asia and the Pacific	18 385 000	9.8	15 919 000	8.5	−13.4
Austria	1 710 000	0.9	1 765 000	0.9	3.2
Belgium	2 853 000	1.5	2 914 000	1.6	2.1
Denmark	2 016 000	1.1	2 277 000	1.2	12.9
Finland	813 000	0.4	792 000	0.4	−2.6
France	14 898 000	8.0	14 827 000	7.9	−0.5
Germany	19 278 000	10.3	18 612 000	10.0	−3.5
Greece	2 048 000	1.1	1 862 000	1.0	−9.1
Iceland	395 000	0.2	429 000	0.2	8.6
Ireland	10 903 000	5.8	11 966 000	6.4	9.7
Italy	8 859 000	4.7	8 802 000	4.7	−0.6
Luxembourg	121 000	0.1	259 000	0.1	114.0
Netherlands	5 777 000	3.1	6 065 000	3.2	5.0
Norway	1 634 000	0.9	1 817 000	1.0	11.2
Portugal	1 010 000	0.5	1 326 000	0.7	31.3
Spain [2]	8 824 000	4.7	8 272 000	4.4	−6.3
Sweden	4 360 000	2.3	3 814 000	2.0	−12.5
Switzerland	4 243 000	2.3	4 459 000	2.4	5.1
Turkey	1 033 000	0.6	949 000	0.5	−8.1
United Kingdom	..	..	..	..	..
Other OECD-Europe	..	..	..	..	..
Total Europe	90 775 000	48.5	91 207 000	48.8	0.5
Total OECD Countries	**143 701 000**	**76.8**	**142 403 000**	**76.2**	**−0.9**
Other European countries	9 502 000	5.1	9 321 000	5.0	−1.9
Ex-Yugoslavia	582 000	0.3	547 000	0.3	−6.0
Latin America	2 200 000	1.2	2 182 000	1.2	−0.8
Asia-Oceania	19 192 000	10.3	21 651 000	11.6	12.8
Africa	11 204 000	6.0	10 294 000	5.5	−8.1
Origin country undetermined	1 352 000	0.7	1 112 000	0.6	−17.8
Total non-OECD Countries	**43 450 000**	**23.2**	**44 560 000**	**23.8**	**2.6**
TOTAL	**187 151 000**	**100.0**	**186 963 000**	**100.0**	**−0.1**

1. Estimates of total number of nights spent in all forms of accommodation, including stays with friends and relatives. Excluding: visitors in transit, visits of merchant seamen, airline personnel and military on duty.
2. Spain includes Canary Islands.

UNITED STATES

ARRIVALS OF FOREIGN TOURISTS AT FRONTIERS

(by country of residence)

	1992	Relative share	1993	Relative share	% Variation over 1992
Canada	18 598 461	39.1	17 293 000	37.8	−7.0
Mexico	11 167 000	23.5	9 824 000	21.5	−12.0
United States	..	..	..	..	..
Total North America	29 765 461	62.6	27 117 000	59.2	−8.9
Australia	486 851	1.0	448 507	1.0	−7.9
Japan	3 652 828	7.7	3 542 546	7.7	−3.0
New Zealand	139 515	0.3	133 746	0.3	−4.1
Total Asia and the Pacific	4 279 194	9.0	4 124 799	9.0	−3.6
Austria	150 663	0.3	164 095	0.4	8.9
Belgium	171 146	0.4	185 836	0.4	8.6
Denmark	100 363	0.2	103 665	0.2	3.3
Finland	83 716	0.2	69 116	0.2	−17.4
France	795 444	1.7	844 644	1.8	6.2
Germany	1 691 663	3.6	1 826 757	4.0	8.0
Greece	55 321	0.1	56 633	0.1	2.4
Iceland	16 221	0.0	18 150	0.0	11.9
Ireland	118 229	0.2	122 435	0.3	3.6
Italy	589 837	1.2	555 785	1.2	−5.8
Luxembourg	13 738	0.0	15 796	0.0	15.0
Netherlands	342 034	0.7	378 904	0.8	10.8
Norway	103 863	0.2	106 437	0.2	2.5
Portugal	45 378	0.1	49 247	0.1	8.5
Spain	343 922	0.7	309 695	0.7	−10.0
Sweden	261 728	0.6	224 281	0.5	−14.3
Switzerland	321 725	0.7	341 591	0.7	6.2
Turkey	35 241	0.1	40 745	0.1	15.6
United Kingdom	2 823 983	5.9	2 999 301	6.6	6.2
Other OECD-Europe	..	..	..	..	..
Total Europe	8 064 215	17.0	8 413 113	18.4	4.3
Total OECD Countries	**42 108 870**	**88.5**	**39 654 912**	**86.6**	**−5.8**
Other European countries	222 395	0.5	258 092	0.6	16.1
Ex-Czechoslovakia	24 100	0.1	23 144	0.1	−4.0
Hungary	24 475	0.1	32 705	0.1	33.6
Poland	45 831	0.1	42 295	0.1	−7.7
Rumania	10 267	0.0	10 335	0.0	0.7
Ex-USSR	90 763	0.2	106 199	0.2	17.0
Ex-Yugoslavia	15 395	0.0	13 034	0.0	−15.3
Latin America [1]	3 255 000	6.8	3 669 107	8.0	12.7
Argentina	342 008	0.7	387 116	0.8	13.2
Brazil	475 266	1.0	555 102	1.2	16.8
Chile	104 550	0.2	120 901	0.3	15.6
Colombia	188 808	0.4	212 688	0.5	12.6
Venezuela	372 313	0.8	444 355	1.0	19.3
Asia-Oceania	..	..	2 027 741	4.4	..
China	411 131	0.9	504 407	1.1	22.7
Hong Kong	191 237	0.4	192 691	0.4	0.8
India	105 790	0.2	102 339	0.2	−3.3
Israel	160 051	0.3	186 409	0.4	16.5
Republic of Korea	341 311	0.7	408 213	0.9	19.6
Philippines	117 031	0.2	115 492	0.3	−1.3
Saudi Arabia	60 966	0.1	66 679	0.1	9.4
Singapore	64 953	0.1	71 628	0.2	10.3
Africa	150 000	0.3	168 969	0.4	12.6
South Africa	58 161	0.1	75 094	0.2	29.1
Origin country undetermined [2]	1 820 196	3.8	..	..	..
Total non-OECD Countries	**5 447 591**	**11.5**	**6 123 909**	**13.4**	**12.4**
TOTAL	**47 556 461**	**100.0**	**45 778 821**	**100.0**	**−3.7**

1. Latin America includes Central America, Carribean, South America.
2. Origin country undetermined includes Middle East only.

MAIN SALES OUTLETS OF OECD PUBLICATIONS
PRINCIPAUX POINTS DE VENTE DES PUBLICATIONS DE L'OCDE

ARGENTINA – ARGENTINE
Carlos Hirsch S.R.L.
Galería Güemes, Florida 165, 4° Piso
1333 Buenos Aires   Tel. (1) 331.1787 y 331.2391
Telefax: (1) 331.1787

AUSTRALIA – AUSTRALIE
D.A. Information Services
648 Whitehorse Road, P.O.B 163
Mitcham, Victoria 3132   Tel. (03) 873.4411
Telefax: (03) 873.5679

AUSTRIA – AUTRICHE
Gerold & Co.
Graben 31
Wien I   Tel. (0222) 533.50.14
Telefax: (0222) 512.47.31.29

BELGIUM – BELGIQUE
Jean De Lannoy
Avenue du Roi 202 Koningslaan
B-1060 Bruxelles   Tel. (02) 538.51.69/538.08.41
Telefax: (02) 538.08.41

CANADA
Renouf Publishing Company Ltd.
1294 Algoma Road
Ottawa, ON K1B 3W8   Tel. (613) 741.4333
Telefax: (613) 741.5439
Stores:
61 Sparks Street
Ottawa, ON K1P 5R1   Tel. (613) 238.8985
211 Yonge Street
Toronto, ON M5B 1M4   Tel. (416) 363.3171
Telefax: (416)363.59.63

Les Éditions La Liberté Inc.
3020 Chemin Sainte-Foy
Sainte-Foy, PQ G1X 3V6   Tel. (418) 658.3763
Telefax: (418) 658.3763

Federal Publications Inc.
165 University Avenue, Suite 701
Toronto, ON M5H 3B8   Tel. (416) 860.1611
Telefax: (416) 860.1608

Les Publications Fédérales
1185 Université
Montréal, QC H3B 3A7   Tel. (514) 954.1633
Telefax: (514) 954.1635

CHINA – CHINE
China National Publications Import
Export Corporation (CNPIEC)
16 Gongti E. Road, Chaoyang District
P.O. Box 88 or 50
Beijing 100704 PR   Tel. (01) 506.6688
Telefax: (01) 506.3101

CHINESE TAIPEI – TAIPEI CHINOIS
Good Faith Worldwide Int'l. Co. Ltd.
9th Floor, No. 118, Sec. 2
Chung Hsiao E. Road
Taipei   Tel. (02) 391.7396/391.7397
Telefax: (02) 394.9176

CZECH REPUBLIC – RÉPUBLIQUE TCHÈQUE
Artia Pegas Press Ltd.
Narodni Trida 25
POB 825
111 21 Praha 1   Tel. 26.65.68
Telefax: 26.20.81

DENMARK – DANEMARK
Munksgaard Book and Subscription Service
35, Nørre Søgade, P.O. Box 2148
DK-1016 København K   Tel. (33) 12.85.70
Telefax: (33) 12.93.87

EGYPT – ÉGYPTE
Middle East Observer
41 Sherif Street
Cairo   Tel. 392.6919
Telefax: 360-6804

FINLAND – FINLANDE
Akateeminen Kirjakauppa
Keskuskatu 1, P.O. Box 128
00100 Helsinki

Subscription Services/Agence d'abonnements :
P.O. Box 23
00371 Helsinki   Tel. (358 0) 121 4416
Telefax: (358 0) 121.4450

FRANCE
OECD/OCDE
Mail Orders/Commandes par correspondance:
2, rue André-Pascal
75775 Paris Cedex 16   Tel. (33-1) 45.24.82.00
Telefax: (33-1) 49.10.42.76
Telex: 640048 OCDE
Internet: Compte.PUBSINQ @ oecd.org
Orders via Minitel, France only/
Commandes par Minitel, France exclusivement :
36 15 OCDE

OECD Bookshop/Librairie de l'OCDE :
33, rue Octave-Feuillet
75016 Paris   Tel. (33-1) 45.24.81.81
(33-1) 45.24.81.67

Documentation Française
29, quai Voltaire
75007 Paris   Tel. 40.15.70.00
Gibert Jeune (Droit-Économie)
6, place Saint-Michel
75006 Paris   Tel. 43.25.91.19
Librairie du Commerce International
10, avenue d'Iéna
75016 Paris   Tel. 40.73.34.60
Librairie Dunod
Université Paris-Dauphine
Place du Maréchal de Lattre de Tassigny
75016 Paris   Tel. (1) 44.05.40.13
Librairie Lavoisier
11, rue Lavoisier
75008 Paris   Tel. 42.65.39.95
Librairie L.G.D.J. - Montchrestien
20, rue Soufflot
75005 Paris   Tel. 46.33.89.85
Librairie des Sciences Politiques
30, rue Saint-Guillaume
75007 Paris   Tel. 45.48.36.02
P.U.F.
49, boulevard Saint-Michel
75005 Paris   Tel. 43.25.83.40
Librairie de l'Université
12a, rue Nazareth
13100 Aix-en-Provence   Tel. (16) 42.26.18.08
Documentation Française
165, rue Garibaldi
69003 Lyon   Tel. (16) 78.63.32.23
Librairie Decitre
29, place Bellecour
69002 Lyon   Tel. (16) 72.40.54.54
Librairie Sauramps
Le Triangle
34967 Montpellier Cedex 2   Tel. (16) 67.58.85.15
Telefax: (16) 67.58.27.36

GERMANY – ALLEMAGNE
OECD Publications and Information Centre
August-Bebel-Allee 6
D-53175 Bonn   Tel. (0228) 959.120
Telefax: (0228) 959.12.17

GREECE – GRÈCE
Librairie Kauffmann
Mavrokordatou 9
106 78 Athens   Tel. (01) 32.55.321
Telefax: (01) 32.30.320

HONG-KONG
Swindon Book Co. Ltd.
Astoria Bldg. 3F
34 Ashley Road, Tsimshatsui
Kowloon, Hong Kong   Tel. 2376.2062
Telefax: 2376.0685

HUNGARY – HONGRIE
Euro Info Service
Margitsziget, Európa Ház
1138 Budapest   Tel. (1) 111.62.16
Telefax: (1) 111.60.61

ICELAND – ISLANDE
Mál Mog Menning
Laugavegi 18, Pósthólf 392
121 Reykjavik   Tel. (1) 552.4240
Telefax: (1) 562.3523

INDIA – INDE
Oxford Book and Stationery Co.
Scindia House
New Delhi 110001   Tel. (11) 331.5896/5308
Telefax: (11) 332.5993
17 Park Street
Calcutta 700016   Tel. 240832

INDONESIA – INDONÉSIE
Pdii-Lipi
P.O. Box 4298
Jakarta 12042   Tel. (21) 573.34.67
Telefax: (21) 573.34.67

IRELAND – IRLANDE
Government Supplies Agency
Publications Section
4/5 Harcourt Road
Dublin 2   Tel. 661.31.11
Telefax: 475.27.60

ISRAEL
Praedicta
5 Shatner Street
P.O. Box 34030
Jerusalem 91430   Tel. (2) 52.84.90/1/2
Telefax: (2) 52.84.93
R.O.Y. International
P.O. Box 13056
Tel Aviv 61130   Tel. (3) 546 1423
Telefax: (3) 546 1442
Palestinian Authority/Middle East:
INDEX Information Services
P.O.B. 19502
Jerusalem   Tel. (2) 27.12.19
Telefax: (2) 27.16.34

ITALY – ITALIE
Libreria Commissionaria Sansoni
Via Duca di Calabria 1/1
50125 Firenze   Tel. (055) 64.54.15
Telefax: (055) 64.12.57
Via Bartolini 29
20155 Milano   Tel. (02) 36.50.83
Editrice e Libreria Herder
Piazza Montecitorio 120
00186 Roma   Tel. 679.46.28
Telefax: 678.47.51
Libreria Hoepli
Via Hoepli 5
20121 Milano   Tel. (02) 86.54.46
Telefax: (02) 805.28.86
Libreria Scientifica
Dott. Lucio de Biasio 'Aeiou'
Via Coronelli, 6
20146 Milano   Tel. (02) 48.95.45.52
Telefax: (02) 48.95.45.48

JAPAN – JAPON
OECD Publications and Information Centre
Landic Akasaka Building
2-3-4 Akasaka, Minato-ku
Tokyo 107   Tel. (81.3) 3586.2016
Telefax: (81.3) 3584.7929

KOREA – CORÉE
Kyobo Book Centre Co. Ltd.
P.O. Box 1658, Kwang Hwa Moon
Seoul   Tel. 730.78.91
Telefax: 735.00.30

OECD PUBLICATIONS, 2 rue André-Pascal, 75775 PARIS CEDEX 16
PRINTED IN FRANCE
(78 95 01 1) ISBN 92-64-14571-0 - No. 47887 1995
ISSN 0256-7598